The Drive for Dollars

The Drive for Dollars

*How Fiscal Politics Shaped Urban Freeways
and Transformed American Cities*

Jeffrey R. Brown
Eric A. Morris
Brian D. Taylor

OXFORD
UNIVERSITY PRESS

Oxford University Press is a department of the University of Oxford. It furthers
the University's objective of excellence in research, scholarship, and education
by publishing worldwide. Oxford is a registered trade mark of Oxford University
Press in the UK and certain other countries.

Published in the United States of America by Oxford University Press
198 Madison Avenue, New York, NY 10016, United States of America.

Library of Congress Cataloging-in-Publication Data
Names: Brown, Jeffrey Richard, 1970– author. | Morris, Eric A., author. |
Taylor, Brian D. (Brian Deane), author.
Title: The drive for dollars : how fiscal politics shaped urban freeways and
transformed American cities / Jeffrey R. Brown, Eric A. Morris, Brian D. Taylor.
Description: New York : Oxford University Press, 2023. |
Includes bibliographical references and index.
Identifiers: LCCN 2022029940 (print) | LCCN 2022029941 (ebook) |
ISBN 9780197601525 (paperback) | ISBN 9780197601518 (hardback) |
ISBN 9780197601549 (epub)
Subjects: LCSH: Urban transportation—United States—History. | Urban transportation
policy—United States—History. | Highway planning—United States—History. |
Urban policy—United States—History. | City planning—United states—History.
Classification: LCC HE308 .B76 2023 (print) | LCC HE308 (ebook) |
DDC 388.40973—dc23/eng/20220811
LC record available at https://lccn.loc.gov/2022029940
LC ebook record available at https://lccn.loc.gov/2022029941

DOI: 10.1093/oso/9780197601518.001.0001

This book is dedicated to the memory of UCLA and UC Berkeley Professor Martin Wachs, whose passions for planning history and transportation finance helped to motivate this book, and whose caring commitment to his students is an enduring inspiration.

Contents

Preface

Our research on this book commenced 36 years ago, meaning its gestation was about as long as it took to construct most of the Interstate Highway System. Brian Taylor was a graduate student in City & Regional Planning and Civil Engineering at UC Berkeley when he was hired in 1985, by Dr. David W. Jones Jr., to assist with a study of the California Department of Transportation (Caltrans). It focused on Caltrans's uneasy, protracted transition from a freeway-building organization to one charged with managing multimodal transportation systems. This research entailed an extensive survey of Caltrans' engineers, many of whom, at the ends of their careers, expressed melancholy. Engineering careers that had begun with the heady excitement of building an enormous, modern system of superhighways were ending with a profound sense of ambivalence. California's planned freeway system was less than half-completed, but construction had by the 1980s slowed to a crawl. Cutting freeways through neighborhoods had proven exceedingly controversial, and community resistance to them was waxing. Freeways, which had initially been seen as promising for finally solving vexing congestion problems, were increasingly clogged with traffic. Los Angeles and many other California cities had become infamous for their smog, much of it attributed to motor vehicle emissions. Funding for freeways, plentiful in the 1960s, was now, in the 1980s, in short supply. And California policymakers—who had charged Caltrans' engineers with building a great freeway system for the future—were pulling back on their commitment to freeways and to the engineers who designed and built them.

How had this near-universal enthusiasm for, and extraordinary commitment to, freeways occurred? And how had the public charge to these engineers to blanket the country, including its cities, with high-speed freeways so quickly unraveled? These were the questions that motivated our early work on this book, and the answers—time and time again—came back to money.

Brian graduated from Berkeley and went on to work as a transportation planner for the San Francisco Bay Area Metropolitan Transportation Commission (MTC) in the late 1980s. He focused on the planning and finance of public transit systems. During his time there he saw repeatedly how the politics of public finance exerted more influence over transportation policy outcomes than the carefully crafted plans ostensibly guiding the work of the MTC. After a few years, Brian entered the Urban Planning PhD program at UCLA. There he wrote his dissertation (under the tutelage of Professor Martin Wachs, to whom this book is dedicated) on how fiscal politics both shaped the design of urban freeways and public transit systems and contributed to their chronic financial woes, entitled *When Finance Leads Planning: The Influence of Public Finance on Transportation Planning and Policy in California.*

Early in his academic career, first as a faculty member at the University of North Carolina at Chapel Hill and then back at UCLA, Brian continued his research on the politics of freeway and public transit finance. In the course of this work, he hired Jeffrey Brown, then an Urban Planning graduate student, to work on two transportation finance research projects. Out of these projects Jeffrey wrote an award-winning master's thesis entitled *Trapped in the Past: The Gas Tax and Highway Finance* and an award-winning doctoral dissertation entitled *The Numbers Game: The Politics of the Federal Surface Transportation Program.* Both projects spurred subsequent research by Jeffrey, now a faculty member at Florida State University, on early urban freeway planning and the politics of transportation finance.

In 2005, Brian began working with Urban Planning graduate student Eric Morris, who was commencing a career shift from Hollywood television writer to transportation academic, as so many do. While at UCLA, Eric wrote a transportation history master's thesis, *From Horse Power to Horsepower: The External Costs of Transportation in the 19th Century City*, which examined the dawn of the motor age in U.S. cities. At that point, Eric, Jeffrey, and Brian began research together on this book, examining how the drive for dollars altered early plans for urban freeways and profoundly shaped American cities and travel in them. This work continued with Eric's graduation and move to a faculty position at Clemson University.

While this book weaves together years of research by Brian, Jeffrey, and Eric, it is an entirely collaborative enterprise. We each contributed to every chapter in an equal research partnership; our names are listed alphabetically by last name and do not indicate any ranking of contribution to the final product. Most of what is laid out in these pages are drawn from original research, sometimes conducted in collaboration with others. First and foremost, Dr. Mark Garrett contributed significantly to our research, and the final product is better because of his efforts. Mark is an accomplished scholar, a research staff member in the UCLA Institute of Transportation Studies, and an expert on transportation, discrimination, and civil rights. Among his other contributions, Mark reviewed and helped us to better understand research on freeways, race, and poverty. He also contributed substantially to assembling and graphically presenting much of the data, helped us to reorganize an early version of this manuscript, and was a discerning and insightful critic of later drafts of this work.

There are many more who helped along the way. Orly Linovski, now a faculty member at the University of Manitoba, helped us to manage our early work on the manuscript in the early 2010s while she was a PhD student at UCLA. Transportation engineering student and UCLA Institute of Transportation Studies assistant Tianxing (Walker) Dai helped us assemble and secure permissions for the visual exhibits and helped clean and format the citations. His successor, Nathan Sharafian, also a transportation engineering undergraduate, helped us proofread the manuscript, and cleaned and formatted the citations as well. Clemson city and regional planning student Anna Wilson reviewed the manuscript and provided us with helpful comments and feedback. UCLA undergraduate Ziyu Zhu helped to make some of the older images more legible. Emily Benitez, Ponneelan Moorthy, and Dorothy Bauhoff at Oxford University Press were very helpful in copyediting our work and guiding us through the logistics of manuscript preparation.

Professor Emeritus Martin Wachs of UC Berkeley and UCLA reviewed not one but two versions of the manuscript and offered enormously helpful comments. Professor Wachs passed away just prior to the publication of this book, which is dedicated to his memory. Professor Emeritus Gregory Thompson of Florida State also reviewed and offered helpful comments on an early draft of the manuscript. In addition, two anonymous reviewers offered numerous constructive suggestions.

Kendra Levine, Director of the Institute of Transportation Studies Library at UC Berkeley, and Matthew Barrett, Director of the Dorothy Peyton Gray Transportation Research Library & Archive at L.A. Metro, were each extremely generous in helping us with archival research and in securing images and permissions. Professor Anastasia Loukaitou-Sideris of UCLA gave us helpful advice on the process of book publishing.

James Cook, our editor at Oxford University Press, is to be thanked for seeing the potential in a manuscript on a subject, transportation finance, which many might at first glance not think would yield a page-turner. He was always a pleasure to deal with and a staunch champion as the manuscript moved through the process.

Finally, the work would not have been possible without the generous financial support of many people and organizations. The University of California Transportation Center (a federally funded University Transportation Center) provided dissertation support to all three of us and later furnished research funding for this work. The California Policy Seminar and the California

Energy Institute also provided research funding. This work was also supported in part by the generous gift to UCLA by Meyer and Renee Luskin.

Finally, the work that went into this exploration of the power of finance was more than matched by the pleasure that all concerned reaped from producing it. We hope the reader feels they have gotten their "money's worth" as well.

PART I
OVERVIEW AND INTRODUCTION

1

Cities, Cars, and Freeways

A modern urban planner equipped with a time machine and sent back to the dawn of the twentieth century would find her world turned upside down. As curious as it may be, given her twenty-first century perspective, in the early decades of the 1900s most urban thinkers considered the automobile and sub-urbanization not the banes of urban civilization but their potential saviors.[1]

Unlike horses, autos didn't kick, bite, or trample children. They didn't de-posit thousands of pounds of manure on city streets each day. With horses and their droppings gone, trillions of flies would never be hatched, which would slow the spread of dangerous diseases like tuberculosis. Hundreds of decom-posing horse carcasses would no longer litter American streets each day. The low growl of the internal combustion engine would be less grating than the clanking of iron horseshoes on pavements.[2]

Many observers believed that traffic crashes and fatalities would fall thanks to vehicles that lacked often-obstreperous minds of their own. Congestion would be reduced as well. Autos traveled at high speeds; they were maneuver-able, particularly laterally; and they took up less street space than the horse-powered vehicles that preceded them. Autos also accelerated quickly, a boon in stop-and-go traffic.[3]

Autos seemed likely to ease parking problems. They were considerably smaller than horse-drawn vehicles, which took up about the same amount of space as a modern delivery truck. Auto storage was a relatively antiseptic af-fair compared with the business of housing the horse; urban stables were one of the nineteenth century's most noxious land uses. Moreover, autos could be left at the curb with less risk of theft and could be counted on to not attack pas-sersby. Autos did not need to be periodically fed and watered. They promised to be easier to repair; it was far simpler to fix a flat tire than a horse's broken leg. Finally, numerous publications calculated that automobiles would be less expensive to own and operate than horse-drawn vehicles.[4]

Many observers at the time also believed that perhaps the greatest benefits of all would come from an auto-driven reshaping of urban form. Many con-sidered cities a great font of social ills. Cities were severely overcrowded; in 1900 the Lower East Side of New York reached a population density of 350,000

The Drive for Dollars. Jeffrey R. Brown, Eric A. Morris, and Brian D. Taylor, Oxford University Press.
© Oxford University Press 2023. DOI: 10.1093/oso/9780197601518.003.0001

persons per square mile, versus 27,500 for modern-day New York.[5] Cities featured inadequate housing, immigrants with "un-American" values, abysmal sanitation, and vice of all sorts (particularly drunkenness). These mixed together to form what was seen by many observers as a dangerous cocktail of crime, disease, poverty, irreligiosity, and moral degeneration. Reform of the city was seen by many as hopeless. The more promising solution: rather than fix the city, abandon it.[6]

Suburbs, on the other hand, promised a lifestyle seen as more in keeping with traditional American values and mores. Lower-density living would be more pastoral in character. A stout American yeomanry would replace the teeming urban proletariat. Individual plots offered space for children's play far from the malign influences of the urban street. The light and air that would come with detached housing would reduce disease.[7]

Middle-class suburbanization in America was not new. It had been proceeding rapidly at least since the introduction of the horse-drawn streetcar in the 1850s, and perhaps even since the 1820s with the opening of steam-powered ferry service from Manhattan to Brooklyn.[8] However, the auto promised to accelerate suburbanization dramatically.

The public was also widely frustrated with the electric streetcar, the predominant mode for longer-distance travel in cities.[9] Service was often unreliable, vehicles were frequently crowded and dilapidated, and the streetcar companies were castigated in the press as greedy, uncaring monopolists. The auto, by contrast, promised comfort, privacy, convenience, and independence. It would liberate travelers from the tyranny of fixed routes and schedules and allow land development away from fixed streetcar tracks. As auto ownership trickled down to the middle classes, whole new segments of the public would be able to acquire an essential—perhaps *the* essential—component of what would soon become the American Dream: a detached, single-family home on its own plot of land within easy driving distance of jobs, shopping, and culture.[10]

Two things are remarkable about this vision of the auto's promise. The first is that, in many ways, it has been realized far beyond its proponents' wildest dreams. Suburbanization *was* greatly facilitated by the privately owned auto. Most Americans today live in suburbs, where ownership of detached single-family homes is the province of the many, not the privilege of the few. Fatalities from crashes *were* greatly reduced, at least on per-capita and per-mile bases.[11] In many ways, sanitation and public health *were* greatly improved; for example, rates of tuberculosis and other communicable diseases dropped sharply after horse-drawn transportation and the flies it nurtured were eliminated.[12] Auto ownership *did* trickle down to the working classes and even the poor. As a group, modern Americans enjoy greater mobility, with greater speed, more convenience, and greater comfort than any people in history.[13]

The other remarkable thing is the degree to which this vision has simultaneously been discredited. Today automobility is viewed by many as a poisoned chalice. Contemporary thinking largely focuses not on promoting the auto but on reining it in, pricing it, taxing it, regulating it, replacing its propulsion system, or supplanting it altogether with alternate modes of travel. How, in the space of a century, did the auto go from the darling of urbanists to their *bête noire*?

There are a number of reasons for the auto's fall from grace. We now know that autos emit pollutants about which early-twentieth-century planners were ignorant. We have seen that congestion cannot be tamed by simply building more roads. Perhaps most importantly, we have come full circle on urbanization. Rather than promoting suburbanization, modern planners generally seek to check it. Instead of turning our backs on cities populated disproportionately by people of color in favor of developing the more homogeneous suburban fringe, many planners and governments across the country endorse limits on peripheral development and promote urban infill and regeneration projects. As tools that permit "sprawl," autos are now blamed for urban decline, rather than being hailed as its remedy.[14]

If the auto is the moustache-twirling villain in this current narrative, it has a henchman: the urban freeway. This innovation was, like the auto, widely hailed in the middle third of the twentieth century as a "cure" for urban transportation ills. Indeed, while some consider the freeway a triumph and others a tragedy (and we maintain the story has elements of both), few would deny that freeways have had an outsized effect on American urbanization and transportation.

The freeways that now encircle and penetrate America's cities are the products of an ostensibly rural-focused program: the Dwight D. Eisenhower System of Interstate and Defense Highways. One of the largest public works projects in world history, the Interstate System's builders acquired an amount of land equivalent in size to the state of Delaware.[15] As we will see, the system's rural orientation is responsible for many of the features of urban freeways that have resulted in the contemporary hostility toward them.

The intercity portions of the system are for the most part regarded as benign, and even beneficial. They have revolutionized rural and small-town life compared to the age when the farmer was "stuck in the mud." They have permitted the integration of previously remote areas into the nation's economy. They have fostered fast and reliable shipment of goods that has contributed to substantial decreases in production and distribution costs, which has helped dramatically increase productivity.[16] Disruption due to land condemnation was generally manageable in the open spaces of the countryside. Rural freeway routing was comparatively noncontroversial; battles were largely waged by rural states and small cities and towns that courted, rather than shunned, connection to the network. Being bypassed by the Interstates was often seen as a municipal death sentence, on a par with being left off the railroad network a century earlier.*

The urban portions of the Interstates also confer substantial benefits. Admirers of the system, such as Cox and Love, have pointed out that urban freeways have saved their users immense amounts of travel time.[17],† They have cut shipping costs and permitted logistical innovations such as just-in-time delivery for producers and ever-faster deliveries of packages for consumers. They have improved access to a host of activities and permitted considerable freedom of location choice for both residents and firms. Compared to urban arterials and local streets, they have drastically reduced road deaths on a per-vehicle-mile-traveled basis. And urban freeways have arguably reduced congestion compared to a world where all traffic moved on lower-speed, lower-capacity surface streets.

However, when many observers today look at urban freeways, they see a planning disaster. To those who live, work, or play near them, freeways are rivers of noise and pollution that cascade through the urban landscape. They are charged with destroying neighborhoods—particularly low-income, Black, and Latinx communities—and with being wedges that divide many more. Freeways are considered auto magnets that have induced travel and heightened congestion rather than relieving and dissipating it. They are seen as enabling wasteful auto-dependent lifestyles that have fueled our addiction to oil, choked off alternative forms of transportation, harmed environments, and hastened climate change. They are blamed for facilitating suburbanization, which opponents charge has encroached on precious open space and exacerbated economic and racial segregation even as it saps central cities of their economic, social, and cultural vibrancy.[18]

What makes freeways such fascinating subjects of study is that all of these claims, both positive and negative, have merit.

---

* This notion of Interstate Highways creating small town winners and losers is widespread. For instance, the popular 2006 Disney Pixar film *Cars* centers on life in the small town of Radiator Springs, which began to decline when the new Interstate freeway passed it by.

† This assertion assumes substantial growth in personal and commercial vehicle travel even in the absence of freeway construction. Such analyses rest on a very large set of assumptions, because, of course, it is hard to know what travel patterns would have been like in a world without freeways.

For better and worse, freeways are the centerpiece of most U.S. metro-politan transportation systems, a feature that distinguishes American cities from almost all others. While many cities around the globe have some grade-separated, limited-access roadways, the metropolitan freeway *networks* that blanket most large American cities, extending into the very hearts of their downtowns, are conspicuously absent elsewhere. No other nation relies on freeways for such a large share of metropolitan travel.[19]

Comprising only a tiny fraction (6%) of urban street and road lane mileage, freeways nationally carry over one-third (36%) of all urban vehicle travel. Freeways actually play a smaller role outside of cities; less than a third (30%) of all rural vehicle travel is on freeways.[20,‡] There is no doubt that the unique land use patterns of twentieth-century American cities—comparatively low densities and with much of the dynamism on the periphery—can be traced in part to freeways.[21] Whether embracing or vilifying them, no one can dismiss the freeways' significance.

To understand the myriad effects of freeways on American cities and travel today, we ask: Were freeways the best—or even a good—way to accommo-date burgeoning urban vehicle travel? Were (and are) there better ways to manage motor vehicle travel in cities? Might smaller, slower-speed freeways configured in denser networks have done the job with less disruption and dis-placement? Why did initial plans for just such networks evolve into the much different system we have today? How did we come to invest so heavily and rely so extensively on metropolitan freeways when so many other countries did not? What impacts have the freeways had on our cities and society? And finally, and most importantly in our analysis, how did the drive for dollars to fund our ambitious freeway systems affect the scale and routing of metropol-itan freeways, and, in turn, cities and travel in them?

We argue that clues to these questions lie in the not-too-distant past when early civil engineers and urban planners began planning cities with few pre-conceived notions about the best ways to accommodate growing motor ve-hicle use. Proceeding through time, we find further clues about freeways, motorization, and their effects on American urban development when we examine why the roads those planners and engineers initially sketched out were not ultimately built as planned. To do this, we build on prior work while adding much new material. We bring previously neglected aspects of the story of fiscal politics and metropolitan freeways into focus, while dismissing some of the more commonly propagated canards.

---

‡ These statistics refer to lane miles and vehicle travel, respectively, on Interstates and other freeways and expressways..

Previous books on freeways have typically taken one of several forms. First are the histories of the Interstate System written for lay audiences, like Lewis' *Divided Highways*; McNichol's *The Roads that Built America: The Incredible Story of the U.S. Interstate System*; and Swift's *The Big Roads: The Untold Story of the Engineers, Visionaries, and Trailblazers Who Created the American Superhighways*.[22] These are readable and informative, but as popular histories they tended to focus on narrative storytelling and emphasize interesting back-stories and personalities of those behind the Interstates. This can come at the expense of analyses of the structural, institutional, economic, political, and other underlying forces behind freeway development.

Second are scholarly histories of the Interstate System, notably Rose's *Interstate: Express Highway Politics* and Seely's *Building the American Highway System: Engineers and Policy Makers*.[23] Both books were written (and Rose's was updated) in the final dozen years of the Interstate era. They focused principally on interest group politics in the political evolution of the federal highway program, the collaborations between states and the federal government in highway development, the significant figures of the freeway era, and how the culture of civil engineering profoundly (and in many cases naively) shaped early highway policy. These were important and insightful contributions, but they focused less on fiscal politics and urban freeway planning than we do.

A third, and considerably larger, set of books examined freeways through more normative lenses. The largest share have titles like *Road to Ruin: A Critical View of the Federal Highway Program*;[24] *Superhighway—Superhoax*;[25] *Highways to Nowhere*;[26] *The Pavers and the Paved: The Real Cost of America's Highway Program*;[27] and *Asphalt Nation: How the Automobile Took Over America and How We Can Take It Back*.[28] They were mostly penned amidst the rise of social and environmental activism in the late 1960s and early 1970s and were harshly critical of the effects of freeways on cities, the folly of auto-dependence, the arrogant indifference of the highway builders, and the power of the auto, oil, and construction industries in advancing the freeway program.[29]

The yin to these freeway critiques' yang is a smaller body of work, including *America's Highways: 1776–1976*;[30] *L.A. Freeway: An Appreciative Essay*;[31] *Driving Forces: The Automobile, Its Enemies, and the Politics of Mobility*;[32] and *The Best Investment a Nation Ever Made: A Tribute to the Dwight D. Eisenhower System of Interstate and Defense Highways*.[33] These works offered spirited defenses of automobility and freeways as a counter-narrative to the many critiques proffered by opponents.

Fourth are more recent works that examine the racial and equity dimensions of freeway development. These most often focused on the displacement

of families and businesses and the carving up of non-White, and in particular Black, communities in order to route freeways through cities. These
books include *Highway Robbery: Transportation Racism and New Routes to
Equity*;[34] *Interstate: Highway Politics and Policy since 1939*;[35,§] *The Folklore of
the Freeway: Race and Revolt in the Modernist City*;[36] and *Dixie Highway: Road
Building and the Making of the Modern South*.[37] They examined highway construction as an instrument of racial segregation, the intentional use of urban
freeway construction for "slum clearance," the explicit routing of freeways to
separate Black and White communities, and the occasionally successful but
more often unsuccessful efforts to oppose the routing of freeways through
Black and Latinx areas.

Fifth, and finally, are works on metropolitan freeway planning
more broadly. Schwartz and Foster (in his 1981 book *From Streetcar to
Superhighway: American City Planners and Urban Transportation, 1900–
1940*) argued that freeways were the products of urban planning at the
time.[38] Schwartz wrote, "Since urban freeways then carried the city planners'
collective seal of approval, there is little merit in the idea that the 1956 Act
(funding the Interstate System) subverted the planners' 'collective wisdom.'"[39]
DiMento and Ellis, in their book *Changing Lanes: Visions and Histories of
Urban Freeways*, disagreed.[40] They detailed architects', highway engineers',
and planners' competing visions for freeways and the roles they ought to play
in cities—a competition largely won by the engineers. We agree with DiMento
and Ellis that the freeway networks eventually constructed in most U.S. cities
were most emphatically not products of city planners' "collective wisdom"—
quite the contrary. We will show how and why decisions made about how to
pay for the freeway program put engineers in the driver's seat, and conse-
quently changed the character and impacts of freeways on cities.

While the authors of these previous books varied widely in terms of their
analysis of the motivating forces behind freeways—ranging from the popular
rise of automobility, to the arc of highway engineering science, to the behind-
the-scenes power of the "Highway Lobby," to the machinations of downtown
and suburban land development interests, to systemic racism—with only a few
exceptions they all tend to treat freeways largely as interchangeable commod-
ities. The key issues in most previous works are the decisions about through
which communities the freeways should pass, or whether to build them at
all. They rarely focus on whether urban freeways—with 160-foot widths and

§ Ostensibly the third edition of Rose's sole-authored book, published in 1979 and updated in 1990, this
coauthored book adds substantial work by Mohl on race, displacement, and metropolitan freeway development, including freeway revolts in Black communities and elsewhere, as well as efforts to tear down particularly unpopular freeway segments.

75 miles-per-hour design speeds—must be such enormous, invasive facilities in the first place. We will show that the urban freeways we know today were far from inevitable, as auto use has grown rapidly in many other developed countries largely in the *absence* of metropolitan freeway networks. As for conspiracies, though it is tempting to assign blame for the system's shortcomings to a cabal of rapacious captains of the tire, auto, petroleum, construction, and trucking industries, this ignores the ironic reality. As we will chronicle, most of the industries that would later come to be known as the Highway Lobby actually began as determined *opponents* of the Interstate System, due mainly to its substantial costs and new tax burdens.

We will also show that, in addition to the popularity of autos, engineering advances, the influence of powerful economic interests, and racial animus or at least insensitivity, the form and function of today's freeways were also the products of hubris, political horse trading, the politics of public finance, and bureaucratic haste. In many ways, the process bore less similarity to rational comprehensive planning than to Lindbloom's vision of planning as "muddling through."[41] A remarkable reported anecdote illustrates this: President Eisenhower, stuck in a traffic jam caused by freeway construction in Washington, D.C. in 1959, was chagrined to discover that Interstates were being built *in* cities, not just *between* them. He demanded to know who was responsible for this, only to learn *he* was; three years earlier he had affixed his signature to the very legislation authorizing federal financing and supervision of the urban Interstates. Eisenhower investigated this state of affairs with an eye toward excising the urban freeways from the plans, but he was too late; the program's momentum was too difficult and politically damaging to alter.[42] If the president himself did not understand the principles behind the Interstate program that would be named after him, neither did many others.

To tell this story, our approach is to "follow the money." Our fundamental argument is that freeways in general, Interstate freeways in particular, and urban freeways most of all were importantly shaped by money—the constraints caused by the lack of it, the means of raising it, the politics of dividing it, the policies for spending it, and the incentives promoted by it. We will show how our modern freeway system and the cities it serves were shaped by fiscal politics. The rules governing the distribution of funds promoted consequential design choices, with rural-style superhighways being deployed in urban areas. The strength and resilience of some revenue sources and the withering of others shaped the power dynamic governing the freeway program. The financial provisions of the enabling legislation turned staunch opponents of the program into ardent advocates. And economic conditions ensured the freeway program's abrupt sunset, just as they had fueled its spectacular rise.

This political-financial dynamic, so central to the story, has typically been ignored. This is a critical oversight because, put simply, money matters.

The story of urban freeways is also about American federalism. While in the eighteenth and nineteenth centuries the federal and state governments not only neglected but actually shunned direct involvement in urban transportation, the mid-twentieth century saw a reversal of long-standing traditions of limited state and, particularly, federal involvement in cities. In fact, the Interstate program was somewhat unique among U.S. public works projects in the degree of active federal control, from planning to finance to routing.[43] There were a number of reasons for this—personal, political, technical, and philosophical—but we will show how this result came about primarily due to the politics of finance.

After describing the origins of municipal, county, state, and national highway planning from local post roads through the approval and initial construction of the Interstate System, we will examine the causes of the abrupt and precipitous decline of the freeway building program in the 1970s.** Prior work has at times descended into a paean to the righteousness of anti-freeway "revolts" or a hagiography of the men and women who made them happen.[44] While the motives and efforts of those who fought urban freeways may have been noble, and while they certainly prevented particular freeway segments from being built, identifying them as the primary causal agent behind the end of widespread freeway building is problematic. We argue that the key to the story was the shifting nature of highway finance, which ensured that the fiscal system that enabled the flowering of the Interstate program also sowed the seeds of its demise.

At the end of our story, we will reset the controls of our urban planner's time machine, taking her back to the present to consider the shape of, effects of, and lessons learned from urban freeways and their nexus with transportation finance. Contrary to the claims of many freeway opponents, we make the case that freeways have conferred tremendous benefits to travelers and shippers. And contrary to the contentions of freeway boosters, we also conclude that freeways have caused significant harm to American cities, and particularly to those who live, work, study, and play adjacent to them. In doing so, we will show that the modern planning process has, in fundamental ways, swung away from the paradigm of the freeway-building era back to resemble the context and process of metropolitan transportation planning in the

---

** While roughly 86 percent of the originally planned system was completed by 1980, it would take nearly two more decades to finish the system, even as some segments, particularly in urban areas, were eventually dropped.

early twentieth century—largely as a result of the experience of building the Interstates.

Finally, we will turn to the future, speculating on the prospects for transportation given the vexing fiscal issues we currently face; we will ask whether current finance mechanisms will support a new era of bold transportation infrastructure investment or whether future planners will have to make do with muddling through. With the nation's transportation finance system at a crossroads, we will consider the promise and pitfalls of the potential paths by which we might stabilize our system of transportation finance. Such financial considerations may strike many as obscure scratching on the ledgers of bean counters in the nation's capital. But, as we will show, questions of transportation finance have the power to cause dramatic and—given the path-dependent nature of transportation facilities and their effect on urban form—enduring impacts on cities and all those who live in them. The story of the interplay between finance, freeways, and urban form in the twentieth century has much to say about which fork in the road we should choose in the twenty-first.

2

Urban and Rural Road Planning and Finance before the Automobile

Long before freeways, local, state, and in a few instances the national governments were involved with paying for and building both city streets and roads between cities. For most of American history, though, relatively little transportation "planning" took place. Until the early twentieth century, the discipline of transportation planning did not even formally exist. Instead, governments generally adopted a laissez-faire attitude toward roads. Planning was a haphazard affair, with roads built and maintained using an irregular and rudimentary finance system. But when planning for roads did occur, there were important differences between planning and paying for roads *within* cities versus *between* them. It is to the origins of urban and rural road planning, and how these were shaped by the systems that funded them, that we now turn.

Planning and Financing Urban Streets in the Pre-Automobile Era

Early American urban street planning was a disorderly affair, as political authority over streets was weak and fragmented. Undergirding this was the economics of a largely property-based system of financing streets. These factors resulted in street systems that were not nearly up to the task of accommodating mass motorization.

In the early years of urban street planning, the hand of government was most evident in the layout of the street network. From the dawn of cities, two antithetical methods of laying out streets have been practiced: (1) the organic method of natural growth, which generally has resulted in convoluted, irregular, and curvilinear street networks; and (2) the regular, planned, geometric gridiron pattern, which first appeared no later than 2600 BCE in the city of Mohenjo-Daro in what is today Pakistan.[1]

The Drive for Dollars. Jeffrey R. Brown, Eric A. Morris, and Brian D. Taylor, Oxford University Press.
© Oxford University Press 2023. DOI: 10.1093/oso/9780197601518.003.0002

Each model appeared in colonial America, with Boston being a classic example of the organic city, while Philadelphia and Williamsburg, Virginia were the prototypical examples of the gridiron one.[2] The grid pattern would eventually come to predominate well into the twentieth century. Regular, straight streets served vehicular traffic better since they minimized the number of bends and turns and eased navigation, and the grid-delineated rectangular land parcels were easy to build on and measure, aiding in property conveyance and tax assessment. The victory of the grid was played out in the planning of New York City. It featured organic growth in lower Manhattan under Dutch rule, with subsequent growth of the English colony north to 14th Street featuring a roughly gridiron but still irregular pattern (sections of grid followed the shifting path of the shoreline and were poorly integrated with each other). This was finally succeeded by a near-perfect grid for all future development further uptown, as was laid out in the Morris-DeWitt-Rutherford "Commissioners' Plan" of 1811 (shown in Figure 2.1).

Despite their rationality, gridiron street systems did have their drawbacks. They were ill-suited for directly routing radial traffic moving to and from the city center, and they sometimes necessitated traversing steep grades, as was the case in San Francisco. Also, as cities expanded, plans for streets in new subdivisions (generally laid out by private developers, not municipal authorities) were poorly coordinated, often leaving gaps, odd angles, or jogs as they connected to the main portion of the network and each other.[3]

Pierre L'Enfant's boulevard designs for Washington, D.C., were also based on the gridiron pattern, albeit interspersed with diagonal, radial boulevards (see Figure 2.2).[4] Detroit, America's "Motor City," was also laid out on a fairly regular street pattern, with some radial streets (see Figure 2.3).

Pre-automobile streets were typically kept narrow and their sidewalks wide. This was in part due to a desire to slow horse-drawn vehicular traffic.[5] More importantly, walking was common, and city streets served multiple purposes besides servicing traffic. They were also places of commerce, culture, recreation, and social life.[6] Also, many major streets grew up in tandem with privately owned and operated public transit. First came horse-drawn, wooden-wheeled omnibuses, then horsecars pulled on rail tracks, and, later, electric streetcars. Because these transit services shared road space with pedestrians and all manner of conveyances for goods, urban street planning, particularly in commercial areas, was from the outset a multimodal, multiuse, and context-sensitive affair.

There was notably little planning for the construction and maintenance of the streets themselves. Street surfaces varied widely, with unimproved dirt roads predominating up through the turn of the twentieth century. Paving

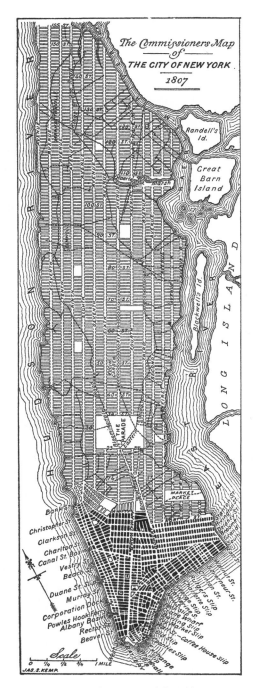

Figure 2.1. The commissioners' plan for New York (1811).

Source: Kemp, James S., and Janvier, Thomas A. June 1893. A modern redrawing of the 1807 version of the Commissioners' grid plan for Manhattan, a few years before it was adopted in 1811 from "The Evolution of New York: Second Part." *Harper's New Monthly Magazine* 87 (542): 23. https://upload. wikimedia.org/wikipedia/commons/a/a6/NYC-GRID-1811.png.

surfaces that did exist (cobblestones, "Belgian" paving, macadam paving,[*] wood blocks, and brick) all had serious drawbacks in terms of expense, durability, suitability for vehicular travel, and/or ease of maintenance.[7]

Up to the end of the nineteenth century, cities did not comprehensively build, operate, or maintain their local streets, nor did they typically collect taxes, fees, or tolls to pay for them. Instead, street improvements and maintenance fell almost entirely to property owners, or "abutters," whose land fronted the street. Groups of property owners would pay for a block or several blocks of adjacent street and sidewalk improvements. According to McShane:

> When a majority of the abutters (or rather those holding a majority of the front footage) along a street decided to pave it, they would hold a block meeting to decide the type of paving. Then, they would petition the city or the ward's city councilor to solicit bids for a paving contract. The city would divide costs among the abutters in proportion to their front footage and enforce this special assessment against any minority owners who objected. The city also guaranteed payment to the street pavers. In some cities the contractor who laid the streets had to collect directly from the abutters, although with recourse to the municipal government for collection in case of default. More commonly, the city paid the contractor, and then collected the special assessment either in a lump sum or in ten or twenty annual payments from the property-holding residents of the street.[8]

But this system had serious drawbacks. Street surface quality and condition could vary wildly, even on the same block, as property owners were more or less attentive to maintenance and varied in their maintenance strategies. For a modern example of this problem, one need look no further than alleyways. Their maintenance is often the responsibility of abutting property owners, and as a result they often vary widely in condition and are frequently poorly maintained.

The fact that abutters wished to minimize their expenses, and had little incentive to serve through traffic, discouraged the creation of integrated networks of high-quality streets, particularly in residential areas. In fact, in a precursor to today's "traffic calming" movement,[†] residential property owners often sought to keep their street's surface just good enough to enable property access, but bad enough to deter through traffic from their neighborhoods.

---

[*] Macadam, developed in the 1820s and named after Scottish road engineer John McAdam, refers to a layer of crushed rock compacted over a dirt road surface to protect it from water and wear. In later years, heated tar was sprayed over the macadam to create tar-macadam, or tarmac.

[†] Traffic calming refers to design and regulatory interventions aimed at slowing motor vehicle travel, particularly in areas with high levels of foot and bicycle traffic.

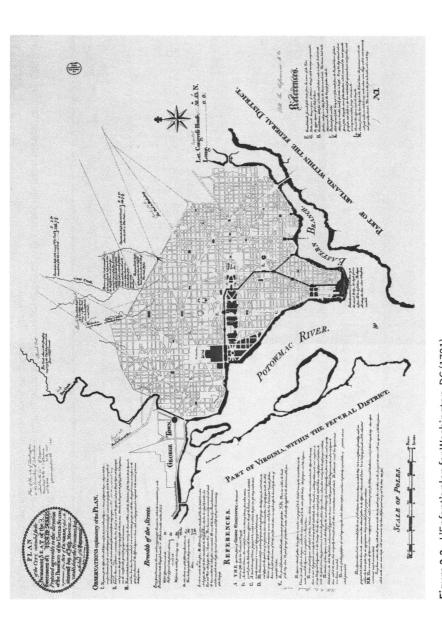

Figure 2.2. L'Enfant's plan for Washington, DC (1791).

Source: L'Enfant, Pierre Charles, Library of Congress, U.S. Geological Survey, and U.S. National Geographic Society. Plan of the city intended for the permanent seat of the government of the United States: projected agreeable to the direction of the President of the United States, in pursuance of an act of Congress, passed on the sixteenth day of July, MDCCXC, "establishing the permanent seat on the bank of the Potomac." Washington, D.C.: Library of Congress, 1991. Map. Library of Congress, Geography and Map Division. https://www.loc.gov/item/97683585/.

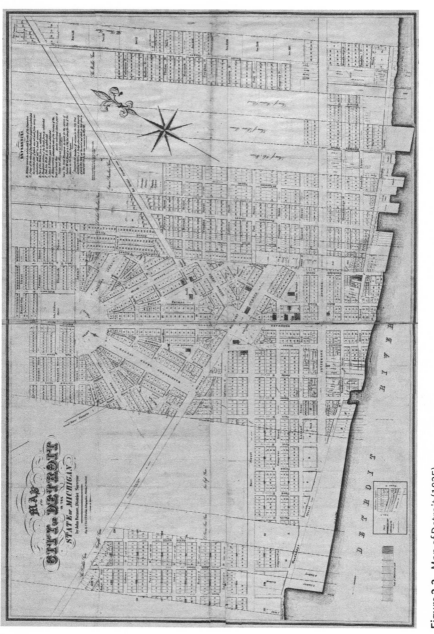

Figure 2.3. Map of Detroit (1835).

Source: Farmer, John, and C. B. & J. R. Graham Lithographers. Map of the city of Detroit in the State of Michigan. [Detroit: Farmer, 1835] Map. Library of Congress, Geography and Map Division. https://www.loc.gov/item/79691130/.

Thus, street improvements (when they took place) tended toward gravel or other cheap, not-very-durable surfaces.[9] In addition, most local street networks were poorly coordinated and aligned, which also slowed traffic and discouraged through-travel.[10] Thus while abutter finance promoted some level of urban property access, it often made traveling through the city a chore.

Requiring urban property owners to fund the construction and maintenance of adjacent streets reflects the "benefits principle," a well-established concept in public finance that has long been a philosophical underpinning of the American road finance system. Under this principle, charges are levied on road system beneficiaries in rough equivalence to the level of benefits they derive from the work being funded.[11] The idea that property owners should pay for the streets and roads that connect their properties to others reflects the view that the primary purpose of streets is private property access, without which parcels are largely worthless. Urban streets give homeowners access to jobs, shopping, and culture; they give business owners access to customers and suppliers; and they give all property owners access to police, fire, and emergency medical services. Thus, the logic of property owners funding city streets is straightforward: public investments in road improvements increase the value and utility of adjacent land and, as a result, property owners should be required to pay for the benefits conferred by them. Thus, abutter finance seemed eminently fair to many at the time.

Among the earliest undertakings to collectivize the maintenance of urban roads involved street cleaning. But these early efforts suffered from a debilitating combination of inefficiency, as cleaning jobs were often handed out based on political patronage with cleaners having little incentive to work diligently, and outright graft. Efforts to outsource this function to private contractors often met with similar outcomes. As a result, streets were often clogged with detritus from both humans and animals, making them unpleasant and unhealthy places. Traffic pushing through this waste often slowed to a crawl, particularly in the winter, when filthy streets were filled with snow as well. The removal of waste, and winter ice and snow, was rare; the latter was particularly problematic for vehicles drawn by horses whose iron-clad shoes provided poor traction.[12]

Traffic regulation was similarly primitive. There were some traffic rules in place in the nineteenth-century city, such as prohibitions against galloping horses on urban streets. But rules were few and traffic enforcement was rare, with no regular traffic police or traffic codes. Most of what we consider today to be rudimentary rules of the road had yet to be devised. Intersections were uncontrolled and often chaotic. Separation of pedestrians and vehicles was in its infancy, and pedestrians entered and crossed traffic streams at will, reflecting the still-prevalent view that streets were spaces for all manner of social life.[13]

In short, nineteenth-century street planning was, by omission and occasionally commission, remarkably ill-suited for traffic service. Government involvement was haphazard due to poor capabilities, a laissez-faire approach, and political imperatives trumping administrative ones. Citizen involvement in decision-making was uncoordinated, often apathetic, and occasionally hostile to improved traffic flows. Financial incentives were at the root of many of these issues.

Around the turn of the twentieth century, American city governments began to assume more responsibility for the construction and upkeep of streets, at least the major traffic-carrying thoroughfares. This began a process, which played out over several decades, in which city engineers replaced abutters as the stewards of streets. This was part of the increasing professionalization of municipal governance, which coincided with the rising notion of scientific management by "apolitical" technocrats.

The professional engineers' mandate came from Progressive-era reformers, most of whom wished to encourage suburbanization as an antidote to the crowding, disease, and vice of the city.[‡] Hence traffic engineers began a process of increasing focus on the fast and efficient movement of traffic and linking emerging suburbs with central cities. Drainage of streets was improved. Cities such as New York and Boston adopted street-widening plans and removed trees that obstructed vehicles. Cities undertook major projects, such as the Brooklyn Bridge (completed in 1883) in New York, to fight congestion by dispersing urban development to outlying locations. Streets' role as places of commerce and social life began to be overtaken by their function as arteries in citywide traffic-circulation networks.[14]

But the most revolutionary development was the introduction of asphalt concrete paving. Asphalt was first laid in the U.S. in Newark, New Jersey in 1871; technical advances over the next few decades greatly reduced its cost. In 1889, asphalt paving began in earnest in New York City. This trend was followed nationwide, and the transition to asphalt across the country was well under way by the early years of the twentieth century. Nevertheless, the conversion was very gradual; by 1907 only about 9 percent of city streets were paved with asphalt, while 56 percent were still dirt roads.[15]

Asphalt had the advantage of being far easier to keep clean, but even more important was that its hard, smooth surface greatly aided vehicular

---

‡ The Progressive Era was a period marked by extensive political and social reform in the United States that extended from the 1890s to the 1910s.

traffic by reducing the energy required to propel a vehicle and enabling less bumpy rides. This was also true of another paving option that appeared soon after: Portland cement concrete, an even harder, more durable surface (albeit a more expensive one). True to form, property owners in some neighborhoods fought to keep their streets from being repaved with these new materials to discourage through traffic. But as power over paving continued to shift from property owners to municipal engineers, such opposition was gradually overcome.[16]

These new paving surfaces facilitated the movement of horse-drawn vehicles. But their greatest impact was literally paving the way for the introduction of the automobile, which began in the 1890s and gathered steam in the first decade of the twentieth century.

Abutter finance could not have funded this revolution in street construction and maintenance since abutters had little interest in paying for expensive street widening or new pavements that would primarily serve automobiles. Instead, cities increasingly took over responsibility for street construction and repair, paid for at first by levying special assessments on larger groups of property owners, and ultimately through citywide property taxes. Widespread adoption of some form of property taxes in the U.S. dates to the mid-nineteenth century,[17] though they were little used for financing streets until the beginning of the twentieth century.[18] But the increasing focus on automobile traffic service for through traffic, particularly on major thoroughfares (which were typically the first streets to be paved), made the switch to property tax funding reasonable under a slightly broader notion of the benefits principle. According to this thinking, since streets were coming to be viewed as part of a citywide traffic movement system, *all* property owners benefited and *all* should collectively contribute. Thus, the transition from abutter finance to property tax finance grew hand in hand with the increasing popularity of the automobile.[19]

By the start of the twentieth century, many cities also required streetcar companies (nearly all of which were private, for-profit businesses in this era) to improve and maintain roadbeds adjacent to their lines as a condition of their franchise agreements.[20] This requirement led to improved road construction and maintenance on portions of the most important streets, which tended to be served by streetcars, at no added cost to the municipality. Instead, the cost was borne indirectly by streetcar passengers, in some cases through higher fares, but also through reduced investment in streetcar service.[21] This subsidy for road travel by transit patrons continued through the early automobile era and was one reason behind the eventual decline of the streetcars.

Before turning to the next stages of urban street finance, let us now consider the parallel evolution of rural highway planning and finance in the pre-automobile era.

Planning and Financing Rural Highways in the Pre-Automobile Era

Throughout most of human history, travel by land was mostly by foot (and in the Eastern Hemisphere by horse), and much of pre-colonial North America was blanketed in a network of well-worn and plied Native American trails. In general, however, water was vastly cheaper, easier, and faster than travel by land. In pre-Revolutionary America, ties between the individual colonies and England were more important than ties among the colonies themselves. This caused the colonies to emphasize transatlantic travel by ship over interregional travel by road. Moreover, the coastal location of most colonial settlements meant that even travel between them was mostly by sea. Even the colonies' inland hinterlands were mainly reached by river. Bridges were very few; streams were forded, and rivers crossed by ferry.[22]

Notwithstanding this, some government involvement in rural road improvement, while limited, dates to colonial times. For example, roads were sometimes improved by eliminating major obstacles such as tree trunks or boulders, and very occasionally near large cities they were accompanied by ditches for drainage and were "paved" with gravel or pounded stone.[23] However, the tools used to fund this work were quite different from those of today. From the seventeenth century to the start of the twentieth, the principal sources of highway finance (loosely defined) were work requirements and, in some localities, poll taxes levied in lieu of work requirements. This system of corvée labor, under which able-bodied males were required to perform a given number of days of road work per year, pay someone to do the work for them, or, early on, send an enslaved person as a substitute, was a relic of the feudal system, having been developed in nations such as France and Britain during the High Middle Ages (ca. 1000–1300 CE) as a replacement for the Roman system of road work by gangs of soldiers or enslaved workers.[24]

This system of road "finance" was ostensibly fair in that all members of the community were equally responsible for maintaining the roads. In practice, however, corvée labor (or "statute labor") was neither equitable, nor efficient, nor effective. With respect to equity, those who could avoid working by buying or bribing their way out, or sending enslaved people in their stead, often did so. Those in sparsely populated areas were often given more work than they could reasonably do. The system was not efficient because the workers lacked experience and expertise, shirking was frequent, road work time often resembled a social occasion, and graft on the part of road overseers who organized the workforce was common.[25] The English practice, begun in 1663, of collecting tolls from travelers was not yet used. Thus, reliance on the corvée system would, as we shall see, persist for a very long time—as would mostly shoddy work on poorly maintained roads.[26]

Colonial intercity roads capable of handling vehicles were initially developed to deliver mail. The first planned highway, laid out in 1673, connected Boston and New York via Providence. Still, such roads as existed were poor; in 1729 it took four weeks for a letter to travel overland from Boston to Williamsburg, Virginia. Among his many achievements, Benjamin Franklin, in his role as colonial postmaster-general, accelerated the process of improving rural postal roads, particularly between Philadelphia and Boston. Mail delivery times dropped dramatically. Thus, the tradition of national efforts in road building being driven (or at least justified) by the needs of the postal service stretches back to the infancy of the nation.[27]

The Revolutionary War, which saw a British naval blockade of the coast, spurred further road development. Even more important were a postwar economic boom and the seizure of land from native populations in the newly acquired western territories, which then required roads to connect them to coastal America. Migration routes heading west started as rough tracks, often originally cut by Native American travelers, which were then used by frontier settlers and their wagons. Over time, many such tracks came to be supplemented by modestly improved roads that typically connected inland settlements to the nearest navigable river. Four roads across the Appalachian Mountains were eventually built.[28]

The first intercity road constructed for the purpose of trade was authorized by the Commonwealth of Virginia in 1792. However, such roads were few in number because of a lack of government interest and capacity. In particular, the states lacked the financial means to invest heavily in roads. They were financially exhausted by the Revolution, and later were hamstrung by a wave of state bankruptcies in the 1830s that resulted in numerous state constitutional amendments prohibiting spending on internal improvements.[29]

There had been some modest federal financial support of road building stretching back to 1796, when land grants aided the building of part of what would eventually become the National Road that opened up Ohio to White settlers. Beginning in 1801, the federal government began granting new states a small percentage of the money it realized from the sale of public lands. This was to be dedicated to the building of roads, as well as canals, schools, river improvements, etc. Vastly more ambitious was an 1807 plan of Treasury Secretary Albert Gallatin that proposed a large-scale and forward-thinking national canal and road system, to be paid for by federal funding. Although this plan was never adopted, the federal government continued to support the extension of the Cumberland Road, and eventually the National Road which would stretch from the Potomac River near Washington, D.C., to Illinois.[30]

But for the most part, early presidents, Congress, and the Supreme Court took a dim view of federal involvement in road building, which was considered constitutionally suspect and a matter for state and local governments. Further, more-developed states that already had relatively good transportation systems resented paying for improvements in less-developed states. President Madison vetoed funding for Gallatin's plan in 1816 on the constitutional grounds that the ability to regulate interstate commerce and provide for national defense were not sufficient rationales for federal involvement in roads. In 1822, President Monroe vetoed an act to fund the maintenance of the National Road with tolls collected by the federal government, which he viewed as unconstitutional. And in the early 1830s, President Jackson vetoed federal funding of the Maysville Turnpike connecting Lexington, Kentucky to the port of Maysville on the Ohio River (today's State Route 68), ruling that this road was a purely local concern. Only one project in this era, the National Road, received federal funds.[31,§]

Between roughly 1785 and 1850, this lacuna was filled by English turnpike-style roads and canals. Turnpikes and canals were privately built, though sometimes with financial support from states, such as by public investment in the enterprise's stock. Pennsylvania in 1791 passed pioneering legislation allowing the state to grant licenses to turnpike and canal builders and, in sparsely populated areas, to subsidize their projects. For the most part, though, the enterprises were expected to recoup their costs from tolls—an early example of the "user pays" principle of finance.

Turnpike operators generally hired professional builders instead of using corvée labor. Given the need to attract paying customers, the roads tended to be well-located and built. Most turnpikes were graded, ditched (for drainage), and paved with gravel or pounded stone. This greatly improved both speed and animal pulling power; one contemporary estimate was that, compared to unimproved tracks, a turnpike raised the total efficiency of freight transportation by 125 percent. Stagecoaches operating on turnpikes attained average

§ The National Road was funded through the sale of public lands with the consent of the states through which it passed. There were significant constitutional disagreements about the federal government's ability to make such internal improvements. Eventually the road was turned over to the states to operate as a turnpike (Weingroff 2017a). Today Interstate 40 travels over much of the original route.

speeds of perhaps five miles per hour. This was twice as fast as canal travel, so the turnpikes tended to be used for passengers and mail, and canals for heavy freight. By the 1850s there were hundreds of private companies operating tens of thousands of miles of turnpikes and canals in the U.S.[32]

However, turnpikes and canals often proved to be poor investments. While there were notable exceptions like the Erie Canal, most toll roads of the era collected about 1.35 cents per ton-mile[**] (or roughly 24 cents per ton-mile in 2021$[††]), not enough to retire their debt and fund operations and maintenance. The lack of traffic on many toll roads was compounded by travelers taking side roads around toll booths, as well as pilfering by toll collectors. As a result, turnpike operators regularly made ends meet by delaying and deferring maintenance, but this strategy only eroded the turnpikes' competitive advantage over free roads, exacerbating their financial difficulties.[33,‡‡]

The coup de grace that ended the turnpike era was the coming of the railroads starting in the 1830s. By 1860, 31,000 miles of rail were in operation, with 5,000 new miles added each year. With its much higher speeds and pulling power, the iron horse would dominate long-distance travel for many decades and retard American intercity road building.[34] In many cases, railroad tracks were laid directly parallel to turnpikes, launching a vicious cycle of declining turnpike traffic, and then falling revenue for maintenance, which led to even less traffic. Unsurprisingly, widespread turnpike bankruptcies followed. Rural roads increasingly played only a subsidiary role to the railroads, primarily by providing short-distance access to railheads and waterways.[35]

The early nineteenth-century flurry in intercity road building also petered out because the sale of public lands failed to produce sufficient revenues to support it.[36] As a result, most rural roads constructed in the latter two-thirds of the nineteenth century continued to be funded by work requirements and poll taxes. This was not widely lamented; while being fans of neither work requirements nor taxes, most Americans preferred the former, as taxes were seen at the time as vaguely "un-American."[37]

The constitutional and political barriers to federal road spending did not apply in the western territories, which were administered directly by Washington. The federal government began to construct roads for military

---

[**] Ton-miles reflect both the mass and movement of goods. Moving one ton (2,000 pounds) of freight one mile is a ton-mile. Moving 20 pounds of freight 100 miles is also equivalent to one ton-mile.

[††] Throughout this book we convert past dollar figures into today's dollars to help the reader understand the magnitudes of sums of money in the past. We notate inflation-adjusted modern dollar figures as "2021$."

[‡‡] Some researchers have argued that early toll road investors were well aware that they would not recover their capital investments. As turnpikes greatly facilitated movement and trade, the resulting indirect benefits to merchants, farmers, landowners, and regular citizens were key justifications for turnpike investment even if profits or dividends were not (Klein 1990).

purposes starting in 1817, to protect New Orleans from possible Spanish attack. The new military roads that followed were also aimed in part at controlling Native American populations. In time, federal officials came to realize that these new roads must serve civilian commerce as well, particularly after California and Oregon were added to the union in the late 1840s. Roads such as the Oregon and Santa Fe Trails played a prominent role in the occupation and development of the West, although these were more often rough, unpaved wagon tracks that carried migrants rather than large-scale interregional commerce. Recognizing their growing importance for civilian use, in 1857 supervision of these roads passed from the War Department to the Department of the Interior. Congress even authorized ambitious plans for improving three transcontinental routes; however, the work eventually performed was modest. Other road development tended to occur only in areas where travel was so light that rail service was economically impractical. So, in the mid-nineteenth century there was no hint of a national road network, even for postal service. Most economic activity clung to railroad stops and navigable rivers.[38]

Urban and Rural Roads at the Dawn of the Automobile Era

In cities, just as automobiles arrived on the scene, streets—for reasons largely independent of the auto—were better maintained than ever before, primarily due to the introduction of new road surface materials, modern paving technologies, and the hiring of professional engineers.[39] All of these developments, however, would not have taken place without the gradual shift from reliance on abutter finance to property tax finance, which made street construction and maintenance the preserve of the entire municipality.

The horsecar, and later the electric streetcar, both of which traveled on rails and not pavement, remained the dominant means of travel for intracity trips longer than walking distance through the 1910s. However, they increasingly shared space with horse-drawn wagons, bicyclists, and pedestrians on street systems that were poorly designed for moving large volumes of through traffic. This logically reflected the tradition of multiple uses for city streets characteristic of the eighteenth and nineteenth centuries, but it proved ever more problematic with the explosive growth of automobile ownership and use that was soon to occur.

In rural areas, rivers, canals, and then railroads were the primary means of intercity and interregional travel. Road travel outside of cities remained exceedingly slow and difficult by modern standards. Spending on building and improving rural roads was paltry. In 1906 only $75 million was spent on rural roads ($2.2 billion in 2021$) versus $800 million on urban streets ($23.4 billion in 2021$).[40] As noted above, because most rural roads were "financed" by corvée labor, they were usually poorly maintained, used primarily for local horse and buggy travel and connecting farmers to railheads by wagon, and formed nothing resembling a national highway network.

Efforts to improve these poor rural roads finally began to take root with the rise of the automobile, the Good Roads Movement, and the beginnings of the highway engineering profession. We turn next to these with the story of the early automobile era and the concomitant revolution in travel.

PART II
PLANNING AND FINANCING ROADS
FOR AUTOS BEFORE FREEWAYS

3

Planning and Paying for Streets in Cities in the Pre-Freeway Automobile Era

Karl Friedrich Benz built a practical gasoline-powered car in Germany by 1885, and he exhibited one at the 1893 Chicago World's Fair. By 1900 he had developed practically all of the basic features of a modern internal combustion engine automobile: an electric ignition, a water-cooling system, a differential gear and surface carburetor, a gearbox for changing speeds, and a fixed rear axle and steerable front stub axles. However, early autos were individually handcrafted and very expensive, ranging in price from $8,000 to $12,000 (about $245,000 to $366,000 in 2021$). During the two decades between 1908 and 1929, though, Henry Ford's mass-produced Model T cut the price to $600 (about $8,000 in 2021$) and the automobile ceased to be a mere plaything of the rich. Instead it became the primary means of high-speed, albeit short-distance, transportation in the United States. Affordable automobiles proved a smash hit with consumers. The number of cars on the road rose from just 8,000 in 1900 to 5.55 million by 1918.[1]

Though it dramatically increased mobility, the auto also brought with it a set of new traffic congestion problems, particularly in urban areas. In response, concerned city officials engaged the services of consulting planners and engineers who developed increasingly sophisticated traffic regulations and proposed major street improvements to accommodate burgeoning automobile use. Their plans reflected a desire for civic grandeur as well as practical solutions to congestion, though the two aspirations were sometimes at odds. As their interventions grew more elaborate, and costlier, new means of paying for urban roads had to be devised.[2]

Avenues as Art: Transportation Planning and the City Beautiful Movement

The earliest city plans in the United States, such as New York's Commissioners' Plan discussed in the previous chapter, were typically layouts for street

The Drive for Dollars. Jeffrey R. Brown, Eric A. Morris, and Brian D. Taylor, Oxford University Press.
© Oxford University Press 2023. DOI: 10.1093/oso/9780197601518.003.0003

systems that sought to impose order on future growth. Early twentieth-century planners of what was known as the "City Beautiful" movement expanded on this approach, seeking not only to use street networks to help shape urban development,[3] but also to use their plans to inspire residents and even mold their attitudes.[4] The monumental boulevard plans that Baron Georges Haussmann prepared for Paris in the nineteenth century were sources of inspiration for City Beautiful planners.[5] This vision of transportation facilities differed from that of the emerging engineering profession, and not surprisingly the two visions found their expression in different kinds of plan making.

Daniel Burnham was perhaps the leading City Beautiful planner, by virtue of the plans he prepared for cities such as Cleveland (1902), Washington, D.C. (1904), San Francisco (1905), and Chicago (1909). His Chicago Plan of 1909 is his most famous and influential one, as it inspired many other planners and cities to pursue similarly ambitious visions. Burnham's approach to the plan's many proposed boulevards and parkways, and its lakeshore drive, was principally aesthetic as opposed to functional; it focused on the monumental scale and form of the facilities, as opposed to their traffic-carrying characteristics (see Figure 3.1).[6] In Burnham's plans, and those of his contemporaries, streets were beautiful public spaces that also facilitated traffic movement.[7] The scale of Burnham's vision for Chicago served to inspire numerous other cities' plans to include a significant aesthetic focus.

The City Beautiful movement came under increasing criticism in the first decade of the twentieth century due to its perceived elitist biases.[8] The movement's critics called for increased governmental activism in the pursuit of greater social justice.[9] A rival planning movement soon emerged, variously called the "City Practical" or "City Functional," whose adherents argued that planning could attain professional legitimacy only when planners acquired and applied formal technical knowledge to solve problems.[10] In doing so, they were firmly within the ethos of the late nineteenth- and early twentieth-century Progressive Era, which stressed the application of engineering, statistical, medical, administrative, and scientific solutions to urban problems, as well as ending the patronage system of public employment by replacing political appointees with impartial, technocratic civil servants. By the time of the 1909 National Conference on City Planning, a watershed event in the rise of American planning, the shift toward a focus on the application of technical knowledge to real-world problems was nearly complete.[11]

However, many planners still combined the use of technical skills to address real-world problems with a sensibility toward aesthetics and design.

Figure 3.1. Boulevard over the Chicago River from the Plan of Chicago (1909).

Source: Burnham, Daniel, and Edward H. Bennett. 1909. *Plan of Chicago*. Chicago: The Commercial Club of Chicago. Plate CXII. Courtesy of the Chicago History Museum, ICHi-059758; Jules Guerin, artist; invoice 31763.

Raymond Unwin, an influential UK-based planner, proposed a street classification scheme that differentiated main roads from residential streets as a means of redirecting traffic away from residential neighborhoods.[12] Yet in addition to this very practical concern, he gave significant attention to the aesthetic qualities of streets and to the roles that streets played as social spaces. A similar approach was taken by Charles Mulford Robinson, whose influential 1911 book *The Width and Arrangement of Streets* helped to popularize function-based street classification to a wider group of planners and engineers.[13] In his classic 1916 text *City Planning*, written against a backdrop of public concern about rapid urban growth and increasing traffic congestion, Robinson called for classifying streets as either main thoroughfares or minor streets as a way to protect residential streets from the increasing nuisance and danger of vehicle traffic.[14] Yet he also emphasized other roles that proper street patterns could play to facilitate land subdivision, define community spaces, and provide opportunities for "architectural accents" where streets intersected.[15] The transitional style of transportation planning championed by Unwin and Robinson emphasized the street's traditional role as a social space, in addition to serving as a traffic conduit.[16] This holistic appreciation for the many, and sometimes competing, uses for street space is entirely congruent with the modern "Complete Streets" movement that emerged a century later.

A similar outlook was present in the work of Frederick Law Olmsted Jr., whose background is a testament to the early multidisciplinary nature of urban transportation planning. He was the son of the prominent landscape architect Frederick Law Olmsted Sr., who designed New York City's Central Park (with its innovative grade separation of roads and walkways that later influenced the design of freeways).[17] While an architect by training, the younger Olmsted's work had a notably practical bent, likely due to the increasingly pressing urban transportation problems of the time and the preferences of his clients. He became one of the leading planning consultants in the country.

Around 1910, city officials began to voice concerns that rising streetcar, horse-drawn vehicle, automobile, and pedestrian congestion collectively threatened the economic well-being of their central business districts (CBDs).[18] Downtown business and property owners were alarmed by the worsening congestion and its potential negative effects on commercial activity and property values. Most cities at the time did not have a staff of professionally trained planners and engineers, so city officials and local business groups turned to outside experts for guidance in coping with ever-rising traffic.

But despite the focus on practical traffic solutions, many of their plans, particularly Olmsted Jr.'s, retained a significant aesthetic component. For example, his 1910 *Pittsburgh Main Thoroughfares* plan examined traffic flows in the downtown Triangle and devised a program that addressed the concerns of city officials and the business community about growing congestion.

The plan included new street construction, two new river crossings into the Triangle, and the development of a regional arterial street network to connect the city with its growing suburbs.[19] And while his plan primarily addressed more efficient traffic circulation, it also paid substantial attention to the aesthetics of transportation infrastructure. The two new bridges were to be based largely on European examples, and the plan called for the development of an elaborate system of parks to parallel the regional arterial network. Olmsted's grand plans for Pittsburgh went unrealized, however, due to their cost.[20]

Aesthetic concerns are also evident in the *Central Traffic Parkway* plan for St. Louis prepared by other like-minded consultants.[21] As in Pittsburgh, St. Louis' downtown business leaders and city officials feared that increasing traffic congestion was causing businesses to move away from the central city, thus reducing downtown property values and property tax receipts.[22] They believed that transportation improvements might stabilize property values by reducing congestion, thereby checking the trend toward suburbanization. The St. Louis City Plan Commission's report illustrates both the aesthetic impulses and appeals to practicality found in many plans of this era. It proposed a monumental central traffic parkway along the lines of Paris' Champs-Elysees, Berlin's Unter den Linden, and Vienna's Ringstrasse to serve as a conduit for traffic, a means to stabilize property values, a guide to future city development, and an aesthetic adornment. "Monumental" aptly describes the proposed facility, which was to include two separate sets of traffic ways, two sets of streetcar tracks, two narrow park strips, and a central boulevard. These would be housed within a right-of-way almost as wide (at 287 feet) as a football field is long, cut through the middle of the city.[23] As in Pittsburgh, prohibitive costs doomed this grand plan.

Urban transportation plans of the 1910s illustrate that, despite the slow move toward a more practical orientation, the City Beautiful ethos of monumental design retained an allure for transportation planners, landscape architects, and engineers, even though it was frequently that costly monumentalism that prevented the plans' realization. Accordingly, their plans reflected a conviction that transportation systems should serve to complement, not clash with, the urban form. But the combination of a dramatic increase in automobile use (and an attendant increase in congestion), the Progressive Era's faith in the ability of science to provide answers to practical problems, the planning profession's desire for legitimacy and status, and the lack of funds to pay for grandiose projects provided new pressure for transportation planning to cast aside its aesthetic pretensions and become a more technical exercise conducted by trained experts.

The Automobile and a New Urban Traffic Congestion Crisis

Between 1910 and 1915, the number of automobiles in the United States increased fivefold, from 469,000 to 2.5 million. Over the next few years, the number of autos doubled, and then doubled again, and then doubled once more, reaching 20 million by 1925.[24] This was in large part due to rapidly falling auto prices, plus the auto's transition from an open-air conveyance to a fully enclosed, all-weather vehicle with amenities like pneumatic tires, electric starters, heating, and windshield wipers. Taken together, these developments caused the automobile to quickly evolve from a plaything of the rich into a means of everyday mass transportation.[25]

The manufacture and sale of large numbers of automobiles soon had a dramatic impact in urban areas. The number of automobile commuters quickly exceeded the number of streetcar commuters in cities such as Los Angeles and San Francisco.[26] This led to increased congestion and slower travel speeds.[27] One author observed, "In New York and, more surprising because of its wide streets and smaller central business district, Washington, D.C., pedestrians could travel faster than cars downtown during rush hour."[28] This obviously did not sit well with motorists, who were rapidly growing in both number and political clout.

As traffic worsened and made downtown shopping and other activities more difficult, businesses began to relocate to less-congested suburban districts in order to be closer to their customers.[29] These new districts catered explicitly to motorists by providing plentiful, typically free, automobile parking. Eyeing the rise of these satellite centers with genuine alarm, downtown merchants and property owners added their voices to the general clamor for traffic relief.[30] With the economic primacy of CBDs now in question, downtown business leaders impressed on municipal authorities that the problem of traffic congestion was undermining the economic health of their cities and costing tax revenues.[31]

In response, officials in cities around the U.S. began to argue that the central goal of urban transportation planning should be to improve travel conditions for motorists, particularly in gridlocked CBDs. As a result, competing objectives—creating beautiful streets, accommodating the myriad social and economic uses of street space, and serving the needs of pedestrians, bicyclists, and streetcars—began to fall by the wayside. Given the ever more intense interest in congestion on the part of the city leaders, the expert consultants who had a few years earlier concentrated on city building as much as traffic relief increasingly focused primarily, even exclusively, on mitigating traffic in order to facilitate automobile travel.

Meeting the Motorists' Need for Speed

As we have noted, while automobiles presented special problems, urban traffic congestion was not at all a new phenomenon; for many years pedestrians mingled with horse-drawn vehicles and later streetcars on typically narrow, winding, or disconnected streets. Local officials had addressed these challenges through a combination of mostly modest measures. These included some basic traffic regulations; William Phelps Eno, an amateur transportation enthusiast, wrote the first manual of traffic regulations for New York City in 1903 and is credited with inventing and/or popularizing innovations such as the stop sign, the yield sign, and the pedestrian crosswalk.[32] In addition to the wider use of asphalt concrete paving, there were other, mostly small-scale infrastructure investments. These mitigated, but never solved, the congestion problem.

But the rapid growth in automobile ownership posed new challenges for America's largely unprepared cities. Motorists occupied considerably more street space than those traveling on foot or by streetcar, and they tended to make more trips than their non-motoring compatriots.[33] Motorists also demanded higher-speed travel. This desire for speed, passionately expressed by automobile enthusiasts and auto club representatives, often went unfulfilled in cities due to rough street surfaces, poorly interconnected street networks, uncontrolled intersections, and competing uses for street space. On the rare occasions when motorists' need for speed was fulfilled, conflicts with slower pedestrians and streetcar users inevitably arose.

Such conflicts contributed to ongoing debates over various users' rights to urban street space. As motorists grew frustrated with chronic traffic congestion, city-dwellers were increasingly agitated by the large numbers of pedestrians, particularly children, who were injured or killed by motor vehicles. The expert consultants to whom cities were turning for help invariably, and largely successfully, addressed pedestrian-motorist conflicts through regulation, primarily by segregating pedestrians to sidewalks and restricting their access to other parts of the street in the interests of personal safety.[34] The congestion problem, on the other hand, proved more intractable, and its relief became a preoccupation of urban property and business owners, motorists, journalists, and public officials. In turn, it became a preoccupation of the leading transportation experts across the country.

Who belonged to this growing cadre of consulting engineers and planners? They were largely believers in the Progressive Era ideal that the application of rational, data-driven methods could overcome just about any societal problem. Men (and they were uniformly men in this era) such as architect-engineer Charles H. Cheney and traffic engineer Miller McClintock, among many others, traveled from city to city as guns-for-hire, arguing that the application of their more "scientific" planning techniques could rid cities of traffic delays for good.[35] Such optimism was quite understandable since technocratic approaches were proving successful in dealing with other urban problems like public sanitation. Surely a similar application of scientific know-how would also solve the problem of urban traffic congestion.

Perhaps the foremost practitioner of this new transportation science was planner-engineer Harland Bartholomew. Widely considered the most important urban transportation planner of the early automobile era, Bartholomew's handiwork is evident today in the many dozens of American cities that retained him as a consultant during his half-century career stretching from 1911 to 1965.[36] Raised in a suburb of Boston, and later in Brooklyn, the twentieth century's most influential advocate for rational, comprehensive urban transportation planning completed just two years of civil engineering study at Rutgers University before dropping out for lack of money. His first professional position was with E. P. Goodrich, a firm that advocated planning to increase the efficiency of cities. Just a couple of years later, Bartholomew was recruited by civic reformers to St. Louis; there he became the nation's first full-time planner working for an American city, a job he held for 37 years.[37] A committed, and in retrospect perhaps naïve, believer that cities could be fully known and optimized through data collection and scientific analysis,[38] Bartholomew published extensively and taught planning and urban design at the nearby University of Illinois from 1918 to 1956, in addition to serving as a presidential appointee on national planning commissions.[39] But perhaps his greatest influence on American cities and planning was through his consulting firm, Harland Bartholomew and Associates, which during his career prepared plans for over 500 cities in the U.S. and abroad.[40] While both greatly esteemed for his commitment to integrated land use and transportation planning, and widely criticized for supporting racial segregation,[41] Bartholomew lived long enough to see many of his ideas—auto-focused suburban development, single-use zoning, and slum clearance—fall out of favor with planners by the time of his death at age 100 in 1989.[42]

Bartholomew, and the growing cadre of transportation professionals employed by cities and/or privately financed traffic committees dominated largely by CBD business interests, wrapped themselves in the cloak of science. This was in higher esteem than ever due to the dazzling rise of scientific knowledge and engineering know-how between the world wars. Early transportation planners and engineers were fond of referring to their work as unbiased and technocratic, despite the fact that it inevitably involved subjective considerations and value judgments—most notably that it was necessary to facilitate ever-increasing automobile travel to and through the centers of American cities. Such self-aggrandizement may well have been sincere, and it certainly proved helpful in selling their plans to public officials and voters.

These planners spent the first few decades of the twentieth century expanding their understanding of motor vehicle traffic and developing larger and ever more elaborate street, and later highway, system plans. They were to have considerable success in formulating theoretical and practical approaches to traffic management, and in many ways their work was both prescient and effective. However, this very success sowed the seeds of subsequent failures. Overconfidence in both the powers of science and their methods meant that some well-intended, rational approaches to understanding transportation in cities ultimately helped to produce unintended and irrational outcomes, particularly from the 1950s onward, as modern urban freeways took shape.

Building a Science of Urban Transportation Planning: The Need for Data

Bartholomew and other transportation experts typically approached their task in a diligent, orderly, and somewhat lockstep manner.[43] All began by collecting data to better understand the patterns of vehicle movement and how they were affected by street layouts.[44] By the 1920s, many states and cities were conducting at least sporadic traffic counts,[45] and in that decade a contemporary of Bartholomew, Miller McClintock of the Erskine Street Traffic Research Bureau at Harvard University, pioneered the "community traffic survey" to inform various traffic regulation and management plans.[46] It was soon to be adapted and adopted by other consultants. In the pages of *The American City* magazine,[*] McClintock outlined the process for conducting community traffic surveys.[47] The surveys collected data on the physical layout and carrying capacity of streets; the operations of streetcars; the directions, speeds, and volumes of automobile traffic; police data on crashes involving motorized vehicles; and, in a few of the more comprehensive surveys, data on pedestrian movement and vehicle parking.[48] Planners could use these

---

[*] *The American City* was an urban affairs and planning magazine published between 1909 and 1942 and read widely by city officials, planners, and urbanists of the day. Its modern counterpart is *Planning* magazine, published by the American Planning Association.

data to produce graphs and maps that identified what were referred to at the time as "desire lines"—straight lines that connect traveler origins with their destinations, the aggregation of which was then used to give transportation planners and engineers a sense as to where larger numbers of people wished to travel. In turn, these desire lines could be used to identify bottlenecks and other areas facing heavy traffic congestion. Planning based on this projected travel demand was intended to avoid problematic land development and to roll out street systems planned explicitly to accommodate desired travel.[49] Importantly, the wealth of data generated through these surveys gave planners the appearance of being both objective and apolitical.[50]

These early surveys could also help to diagnose the underlying causes of traffic congestion, with population growth and ever-rising automobile ownership being the most widely cited reasons. But urban leaders had little control over these, so they were taken as given. Other, more readily addressed factors included (1) still-inadequate rules of the road, (2) insufficient street capacity, (3) the mixing of different classes of traffic (auto, truck, streetcar) on the same streets, and (4) the absence of facilities to separate local and through traffic.[51]

The Rise of the Rules of the Road

Eno's work had advanced the science of traffic regulation, but modern right-of-way rules were still not fully developed or deployed in the early decades of the twentieth century. Cross traffic and turning movements posed substantial obstacles to through traffic, as did pedestrians who routinely crossed streets whenever and wherever they chose.[52] Motorists parked wherever they found space, including on sidewalks or in traffic lanes. Local regulations for speed, parking, and emissions were inconsistent, and at times contradictory, from place to place, which proved problematic for often-unwitting motorists who fell afoul of the varying rules.[53] The first task, then, was to impose order through consistent traffic regulation.

Out of concern for pedestrian safety in addition to vehicle movement, McClintock built on Eno's work by using his survey data to help draft new traffic regulations. These addressed chaotic street conditions through rules governing the movements of pedestrians, streetcars, and motorists. A particular focus was the adoption of anti-jaywalking laws. In doing so, McClintock's work accelerated the transformation of city streets from their historic role as community economic and social spaces into traffic ways.[54] McClintock did not invent these regulatory ideas, but he developed an elaborate analytic framework that legitimated them, codified them in traffic ordinances, and worked tirelessly to spread them through his consulting work. McClintock personally drafted the ordinances for San Francisco (1927), Boston (1928), and Kansas City (1930), among many other cities, and he and his adherents spread similar ordinances to cities around the country. Most clients were civic and business organizations, audiences that were particularly eager to smooth traffic flows to and from properties and businesses.[55] McClintock often cited the formation of business-dominated traffic committees as an essential component of effective urban transportation planning.[56]

Cities across the country rushed to adopt new traffic ordinances, and intersection control and traffic-signaling systems began to be installed shortly thereafter.[57] Stop signs first appeared in 1911. Traffic signals began to be introduced around 1920; though they were initially manually operated, timed lights were first introduced in 1922 and traffic-actuated lights in 1928.[58] Their spread did indeed increase traffic throughput by unclogging many previously jammed intersections. McClintock also devoted attention to the issue of on-street vehicle parking and urged cities to impose parking bans on particularly busy streets so that scarce road space could be devoted to moving traffic as opposed to storing vehicles.[59] Parking was an important issue in most plans of this era. If a central goal of cities was to increase social and economic activity, then these new ordinances and signalized intersections were unambiguous successes, as more people and goods could move to, from, and through central cities faster, safer, and more reliably.

The rise of the rules of the road had broader—and in some ways pernicious—effects as well. The deployment of local, county, and state police and sheriffs to enforce the new traffic laws greatly expanded the role of policing in America. Police forces were enlarged, often substantially, to apply the new laws. Such enforcement was abetted by a series of narrow court interpretations of the Fourth Amendment—which constitutionally protects against unreasonable searches and seizures—as applied to traffic enforcement. This meant, and still means, that most Americans' contact with police is from an automobile. The broad discretion granted to police in enforcing traffic laws has been a source of ongoing social tension and civil rights struggles for many decades. In particular, racially biased traffic enforcement—of "driving while Black"—increasingly caught on camera for all to see in recent years, remains a troubling legacy of the rise of traffic regulations and enforcement at the dawn of the automobile era.[60]

While traffic signs, signals, and regulations increased traffic throughput, reduced crashes, and increased the scale of policing, they most decidedly did not tame traffic congestion. Despite sometimes-dramatic increases in the traffic-carrying capacities of streets, congestion inevitably reappeared as a rising tide of vehicles quickly overwhelmed even the most farsighted efforts to squeeze more traffic through city streets. These improvements, in other words, were victims of their own success. But rather than reconsider the myopic focus on traffic relief, McClintock and his peers remained unshaken in their belief in traffic science and redoubled their efforts to sate the ever-rising demand for auto and truck travel.

The Rationalization of City Street Layouts

Transportation planners of the era broadly agreed that inadequate street systems were at least partly responsible for chronic traffic congestion. Many streets were too narrow for the traffic volumes they carried, as pedestrians, automobiles, horse-driven vehicles, and streetcars competed ever more aggressively for limited road space. For example, the typical 40-foot-wide street of that era had room for a traffic and parking lane in each direction, but with no space for left turn pockets to keep turning vehicles from holding up traffic; further, there was frequent double parking by motor vehicles due to limited off-street parking.[61] As a legacy of the piecemeal growth of urban road networks, many streets contained dead ends or awkward jogs at cross streets that required frequent turns by through travelers.[62]

The new generation of transportation planners and engineers argued that there was an ideal ratio of street area to building area in downtowns. Failing to meet this ratio would result in unacceptable traffic congestion. They criticized cities such as Los Angeles for falling short of this ideal; 21 percent of its downtown land area was dedicated to streets, while San Francisco devoted 30 percent and Washington, D.C., more than 40 percent. They criticized other cities for the poor layout of their street systems. For example, Oakland, California, was singled out for having nearly 200 sudden twists and turns, and abrupt dead ends, on its major streets.[63]

The logical response to both shortcomings was to build more, better-connected, straighter, and larger streets, as cities had begun doing at considerable cost even before the automobile arrived.[64] Planners, not surprisingly, advised that greater foresight was required, and that interconnected street systems should be planned in advance of, or in conjunction with, new development so as to avoid wasteful and unnecessary future construction expenses. The planners, in other words, advised planning.

Figure 3.2. Traffic Jam at 7th and Hill, Los Angeles (1936).
Source: Los Angeles County Metropolitan Transportation Authority.

The Development of Street Classification

City streets were also asked to host a diverse, and often conflicting, array of conveyances. Bartholomew referred to this as the "promiscuous" mixing of different modes of traffic,[65] including everything from the latest fast-moving automobiles to bulky streetcars to lumbering heavy trucks to pedestrians to the occasional horse-drawn wagon.[66] While, as we have noted, conflicts between cars and pedestrians were dealt with mostly through regulation, streetcars posed another set of problems. They were inflexibly lashed to their street rails and made numerous stops to gather and discharge passengers, generally in the middle of the street. Conversely, increasing automobile and truck traffic interfered with the smooth operation of streetcars, particularly when double-parked delivery vehicles blocked traffic and when moving vehicles endangered streetcar passengers' boarding and alighting (see Figure 3.2).[67] Most transportation planners of the day saw inflexible street railways as a major cause of congestion, and many advocated relocating transit routes (which were almost exclusively privately owned and operated) to less heavily trafficked parallel streets so as not to disrupt faster-moving cars.[68] Harland

Bartholomew was particularly insistent that streetcar and automobile traffic be separated, citing the "improper" routing of transit lines as a common problem in congested centers.[69]

To address this problem, experts like Bartholomew recommended classifying streets into a hierarchy based on their functions, and then segregating traffic types by function (see Figure 3.3). The idea of street classification was not a new one, as it had appeared earlier in work by Unwin and Robinson, but the classification schemes that emerged in the 1920s were more formally structured. The idea caught on, and street classifications are used by transportation planners and engineers to the present day. But in contrast to the holistic, multimodal street classification systems increasingly employed in the 2020s, the classifications developed a century earlier characterized a street's function solely in relation to the carriage of motor vehicle traffic. Some streets were designated as major high-speed traffic carriers; these eventually became modern-day arterials (often called boulevards or urban highways in modern parlance). Lower-level classifications eventually included modern-day collectors (streets scaled between arterials and local streets), and minor, property-serving local streets. Planners and engineers of the day specified minimum desirable roadway designs and widths for each street class in the hierarchy.[70]

Street classification strategies were effective in concentrating heavy volumes of higher-speed traffic on larger streets and largely excluding it from others, thus increasing the network's vehicle-carrying capacity while reducing through traffic on some streets. This enhanced safety for motorists and, at least on the minor streets, pedestrians as well; it also allowed resource-strapped cities to focus their road building resources on the "most important" traffic-bearing arterials. But this increasing focus on traffic service came at a price; many major city streets evolved from lively, if chaotic, venues of social and economic activity to mere conduits of vehicular traffic.[71]

Accommodating Through Traffic

Transportation planners also diagnosed a fourth cause of congestion: the lack of adequate crosstown routes for through traffic.[72] In cities with radial street patterns, for example, traffic moving from one end of a metropolitan area to the other was often funneled through the CBD on already crowded local streets. Some business owners initially viewed crowded streets as a sign of prosperity, indicating the presence of many potential customers.[73] But when it became clear that many vehicles were just passing through, and in doing so might be making it harder for customers to access their businesses, CBD merchants began to view through traffic as a problem.

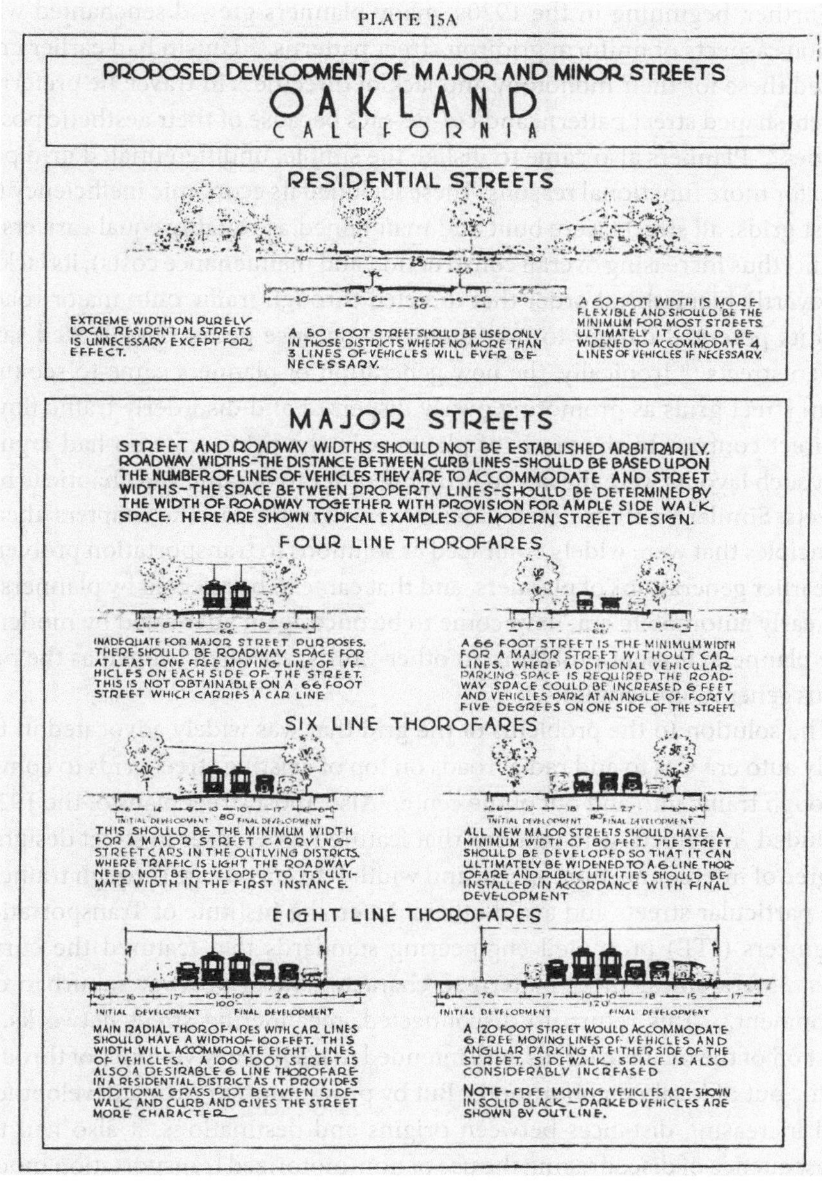

PROPOSED DEVELOPMENT OF MAJOR AND MINOR STREETS
OAKLAND
CALIFORNIA

RESIDENTIAL STREETS

EXTREME WIDTH ON PURELY LOCAL RESIDENTIAL STREETS IS UNNECESSARY EXCEPT FOR EFFECT.

A 50 FOOT STREET SHOULD BE USED ONLY IN THOSE DISTRICTS WHERE NO MORE THAN 3 LINES OF VEHICLES WILL EVER BE NECESSARY.

A 60 FOOT WIDTH IS MORE FLEXIBLE AND SHOULD BE THE MINIMUM FOR MOST STREETS. ULTIMATELY IT COULD BE WIDENED TO ACCOMMODATE 4 LINES OF VEHICLES IF NECESSARY.

MAJOR STREETS

STREET AND ROADWAY WIDTHS SHOULD NOT BE ESTABLISHED ARBITRARILY. ROADWAY WIDTHS—THE DISTANCE BETWEEN CURB LINES—SHOULD BE BASED UPON THE NUMBER OF LINES OF VEHICLES THEY ARE TO ACCOMMODATE AND STREET WIDTHS—THE SPACE BETWEEN PROPERTY LINES—SHOULD BE DETERMINED BY THE WIDTH OF ROADWAY TOGETHER WITH PROVISION FOR AMPLE SIDE WALK SPACE. HERE ARE SHOWN TYPICAL EXAMPLES OF MODERN STREET DESIGN.

FOUR LINE THOROFARES

INADEQUATE FOR MAJOR STREET PURPOSES. THERE SHOULD BE ROADWAY SPACE FOR AT LEAST ONE FREE MOVING LINE OF VEHICLES ON EACH SIDE OF THE STREET. THIS IS NOT OBTAINABLE ON A 66 FOOT STREET WHICH CARRIES A CAR LINE

A 66 FOOT STREET IS THE MINIMUM WIDTH FOR A MAJOR STREET WITHOUT CAR LINES. WHERE ADDITIONAL VEHICULAR PARKING SPACE IS REQUIRED THE ROADWAY SPACE COULD BE INCREASED 6 FEET AND VEHICLES PARK AT AN ANGLE OF FORTY FIVE DEGREES ON ONE SIDE OF THE STREET.

SIX LINE THOROFARES

INITIAL DEVELOPMENT 80 FINAL DEVELOPMENT

THIS SHOULD BE THE MINIMUM WIDTH FOR A MAJOR STREET CARRYING STREET CARS IN THE OUTLYING DISTRICTS. WHERE TRAFFIC IS LIGHT THE ROADWAY NEED NOT BE DEVELOPED TO ITS ULTIMATE WIDTH IN THE FIRST INSTANCE.

INITIAL DEVELOPMENT FINAL DEVELOPMENT

ALL NEW MAJOR STREETS SHOULD HAVE A MINIMUM WIDTH OF 80 FEET. THE STREET SHOULD BE DEVELOPED SO THAT IT CAN ULTIMATELY BE WIDENED TO A 6 LINE THOROFARE AND PUBLIC UTILITIES SHOULD BE INSTALLED IN ACCORDANCE WITH FINAL DEVELOPMENT

EIGHT LINE THOROFARES

INITIAL DEVELOPMENT 100 FINAL DEVELOPMENT

MAIN RADIAL THOROFARES WITH CAR LINES SHOULD HAVE A WIDTH OF 100 FEET. THIS WIDTH WILL ACCOMMODATE EIGHT LINES OF VEHICLES. A 100 FOOT STREET IS ALSO A DESIRABLE 6 LINE THOROFARE IN A RESIDENTIAL DISTRICT AS IT PROVIDES ADDITIONAL GRASS PLOT BETWEEN SIDEWALK AND CURB AND GIVES THE STREET MORE CHARACTER.

INITIAL DEVELOPMENT 120 FINAL DEVELOPMENT

A 120 FOOT STREET WOULD ACCOMMODATE 6 FREE MOVING LINES OF VEHICLES AND ANGULAR PARKING AT EITHER SIDE OF THE STREET. SIDEWALK SPACE IS ALSO CONSIDERABLY INCREASED

NOTE—FREE MOVING VEHICLES ARE SHOWN IN SOLID BLACK—PARKED VEHICLES ARE SHOWN BY OUTLINE.

Figure 3.3. Street classification in the 1920s.

Source: Harland Bartholomew and Associates. 1927. "A Proposed Plan for a System of Major Traffic Highways: Oakland, California." Oakland, CA: Major Highway and Traffic Committee of One Hundred. Plate 15A, 50. Permission granted by Barry Hogue for Parsons (inheritor for Harland Bartholomew and Associates).

Further, beginning in the 1920s, many planners grew disenchanted with various aspects of uniform gridiron street patterns.[74] Unwin had earlier criticized these for their monotony and lack of directness in travel; he preferred a web-shaped street pattern, and cul-de-sacs because of their aesthetic possibilities.[75] Planners also came to dislike the simple, undifferentiated grid pattern for more functional reasons. These included its economic inefficiency (in most grids, all streets were built and maintained as roughly equal carriers of traffic, thus increasing overall construction and maintenance costs), its lack of an overtly hierarchical order that directed through traffic onto major roads, and its potential danger to non-motorists because pedestrians lacked safe-haven streets.[76] Ironically, the new generation of planners came to see uniform street grids as promoting overly dispersed and disorderly traffic flows, a direct contrast to the views of planners in the prior era who had argued that such layouts were the key to bringing order to organic and chaotic urban streets. Similar to other developments we will outline in the chapters ahead, principles that were widely embraced as solutions to transportation problems by earlier generations of planners, and that came to be rejected by planners in the early automobile era, have come to be once again advocated by modern-day planners. Present problems, in other words, are often framed as the previous generation's solutions.

The solution to the problems of the grid that was widely advocated in the early auto era was to add radial roads on top of existing street grids to convey through traffic into and out of the center. Also, most street plans of the 1920s included "modified" grid patterns that featured differences in street design—degree of interconnection, speed, and width—to encourage through traffic to use particular streets and avoid others. Later, the Institute of Transportation Engineers (ITE) promoted engineering standards that featured the curvilinear, hierarchical street pattern so characteristic of postwar suburban development.[77] This return to disconnected, meandering street networks, at least off of the major arterials, was intended to keep heavy volumes of through traffic out of local neighborhoods. But by promoting sprawling development and increasing distances between origins and destinations, it also had the consequence of discouraging the use of non-motorized transportation modes (such as walking and biking) and public transit.

The Major Traffic Street Plans

The so-called major traffic street plan was the principal mechanism through which the transportation experts of the 1920s promoted their ideas. The primary inputs to these plans, obtained from community traffic surveys, were traffic and street network inventories combined with current and forecast population, land use, and economic data.[78] These data were used to apply functional street classification systems, street design standards, and traffic segregation schema. To their proponents, the major traffic street plans were built on a careful, rational methodology that could be applied in any city, but would result in outcomes specific to that city's context.[79] However, while the plans varied substantially in specifics from city to city, they were strikingly similar in the general types of improvements proposed.

Though most of these plans had a narrow focus on relieving traffic congestion, a few linked street planning with land use planning on the premise that a coordinated approach to both road and land development would bring the best long-term congestion-reducing results.[80] However, unlike the earlier grand plans by Daniel Burnham and his peers, and even the transitional work of planners like Olmsted, the major traffic street plans paid little if any attention to aesthetic and social issues. The transition from City Beautiful to City Practical was complete.

The Major Impact of Major Traffic Street Plans

Bartholomew was among the most important proponents of the major traffic street plans. His *Major Street Plan for St. Louis* established a template that, with slight modifications, was the model for most of his other plans.[81]

As was so often the case in U.S. cities, St. Louis city leaders and downtown business groups fretted that motor vehicle congestion had pushed businesses out of the CBD.[82] The City Plan Commission, whose membership was dominated by downtown interests, commissioned Bartholomew to prepare a plan to address traffic congestion in the downtown core.[83] Bartholomew's plan, which was prepared after "securing all available information and after having carefully weighed and considered its value,"[84] featured a highly standardized system of arterial streets, local streets, and minor streets.[85]

The plan proposed a system of major arterials to improve motor vehicle access into and around the CBD; Bartholomew urged the city to devote most of its limited resources to this system.[86,†] The downtown business community supported his recommendations, and city officials quickly implemented his utilitarian and relatively cost-effective plan.[87] This stood in stark contrast to their mothballing of the monumental, grandiose, and expensive City Beautiful plan the city had commissioned just a few years earlier.

---

† The Bartholomew plan considered public transit, but largely in the context of separating streetcars from major streams of auto traffic (Bartholomew 1917). Later in his career, Bartholomew embraced a more multimodal approach to transportation planning (Brown 2005).

Bartholomew followed this with similar assignments in other cities. His 1921 *Plan for Pittsburgh,* developed 11 years after Olmstead's extravagant plan for the central Triangle, was much more modest in scale and utilitarian in character. It paid scant attention to non-traffic-related concerns.[88] After conducting a survey of the street layout and traffic flows, Bartholomew developed a plan that included the classification of all streets according to his now-standard functional formula, the widening of 100 miles of existing streets, and the creation of 22 miles of new streets.[89] As in St. Louis, his clients enthusiastically greeted these data-informed, practically minded traffic relief prescriptions.

Of note among Bartholomew's other major recommendations was a call for the development of a "regional major street system" that would provide direct, high-speed vehicle access between the CBD and the suburbs, as well as a system of crosstown routes that would allow non-CBD traffic to avoid downtown.[90] What he envisioned in the Pittsburgh plan were not quite modern freeways, but the proposed regional major streets proved forerunners for a new type of higher-speed, higher-capacity metropolitan highway that soon came to dominate the thinking of urban transportation planners.

Scientific Transportation Planning in Los Angeles

Los Angeles, widely viewed as perhaps the exemplar automobile city, serves as an instructive illustration of the transportation planning approaches of the time. The city's Mediterranean climate, relative affluence, and low-density development patterns were conducive to the rapid adoption of the automobile. Indeed, vehicle registrations surged from 110,000 in 1918 to more than 400,000 five years later. The swift development of the city meant that it was afflicted with a hastily arranged street system, with many disconnected street segments of highly variable width and condition.[91] In short, Los Angeles in the 1920s suffered from the sorts of traffic problems that afflicted most other growing cities, only more so.

The city was also home to civic groups striving to find solutions to these problems so that they would not inhibit growth. The most important was the business-dominated Los Angeles Traffic Commission (LATC), which was widely cited as a model for other cities.[92] The LATC was formed to study the city's traffic problems and develop solutions that would maintain the economic stability of the CBD and enhance the region's future economic prospects. It claimed, "It is not too much to say that the onward march of Los

Angeles toward its place of destiny will be made immeasurably slower unless a solution is found for the traffic problem."[93]

In the early 1920s, City Engineer John Griffin advised the LATC and city officials that a program similar to that being developed in St. Louis held the answer to the city's congestion problems.[94] The LATC, in partnership with the Automobile Club of Southern California (ACSC), unveiled a locally developed plan that included more than 200 specific street-widening and construction projects, designated major traffic streets, and called for the separation of grade crossings[‡] both in congested districts and at major railroad crossings.[95] The LATC emphasized that the plan's success depended on alerting the public to the long-term dangers of traffic congestion and encouraging public enthusiasm for the plan's solutions.

The plan garnered favorable press but little immediate action, so its members decided that a more detailed investigation, to be prepared by "neutral," "objective," and influential outside experts, was required. The Commission retained the services of three of the biggest names in the field: Bartholomew, Olmsted, and Cheney. Olmstead and Cheney, like Bartholomew, had been active in the preparation of similar plans for other cities.[96] In a display of civic spirit, local Boy Scouts conducted the required traffic counts for the community traffic survey. (Boy Scouts were called upon to perform this task in other cities as well.)[97] Public transit expert R. F. Kelker and traffic regulation guru McClintock were also retained to contribute their expertise, although Kelker's transit plan was eventually for naught.[§]

The American City magazine praised the city for commissioning these "technical men" to conduct their scientific study of its traffic congestion problem. Bartholomew, Cheney, and Olmsted were asked to focus principally on the downtown portion of the city, but they soon decided to take a more comprehensive view of countywide travel. Even so, *A Major Traffic Street Plan for Los Angeles* largely reflected the traffic-related concerns and objectives of their downtown clients.[98] Due to the planners' reputations, their study was widely perceived as a sound one, and their report was greeted with much fanfare when it was released in 1924.[99]

[‡] A grade crossing in this context was a point where a road and a railroad track intersect at the same level. The term can also refer to a point where two roads intersect. Later, urban freeways eliminated all crossings at grade along their routes.

[§] Kelker proposed a plan to improve Los Angeles' transit operations through a radial system of new subways and elevated rail transit lines, tied into an extensive feeder bus network in outlying areas. Covering over 100 miles, the project's price tag was an estimated $133 million (about $2 billion in 2021$). Public subsidies would be needed to supplement farebox revenues. Voters defeated Kelker's plan due to a combination of anti-transit attitudes and suburb-versus-CBD political disputes (Bottles 1987; Foster 1981). Suburb-versus-CBD rivalry marked many of Los Angeles' subsequent transportation efforts, including the 1980 decision to fund the region's rail transit system (Richmond 2005).

The planners diagnosed the causes of the city's traffic congestion as the by-now-familiar combination of the area's rapid growth of population and automobile ownership; an "unscientific width and arrangement of streets"; the "promiscuous" mixing of auto, truck, and streetcar traffic; and the presence of both local and through traffic on city streets. Their plan articulated an elaborate classification scheme that included six distinct categories of streets (distributor streets, radial thoroughfares, inter-district thoroughfares, truck-hauling thoroughfares, parkways and boulevards, and minor streets), each with a standardized width that could best serve its appointed traffic function.[100] The planners used this scheme, and a program of grade-separation at major road crossings, as a means of segregating streetcar and auto traffic (see Figure 3.4). The more visionary elements of the plan included proposals for the creation of a regional parkway network to facilitate intraregional travel and a truck "speedway" to facilitate goods movement between downtown, the city's port at San Pedro to the south, and the San Fernando Valley to the northwest. The planners argued that completing their far-reaching program would result in a dramatic improvement in the entire area's traffic situation.[101],**

The celebrated planners were reluctant to put a price tag on their plan, perhaps because it was obvious that the ambitious program would require many years and hundreds of millions of dollars (equivalent to many billions today) to complete. They did, however, compile a list of $25 million (about $378 million in 2021$) worth of priority projects that were selected, they asserted, based on an analysis of traffic flows and not interest-group pressure. Because they claimed that the projects would benefit all Los Angeles residents, they recommended that the program be paid for with a combination of general tax revenues (derived primarily from property taxes), special assessments on property owners, and bonds (perhaps to be repaid with state motor fuel tax revenues).[102] The LATC worked with the Los Angeles City Council to present the plan, and an accompanying $5 million (about $76 million in 2021$) bond measure, to Los Angeles voters.††

** The planners also wrote that Los Angeles might one day have to distinguish between "important" and "unimportant" types of vehicular travel. For example, they wrote that in severely congested conditions the streetcar's travel should be expedited over that of the automobile because of its larger person-carrying capacity (Olmsted, Bartholomew, and Cheney 1924). They also developed parking restriction proposals for particularly busy streets and called for the future development of a subway system to remove streetcars from the busiest roads. Their transit recommendations echoed the work then being done by R. F. Kelker on a regional transit plan, which met with an unsuccessful result, as noted above (Wachs 1984; Bottles 1987).

†† The bond sale would be used to pay between 10 and 20 percent of the cost of each "priority" project in the city, while adjacent property owners would bear the remaining 80 to 90 percent of the cost (Foster 1981; Bottles 1987).

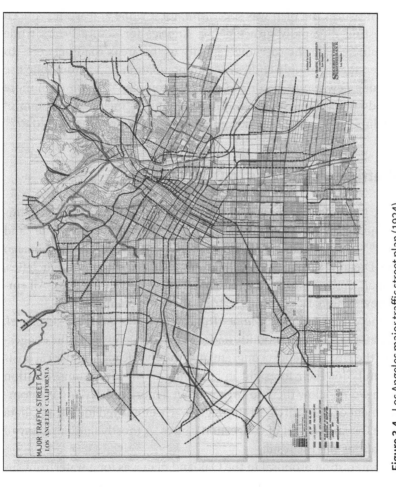

Figure 3.4. Los Angeles major traffic street plan (1924).

Courtesy of Barry Lawrence Ruderman Antique Maps Inc. *Source:* Olmsted, Frederick Law, Harland Bartholomew, and Charles Cheney. 1924. "A Major Street Plan for Los Angeles." Los Angeles, CA: Committee on Los Angeles Plan of Major Highways of the Traffic Commission of the City and County of Los Angeles. Map. Permission granted by Barry Hogue for Parsons (inheritor for Harland Bartholomew and Associates).

The plan was backed by auto enthusiasts and a broad coalition of downtown and suburban business and real estate interests; even local streetcar companies professed belief that the plan was in their best interest, in no small part because of the collective gravitas of the report's authors.[103] Newspapers touted the beneficial effects of the plan on Los Angeles' future growth.[104] In the end, voters approved the plan, and the accompanying bond issue, by a large margin.

By many measures the plan was successful, for a while at least. It reduced traffic congestion in rapidly growing Los Angeles for several years while dramatically increasing the carrying capacity of the area's road network. In time, however, the seemingly endless rise in population and automobile use brought about a new round of congestion that prompted calls for even more elaborate and far-reaching solutions. These eventually included a system of high-speed, limited-access, grade-separated freeways, as we discuss below.[105]

Major Traffic Street Plans in Other Cities

Cheney and Bartholomew parlayed their work in Los Angeles into similar assignments for other California cities, including Riverside and Sacramento.[106] Major traffic street plans were also prepared for Chicago (1925), San Diego (1926, 1930), Vancouver (1928), and many other cities, large and small, around North America in the 1920s and early 1930s. All employed the new systematic approach to transportation planning.[107]

Bartholomew prepared his *Major Traffic Highways Plan for Oakland, California*, before rising automobility had triggered a perceived traffic congestion crisis in the city. His report congratulated the civic leaders and local business community for their foresight in attending to the city's transportation needs, which would allow them to "bring about a more orderly and economical development of the entire East Bay region." He employed local traffic data to illuminate the familiar set of congestion causes. A mostly familiar array of recommendations was the result.

The most interesting proposal in the Oakland plan was for a waterfront superhighway to provide a high-speed through-traffic connection between the growing East Bay communities and the proposed Oakland–San Francisco Bay Bridge.[108] It would be enormous even by today's standards: rail rapid transit in the median, two lanes in each direction for truck traffic, and four lanes in each direction for faster automobile traffic in a grade-separated facility within a 180-foot right-of-way.[109] Bartholomew also included a proto-freeway in his 1928 plan for Vancouver, British Columbia.[110] Neither of these facilities was built, but the idea of a higher class of traffic-serving road was intriguing and would soon be adopted by other similarly minded planners. Such roadways were the next logical step in the ongoing efforts to accommodate ever-increasing numbers of motor vehicles, as it became increasingly clear that efforts to straighten, widen, classify, and interconnect city streets had only slowed, but not halted, the traffic congestion crisis.

Paying for City Streets in the Early Automobile Era: The Rise of Property Tax Finance

Just as urban transportation planning changed significantly between 1908 and 1929, the finance system used to support urban streets changed as well. Cities assumed increasing responsibility for pavement installation, street relocation and expansion, and maintenance, and they also assumed more responsibility for paying for these improvements. While purely local streets still tended to be financed entirely by abutters, improvements on major streets were increasingly funded by mandatory special assessments on larger groups of property owners.[111],[‡‡]

However, the logic of the abutter/special-assessment finance nexus begins to break down when arterials, avenues, boulevards, and other roadways host mostly through traffic, as was the case with the elaborate road improvements proposed as part of major traffic street plans. It seemed fair to expect a homeowner to pay for his local street, but not a roadway through his neighborhood carrying unwanted through traffic that not only generated limited benefits for him but occasioned substantial costs, such as noise, emissions, and traffic delays.[§§]

Thus, with the emergence of mass motorization, faster travel speeds, longer-distance vehicle trips, and an ever-larger proportion of through traffic on city streets and roads, special assessments proved to be philosophically and politically ill-suited to the task at hand. The nexus between property abutters, property access, and road finance was beginning to unravel.

[‡‡] In Los Angeles, for example, special assessments remained routine into the 1920s, contributing 78 percent of the revenues used to amortize street and highway bonds in 1928 (Jones 1989).

[§§] To take a modern example, while proximity to a present-day freeway interchange can enhance the accessibility and value of residential property, freeway *adjacency*, which exposes residents to the noise and pollution of freeways with no added access relative to those living a bit further away, diminishes the value of residential (if not so much commercial) property. The beneficiaries from the mobility that freeways confer are often through travelers whose trips begin and end across larger geographies that often reach well beyond the neighborhood and even the city and county; these drivers do not contribute property taxes toward the roads' upkeep while reaping their benefits.

This inequity was not lost on property owners at the time. For example, some of the most vocal opposition to the 1924 Los Angeles bond issue came from members of homeowners' groups. They objected that assessing those whose property was adjacent to the improved major streets to retire even part of this bond issue was unfair because most benefits of the improved boulevards would accrue not to property owners but to non-resident through travelers.[112]

Thus cities increasingly moved toward paying for streets and roads out of annual taxes levied on all property owners citywide. Voters were often asked to approve the issuance of bonds to be retired through combinations of special assessments, property taxes, and general funds. By the 1920s, property tax finance of urban streets and roads had become commonplace. In addition to adhering to the benefits principle—that those who accrue tangible returns from roads (including through travelers) should pay for them—property taxes have the practical benefit that they are relatively easy to levy and are difficult to evade. Given their effectiveness, efficiency, and equity, property taxes (along with some special assessments) are still today the primary instrument by which local streets are funded in cities across the U.S.

In addition to property taxes' conceptual appeal, in practical terms they generated bounteous revenue for local governments as rapid urbanization and land value appreciation took place during the boom years of the 1920s. Between 1922 and 1927, property tax revenues nationwide increased a remarkable (and unsustainable) 9 percent per year amid a speculative real estate fervor. By 1927, 82 percent of all local government revenue came from property taxes.[113] Property taxes and special assessments collectively accounted for over 70 percent of all local government revenues for streets and highways, and in many cities streets and highways were paid for entirely by property taxes.[114] Property tax revenue helped pay for a dramatic increase in spending on urban streets; this rose from $337 million ($5.14 billion in 2021$) in 1921 to about $800 million ($13.08 billion in 2021$) by 1930.[115]

Yet this burgeoning revenue source soon proved to be a mixed blessing. With rapidly increasing growth in property tax revenue came increasing dependency, and hence vulnerability. This became abundantly clear at the close of the decade with the coming of the Great Depression, as a wave of property foreclosures, plummeting real estate values, widespread property tax defaults, and subsequent property tax relief efforts to stem those defaults brought a dramatic decline in revenues. Between 1929 and 1936, property tax assessments nationwide dropped nearly 20 percent, from $167.6 billion to $136.2 billion (in both years the 2021 equivalent was $2.5 trillion due to rapid deflation).[116] Collections were down as well, declining 13 percent between 1927 and 1934; it would be another 17 years before property tax revenues again reached their 1927 levels. No area of the nation was spared, but rapidly growing Midwestern and Western cities were hit hardest. Between 1929 and 1936, property tax revenues in Illinois dropped 40 percent, and in Arizona 50 percent.[117]

Despite the fact that deflation cushioned some of the blow from falling tax revenues, funding for local streets and roads declined even more dramatically than overall property tax receipts because road construction and maintenance were easier to cut than many other city services. Funds allocated by all local and county governments to streets and highways nationwide dropped 44 percent, from $1.8 billion in 1930 ($27.5 billion in 2021$) to just $1.0 billion ($18.7 billion in 2021$) in 1939. For municipalities, the collapse in property tax revenues for streets and roads over the same period was even greater, dropping 73 percent from $1.2 billion in 1930 ($18.4 billion in 2021$) to $329 million in 1939 ($6.2 billion in 2021$).[118] In Los Angeles, general and special assessment district funds for streets and roads plummeted 90 percent from over $27 million in 1929 ($413.0 million in 2021$) to less than $3 million ($55.7 million in 2021$) by 1935.[119] What appeared to be the answer to the question of urban road finance just a decade earlier had largely collapsed by the mid-1930s.

This painful contraction was not the only pitfall of depending on the property tax to fund metropolitan streets. It soon dawned on city officials that many through travelers actually came from outside their borders. In response to this growing realization, the rationale for shifting the financial burden from people who lived on streets to the motorists who traveled on them was described this way:

> [The] point is taxation apportionment. To be on an equitable basis it must properly reflect use, wear, and benefit. It seems to me that more study and effort should be devoted towards locating the real origin of traffic—the user. The high percentage of "urban" origin is impressive, but it does not prove the justice of a small city bearing the expense of an overwhelming foreign through traffic from its big neighbor.[120]

Thus, fiscal, political, and equity concerns demanded shifting the tax burden for streets and highways hosting mostly through traffic from the property owner to the motorist. To do this, a new form of urban highway finance was needed.

Urban Road Planning and Finance at the End of the 1920s

By 1929, the regulatory and infrastructure improvements deployed under the major traffic street plans had imposed some order on the movement of traffic and had addressed many inadequacies of existing street systems. Yet as more motor vehicles crowded into cities, the hungered-for "solution" to the traffic congestion problem remained as elusive as ever. To implement the increasingly expensive recommendations of these plans, cities continued to broaden their tax bases for financing urban streets from abutter finance, to special assessments on adjacent property, to more broadly based property taxes. These new taxes generated sufficient revenue for progress to be made on many plans, but their revenue-generating capabilities were ultimately undercut by the financial collapse of the Great Depression. Planners and engineers thus began to look to new strategies to address traffic congestion and to new financial tools to pay for them.

Fortunately, there was just such an alternative available: the recently developed motor fuel taxes whose story we will turn to next. Unfortunately for cities, however, it would prove difficult for them to tap this revenue source. This was, in time, to have dramatic effects on transportation in cities, not all of them positive.

The situation for rural and intercity highways was much different, and it is to them that we now turn.

4
Planning and Paying for Highways between Cities in the Pre-Freeway Era

In rural areas, where major roads in the late nineteenth and early twentieth centuries were largely the responsibility of counties and the states, highway officials faced pressure for better roads, first from bicyclists and then from motorists. They initially responded with piecemeal road improvements and later with interconnected rural and intercity highway systems. Like their urban counterparts, state officials struggled with how to finance these investments. They ultimately turned to a new fiscal innovation: motor fuel taxes.

Rural and Intercity Roads in the Post–Civil War Era

With the widespread bankruptcy of their operators, the early turnpikes were typically subsumed into the county-administered road systems. In wealthier counties, the former turnpikes were sometimes kept up reasonably well, which was made easier by the fact that they generally now carried much less traffic. But often, particularly in poorer counties, turnpikes were allowed to markedly degrade. The county road systems they joined were in little better condition, generally consisting of winding, unimproved tracks whose siting was determined by the evolution of use over time as opposed to any plan. They typically followed the boundaries between farms or traversed areas that were poorly suited for agriculture. They paid little heed to the needs of travelers from other jurisdictions. These mostly poorly engineered roads were mostly poorly maintained using corvée labor, the problems with which we discussed earlier.[1]

In the West, there was more order to the rural road system. "Public land states" (all states but the original 13 colonies) had been subdivided into a roughly gridiron pattern of rectangular townships by the Land Ordinance of 1785. Farms had been laid out along the township boundaries, and these boundaries were thus a path of least resistance for rural roads to follow.

The Drive for Dollars. Jeffrey R. Brown, Eric A. Morris, and Brian D. Taylor, Oxford University Press.
© Oxford University Press 2023. DOI: 10.1093/oso/9780197601518.003.0004

Although this layout made diagonal travel difficult and often caused steep grades in hilly terrain, it did impose order on the rural road system.[2]

Over time, there was some improvement to rural roads, as some of the more important routes were ditched for drainage, graded, and even surfaced with gravel. However, such improvements were few and far between. Thus, roads between cities were, even more so than their urban cousins, mostly very rudimentary.[3]

The Beginning of the Good Roads Movement

The first major call for the improvement of rural American roads in the post-turnpike era came in the late 1870s with the development of the bicycle. At first it was largely a recreational toy for the affluent. However, technical improvements, including the elimination of the early, ungainly giant front wheels (1884), the advent of pneumatic tires (1888), and a rapid drop in price resulting from mass production, turned the bicycle into a mass-market, utilitarian vehicle. It could, in favorable conditions, achieve greater speeds than a horse and carriage. As a result, a bicycle craze swept America, and, by 1896, Americans owned four million of them.[4]

However, bicycle travel was hampered by the poor state of nineteenth-century roads, both within and outside of cities.[5] Urban bicyclists who traveled to the countryside for rallies, road races, and weekend excursions lamented the poor condition of rural roads.[6] In response, leading bicycle manufacturers formed an interest group called the League of American Wheelmen (LAW) in 1880. This organization eventually reached a total of 102,000 members. Vocal evangelists for better roads, the Wheelmen began publishing *Good Roads Magazine* in 1891, which garnered a circulation of one million within three years.[7] The league's leaders argued that improved roads could serve higher public purposes by raising land values, fostering economic development, facilitating goods movement, opening markets, reducing rural poverty, increasing political participation by rural inhabitants, and promoting school attendance. *Good Roads* also included educational material on methods for constructing better roads. It sought to shame Americans by comparing their roads unfavorably to those in Europe, particularly France. The League also sponsored the first national roads conference in 1894.[8]

The League also built high-quality demonstration roads. It had some success in securing improvements in urban and suburban areas, though not nearly as much on intercity routes. Moreover, the League's calls for state aid for roads met with only limited success. Thus, despite the considerable improvement in urban roads beginning in the 1890s, rural roads remained in a state of relative underdevelopment. Still, the organization managed to focus popular and political attention on the need for better roads after decades of relative inaction.[9]

The bicycling craze waned after 1897, but the growing corps of automobile enthusiasts soon joined the cause. Picking up the baton from the LAW, motorists came to form the nucleus of the "Good Roads Movement" beginning in the early 1890s. Pro-road agitation was spearheaded by the National League for Good Roads, founded in 1892, and a lobbying group called the National Good Roads Association. In addition, by 1902 there were 18 state good roads associations and an additional 40 local ones. Their efforts were supplemented by 32 chapters of the Automobile Club of America. Most good roads associations did not collect dues, but were financially supported by commercial interests such as automobile manufacturers, materials producers, and railroads.[10]

The Good Roads Movement held conventions and staged public events to promote improved highways. It operated "Good Roads Trains" which traveled the country, showcasing the latest in road-building techniques for the benefit of local officials and the public. At stops, crews of roadworkers employing the latest technology built short stretches of demonstration roads. In addition, the movement lobbied state governments to become involved in road building.[11]

Slowly Replacing Corvée Labor

The Good Roads Movement also lobbied for the replacement of corvée labor with professional road construction and maintenance crews. If the corvée system was disliked by road engineers, it was loathed by those periodically compelled to do roadwork. Thus, by the early 1900s, many parts of the country shifted away from work requirements and toward raising money to pay professional roadworkers. Property tax funding was one source of revenue, with rates that dramatically varied by county. Another revenue source was a flat per-head poll tax of a few dollars per year levied on all county residents. Yet given sparse rural populations and the great distances rural roads needed to cover, these revenue sources were inadequate. In 1904, nationwide property and poll taxes for rural roads raised about $53.8 million (about $1.64 billion in 2021$), an amount that may sound large, but which was spread over a road network of 2.1 million miles. Further, not all states permitted counties to borrow money to finance roads, and, even when they did, it was quite rare: as of 1914 only ten states had county road indebtedness of more than $10 million

($260 million in 2021$). So corvée labor continued to play a significant role in road maintenance. In 1904, 25 states still had work requirements, and the labor of conscripted citizens was valued at about one-fourth of total road expenditures; as late as 1914, 18 states still relied heavily on corvée labor for roadwork.[12]

In the early twentieth century, much of the South shifted from mostly White corvée labor to mostly Black convict labor organized in chain gangs. Ingram argues that this allowed White Southerners to haltingly embrace the Good Roads Movement while maintaining the White supremacy central to Jim Crow.

[S]outherners' steadfast commitment to the racialized, locally controlled convict-labor system preserved chain gangs as a major resource for southern roads, slowing the work of the highway lobby for years to come and reopening old divisions within the Good Roads Movement at a critical juncture in its history.[13]

Reliance on convict labor was not cheap, as the cost of transporting, housing, feeding, and guarding prisoners was high, often exceeding the cost of private contracting for roadwork. But convict labor maintained local (mostly county) control over roadwork in the South and allowed resistance to state and federal interference while preserving racial hierarchies.[14]

Getting the Farmer Out of the Mud

Ironically, even though the potential for improved roads to transform the life of the farmer was noted early on, it was in rural areas that political support for good roads was weakest. Despite their troubles with isolation due to rough, often-muddy roads, many farmers initially viewed road building as a scheme to funnel rural tax dollars into infrastructure that mostly benefited the interests of wealthy urban drivers and bicyclists.[15]

Rural anti-good-roads sentiment began to diminish with the establishment of Rural Free Delivery by the U.S. Post Office. Prior to this, rural residents often lacked both mail delivery and telephones, and were also often served by roads that were sometimes impassable due to weather, resulting in profound isolation. Despite skepticism that it would not be economically feasible, beginning in 1893 the Post Office began testing, and then expanding, a service of free mail delivery to rural residents. The program succeeded and, by 1903, 8,600 carriers were delivering mail to 5 million rural homes. However, delivery was offered only to houses accessible by serviceable roads, which proved a powerful spur to hundreds of counties to improve their roads.[16]

Rural Free Delivery also prompted the federal government to promote rural road improvements, at first by dispatching inspectors to inform localities about needed road improvements, and later by furnishing technical advice on how to effectively improve roads. However, a series of bills proposing federal funding of postal roads failed in Congress starting in 1903, so for the next dozen years localities bore the entire expense of postal roads. Eventually, Congress passed a law in 1912 instructing the secretary of agriculture and the postmaster general to appropriate funds directly to counties to subsidize the construction of a limited number of high-quality demonstration postal roads. The program was unsuccessful, however, because the terms of the grants (for example, by forbidding convict labor and mandating an eight-hour workday) often violated state laws or policies. Further, the federal government coordinated the work directly with the nation's 3,000+ county governments, which proved administratively unwieldy and politically fraught. A few roads were eventually built, but perhaps the greatest legacy of this project was to motivate federal officials to work almost exclusively with states for many decades and eschew engaging directly with counties or other local governments.[17]

In addition to Rural Free Delivery, in time gasoline-powered trucks that could haul produce to market sparked farmers' interest in good roads.[18] When rural interests began to take an interest in roads, they had a ready-made constituency in state legislatures, which throughout this period had strong rural orientations. State activism in rural road building got a boost from an 1891 traffic count study in New Jersey, which found that much of the traffic in Garden State townships consisted of through travelers, and not township residents. Supported by the LAW, the townships that commissioned the study used its findings to successfully advocate for legislation that made the state responsible for one-third of the cost of county roads (10% was to be paid for by the property owners along the roads, and the remainder by the county). The principle that rural roads were used by, and should be paid for at least partly by, all state residents established an important precedent that was eventually embraced across the nation.[19]

Two years later, in 1893, Massachusetts made a dramatic leap forward by funding an interconnected state network of roads that were to be built to (for the time) high standards. The plan established the first state highway commission and greatly expanded the state's powers vis-à-vis road building and maintenance compared with what New Jersey had enacted. Other states followed Massachusetts's lead, and by 1905, 14 states had highway commissions. By 1917, all states were involved in supporting rural road building in some way.[20]

Yet despite these developments, in the early years of the twentieth century, intercity and rural highways improved only very slowly. In addition to the dismal state of the road surfaces, roads lacked signage and motorists lacked reliable maps. There were few places offering fuel or repairs, and they could be difficult to find. Cross-country auto trips were arduous enough to be heavily publicized, as in 1903 when it took a pair of drivers 63 days to travel from San Francisco to New York, which at the time was actually celebrated as a surprisingly speedy trip.[21] The cross-country driving time subsequently fell precipitously as the quality of rural roads gradually began to improve; the current record, as of 2021, is under 26 hours.[22,*]

In 1904, less than 8 percent (154,000 miles) of the 2 million miles of American roads had been improved in any way.[23] Most unimproved roads remained simple, rutted dirt wagon tracks that turned into impassable swamps of mud whenever it rained. In the North, spring thaws were particularly problematic, while in the South, soft, deep sand was a chronic problem.[24]

Even when improved, most roads at the time were a far cry from modern standards. The most common improvement was simply grading dirt roads to remove the bumps and ruts. When more was done, typically only a single lane was paved and cars were expected to pass one another on unpaved shoulders. Paving materials were also primitive, with sand-clay paving, gravel, and macadam paving all having serious shortcomings, particularly for heavy vehicles. These problems were only solved with the introduction of asphalt, and later Portland cement, though their use on rural roads was extremely limited at first.[25]

The Establishment of the ORI: Washington Takes Up the Cause of Rural Road Building

Up to this point, federal involvement in funding or constructing roads had been explicitly rejected on several occasions on the grounds that it would slow the road-building process, sap local initiative, and violate the Constitution.[26] Outside of a few spotty efforts, the first active federal involvement in building

---

* The so-called Cannonball Run is an unsanctioned race against the clock (and, since World War II, the police) for a high-speed drive between New York and Los Angeles. By 1915, the record for the more than 2,900-mile one-way trip was 11 days, 7 hours, and 15 minutes; 18 years later (in 1933) it was down to 2 days, 5 hours, and 30 minutes. The especially light traffic during the early months of the COVID-19 pandemic caused the record to fall three times (all under 26 hours) in quick succession, with *average* speeds of 106, 108, and 110 miles per hour (Wikipedia 2021). While the prudence of this record setting is very much in question, what is not in question is whether the roads today are of sufficient quality to host such high-speed driving.

and maintaining roads came only in 1893, when, thanks in large part to agitation from the LAW and the Good Roads Movement, the Department of Agriculture set up the Office of Road Inquiry (ORI). Its chief, General Roy Stone, opined that Americans had "the worst roads in the civilized world" and that the costs of inhibited mobility—in terms of time loss and squandered productivity—dwarfed the costs of improving the roads.[27]

The establishment of the ORI was of great symbolic import, as it established a greater federal role in rural and intercity road building and maintenance. The ORI became the Office of Public Roads Inquiries, or OPRI, in 1899. The ORI/OPRI contributed to the study of nationwide road conditions through surveys of state and territorial governors, secretaries of state, members of Congress, geologists, and railroad men. For some states, it created maps showing the condition of the improved road networks. The OPRI conducted road-engineering research in its laboratory, established in 1900. Perhaps most importantly, the evolving organization was increasingly a font of state-of-the-art technical advice to states and counties on road construction and maintenance. For example, taking a cue from Massachusetts, it supervised and partially funded the building of "object-lesson" demonstration roads that exemplified the latest engineering and construction techniques.[28]

The ORI/OPRI's second thrust was promotional. Its staff advocated for road building and improvement through public relations efforts like distributing pro-road pamphlets and making convention appearances. It also published the proceedings of good roads conferences, including the text of their pro-road speeches.[29,†]

The ORI/OPRI advanced all manner of arguments in favor of better roads. For example, it demonstrated that rural school attendance rose sharply when roads were improved. It also showed that moving goods long distances on roads was 50 times more expensive than by rail, and that the cost of moving a ton of freight was cut in half after proper road surfacing. Another well-publicized study found that shipping costs for a Georgia farmer transporting a bushel of peaches 20 miles to Atlanta over bad roads were higher than those for a California farmer shipping the same peaches cross-country by rail.[30]

Road marketing campaigns notwithstanding, political reality blunted General Stone's ambitions. The ORI/OPRI's mandate extended only to investigating and disseminating information. It was a shoestring operation; at the outset, Stone had a staff of two and an annual budget of $10,000 (about

---

† Interestingly, the railroads were early supporters of road building, as they saw roads as complements to rail shipping and a means of easing demand on the rail system during peak periods; indeed, they were roads' strongest corporate supporters until the 1916 federal legislation discussed below (Seely 1987; USDOT, FHWA 1977).

$275,000 in 2021$). Further, the ORI/OPRI was prohibited from direct involvement in political activities, such as advocating for state legislation, and needed to be at pains to assure skeptics that it was not seeking to establish a direct federal role in road building. So, its role was limited to technical and promotional efforts, but in that role it did indirectly advance the cause of road building politically.[31]

Logan Page, the OPR, and the Expanding Federal Role

The Office of Public Roads (OPR), successor to the ORI/OPRI, was founded in 1905 with triple the budget of the OPRI. Under the leadership of its first director, Logan Page (who served from 1905 to 1919), the OPR continued to promote technical progress in road building. Page had been director of Harvard's road materials laboratory and had also served as a geologist and testing engineer for the Massachusetts State Highway Commission before serving at the ORI. As was the case with the early urban transportation planners, Page was steeped in the ethos of the Progressive Era, with its emphasis on science, technological expertise, honest apolitical administration, social activism, and optimism about the government's ability to solve society's problems. Under Page's supervision, the OPR grew in influence and size, from a budget of $50,000 in 1905 to $279,000 in 1914 (about $1.3 million to $7.3 million in 2021$). In the latter year, it employed 218 people.[32]

The OPR greatly expanded ORI/OPRI efforts to collect and disseminate information on the condition of the U.S. road system. The OPR sent tens of thousands of surveys to county roads officials, to organizations like motorists' clubs and chambers of commerce, and even to private citizens such as postmasters and attorneys to gather information on roads. These efforts culminated in 1914 in a systematic survey that produced by far the most complete picture to date of America's highways. It showed that in the past decade road spending had almost tripled, to $240 million ($6.5 billion in 2021$), with much of this coming from borrowing (as we shall discuss further below). The U.S. road system had grown from 2.15 million miles in 1904 to 2.45 million in 1914, but still only about 10.5 percent of this mileage was improved in any way beyond simple dirt surfaces, and just 0.6 percent had high-quality asphalt, brick, or cement paving.[33]

The OPR also continued the work of the ORI/OPRI by generating data on construction, paving techniques, and material and equipment standards using its testing laboratory and field experiments. The techniques it explored included using bituminous substances as a pavement binder to hold down road dust, which ultimately led to testing and improving asphalt road surfaces. It also studied paving with brick and Portland cement. Aided by industry trade associations and national engineering groups, the OPR used the results of these experiments to formulate and propagate construction standards nationwide. Page opposed the prior emphasis on relatively expensive macadam paving. Instead, he advocated for the use of earth, clay, and sand as a cheaper alternative until such time as the level and speed of traffic demanded upscaling to a more durable and smoother pavement. This "stage construction" was one of the guiding principles of federal road construction for decades, although, as we shall see, policy would swing to the other end of the spectrum in the Interstate era.[34]

In addition to promoting technical expertise, the OPR disseminated new ideas about road administration. Poor management on the part of local authorities was often the rule for rural roads in the nineteenth century. Page formed a team of inspectors that traveled widely to introduce better techniques, including improved administrative procedures and financial management. Moreover, federal engineers were dispatched to localities to supervise projects and train local officials, engineers, and workers. In time, they assisted 144 counties in 28 states. It was clear, however, that a shortage of trained engineers hampered their efforts—it was estimated that one-quarter to one-third of road expenditures were wasted due to a lack of engineering expertise, which resulted in poorly located and drained roads. So, Page established a one-year postgraduate course in highway engineering at the OPR that trained 70 engineers in its labs and on its field teams between 1905 and 1915. It also supported universities in establishing road-engineering programs, following the lead of Harvard in the 1890s.[35]

Perhaps most importantly, Page and the OPR abetted state highway departments. Although many states had formed or were in the process of forming such departments, many had not. Moreover, even where departments existed, their efforts were often hamstrung by poor administrative techniques, a lack of funding, and/or insufficient personnel. The OPR's primary emphasis was on the removal of political appointees and their replacement with ostensibly impartial, apolitical, and well-trained engineers. In order to avoid the strictures against direct political activity by the OPR, Page was instrumental in founding, in 1911, the American Association for Highway Improvement (AAHI), a nongovernmental organization (NGO) closely coordinated with the OPR, which engaged in political lobbying. The

AAHI drafted model state-aid highway legislation that could be adapted and adopted by state legislatures in order to structure their highway departments. It also sponsored the First American Road Congress in 1911, whose delegates supported resolutions calling for more federal and state financing of road building and maintenance. The AAHI also supported new rules of the road, such as requirements that vehicles use lights at night, regulations keeping slow-moving traffic on the right, uniform speed limits across jurisdictions, and the posting of road signs with directions and distances.[36]

After initially eschewing a high public profile, Page came to understand the importance of cultivating public opinion. His staff prepared short articles that appeared in thousands of newspapers, and the agency dispatched lecturers who delivered 1,135 talks in 1912 alone. The OPR sponsored popular exhibits on roads and road technology at fairs and ran "Road Improvement Trains" to demonstrate state-of-the art road-building techniques across the country.[37]

Page's focus was almost exclusively on rural roads, as he saw his primary mission as "getting the farmer out of the mud." The idea that mud-bound farmers deserved the same social, political, religious, and educational opportunities as urban residents provided the social justification for the technical programs of the OPR. Poor rural roads came to be seen as a moral wrong and their improvement a matter of democratic fairness.[38]

In 1912, the Post Office Appropriation Act allocated $500,000 ($13.3 million in 2021$) to pay one-third of the cost of constructing rural postal routes as selected by the postmaster general and the secretary of agriculture.[39] The states contributed the remaining two-thirds of the cost of roads constructed under the program, which came to be regarded as a success by all involved and demonstrated that federal-state cooperation on road building was possible. However, some states refused to participate in the program, sometimes citing constitutional grounds.[40]

The work of the OPR came at a pivotal time in the history of American transportation. While the ORI had focused on roads to serve horse-drawn, steel-wheeled traffic at speeds of six to eight miles per hour, the OPR oversaw roads during a period of breakneck growth of automobile ownership and use. Page and his organization helped shepherd the beginnings of the transition to building roads to serve a qualitatively, and quantitatively, different type of traffic.[41]

One major problem was that automobile wheels and tires did tremendous damage to the two most common paving surfaces of the time, macadam and gravel, as rubber tires gripped and scattered the road surfaces. Given the rapid growth in automobile ownership and use, it quickly became clear that more advanced road materials such as asphalt and Portland cement were needed.[42]

The Beginnings of a National Highway Program

One problem with rural and intercity road development was that coordination among state highway departments was lacking. Even as late as 1941, it was not possible to cross the U.S. from coast to coast on any rationally planned route.[43] Hence the first major effort to create interstate highways came from private booster groups, like the Lincoln Highway Association, the Dixie Highway Association, the Dixie Overland Highway Association, and the Lee Highway Association.[44] These associations were not road builders so much as road boosters, whose work consisted mostly of marking proposed routes and publishing maps of them—an accomplishment in its own right in an era when both signage and road maps were in short supply. By far the most successful of these was the Lincoln Highway, a transcontinental New Jersey–San Francisco route. It was launched in 1913 by entrepreneur Carl G. Fisher, who recruited the support of public officials in towns along the route and collected subscriptions for improving it. Millions of dollars were eventually raised. It was the only private association highway that resulted in any new construction, though the amount of actual work was modest and limited to short sections of demonstration road. However, the lasting effect of the Lincoln Highway was not in moving vehicles, but in spurring debate about the feasibility and desirability of a national highway system.[45]

In the early 1910s, the National Highway Association, headed by wealthy businessman Charles Henry Davis, produced the most ambitious private plan. It called for a 51,000-mile national highway system centered on three east-west and three north-south highways, plus an extensive feeder network. This plan spurred plenty of talk but no action, thanks to the then-unheard-of estimated price tag of $30,000 per mile (about $770,500/mile in 2021$) and also to rural opposition to spending on roads that rural residents believed would be used primarily by urbanites. However, motorist organizations like the American Automobile Association (AAA) strongly supported this sort of network of high-quality, intercity, cross-country roads.[46]

With private efforts yielding little progress, it was clear that it would fall to the government to build a national highway network if one were to be built at all. However, the efforts of organizations such as the OPR notwithstanding, the scale and capacity of the public sector in the 1910s was not nearly what it is today, so numerous questions about a government-built national highway network loomed. Perhaps the most fundamental was about the relationship between federal, state, and local authorities. On one side were those like the OPR's Page, who advocated leaving states to develop roads, with the federal role limited to providing encouragement, expertise, and some funding. In Page's view, a federally directed national highway system would be wasteful and unnecessary.[47] Others, by contrast, believed that a truly national system could only be planned, financed, and built by the federal government.

In addition, there was the question of whether the system should primarily serve farmers or intercity travelers. Page favored the former, with an emphasis on farm-to-market roads and rural mail delivery. Similarly, advocates of "business roads" argued that driving could never be as fast and efficient as railroads, so the primary function of roads for intercity travel should not be to connect cities directly but to connect travelers to the nearest railhead. However, many urbanites, along with auto executives and motorists' associations, favored a national network of very high-quality "touring roads" focused on long-distance, cross-country car travel.

Given these disparate visions, a wide variety of proposals for intercity roads were put forward in this era. In 1913 alone, approximately 50 national road bills were proposed by members of Congress, including plans to float construction bonds, provide direct federal aid to states, and expand the postal road system.[48] Among this cacophony of bills, only the 1912 bill providing limited federal aid for postal road construction was signed into law.[49]

But momentum for bigger and better roads was building. A congressional committee was empaneled to study the problem. Addressing rural concerns, it concluded that the state of American roads was highly costly to farmers; for example, it cost French farmers only 40 percent of what it cost American farmers to haul produce to the nearest railhead. Bad roads were estimated to result in an annual economic loss 40 times the government's annual expenditure on roads. Bad roads were also blamed for shoddy rural education and the exodus of young people from rural areas to the cities. When the committee issued its report in 1915, it unanimously concluded that federal support for road building was both desirable and constitutional.[50]

The Federal Aid Road Act of 1916 Puts Washington into the Road-Building Business

A watershed moment in American highway planning came with the passage of the 1916 Federal Aid Road Act. This landmark legislation finally established a direct, active, and continuing federal role in rural road building. The ostensible constitutional prohibition against federal road building was swept away through a combination of rationales: new roads were held to be crucial for mail delivery, interstate commerce, "general welfare," and, with the coming

of World War I, national defense—all powers specifically granted to the federal government by the Constitution.[51] Constitutional objections to a waxing
federal highway role were further blunted by the fact the states and localities
would build, maintain, and own the roads. The legislation was largely crafted
and promoted by two groups: the AAA and the American Association of State
Highway Officials (AASHO),[‡] the latter a lobbying group composed of senior
state and federal highway administrators that was established with the help of
Logan Page in 1914. In addition, the 1916 Act owed a great deal to Page and
the OPR, which furnished technical and political assistance throughout the
legislative process.[52]

The provisions of the 1916 Act introduced the first large-scale federal
funding of road projects. Although the federal government would not contribute to right-of-way acquisition, the Act created a matching grant program whereby $75 million (about $1.88 billion in 2021$) in federal funds
supplemented state rural road construction over a five-year period through
1921. The states had to match federal funding on a 1:1 basis.

The federal share of the match could not exceed $10,000/mile ($249,000/
mile in 2021$). This provision ruled out federal support for the most du-
rable pavements and widest roads, which by the end of World War I could
cost $40,000 to $50,000/mile ($996,000 to $1.3 million/mile in 2021$). This
was a victory for those who supported farm-to-market and business roads to
railheads instead of a more elaborate cross-country intercity system built to
accommodate high volumes of traffic. Federal support was limited to postal
roads only (albeit generously defined as any rural road over which the mails
were or could be carried), another concession to those who believed that roads
should be planned only with a short-distance, farm-to-market rationale; this
provision ultimately proved to be a handicap for highways through sparsely
populated desert, mountain, and prairie areas, particularly in the West. In
terms of administration, the federal role increased but primary responsibility
fell to the states. States chose routes and performed the planning, engineering,
construction, and maintenance, though with federal technical assistance and
subject to federal inspection and approval. Money flowed only to states with
established highway departments. (In 1916, 11 states still did not have such
departments, and five others were widely considered highly susceptible to political influence.) Hence, the legislation played a key role in forcing the modernization of state highway administration.[53]

The 1916 Act made the rural bias in the federal-aid program explicit.
Congressional debate on the legislation was almost exclusively focused on

‡ Known today as the American Association of State Highway and Transportation Officials (AASHTO).

the formula to be used to apportion the money among states, with wealthier, more urbanized states protesting that they would not receive back funding commensurate with the taxes they paid (an argument which, as we will see, continues to the present day). The final formula for the apportionment was a victory for the rural states, as it gave state population only a one-third weight, with geographic area also counting for one-third, and the mileage of the state's postal road system counting for the final third. Other rural victories were that "cities" with over 2,500 inhabitants received almost nothing. The Office of Public Roads was renamed the Office of Public Roads and Rural Engineering (OPRRE), although it remained lodged in the Department of Agriculture. In all, the program reflected Page's beliefs in the social goal of improving rural life and in not aiding urban intercity travelers.[54]

The 1916 Act did not establish a unified national system of roads since there was no provision for coordinating the efforts of the states or connecting the routes they were constructing. Page and other advocates of state control maintained that such a system would develop organically. AASHO was deadlocked on this point, and by a 20–20 vote it failed to recommend the creation of a national highway commission to play this coordinating role. Also, there was also almost no federal role in determining uniform, nationwide construction standards, although once such standards were agreed upon by AASHO, the OPRRE would subsequently enforce them.[55]

As groundbreaking as the 1916 Act was on paper, its effects took time to materialize. Though fast progress was expected, and many states ramped up budgeting for roads, World War I intervened. There was an initial plunge in road building due to the imperatives of the war, such as the need to free up overtaxed rail capacity by restricting the transport of road construction materials, far-reaching federal intervention in the economy that diverted materials away from road construction, dramatic increases in the costs of labor and road-building materials, and the transfer of civil engineers to assist with military efforts in Europe.[56] By 1918, federal-aid road work was limited to those routes deemed essential to the war effort; these were numerous enough, however, to cause federally funded road construction to actually increase over the course of the war.[57]

Another limit to the impact of the 1916 Act was that its "improved" roads were not necessarily of high quality. Officials in Southern and Western states in particular did not see a need for extensive macadam or asphalt paving, given the light traffic on most of their roads. Thus, the Act allowed the funding of gravel, sand-clay, and earthen roads; by the beginning of 1918, 80 percent of the mileage on which federal-aid money had been spent was for such lower-quality roads.[58]

Moreover, there was much administrative confusion because, as we have noted, not all states had highway departments in 1916, and many others were not capable of administering federal funds or managing construction. At the time of the Act, only California had highway laws completely in conformity with OPRRE standards. OPRRE leaders found many state highway departments and officials incompetent, while those officials often resented what they saw as imperious federal meddling. These battles delayed progress, so that by the war's end 572 federal-aid projects had been approved but only five completed.[59]

Still, the years of World War I and its immediate aftermath were not entirely a period of torpor. In the long run, the war stimulated road travel and building. The railroads were strained during the war: there was unprecedented demand for hauling raw materials and finished goods for military production, many railroad workers left for the military or for other jobs to support the war effort, and severe congestion in and around railway and port terminals was commonplace.[60] These problems helped to birth the trucking industry as shippers sought an alternative to rail, with trucks progressively taking more and more traffic from the railroads and carrying it longer and longer distances. Trucks themselves were also being shipped to France, and the government opened routes for trucks to drive from Midwestern factories to East Coast ports instead of being carried by train, proving the feasibility of long-distance truck travel. Truck production was not limited during the war, so the number of trucks on the nation's roadways swelled as shippers discovered the door-to-door speed, flexibility, and, in some respects, cost advantages of truck transport compared with rail. Trucks also performed very effectively in France. Thus, during and after the war, trucks made decisive progress toward displacing horses as the primary non-rail haulers of freight.[61]

This war-related rise in trucking turned more attention to road maintenance and improvement since wartime efforts to ship goods by truck were limited significantly by the quality of intercity highways. While improvements slowly progressed, few of the improved roads were built for heavy truck traffic. To make matters worse, truckers had incentives to overload their vehicles since few states had truck weight limits and those that existed were poorly enforced. The problem was compounded by the fact that trucks of the day ran on solid rubber tires, which did more damage to roadbeds than pneumatic tires. These issues prompted calls for both intercity highway improvements and restrictions or outright bans on heavy vehicles from most roads. During the war, truck manufacturers and road builders agreed on a weight limit of 7.5 tons, though debates over the costs that heavy vehicles inflict on roads continue to the present day.[62]

In the year following the end of the war, the military publicized the inter-city highway problem by sending a convoy of 72 trucks and other vehicles on a demonstration cross-country road trip from Washington, D.C. to San Francisco. The trip took 62 days and encountered numerous daunting obstacles in terms of terrain and road conditions. Media coverage highlighted the need for better roads with more durable pavements and helped to spur subsequent postwar road-construction efforts. Modern commentators have made much of the fact that the experiences of one participant in the military convoy, then-Bvt. Lt. Colonel Dwight D. Eisenhower, would shape his thinking as president in setting the direction of U.S. highway policy.[63]

Thomas MacDonald and the Development of the Federal Highway Program

With a legislative framework in place after the 1916 Act and World War I highlighting the need for better roads, America now needed the personnel to execute the new policy. In 1919, upon the death of Page, it settled on the formal, reserved, and austere Thomas Harris MacDonald, who became chief of the OPRRE, now rechristened the Federal Bureau of Public Roads (BPR). MacDonald would lead the agency for 34 years, until 1953.

There is often danger in writing history as the story of great men, but observers, both at the time and today, agree that MacDonald would prove a pivotal, even dominating, figure in the history of American road development. By the end of his 34-year tenure, he was the longest-serving high-ranking official in the entire federal government, having served seven presidents. When he assumed leadership of the BPR, there were about 250,000 miles of improved roadway in the country, almost all of which was unpaved; by the time he retired, there were 3.5 million miles of hard-surfaced highway.[64]

A product of the Iowa countryside, where rains turned roads into impassable rivers of muck (known locally as "gumbo"), MacDonald was trained as a civil engineer by Anson Marston, a Good Roads Movement advocate. Marston stressed the importance of by-now-familiar values like technical expertise, experimentation, scientific fact gathering, and engineering-oriented solutions to problems. MacDonald wrote his senior thesis on the problem of Iowa mud for road transport. Hence, like Page before him, MacDonald had a rural orientation; he believed good roads would solve rural problems, foremost among them the trend toward rural depopulation. MacDonald was convinced that providing these roads was among the government's foremost purposes.[65]

Prior to his BPR post, MacDonald was an assistant professor of civil engineering at Iowa State College and then was appointed as the first—and only—employee of the road commission in Iowa. There he adopted both Marston's Progressive-Era values and the federalist methods of Page and the OPR, establishing a cooperative relationship between his office, which provided technical assistance and advice, and local road-building authorities. Despite a tiny staff and budget, and in the face of a system of cozy political arrangements by contractors who often rigged bids and skimped on construction, MacDonald successfully reformed the Iowa road system, breaking up road cabals, raising construction standards, and improving roads greatly in both quality and extent.[66]

In part, this was achieved through appeals to political and public opinion. Despite being an uninspiring writer, a poor public speaker, and a manager who in many ways failed to inspire his subordinates, MacDonald disseminated his views and managed to secure a political about-face in statewide attitudes toward government support for road improvement. MacDonald balanced local and state needs by leaving intracounty routing in the hands of county officials but using state supervision to ensure that the roads formed a connected statewide network. This proved a foretaste of developments he would lead at the national level. MacDonald was active in AASHO and a pivotal figure in crafting the federal-aid legislation of 1916, which gave him a national reputation and led to his appointment as chief of the BPR.[67]

As noted above, the federal-aid program had made almost no progress in terms of actual road construction when MacDonald arrived in Washington in 1919. But his background as a former state official and his considerable political savvy made him well suited to head the Bureau. Upon assuming office, MacDonald successfully moved to ease tensions that had grown between the OPRRE/BPR and the states under his predecessor. He did so by stressing to his staff the need to proceed in a collaborative manner, including consulting with the Executive Committee of AASHO, streamlining federal approval and inspection procedures, allowing states some (though not complete) flexibility in terms of engineering standards and budgeting, and other measures. When states lacked the technical or administrative capacity to deal with the surge in available federal-aid funds, the Bureau assisted with advance engineering planning, discouraged the construction of poor-quality roads, helped implement safeguards against waste and fraud, and propagated techniques such as using local materials and phased, or staged, construction[§] where possible (though,

---

[§] As a reminder, this entailed constructing or reconstructing segments of roadways to meet existing needs, with any upgrades or expansions coming later as warranted.

as we discuss later, MacDonald would eventually become a determined opponent of phased construction). So, although the federal role in road building rapidly expanded, care was taken that this involvement not be undertaken in an overbearing manner vis-à-vis the states. This new, more collaborative approach was generally well received by the state highway departments.[68]

MacDonald was also successful in maintaining the BPR's independence within the federal government and warding off efforts at interference with what he perceived to be the Bureau's mission. He was highly effective at lobbying for his positions on Capitol Hill.[69]

Although less a proselytizer and more a technician than Page, MacDonald jump-started the federal highway program by undertaking a public information campaign featuring speakers, publications, scholarships for road engineers, and, most importantly, the promotion of AASHO.[70] Through these efforts, the Bureau enlisted non-highway-department stakeholders, including farmers, pleasure motorists, defense officials, and, unsurprisingly, trade associations of firms related to highway building.[71]

Under MacDonald, the BPR continued its role inherited from OPR as a font of scientific expertise and sound engineering principles. The Bureau worked collaboratively with states, universities, and trade associations (such as those of the asphalt and cement producers). It also largely founded, guided, and financed the Highway Research Board,** a national facilitator of dialogue between engineers in the BPR and state highway departments and a "collator" of highway research. Moreover, the BPR itself performed extensive engineering and scientific research on soils, road-construction techniques, and materials, using its laboratory facilities in Virginia. It also conducted traffic surveys across the nation. In 1920, for example, Bureau spending on research comprised one-third of all road-research spending in the country, meaning that only the Bureau had the capacity to undertake large-scale and costly research projects.[72]

The BPR also supervised research on highway economics, including on how states could best raise funds to pay for road improvements, as well as on accounting procedures and benefit-cost analyses. In addition, and like planners working in parallel in cities, the Bureau developed the science of measuring and predicting traffic flows using surveys to study vehicles, trips, origins, destinations, driver behavior (such as speeds, adherence to traffic laws, and response to varying road conditions), and trip purposes. These would inform early state and regional plans that attempted to forecast traffic levels in the

---

** Known today as the Transportation Research Board (TRB), which is part of the National Academies of Science, Engineering, and Medicine.

future and proactively meet these needs with construction in advance of use; such studies came to powerfully shape policy on the purpose, form, and function of the federal-aid system, as we explore in later chapters. The BPR also determined that heavy trucks with solid rubber tires did tremendous damage to roadways, which ultimately contributed to the adoption of the pneumatic tire, as well as truck weight taxes and limits. In all, the Bureau moved toward the conclusion that the modest engineering standards of existing rural and intercity highways were inadequate for the heavier and faster vehicles being produced, and that higher design standards were needed to ensure safe and efficient travel.[73]

The results of this work, as well as that by researchers in state highway departments and universities, were disseminated in the Bureau's journal, *Public Roads*, which from 1918 on was the leading source of information on highway research. By the 1930s, more than two-thirds of all highway research funding came from the BPR, which solidified its reputation as the foremost source of technical expertise. Thus, as was the case with planning, the Bureau became a leader in highway research due to superior knowledge and resources, plus MacDonald's increasingly authoritative presence.[74] This leadership role came to be widely accepted despite—or more likely because of—the fact that MacDonald went to great pains to maintain a collaborative relationship with the states, industry, and academia.

The BPR was highly effective in promulgating engineering and construction standards, continuing the process that had begun under Page. This led to an accelerating standardization of highway design practices, owing in part to the Bureau's de jure supervisory role over federal-aid construction, but due even more to its reputation for expertise. In 1926, a survey of state highway engineers revealed that they believed the federal standards were the BPR's most important contribution to the cause of road building. As was typical of MacDonald's style, AASHO was used as an intermediary that masked federal direction of the process, but, since BPR engineers chaired every AASHO technical committee, the standards AASHO developed were very much a product of the Bureau. These included standards on road geometry, design, construction, materials, and accounting procedures. States were granted considerable leeway, but basic federal benchmarks for quality had to be met.[75]

MacDonald also encouraged professionalism. State highway departments were improved with BPR help and the very occasional sanction. In time, trained construction and maintenance workers increasingly replaced weekend gatherings of farmers and convict chain gangs for road work and repairs.[76]

MacDonald's efforts soon bore fruit. Although road construction was initially hampered in the immediate postwar period due to materials and labor shortages, concomitant cost inflation, and an inability of states to float the bonds necessary to finance their ambitious highway-construction plans, road construction under the federal-aid program soon boomed. Aided by new mechanization techniques that cut down on labor needs, plus the acquisition of war surplus material like trucks and TNT by the Department of Agriculture, by 1920 construction was under way on 1,835 projects that totaled 14,490 miles of roads. Given all of this activity, the White House, Congress, state highway departments, and the public at large increasingly came to appreciate the Bureau's work.[77]

Planning for a National Highway Network

Despite progress on many fronts, the debate over the fundamental purpose of the nation's highways remained unresolved. Should rural roads focus on farm-to-market or intercity travel? To what extent should the federal government bring about an interconnected, "national" highway system? A rift had grown in the Good Roads Movement: the AAA, the National Automobile Chamber of Commerce (which represented the trucking industry), and other urban interests supported a national intercity system, while AASHO and others advocated continuing the piecemeal approach focused on farm-to-market roads, with the states taking the lead in routing and pavement decisions.[78]

Moreover, the federal-aid program was buffeted by a dispute pitting the states of the Northeast and Upper Midwest against those of the South and West. The former focused their efforts on a limited number of high-quality intercity roads, while the efforts of the latter were diffused across many disconnected roads, resulting in extensive, but piecemeal and low-quality, roads unlikely to ever coalesce into an interconnected highway system.[79]

MacDonald approached this ongoing debate differently than Page. While both had rural roots, MacDonald did not share his predecessor's moral fervor. His interests were more technical, economic, engineering oriented, and pragmatic: reduce wear and tear on vehicles, move freight more quickly and inexpensively, and save travel time. Traffic service, MacDonald repeatedly professed, was the purpose of highways.[80]

Still, this engineering focus led him to many conclusions similar to Page's. Because it was increasingly apparent from BPR surveys that long-distance intercity highway traffic remained relatively sparse, MacDonald concluded that there was no immediate need for a national highway system (though surely an underdeveloped and disconnected road network was depressing intercity travel demand). With the vast majority of road traffic being local in nature, he argued that local economic development needs today should take precedence over intercity travel needs in the future. In practice, this meant that agricultural needs should take primacy, and hence more than 50 percent of the federal-aid mileage and 40 percent of federal funds were devoted to farm-to-market roads. As we have noted, urban highways were not part of the federal-aid system.[81]

MacDonald's belief in state and local control led him to oppose a potentially far-reaching plan put forward by Michigan Senator Charles E. Townshend at the end of World War I. It proposed ending the 1916 federal-aid program and replacing it with a national highway system with full authority vested in the federal government. In an obvious tip of the hat to state representation in the U.S. Senate, this new program would have created a network of at least two federal highways through each state, large or small. Townshend's proposal was initially popular, but infighting, legislative maneuvering, the high cost of the proposed system, and MacDonald's argument that highways were primarily tools for local traffic and economic development carried the day; the initiative was shelved.[82] Notwithstanding this setback, however, federal assistance for state highway programs would continue to grow.

The Federal-Aid Highway Act of 1921 and the Genesis of a National Highway Network

Responding to widespread public demand for better roads, and the shambles in which the roads had been left due to wartime overuse and neglect, in 1919 Congress allocated the federal-aid program an additional $200 million ($3.2 billion in 2021$) to be spread over three years.[83] The new Act also dropped the federal:state matching ratio from 1:2 to 1:1. In a victory for the intercity highway enthusiasts, and at the expense of those who favored farm-to-market roads, it raised the cap on federal spending to $20,000/mile (about $315,000 in 2021$). It also stretched the definition of "postal" road to be so broad that nearly all roads qualified, ending the pretense that mail delivery was the primary justification for federal involvement in road building. The principle of federal funding of the highway network was now firmly established.[84]

The federal-state highway partnership took another leap forward in 1921 with the passage of new legislation shepherded by AASHO, with MacDonald and the BPR orchestrating in the background. The Federal-Aid Highway Act of 1921 upped the federal ante further to $75 million (about $1.0 billion in

2021\$) *every* year, and, ultimately, the actual amounts spent would, for various reasons, be even higher.

Of even greater importance, for the first time the new Act imposed a degree of central coordination on the nation's inchoate road network. The 1921 Act extended the federal-aid program from rural postal routes to a broader category of roads, particularly a so-called primary system. This consisted of the most important highways that were eventually to be fused into a national intercity highway system.[85] According to the amendment's provisions, 7 percent of each state's rural road mileage, as selected by the state, would be designated as deserving federally backed improvement (the federal-aid system). Included in this total were 3 percent of the roads that were to be knit into the network of primary roads designed to serve long-haul, interstate travel.[86,††] This network would not include many key intercity routes, even after Congress increased the mileage in 1936.[87] But in general the routes selected by the states conformed well to the BPR's estimations of where high-quality roads were needed, based on county-level population and economic activity. In sum, these roads would collectively constitute America's first truly interstate highway network; by the BPR's calculations, when the proposed system was completed, more than 90 percent of the U.S. population would live within 10 miles of a federal-aid road, and the system would directly connect 94 percent of cities with a population greater than 5,000. This principle of a national network involved something of a *volte face* for MacDonald, though, in keeping with his federalist principles, states would be the prime movers in designating the routes. Ultimately the 1921 Act brought quality intercity road connectivity to every major city and town in America.[88]

The Act provided a minimum share of funding to all states. To be sure they could construct at least some highways, very small states like Delaware and New Hampshire were accommodated with a revenue floor of one-half of one percent of the total apportionment. At the other extreme, large Western states with vast sizes, low populations, and much non-taxable federal land also benefited from special provisions to secure extra funding for them.[89]

Because of its central role in establishing the first truly national highway network, some have argued that the Federal Aid Highway Act of 1921 was the most important piece of highway legislation in American history, more so even than the acts creating and later funding the Interstate System.[90] The process was a political triumph for MacDonald and the BPR; in response to

---

†† The 7 percent figure was ultimately devised by MacDonald, though we don't know how he derived it. One theory is that it was based on the percentage that would give a pair of Western senators a highway in each compass direction though their states. Another theory is that it was ultimately derived from MacDonald's experiences in Iowa (Swift 2011).

a poll, 36 state highway department officials reported that they supported the federal-aid system, while only four supported Senator Townshend's proposed national highway system. The 1921 Act cemented MacDonald's position as America's leading authority on roads. His formula of behind-the-scenes persuasion, cooperation with the states, and assuming the mantle of apolitical technical expertise proved a potent one. Even Townsend plan supporters, such as the AAA, were ultimately happy with the 1921 legislation because they felt that MacDonald and the BPR would bring new vigor and professionalism to road building.[91]

In other respects, the 1921 Act was similar to its predecessor: states not only selected the routes, but were also responsible for planning, design, construction, and maintenance, subject to federal standards and approval. However, as events unfolded, the balance of power on the ground shifted. As had always been the case, the BPR generally (though not always) avoided using its statutory authority to reject state plans or withhold funding. But at the same time, its de facto influence was far greater than the letter of the law would suggest. Given its superior technical expertise, the BPR was generally better placed than its state counterparts to take the lead. Thus, while on paper the federal government was the junior partner, in reality its role was active and central. Yet at the same time, due to its great efforts to show ostensible deference to the states, federal direction was rarely resented. Perhaps the ultimate testimony to the success of the federal-state partnership was the fact that states voluntarily requested a great deal of assistance from the BPR even on state roads that were outside of the federal-aid system.[92]

Though state and federal involvement in road building was rapidly increasing, most rural roads still remained county affairs. In 1921, about three-quarters of all road capital spending was by county and local governments. Further, particularly in more rural states, the stage construction technique meant improving roads up to relatively low standards since current traffic levels did not justify expensive pavements or wider rights-of-way.[93] However, most counties eventually adopted standards patterned after the federal-aid ones.[94] Moreover, the 1920s saw a steady transfer of road authority away from the counties (which were viewed by BPR staff as mostly unprofessional) and to the states (which under BPR guidance were increasingly professional and sophisticated).

The BPR-state partnership rapidly produced results. Thanks to the steadily rising federal financial commitment, to the fact that federal support was now budgeted years in advance so states could do advance planning, and to a fall in construction costs, in fiscal year 1922 alone 10,247 miles of road improvements were made, 3½ times as much as had been accomplished over the entire life of the federal-aid program through 1921. By 1929, 90 percent of the federal-aid system had been improved in some way (though that could simply mean simple grading and ditching to aid water runoff).[95]

Financing Highways Outside of Cities in the Pre-Freeway Era: Reliance on the Property Tax

In this period, road construction and maintenance saw a welcome shift away from citizens reluctantly fulfilling their work requirements and convict chain gangs forced to do road work, all working under the eyes of inexperienced, untrained, and often-disinterested overseers. This model was increasingly supplanted by trained, paid work crews under the direction of professional engineers. This shift did, of course, cost money. Further, thanks to the financial incentives of the federal-aid program, states now needed to raise considerable funding to receive their federal matches. Thus, by 1917, every state was involved in funding highways, whether through reimbursement programs for local governments or more directly through financing the construction of rural highways themselves.

From where was this money to come? Even as late as 1904, work requirements and poll taxes comprised 59 percent of the $80 million ($2.2 billion in 2021$) raised for road building by state and local governments. However, as was the case in cities, the use of property taxes steadily increased, comprising 34 percent of state highway revenue by 1904 and ultimately becoming the dominant funding mechanism in the early decades of the twentieth century.[96]

Yet there were three principal problems with reliance on the property tax for rural roads. First, there was a limit to how high the tax rates could go. Both state and local governments independently funded their myriad expenses, including for road building, from property taxes. Property owners frequently complained about over-taxation, and some observers feared that increasing taxes might spark a large-scale property tax revolt. Second, many areas requiring rural and intercity roads had too few local property taxpayers to provide the needed financial support; this problem was particularly acute in many Western states, where much of the land was in public hands and, thus, untaxed. Third, even as the potential to raise additional property tax revenue was constrained, demand for that revenue spiraled upward with the ever-increasing number of motorists and their growing use of the roads. Thus, the property tax financing system adopted widely to finance urban streets ultimately proved inadequate to fund rural roads.[97]

As a result, the consensus that property owners in rural areas should bear the cost (though their labor, and later financially) of nearby roads began to fray. Rural landowners argued that automobiles, mostly owned by city dwellers, imposed increasingly burdensome demands on rural road systems, and that those demands were far beyond those imposed by local residents. Hence it became more and more apparent that road users themselves should bear at least some of the burden for highway construction and maintenance, particularly for through roads whose primary function was not local access. Few people advocated a complete abandonment of property tax and local general revenue support for roads, but still it was becoming clear that an alternate method of reapportioning the fiscal burden would be necessary.[98]

At first, states turned to borrowing backed by future state revenues. Massachusetts in 1893 and New Jersey in 1894 were the first to issue road-building bonds, though California, Connecticut, Maryland, and New York followed soon thereafter. In the years immediately following World War I, the rush by states to sell bonds for highway construction flooded the market to the degree that it became difficult to find bond buyers.[99] Unsurprisingly, a financing schema, like bonds, that permitted costs to be pushed to the future had considerable political allure.

But this approach had its drawbacks as well. Roads in this era often broke down quickly due to damage caused by the increasing numbers of vehicles, especially trucks, and to new road-building geometries demanded by newer generations of faster motorized vehicles. (The engineering strategies to cope with higher-speed vehicles included gentler curves, flatter grades, better sightlines, improved highway-railroad intersections, wider roadways, more emergency stopping places, striping of centerlines, and sometimes abandoning highways entirely in favor of new routes that more easily hosted these improvements.) These measures were seen as necessary not only for accommodating higher vehicle speeds, but also for addressing safety problems since there was a national uproar over skyrocketing crash rates as more and more Americans took to the roads. Of course, engineering for higher speeds had the effect of encouraging ever-faster driving, which meant further engineering for even higher speeds, and on and on.[100]

The upshot of all of this was that, because of the relatively short lives of crudely improved roads, often a government would have to issue a new bond to rebuild a road whose original construction costs were still being paid for by a bond that had yet to be retired. Bonds of that era typically had lives of 25 to 30 years, which was substantially longer than the lives of the often rudimentarily constructed roads that lasted 15, 10, or even just 5 years. Given the scale of road building and maintenance necessitated by rising auto traffic, debts accumulated and consumed ever-larger proportions of state budgets. Total road-building bond indebtedness in the United States that totaled $229 million in 1915 had skyrocketed to $1.2 billion by 1922 (from $5.9 billion to $18.6 billion in 2021$). This mounting debt placed enormous stress on state budgets. By 1922, California devoted nearly 44 percent of all state government revenues either to directly fund the state highway program or for debt service on the bonds issued to support that program.[101] States typically repaid bonds with general revenues, which often came substantially or even principally from property tax receipts that were subject to all the limitations discussed above.

The Shift to User Fees

With borrowing reaching its limits, public officials began to look increasingly to road users for funds. Tolling is the most direct form of user finance, and its use in America dates, as we have seen, from the turnpike era in the early nineteenth century. But in most places toll roads were impractical: they required heavy traffic to cover costs, the tolls were expensive and onerous to collect, and toll booth attendants were challenging to supervise. In addition, manned toll booths needed to be placed at many points on a toll road in order to collect from a large share of users, which was not only expensive but required travelers to frequently stop in order to pay; this directly undermined the utility of the toll roads for travelers. Toll evasion was also quite common, such as by detouring on side roads in order to avoid tollbooths. Federal policy actively discouraged the use of tolls on federal-aid roads; in general, tolls were seen as warranted only for large bridges with especially high capital costs and semi-monopoly positions in the road network, and even then, tolls were widely seen as appropriate only to pay off the debts incurred for the facilities' construction.[102]

Thus, the return to the "user pays principle" in the twentieth century came, at first, not from tolls but from driver's license and vehicle registration fees. New York pioneered the state vehicle registration fee in 1901, charging $1 (about $30 in 2021$) per vehicle.[103] Initially, it was a one-time fee, just high enough to cover the expenses incurred in identifying the vehicle. However, the revenue-generating potential of this levy proved tempting to public officials, and by 1915 every state had adopted annual registration fees with the proceeds typically devoted, at least in part, to support highways.[104] Between 1910 and 1920, vehicle registration fees produced a total of nearly $1 billion for the states (approximately $25 billion in 2021$).[105] Spurred in large part by the road damage caused by trucking in World War I, states also began to graduate registration fees based on vehicles' weight and/or carrying capacity in an effort to apportion more of the finance burden onto the heavy trucks that did a disproportionate share of the road damage. In addition, some cities and villages began to enact "wheel taxes" for the privilege of driving on their streets, and a few states extended their property taxes to cover the value of automobiles.[106]

The Arrival of the Motor Fuel Taxes

Extending the search for ways to tax road users, the states looked to Europe, where motor fuels were taxed. In 1919, Oregon, which due to its sparse population and rugged terrain had reached the limits of what could be raised for roads through bonding, was the first U.S. state to adopt motor fuel taxes. The idea of taxes on motor fuels, mainly gasoline and diesel fuel, with the proceeds dedicated to roads, was immediately and widely popular with state officials. Following Oregon's lead, fuel taxes were adopted by New Mexico, Colorado, and North Dakota later that same year, and by Louisiana, Kentucky, Connecticut, Florida, Georgia, North Carolina, and Pennsylvania in 1920 and 1921.[107] By 1923, 34 states had adopted motor fuel taxes, and by 1929 all 48 states and the District of Columbia had implemented them.[108]

Taxes on motor fuels were adopted quickly and widely for several reasons. First, although theories of justice may not always (or even often) sway the political process, an important factor in the fuel tax's favor was its merits according to the "benefits principle" of taxation. Fuel taxes did not precisely target those who benefited from a particular road, as tolling might. But since fuel consumption varied roughly with vehicle miles traveled, and since, barring the widespread use of tolling, vehicle miles traveled was as good a measure as could be realistically devised for judging the benefits received by a motorist from using the road system, the fuel taxes acquitted themselves well in terms of fairness.

Moreover, the taxes performed well according to the "costs imposed" finance principle. This justifies taxing those whose activities generate burdens on the public at large, in this case the burden of building and maintaining roadways. In addition to varying with distance driven, fuel consumption also roughly varied with vehicle axle weight and speed, which are the principal factors contributing to roadway wear and tear. Hence fuel taxes fell roughly proportionally on those responsible for the ruinous cycle of constant road rehabilitation and reconstruction. Thus, in all, the motor fuel taxes were a philosophical step forward, and this generated a widespread sense of their fairness.

Several other factors combined to make the motor fuel taxes a triumph of fiscal politics. First, the concept had been "road tested" in Europe for a decade. Second, the fuel taxes were simple to administer. The taxes were collected not at the pump or even from individual gas stations, but from motor fuels wholesalers and distributors, which were relatively few in number. As a result, the cost of administering the taxes during the 1920s was an average of only 0.5 percent of revenues,[109] which was vastly less than that for tolls or even other taxes, such as property taxes. For example, administration costs for vehicle registration fees accounted for up to 40 percent of tax proceeds in some states.[110] Third, the fuel taxes fell on out-of-area and even out-of-state motorists, not just local property owners; in some states, "foreign" (out-of-state) drivers comprised a significant proportion of highway users.[111] This was a particularly important issue in both Oregon and Colorado.

Three more advantages of the motor fuel taxes stemmed from the failure of motorists to appreciate their actual financial burden. First, at least in their early years, the taxes were hidden in the retail fuel price that motorists paid at the pump. The wholesale fuel distributors who directly paid the taxes were well aware of how much they affected the price of fuel, but the retailers and motorists who set and paid the retail price for gasoline and diesel fuel were not so directly cognizant of the tax's effect on prices. As such, legislators enjoyed a certain degree of protection from wrathful consumers, who were more likely to blame oil companies than statehouses for price increases. It was not until 1925 that the petroleum companies, by that time increasingly chary about the fuel taxes, began to post the per gallon tax rate at the pump. With the retail equivalent of the taxes exposed, the relative anonymity of the fuel taxes was diminished.

Another advantage of the fuel taxes was that motorist opposition was blunted by the fact that the taxes were paid only a few pennies at a time. While over the course of a year the amounts paid by motorists could grow quite large, paying in small amounts over many transactions made the burden seem relatively trivial. Moreover, gasoline prices dropped sharply during the fuel taxes' early years, camouflaging any pain from tax increases.

Finally, one reason to love the fuel taxes stood out as more important than all others in the eyes of state officials: the taxes were phenomenal money-spinners. Starting at modest levels, fuel tax revenue grew dramatically. In 1921, the new fuel taxes constituted only 3 percent of state motor vehicle tax receipts (registration fees supplied the majority of the rest). But the relentless increase in the number of autos (sales rocketed from 1.6 million in 1921 to 5.3 million in 1929) and the concomitant rise in miles driven meant that by 1926, fuel tax revenue was up to 40 percent of total vehicle tax revenue. By 1929, fuel tax revenue surpassed registration fee revenue and, by 1931, it tripled it. Between 1921 and 1929, state revenue for road construction increased by a factor of six. During that period, state highway budgets almost tripled to $1.3 billion (about $19.6 billion in 2021$), yet in 1929, fuel tax revenue entirely covered these engorged state highway expenditures plus an $81 million surplus ($1.28 billion in 2021$).[112] States had at last found the "cash cow" to fund highways between cities. In part due to their newfound financial power, during the 1920s states began paying for the costs of constructing county and local roads post hoc when these were incorporated into state highway systems.[113]

In sum, due to effectiveness, efficiency, equity, and other advantages, the taxes on motor fuels had much to recommend them. While not a perfect mirror of costs imposed and benefits received, the utility of the motor fuel taxes was so great that they quickly became a cornerstone of transportation finance.

Given their many merits, the fuel taxes were a rare case of taxes that were widely popular politically. Even interest groups that might have been expected to oppose the taxes supported them, or at least were muted in their opposition. In many cases, automobile clubs actually *led* the fight for the fuel taxes because they promised new revenues for new roads. The automobile industry supported the taxes because it needed new roads in order to sell more cars. And the petroleum industry, while far from enthusiastic, was noticeably absent from the field of opponents—at least early on.

The oil companies generally chose to keep silent for two reasons. First, they recognized, if reluctantly, that the auto industry arguments had validity and better roads meant more cars and more driving, which in turn meant an increasing market for petroleum products. Second, the low rates of the earliest taxes did not seem to substantially affect fuel sales.[114] If the initial level of the taxes had been higher, the petroleum industry might have put up a more concerted fight against them early on.

Soon enough, however, the oil companies turned against the motor fuel taxes. But this change of heart had little effect on the public's attitude toward the taxes due to the general unpopularity of the oil industry at the time. This was, after all, the era when Standard Oil was a favored target of those such as populist demagogue Huey Long of Louisiana. As a result, the petroleum industry was relatively isolated in its opposition to motor fuel taxes and on the defensive as it watched the taxes expand in both scale and scope.

However, despite the taxes' broad popularity, public and pressure group approval did not come without strings. Motorists and members of the "Highway

Lobby" demanded commensurate benefits, insisting that fuel tax revenue be directly plowed back into road construction and upkeep and not diverted to unrelated public expenditures, as was the practice in Europe. So, when new fuel taxes were imposed, state officials often explicitly promised that these new revenues would be used to retire highway bonds. While state and federal trust fund accounts reserving motor fuel tax funds for transportation expenditures would come later, fuel tax revenues deposited in state general funds were roughly linked with state highway expenditures.[115]

For example, in 1929, New York Governor Franklin D. Roosevelt pushed a two-cent motor fuel tax through the New York legislature. It was billed as a user fee whose revenues were earmarked—at first informally and later officially—for roads. In adopting the tax, legislators explicitly rejected the idea that roads were public goods that ought to be paid by all, regardless of how much they traveled. Ironically, by shifting the financial burden of paying for roads from property owners to drivers, motor fuel taxes created a nascent interest group in the process.[116] This new group of road proponents fought an ongoing struggle against the states' creeping diversion of fuel tax proceeds for non-road purposes during the Depression years.

The Pershing Map and the Delineation of a National Highway System

As a result of more revenues and more effective spending, the American highway system grew rapidly. State road systems increased in extent from 203,000 miles in 1921 to 324,000 miles in 1930, and the total mileage of surfaced roads in the nation nearly doubled from 387,000 miles to 694,000 miles during this period. The federal-aid portion of the rural road system grew more slowly, from 169,000 miles in 1921 to 194,000 miles in 1930, but this masks the fact that these new roads tended to be built to high standards. By 1925, 49 percent of all state highway construction funds were allocated to federal-aid roads.[117] On the federal side, between 1921 and 1932, the government provided $1.2 billion (approximately $18.3 billion in 2021$) in aid to the states under the conditions established by the 1921 Act.[118]

In the early 1920s, federal and state authorities selected the routes to be included in the federal-aid system. Once more, this process involved collaboration between Washington and the states, with the states taking the leading role in laying out the initial proposals. As usual, the BPR role was theoretically secondary, but in practice it was far more robust. Since defense was a major constitutional justification for the federal role, the BPR asked the War

Department to designate roads it considered crucial for military preparedness. In consultation with MacDonald, the War Department agreed early
on there would be no separate network of military roads but a combined
military-civilian system.

In 1922, the army created the "Pershing Map" (named for General John.
J. Pershing), which laid out a plan for an enormous 75,000-mile, interconnected, border-to-border, coast-to-coast highway system. This map served as
a basis for further work by MacDonald and the BPR. In particular, Bureau
engineer Edwin W. James conducted a survey of conditions nationwide and
assigned each state road mileage and route designations based on state and
county population and economic productivity. The revised map that resulted,
which included 168,881 miles of roadway (about 5.8 percent of total U.S. road
mileage), delineated a system accessible by roughly 90 percent of the nation's
population. Ultimately the Pershing Map very closely resembled the actual
routing of the federal-aid highway system, and it would later serve as a basis
for the future Interstate Highway System.[119]

In addition to route selection, MacDonald and the BPR brought order to
route designations. Prior to 1924, the nation was crisscrossed by at least 250
named routes (like the Lincoln and Dixie Highways). These were designated
by private "trail associations" of road enthusiasts. These routes often over-
lapped, so that in one spot a road could go by several different names, with
confusing signposting to match. In 1924, AASHO recommended that the
system be reorganized, with continuous routes no longer bearing names but
one- and two-digit numbers, with three digits being used for spurs or variants
off the main routes. North-south roads would bear odd numbers and east-
west roads even ones, with the lowest numbers in the far Northeast; the most
important east-west routes would end in "0" and the most important north-
south routes would end in "1." A public participation process at the time saw
the route mileage increase by 50 percent, since many cities clamored to not be
left off of the numbered system. After the design was unveiled in an AASHO
manual, the now-familiar uniform "U.S." road signs with their distinctive
shields began to appear in 1926 (see Figure 4.1). (Incidentally, this manual
also for the first time standardized the shape and color of danger and regulatory road signs, such as the familiar red octagon for the "stop" sign.)[120]

Engineering Rural Roads

By the late 1920s, the influence of private highway associations had waned;
the Dixie Highway Association closed in 1927, and the Lincoln Highway

Figure 4.1. Highway shield for the famous Route 66.
Source: Public Domain-wikipedia: Levente Jakab creator. *Source:* Levente Jakab. 2009. 16 x 16 U.S. route shield approximated to the 1948 standards, modified to use the 1926 font set. https://comm ons.wikimedia.org/wiki/File:US_66_Arizona_1926.svg.

Association shut its doors a year later. But before closing shop, the latter moved the highway debate forward with a proposal for engineering and construction standards for a national system. Based on a questionnaire mailed to 4,600 highway engineers, the Association determined that the ideal highway would have a right-of-way at least 100 feet wide, two traffic lanes in each direction, five-foot grass shoulders, and narrow sidewalks. Alignments were to be as straight as possible, with curves banked with radii of at least 1,000 feet, which would allow cars to take the turns safely at 35 miles per hour and trucks at 10 miles per hour. Closely adjacent roadside ditches and advertising were ruled out. One survey-endorsed specification later rejected by MacDonald was that all roads be surfaced with 10 inches of reinforced Portland cement concrete, since he felt that in many places traffic would not require what remains to the present day the gold standard of road surfaces.[121]

However, despite these lofty principles, the roads actually constructed were mostly quite modest. Breadth of effort was generally preferred to depth in quality in order to maximize paved mileage—a strategy that became known as "ribbon construction." Pavements were narrow and relatively thin. In the more heavily trafficked eastern U.S., Portland cement and asphalt were often used, but in the then-sparsely-settled West, surfaces were generally still gravel or sand-clay.[122] Roads were normally one lane in each direction, with narrow shoulders, and were often routed to reflect local idiosyncrasies. These modest design practices fit with the stated goals of the federal-aid program: bringing farm produce to market, allowing postal service, and facilitating troop and materiel movements. None of these purposes required a high degree of road durability. Thus, while the routes were now part of an impressive national numbering system, they were still geared primarily to local uses.

Crucially, the roads almost always lacked full grade separation (where crossing roadways and railways pass over or under one another) and access control (where roadways can only be entered into or exited from designated interchanges and not from or to adjacent property). This meant slower traffic speeds through towns due to numerous stop signs or signals, as well as traffic that entered and exited the traffic stream in an uncontrolled fashion, particularly to and from the businesses that often lined highways.[123] Thus, by 1930, there was a flurry of lobbying for stricter access control, complete grade separation, limitations on roadside development, and a ban on non-auto traffic (horses, bicycles, pedestrians, etc.). The familiar cloverleaf intersection, pioneered in Woodbridge, New Jersey, was proposed for major road interchanges.[124] Still, for several more years these proposals remained only proposals.

Though it was but a foretaste of what was to come, progress on the rural road system during the 1920s and early 1930s was, in all, impressive. Although construction standards were not always high, they had vastly improved, and by the mid-1930s a basic national highway network was already in place. By that time, few Americans lived further than ten miles from an improved, numbered U.S. highway. Hence, well before the advent of the Interstates, America had embarked on the incremental construction of a mammoth highway system. Many scholars attribute this to the work of MacDonald, and certainly he was a central and energetic actor. But ultimately the motive force for the highway-building movement was the American motorist, as auto ownership grew by two and a half times from 10.5 million to 26.7 million in the 1920s alone.[125] Drivers, and the growing auto-related industries that served them, demanded roads that would accommodate safer, high-speed travel—and American governments at all levels began to oblige.

Rural Highways for Urban Areas?

One final question loomed. Should the nascent national network include urban roads, which the 1916 Act expressly forbade? Initially, intercity routes like the Lincoln Highway tended to run directly through town centers. But this arrangement imposed considerable delay for through traffic. To avoid this, bypass and belt highways were promoted from the early 1920s on. However, their effectiveness was limited because they tended to attract development that in turn generated local traffic and slowed through-traffic speeds. In any event, whether the focus was on the farmer or the intercity traveler, there seemed little place for national or state highways dedicated to serving intraurban traffic, due ultimately to financial constraints.[126] As we will see, this exclusively rural focus began to change only with the onset of the Great Depression and its associated public works programs. Yet even then, work on urban roads would be piecemeal, not part of any greater plan to fundamentally alter the form or function of highways in cities, include them in the interstate network, or bring them under state and federal purview. This general aversion to adding urban segments to national and state highway networks would not begin to change until the late 1930s.

Motor Fuel Taxes in the Great Depression

As we have noted, the onset of the Depression meant a fiscal disaster for urban road building as property values, and thus the property tax revenue by which urban streets were funded, plummeted. Remarkably, however, the motor fuel taxes on which states increasingly depended to fund roads outside of cities remained robust. While burgeoning motor vehicle ownership after World War I meant that cars were no longer simply playthings for the rich, they remained relatively rare among the working class and poor between the world wars. Thus, motor vehicle use declined less during the Great Depression than did public transit ridership, the latter of which was the principal means of conveyance among those hit most severely by economic hard times. Transit ridership plummeted by a third, or 5.7 billion annual passenger trips, during the darkest years of the Depression (between 1929 and 1933), and by 1939, passenger counts were still more than 25 percent below 1929 levels.[127]

In contrast to transit, the Depression story of motor vehicle ownership and use was not so, well, depressing. Ownership of cars and trucks did dip somewhat (about 10.6%) during the Depression's early years between 1929 and 1933, meaning that revenue from vehicle registration fees was roughly 6–8 percent lower than it had been in 1929. However, during this same period, fuel consumption, and thus fuel tax revenue, rose dramatically; the extra $55.5 million (about $902 million in 2021$) in fuel tax receipts during this period more than doubled the losses from fewer vehicle registrations and declines in other fees.[128] In short, driving remained remarkably robust. Further, as the Depression progressed, vehicle ownership levels recovered and resumed their ascent, increasing 13.6 percent overall between 1929 and 1939.[129] While reliable vehicle travel data go back only to 1936, between 1936 and 1939 vehicle miles of travel increased 13.2 percent.[130] Thus auto ownership and driving were relatively resilient at a time when nearly all other forms of economic activity cratered, until fuel rationing and the almost-complete cessation of auto production were adopted during World War II.[131]

Conclusion: Road Planning and Finance for Autos Before Freeways

The automobile's arrival brought major changes to the planning and financing of roads in both urban and rural America. In cities, planners and engineers confronted the problem of traffic congestion, first by regulating street use, and then by implementing ever more ambitious programs of street improvements and capacity expansions as recommended by the major traffic street plans. It was widely believed that urban areas could and should take care of their own needs since they were home to more people and economic activity. Thus, cities moved beyond abutter finance to fund their increasingly elaborate and expensive road treatments, first with special assessments and then with general property taxes. These efforts brought some short-term relief, but were ultimately overwhelmed by the ever-rising tide of automobiles. Further, improvements to urban transportation systems were hamstrung by the fact that property tax revenues collapsed during the Depression and were ultimately bounded in the revenue they could generate without causing widespread hardship and anger.

In rural America, state governments and then the federal government returned to the road-building field. As a result, America's rural and intercity highways underwent a radical transformation. A partnership emerged between the states and the federal government to improve rural and intercity highways, and significant progress was made in doing so. Beginning with small-scale, piecemeal efforts to get farmers out of the mud, improve postal roads, and put an end to rural isolation, by the end of the 1920s a federally supported but state-administered national system of rural and intercity highways had emerged that enabled the deeper economic integration of the country. New industries began to soon appear, such as intercity trucking. Rural America was no longer as isolated as it had been in the past.

This system was built by a new breed of highway engineers to increasingly uniform standards. It prioritized economical traffic service over the social objectives that had motivated some earlier rural roadway advocates.

A key difference between urban and rural roads was the means used to pay for them. In contrast to the cities, the states had come across a money-spinner in the form of the motor fuel taxes that had broad public acceptance and that generated increasing revenue in tandem with ever-advancing American motorization. This was a trend that even the Great Depression could not derail.

Figure 4.2 shows the amount of street and highway funding that came from motor fuel taxes (gasoline and diesel) and vehicle excise taxes (including registration fees, wheel taxes, commercial vehicle fees, taxi permits, and other miscellaneous fees and licenses). This is compared to the percentage of available funding from property taxes and assessments in both urban and rural areas between 1921 and 1945. The relative roles played by these tax instruments essentially switched places during the two-and-a-half decades between end of the two World Wars, with fuel taxes ascendant and property taxes in decline.[132]

This shift was striking. Roads within cities faced penury, while roads between them enjoyed prosperity. The fact that roads within cities and roads

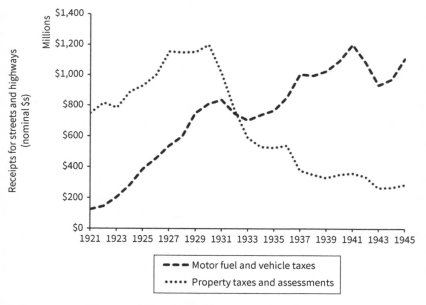

Figure 4.2. Property and motor fuel and vehicle taxes available to all levels of government for street and highway finance, 1921–1945.

Data source: U.S. Department of Transportation, Federal Highway Administration, Bureau of Public Roads, Highway Statistics, Summary to 1965, Table HF-201, United States Government Printing Office, Washington, D.C., 1967.

Note: Fuel taxes and vehicle fees exclude amounts allocated for collection expenses and expenditures for non-highway purposes.

outside of them were funded in very different ways, with the revenues controlled by different levels of government, would ultimately have dramatic effects on the shape of the American highway system and American cities. Meanwhile, urban and rural highway planners began pursuing decidedly different paths to moving increasing numbers of vehicles through their respective territories, setting up a fundamental conflict over the future of highway transportation that would have to be resolved before the era of massive freeway construction could begin. The next two chapters tell these stories.

PART III
PLANNING AND FINANCE IN THE EARLY FREEWAY ERA

5

Planning Highways in Cities in the Pre-Interstate Era

The development of a comprehensive system of parkways today finds its justification primarily in the need of the community for rapid trafficways radiating from the center of the city to the suburbs, and connecting the various suburbs with one another.

—Swan (1931, 84)

Innovations in traffic regulation and the major traffic street plans of the 1920s greatly facilitated motor vehicle movement. But rising automobile ownership and usage, paralleled by an accelerating decline in public transit patronage, resulted in a continuing flood of new traffic onto America's urban streets. Worried city officials and local business interests, particularly those situated in CBDs, continued to turn to the growing cadre of transportation planning and engineering experts for relief. One new potential solution was at hand, suggested by the recreational parkways designed for pleasure driving; it would ultimately sow the seeds of a revolution in urban road construction.[1]

The Development of the Parkway

The origins of the parkway lay in the parks movement of the middle and late nineteenth century. The earliest parkways, deployed in major cities such as New York and Boston, were roads through municipal or regional parks or along streams.[2] The roads were limited to recreational vehicles* (usually carriages) and commercial traffic was almost always banned. During the first decade of the twentieth century, planners began redeveloping the polluted

---

* At the time, the term "recreational vehicles" implied those used for driving or riding for pleasure (most often by the upper-middle classes and well-to-do). Today, by contrast, the term and its acronym (RVs) refer to vehicles designed for camping or living in while on the road.

The Drive for Dollars. Jeffrey R. Brown, Eric A. Morris, and Brian D. Taylor, Oxford University Press.
© Oxford University Press 2023. DOI: 10.1093/oso/9780197601518.003.0005

Bronx River Valley in New York as a parkway for pleasure travel by foot, bicycle, horse and carriage, and automobile. By the time construction actually began, the road was redesigned as an exclusive motor vehicle parkway, but one still specifically for leisure travel. One of the earliest examples of a controlled-access highway, its construction began in 1917 and the entire parkway opened for traffic in 1923.[3] Other parkways soon followed.

These early automobile parkways were consciously planned and built as recreational spaces.[4] They provided their users with a leisurely, enjoyable traveling experience (see Figure 5.1). The landscaped and architecturally pleasing facilities were designed to fit hand-in-glove with the natural topography.

However, despite their recreational focus, the parkways introduced several design features that were of keen interest to more utilitarian-minded engineers and planners. First, travel was often limited to a single direction on each side of a divided road, which greatly reduced the chance of head-on collisions. Second, many at-grade crossings were eliminated by over- and underpasses, called "grade separation." As a result, stops at intersections were mostly avoided, which not only increased average travel speeds but also removed the risk of dangerous right-angle "T-bone" crashes. Third, the number of entry and exit points was controlled, thereby limiting parkway access.[5] Parkways were often bordered by strips of parkland, which in addition to their aesthetic

Figure 5.1. Bronx River Parkway.
Courtesy of the Westchester County (NY) Archives.

appeal freed planners from having to provide direct access to properties along the route, avoiding the legal obligation for urban streets to accommodate abutters.[6] Limiting access removed a hindrance to traffic by minimizing disruptive merging and turning movements, and also improved safety by eliminating many of the conflicting "frictions of movement" that caused crashes.[7] Together, these features enabled parkways to carry motor vehicles more safely, at considerably higher speeds, and in much larger numbers than could cramped local streets or traditional urban thoroughfares.

By the early and mid-1920s, planners near New York City devised additional systems of recreational parkways, exclusively for the use of passenger automobiles on Long Island.[8] These largely suburban and rural facilities proved enormously popular with the motoring public, as they provided direct access from the crowded city to nearby beaches, parks, and other recreational areas. Robert Moses, the key figure behind the development of the Long Island parkway system, built similar facilities in other parts of New York State to connect its various parks.[9] Further, several parkways were constructed in Westchester County, a tony suburb to the north of the city. In this case, the purpose of the roads was not to carry motorists on pleasure drives to recreational facilities, but to bring commuters into and out of New York City. Due to the Westchester parkways' access benefits, they raised the value of adjacent property considerably. These facilities received considerable positive publicity in both the popular and engineering press, and engineers and planners across the United States began to emulate New York by building their own suburban and rural parkways, often relying on state funds (including motor fuel tax revenues) to do so.

From the Parkway to the Freeway

Back in the city, transportation planners and engineers watched the rural and suburban parkway boom with keen interest as motorists flocked to these facilities. Given the parkways' considerable improvements in speed, safety, and carrying capacity, it's not at all surprising that planners and engineers of the day quickly recognized their potential in the ongoing fight against traffic congestion.

Urban transportation planners and engineers would thus adapt the new parkways' design principles for more utilitarian, traffic-serving purposes.[10] The facilities they devised went by a variety of names—limited ways, motorways, expressways, and superhighways—before famed planner Edward Bassett eventually coined the term "freeway." Bassett defined a freeway as "a strip of public land devoted to *movement* over which the abutting property owners have no right of light, air or access."[11] The emphasis on movement, as opposed to recreation, distinguished freeways from parkways. The freeway was simply a major street, quite similar to the broad boulevards contained in proposals such as the 1909 Burnham Plan for Chicago, to which the three distinguishing design features of parkways were added: divided traffic, grade separation, and limited access.[12] For consistency and simplicity, we henceforth use the generic term "freeway" to refer to any of the variously named facilities that possessed these three design attributes and were open to all types of vehicular traffic.

Most early metropolitan freeway plans, like the major traffic street plans before them, were prepared by a small, and by now familiar, group of consultants. They again worked most often for downtown-based business associations,[13] though occasionally their work was commissioned by local governments.[14] Although the plans differed in their details, they shared many features. They were often multimodal, containing both an automobile and a rapid transit component (such as rail transit in the median strips of freeways). They typically called for relatively dense networks of small-scale freeways (often only two traffic lanes in each direction) with moderate design speeds (maximums of 35, 40, or 45 miles per hour) (see Table 5.1). The footprints of these facilities were far smaller than those of the mammoth high-speed freeways we have today, making them easier to integrate into the urban fabric with less disruption of adjacent communities.[15]

Table 5.1 Selected Metropolitan Freeway Plans of the Pre-World War II Era

City	Year	Client	Extent and Cost	Design Standards
Detroit	1924	Detroit Rapid Transit Commission	217-mile network. No cost estimates.	Design speed: 35 miles per hour. Facilities: 204-foot right of way, 84-foot center reserved for transit. Full grade separation. Limited access.
Chicago	1932	Chicago Committee on Traffic and Public Safety	160-mile network. Cost: $100 million.	Design speed: 40 miles per hour (passenger vehicles only). Elevated facilities. Full grade separation. Limited access.
New York City	1938	NYC Committee on City Planning	65 miles of expressways, plus arterial highways. Cost: $150 million.	Design speed: 35 miles per hour. Two traffic lanes in each direction. Full grade separation. Limited access.

Sources: Rapid Transit Commission (1924) for Detroit, McClintock (1932) for Chicago, and Moses (1938) for New York City.

The metropolitan freeway plans of the 1920s and 1930s were usually part of larger planning efforts that considered the transportation system, and freeways in particular, in relation to adjacent land uses.[16] Nearly all these early freeway plans were concerned with providing better automobile and rapid transit access to congested downtowns. As with the major traffic street plans, downtown business groups, city governments, and the consultants whose services they engaged saw the freeway as a means for maintaining the economic viability of downtowns through better motor vehicle connections with expanding suburbs.[17] These ambitious plans, which began to be prepared in 1924, extended well beyond the prototype grade-separated arterials that had been included in urban road planning up to then, and the facilities they included would be decidedly more expensive than anything yet proposed.

The 1924 Detroit Superhighway Plan

> *The Super-Highway is unique. It is a new and necessary departure in transportation planning for the modern city. Not only does it provide for a cheaper form of rapid transit on rails and for the ordinary highway motor-traffic of today, but it will also do something never before proposed—it will furnish an express motor traffic highway upon which automobiles can travel continuously at a maximum speed with safety, because all grade-crossings will be eliminated. In other words, the Super-Highway will become the major traffic artery of the future city, for both rail and automobile rapid transit services.*
>
> **—Turner (1925, 373)**

The first large-scale, utilitarian metropolitan freeway plan was, fittingly, prepared for the Motor City in 1924. The plan opened with a description of Detroit's problems, which were shared by many other cities, and expressed optimism for their solution:

> Detroit is now being strangled for lack of sufficient circulating facilities for its people—for lack of a system of streets of adequate width to accommodate its enormous amount of automobile traffic that is growing by leaps and bounds year after year. All other great cities in the country, and many of the smaller ones, too, are in similar distress, and from the same cause—excessive traffic congestion. Such a state of affairs is not strange in the light of the transformation from the horse to the automobile that has taken place in less than a single generation; and in the light of the further fact that our cities are being piled up layer upon layer almost

without limit, so that the streets that were once intended to serve 2 and 3 story buildings are now required to accommodate the massed office workers of 20, 30, and 40-story skyscrapers. The chief purpose of this report is to show how the traffic congestion of today resulting from the above conditions may be largely reduced in the future, in the Detroit of 1950, and the Greater Detroit of the year 2000, provided there is vision to plan and courage to execute.[18]

The planners' solution to these problems was a combined grid-radial system of 217 miles of freeways (referred to as superhighways in this plan) extending more than 15 miles outward from the city center. The freeways required enormous 204-foot-wide rights-of-way in the outer parts of the region, and generous 120-foot-wide rights-of-way in the downtown district.[19] In the outer sections, the rights-of-way included an 84-foot center for rail rapid transit lines flanked by landscaping, two 20-foot express roadways surrounded by 5-foot plantings, two 20-foot local roadways, and two 15-foot sidewalks (see Figure 5.2). In the downtown district, the rapid transit lines ran in a subway, and thus the necessary right-of-way was reduced. The rapid transit system featured stations at half-mile intervals.[20]

According to the plan's authors, the multimodal nature of the proposed facility was among its key strengths:

> A super-highway makes possible mass transportation on rails, with less cost for the structure than in any other form. Costing less money, rapid transit can be provided along these super-highway routes at a much earlier date than if either of the more expensive forms, such as elevated and subway, must be used. It also makes possible, adjacent to the rapid transit right of way, an express movement of motor vehicles with safety to the public that is not now provided anywhere in the world, and that will make an entirely new era in the usefulness of the motor vehicle.[21]

The authors noted that a single lane of superhighway had an hourly capacity from seven to ten times what the same lane would have in a 120-foot-wide street at the business center, an advantage of "incalculable value."

The express roadways had no at-grade crossings, and access points were limited. Travel speeds were expected to be a rapid 30 to 35 miles per hour, which was five to six times faster than the then-current average speed of 6 miles per hour on local streets.[22] The potential effects of the new facilities on relieving congestion were thus seen as extraordinary, indeed almost miraculous.

The authors intended that their freeway program be coordinated with land use planning throughout the region so that transportation and land use could work in harmony to achieve a more desirable urban form[23]—which at the time

TRANSITION FROM 204 FOOT HIGHWAY
TO
120 FOOT THOROUGHFARE
RAPID TRANSIT COMMISSION
DETROIT MICH. APRIL 10 1924

Figure 5.2. A super-highway from the Detroit super-highway plan (1924).
Source: Rapid Transit Commission. 1924. "Proposed Super-Highway Plan for Greater Detroit." Detroit, MI: Rapid Transit Commission. *Illustration:* Transition from 204-foot highway to 120-foot thoroughfare.

was thought to be a modern CBD, well connected with idyllic suburbs. This focus on integration with, and influence on, urban development would be present in many subsequent metropolitan freeway plans developed for other cities. Key considerations were stemming the decline of the CBD through increased accessibility and guiding the future growth of the region using the new freeways as a framework for decentralized development, which would align along the freeway corridors. Thus, the plan was not only a highway plan, but a transit and land use plan as well.

The Detroit plan was adopted but never fully implemented.[24] The financial resources and political support necessary to build out all of the plan's elements proved lacking, especially for the rail rapid transit components.[25] As in other cities, transit was still a privately owned, for-profit industry, and transit company owners were viewed with considerable distrust by a public angry over what it viewed as unreasonably high fares and poor service.[26]

Still, the ambitious plan generated significant interest in the transportation-engineering and city-planning communities, including notice in the pages of *The American City* and in the speeches of Thomas MacDonald, who championed many of the plan's ideas. MacDonald advocated the use of roads in park systems or in park-like strips, such as in the Detroit plan, as devices for relieving congestion.

The Detroit plan soon inspired other engineers and planners to develop their own adaptations of the parkway. Freeway-like facilities began to appear as minor elements in the major traffic street plans prepared by Miller McClintock, Harland Bartholomew, and their contemporaries.[27] Robert Moses began developing parkways in increasingly urban parts of New York City at about the same time.[28] By the end of the 1920s, a series of freeway-centered metropolitan transportation plans had emerged, including for cities such as New York, Chicago, Boston, San Francisco, St. Louis, and Los Angeles.

Most plans' underlying philosophy was that the key to solving the congestion problem was to provide for unimpeded, higher-speed vehicle movement throughout the city, particularly into and out of the CBD.[29] In retrospect, of course, it is ironic that freeways were embraced by so many at the time as saviors of downtowns, when, a half-century later, their critics would blame them for sowing the seeds of central cities' demise. Engineers were often skeptical of planners' faith in the resuscitating effects of freeways on downtowns, but still championed the new facilities as traffic carriers par excellence.

Two Early Visionaries of Urban Freeway Development: Bartholomew and Moses

City planning is neither extravagant nor grandiose; it is nothing more than practicality, avoidance of needless future expense by exercise of wise forethought.
> **—Harland Bartholomew (quoted in Lovelace 1993, 4)**

Doctors, we are told, bury their mistakes, planners by the same token embalm theirs, and engineers inflict them on their children's children.
> **—Robert Moses (Moses and Andrews & Clark Consulting Engineers 1949, 5)**

Among those who led the early planning of metropolitan freeways, two stand out: Harland Bartholomew and Robert Moses.[30] Both men would eventually leave their imprint on urban Interstate Highway development in the United States. Bartholomew was a vocal advocate for the more local-oriented, multimodal, integrated transportation/land-use style freeway planning that emerged in the 1920s and 1930s. Moses, on the other hand, became an advocate for the no-nonsense, utilitarian, traffic-service mindset that would dominate Interstate Highway development in the postwar period. Bartholomew's influence was felt through the plans he prepared for cities around North America throughout the 1920s and 1930s. Moses also developed plans for cities around the country but left his most indelible mark on New York.

Harland Bartholomew and Early Urban Freeway Development

Harland Bartholomew was trained as an engineer, but his outlook on transportation planning problems was much broader than that of most engineers. In Bartholomew's view, the transportation system was a critical component of a linked land use and transportation system whose interrelationship was critical for the future development of the city and the success of its residents.[31] His early street and highway plans for cities such as Los Angeles, Oakland, St. Louis, and Vancouver took account of their potential influence on development patterns, neighborhood structures, and downtown property values in addition to traffic service concerns.[32] Bartholomew was an important proponent of the vision of the metropolitan freeway as essentially a peculiar type of land use with important potential impacts—both positive and negative—on both transportation and urban form. His plans of the 1930s and 1940s reflect this perspective,[33] which became predominant in urban transportation planning circles in the 1930s. Bartholomew served on the Interregional Highways Committee, whose report to President Roosevelt on postwar U.S. highway planning was a direct precursor to the Interstate Highway System.

Proto-freeways, which Bartholomew variously referred to as "speedways," "parkways," and "industrial thoroughfares," appeared in some of his major street plans in the 1920s.[34] By the 1930s, these facilities, now called "freeways," were central features of a transportation system and important tools to direct future development activity along "certain desired lines."[35] In his view, the freeway was part of a broader program of urban renewal that included enhancing accessibility to the CBD and clearing out central slum districts in order to reclaim the land for future commercial growth. The latter goal was justified on the now-discredited assumption, common among planners at the time, that a principal cause of poverty and decline in poor, Black, and other minority neighborhoods was physical blight. Maximizing traffic service, on the other hand, was a secondary function in Bartholomew's freeway planning calculus. In fact, Bartholomew worried, presciently it would turn out, that, "if the capacity is increased beyond that of a city major street, congestion and confusion will result at the points of junction with major streets of the city."[36]

In addition to providing consulting services to dozens of cities, Bartholomew developed a series of freeway plans for his firm's home base, St. Louis.[37] His earliest freeway plan for the area, the 1930 plan for St. Louis County,[38] was modeled explicitly on the 1924 Detroit plan. In it, he called for the development of 42 miles of freeways that would provide increased access between the suburbs and the St. Louis CBD. The freeways had 150-foot-wide rights-of-way, included separate roadways for express and local traffic, and featured a 26-foot rapid transit right-of-way in the center, surrounded by two 20-foot express highway sections and two 20-foot frontage road sections. Grass strips separated all of the road sections. Bartholomew estimated that the facility could accommodate eight lanes of vehicles, six for moving vehicles and two for parked vehicles—the latter a feature conspicuously absent from modern freeways. All road crossings were grade separated, and access to adjacent property was limited. The roads were sited after a careful study of present and projected population and land use distributions.[39] Bartholomew would revisit his freeway plan for St. Louis in the 1940s after national developments had begun to transform the focus of urban freeway planning.

Robert Moses and Early Urban Freeway Development

Robert Moses is perhaps the most famous builder of infrastructure in U.S. history. He presided over a number of public authorities and commissions, serving in local and state government in both New York City and State for more than four decades. During this time, he presided over the construction of everything from bridges, tunnels, power plants, and dams to university campuses, parks, housing projects, cultural and recreational facilities, and a network of highways that crisscrossed the city and state.[40]

Moses had little patience for the long-view, comprehensive planning espoused by Bartholomew and Moses's occasional adversaries in the Regional Plan Association (RPA) of New York. Moses and his team designed and built roads largely without reference to a larger city plan. They were designed either as stand-alone facilities or, later, in relation to other parts of larger road, bridge, and tunnel networks. But by default, the consequences of the roads Moses built, and their traffic, became the de facto city plan. Moses dismissed most planners as dreamers who produced little of practical significance, occasionally referring to them as "municipal smart alecks."[41] He saw himself as a "doer," and he charged his staff with preparing blueprints for immediately buildable projects.

Moses began his highway-building career in the 1920s with the construction of recreational parkways that connected New York City with the parks and beaches on Long Island. Those projects, as discussed earlier, were extensively landscaped, and focused on aesthetics and recreation. His 1930 arterial roadway plan for greater New York City proposed the same "road-as-landscape-architecture" treatment for hundreds of miles of parkways.[42] Throughout the 1920s and 1930s, Moses's roads were modestly sized, relatively low-speed facilities that were similar to the early freeways proposed by planners elsewhere in the country. At the time, Moses viewed higher-speed roads as extravagant wastes of public resources.[43] Moses's roads differed from Bartholomew's freeways, not only because they were built with little reference to any overarching vision of urban development, but also because they offered no accommodation for public transit.

Moses's road-building efforts were frequently criticized by the members of the Regional Plan Association. Founded in 1922 by a group of wealthy philanthropists, the RPA sought to survey, analyze, and plan the future growth of the New York metropolitan region. In 1929 it published its *Regional Plan of New York and Its Environs*. The plan was financed by the Russell Sage Foundation and was prepared under the auspices of a committee of leading local businessmen and financiers chaired by Frederic Delano (who was later a member of the Interregional Highways Committee).[44] The multivolume plan touched on everything from land use to recreation to transportation. Among its numerous transportation recommendations was a call for the development of an elaborate regional highway network consisting of radials, bypasses, and beltways, all inspired by parkways. The highway facilities would be planned in a manner that would support the plan's larger objective of controlled, decentralized development of the metropolitan region. Transportation and land use were considered jointly as components of a single urban problem.[45]

But, as with many such visions, the RPA had no money to translate the plan's many ideas into reality. It could influence others to act in its spirit, but it lacked both the statutory and fiscal wherewithal to compel action. The plan's wide-ranging recommendations and explicitly regional focus meant that it also lacked the political support of downtown land and business owners, which was key to translating privately sponsored plans into action across the region's many cities and boroughs. On the other hand, Moses, given his many public-sector roles, had the means to turn his own vision for a belt urban highway network into reality. In contrast to the RPA's vision, Moses's system was largely disconnected from land use or urban development.[46]

The key to Moses's power and lasting influence was money; he had discovered a way to finance his increasingly ambitious projects so that his plans came to fruition while many other freeway plans languished. He financed his plans in two principal ways. First, he leveraged toll income from his various public enterprises.[47] Moses quickly discovered that motorists were quite willing to pay a toll to cross a new bridge or to use a new tunnel or limited-access roadway as opposed to traveling on a crowded city street. His new roads, bridges, and tunnels frequently filled to capacity soon after they opened, and as toll revenues grew, they were then used to back the issue of bonds to build yet more facilities.

The other key to Moses's success was that he was a master grantsman, tapping numerous Depression-era state and federal public works programs.[48] Some of these grants were made available starting under the National Industrial Recovery Act of 1933 and the Hayden-Cartwright Act of 1934. These acts played important roles in highway planning and construction, since these and other pieces of New Deal† legislation brought federal dollars into cities for highway construction in order to provide jobs.[49] Federal public works monies funded street and highway projects in numerous cities across the country, including, for example, Chicago's Lakeshore Drive. But Moses proved particularly adept at obtaining these dollars for New York.

Thanks to Moses and his contemporaries, New York stands out for its accomplishments in freeway construction during the 1930s. By 1933, 103 miles of freeways in the region were either open to traffic or about to begin construction.[50] Much additional mileage soon followed in the years preceding World War II, with each new link celebrated in a Moses-issued glossy report and the local newspapers.[51]

Importantly, however, the facilities built in New York during the 1930s bore only limited resemblance to modern Interstate Highways. With a typical maximum speed limit of 35 miles per hour, two traffic lanes in each direction, and generous landscaping, the roads looked more like parkways than

---

† The New Deal is the moniker used to describe the many programs, public work projects, and financial regulations shepherded by President Franklin Roosevelt in the 1930s to address the economic problems and hardships wrought by the Great Depression.

modern freeways, despite the fact that they increasingly served more utilitarian traffic.[52]

Moses's influence also extended nationally through his expert testimony to Congress and the many plans he and his staff prepared for other cities.[53] One of his earliest commissions outside of New York, received just prior to World War II, resulted in (yet another) plan for arterial improvements in Pittsburgh.[54] Much like in the major street plans of the 1920s, Moses argued that his road-straightening and widening program would offer a great deal of relief to harried motorists and improve access to the CBD. But much of his report focused on aesthetic treatments, urging the people of Pittsburgh to develop a beautiful parkway extending from the suburbs to the city center, the Triangle.[55] So while he remained skeptical of weaving urban freeways into larger urban and regional plans, as late as 1939 Moses remained a proponent of recreational parkways, having resisted the entirely utilitarian, traffic-service-only focus of his many engineering brethren. Pittsburgh officials eventually implemented most of Moses's recommended street improvements, although not the proposed parkway.[56]

U.S. Urban Freeway Planning in the 1930s: Big Plans, Limited Results

Over time, however, attention to freeway aesthetics began to wane. Instead, planners increasingly developed new freeway plans because of the widely held consensus that freeways would prove the ultimate, long-sought solution to urban traffic congestion. For example, planner Robert Whitten optimistically opined in 1932:

> It is sometimes said that it is useless to increase street capacities in central areas, as any additional capacity provided will be immediately taxed to the saturation point. This assumption may be valid in certain situations as applied to local business streets, but has no validity whatever as applied to any major traffic artery . . . [or] to any street that is an essential part of a comprehensive thoroughfare plan.[57]

This rather naïve view of both the behavior of motorists and capacity of new urban highways influenced many of the plans prepared in this period. The idea that freeways were exempt from saturation effects that had repeatedly plagued straightened and widened surface streets was an article of faith among planners of the time, so sure were they that dramatically higher traffic volume capacities per lane could fully absorb any increased demand. Most planners writing at the time appeared to truly believe that they had found the ultimate answer to urban traffic congestion: freeways, ideally coordinated with public transit and comprehensive land use plans, would solve the congestion problem and encourage future urban development to proceed on more rational lines.

However, despite the significant amount of freeway planning that occurred during the 1930s in Chicago, Boston, San Francisco, and countless other cities, most places had much less success than New York in moving from freeway planning to freeway construction. Chicago's 1928 Avondale Highway proposal,[58] its 1932 *Limited Ways: A Plan for the Greater Chicago Traffic Area*,[59] its 1939 *A Comprehensive Superhighway Plan for the City of Chicago*,[60] and its 1943 freeway plan[61] all failed to be implemented. Both Boston's 1930 *Report on a Thoroughfare Plan for Boston*[62] and San Francisco's ambitious 1937 *Limited Ways Plan for San Francisco*,[63] the latter of which proposed placing 84 percent of the densely developed city's population within one-half mile of a freeway, met similar fates.

These failures of implementation were due primarily to insufficient financial resources. Cities outside of New York by and large lacked access to substantial bridge and tunnel toll revenues, and, as we have seen, state motor fuel tax revenues were used exclusively to finance rural and intercity roads and highways.

The federal government's Depression-era public works programs—the National Industrial Recovery Act, the Hayden-Cartwright Act, and other pieces of New Deal legislation— financed individual road projects in some cities. But the New Deal's focus on immediate, short-term job creation meant that it did not provide the longer-term, large-scale financial commitments required to implement the ambitious freeway plans proposed by many cities.[64]

Cities were thus left to raise the necessary fiscal resources for freeways on their own, which proved nearly impossible during the Depression due to the significant decline in property tax revenues outlined earlier. So, the plans for metropolitan freeways had to await a new way to pay for them.

The Postwar Urban Transportation Crisis

The onset of World War II saw a hiatus in urban highway planning. During the war, gasoline and tires were rationed and auto plants were converted to defense production so that the production of new cars almost entirely ceased. In response to government programs aimed at reducing draws on petroleum reserves and burdens on the highway system, millions of Americans took up ride-sharing, walking, and riding public transit, or deferred travel entirely. As a result, highway traffic levels dropped 35–40 percent. This gave many cities some respite from their ongoing struggles with congestion. One problem, however, was that the fuel tax revenues, on which states depended, dropped as well since vehicle travel fell 37 percent and fuel consumption fell 33 percent. This was particularly an issue for states that diverted a large share of those revenues and depended on them for needs unrelated to driving. Another major issue, similar to that experienced during World War I, was the severe damage done to highways by heavy truck traffic related to defense industries. Truck mileage doubled during the war years, and axle loads of over 18,000 pounds grew by a factor of almost five, for a total increase in axle loadings of 1,100 percent.[65]

Compounding these problems was that Americans' pent-up demand for automobiles and driving exploded as soon as the war and its rationing ended. Automobile registrations soared, growing from 32.5 million in 1940 to 37.8 million in 1947 and 44.7 million by 1949, a nearly 40 percent increase in less than a decade.[66] By 1956, motor vehicle registrations reached over 65 million, more than twice the 1940 level.

Automobile use also surged. By 1949, vehicle miles traveled (VMT) doubled from the wartime low of 208 billion in 1942, and by 1956, the 631 billion VMT was three times the 1942 level.[67] More Americans traveled by automobile, and those travelers traversed longer distances than ever before, thanks in large part to the postwar growth of suburbia. Many of these newly suburban Americans crawled along on heavily congested, worn-out arterial roads that had not been improved, or in many cases even maintained, during the war.

Rising suburbanization only intensified the concerns of local politicians and downtown business groups about the decline of CBD investment and activity. Suburban residential development had not yet dethroned the CBDs from their premier economic position, but it was nevertheless a rapidly rising threat. Recall that retail activity began to decentralize in response to the auto as early as the mid-1920s in places like Los Angeles, where auto-oriented shopping districts soon emerged to compete with downtown.[68] Gradually, other functions that had previously been overwhelmingly located in the CBD, including banking and office activities, began to move outward as well. As we have seen, most CBD property owners and their political allies viewed commercial decentralization as the result of chronic downtown traffic congestion. Hence, they frequently argued that the answer to the problem was to improve public transit and, more importantly, to improve automobile accessibility to and parking in the CBD. As they had in the prewar era, local officials turned to transportation planners to devise solutions to the congestion problem. As before, these planners had lots of ideas—foremost among them, the freeway.

Robert Moses and Evolving Urban Freeway Planning in the 1940s

As World War II neared an end and metropolitan freeway planning resumed in earnest, much of New York's freeway system was coming into being, thanks to the work of Robert Moses. Further, his reach continued to go far beyond New York. In the 1940s, he busied himself not only with Gotham but also with freeway plans for Baltimore, Hartford, New Orleans, Pittsburgh, and Portland, among other cities. Moses's team primarily prepared these plans for local government clients who had wide-ranging transportation and non-transportation concerns; their earlier plans were characterized by freeways playing an important role in a larger scheme of urban development and redevelopment. However, as Moses's outlook shifted with the prevailing winds, his team's later plans tended to reflect an ever-narrower focus on traffic service, in line with the mindset of most state highway engineers.

In 1943, Moses unveiled a comprehensive plan for Portland, Oregon. It touched on ports, parks, playgrounds, and schools, but arterial improvements, and in particular freeways, were its central feature.[69] In a shift from his work for Pittsburgh, Moses proposed the development of freeways that resembled modern urban interstates in many respects: stark, minimally landscaped facilities designed first and foremost for moving vehicles (see Figure 5.3). Nevertheless, they had lower design speeds, fewer lanes, and were

Figure 5.3. Freeway planned for Portland, Oregon (1943).
Source: Moses, Robert (Director). 1943. "Portland Improvement." Prepared for the City of Portland and Multnomah County. Portland, OR. Illustration: Typical Thruway Development, 27. Courtesy of the City of Portland (OR), Archives A2004-001.858.

better coordinated with local land use development than their post-1956 counterparts would be. Portland adopted the plan, but it was better than a dozen years before it was meaningfully funded, due to uncertainty over whether state and federal aid would materialize.[70]

Moses followed his work in Portland with a commission to propose solutions to growing traffic problems in Baltimore. In keeping with his evolving outlook on the role and design of the freeway, his proposed Franklin Expressway bore an even greater resemblance to the modern utilitarian freeway than had his Portland designs. However, urban redevelopment and aesthetics had not yet fallen entirely by the wayside; the Franklin Expressway featured some parkway landscaping.[71] At this time he still cited the lower-speed, heavily landscaped, prewar Long Island parkways as examples of how these new roads could enhance areas, overcoming the concerns of residents who were skeptical about freeways' potential negative effects on surrounding property values.[72] The conflation of park-like, low-speed parkways, which did indeed often increase the value of adjacent property, with increasingly utilitarian high-speed, high-volume freeways that depressed adjacent residential (if not commercial) property values characterized many freeway plans in the 1940s.

Moses expressed outright hostility toward poor and non-White neighborhoods, and over the years had come to adopt the views of many urban planners of the era regarding the desirability of using freeways as tools for slum clearance. In touting his Baltimore plan, Moses assured his clients in the harshest possible terms that the expressway would help the city with urban blight: "Some of the slum areas through which the Franklin Expressway passes are a disgrace to the community and the more of them that are wiped out the healthier Baltimore will be in the long run."[73] The Franklin Expressway alone would have displaced 19,000 people, including 880 homes and 68 businesses in the predominantly Black, middle-class Rosemont community, where 70 percent of the families owned their homes.[74]

Such disregard for the residents of Black and poor neighborhoods was not confined to the planners of this era. Engineers often argued that routing through Black and poor neighborhoods was justified because costs were lower, both because land was cheap and also because such neighborhoods wielded less political power to oppose freeways.[75] Whether the product of explicit racial animus, instrumental indifference toward the poor and less well-connected, or some combination of the two, the result was the displacement of African Americans in cities around the U.S. This sordid history "ultimately produced much larger, more spatially isolated, and more intensely segregated second ghettos,"[76] a story to which we will later return.

The people of Baltimore chose to ignore Moses's advice on expressways and slum clearance, due largely to a lack of money to implement the plan. City officials began a freeway construction program several years later when Interstate funding finally materialized,[77] but delays in construction ultimately allowed anti-freeway groups to successfully oppose many of the proposed projects that would entail substantial displacement.[78] However, while few of Moses's planned freeways for Baltimore were ultimately built, standing plans to clear land to make way for proposed freeways led over the years to disinvestment and decay because, according to Lieb,[79] "[p]ublic policy declared over and over again that Baltimore's black neighborhoods were disposable."

Undeterred by his failure in Baltimore, Moses continued his work as an expert for hire with his 1946 plan for New Orleans.[80] There, he advised city officials to build an elevated freeway near the French Quarter that would offer direct, high-speed access to the downtown and the Vieux Carré from the east and west. Moses argued that removing traffic from local streets onto the freeway would benefit the city, but the proposed facility became highly controversial and was ultimately canceled in 1969.[81]

Moses's plan touched on many facets of the New Orleans transportation system.[82] Among his many non-highway recommendations was that the city's streetcar system be retained;[83] indeed, the iconic St. Charles Streetcar is today the oldest continuously operating streetcar line in the world and a local tourist attraction. He also discussed the need to provide parking facilities for motor vehicles, recommending that they be built in tandem with the expressway.[84]

In 1949, Moses prepared a freeway plan for Hartford, Connecticut. While expressways were ultimately built in the locations he suggested, his other recommendations for urban renewal were not followed.[85] In his Hartford plan, Moses devoted considerable space to criticizing a previous recommendation by the state highway department, made largely on financial grounds, to take part of a park for use as freeway right-of-way.[86] Moses took great offense at proposals to "invade" parks because their rights-of-way were free or very inexpensive. Members of Moses's consulting team rerouted the proposed east-west freeway to avoid taking park property and to minimize residential and commercial takings as well. But despite Moses's admirable instincts to preserve parkland, the alternative he suggested was itself pernicious; the road was instead routed through a poor neighborhood so that urban renewal funds could be used to help finance the project.

This again reflected the prevailing view at the time that "slum clearance" was an effective way to renew depressed areas. This bulldozer approach to community revitalization has come under withering and enduring criticism; this began in the early 1960s with critiques by prominent public intellectuals like Jane Jacobs and James Baldwin, the latter of whom described urban renewal schemes as "Negro Removal."[87] Those who were displaced by urban freeway construction were forced to relocate, most often to other economically depressed neighborhoods.[88] Those who remained behind had a noisy, polluting freeway added to their economically struggling community—hardly a recipe for revitalization.

In sum, Moses's urban freeway plans in the immediate postwar era tended to incorporate broader urban concerns, whether for benign purposes (such as aesthetics) or malign ones (slum clearance). But increasingly he keenly felt the pressures of ever-escalating vehicle congestion. It seemed that every time he completed a project in his hometown of New York, traffic quickly overwhelmed the facility.[89] Pressure from motorists frustrated with worsening congestion compelled Moses and New York City to build ever higher-capacity and more utilitarian facilities designed simply to move large volumes of traffic.[90] These later facilities more closely resembled modern no-frills Interstate Highways, though typically at a smaller scale. While he often claimed that his roads were not the "gasoline gullies" being "perpetrated" by road engineers on other communities,[91] they gradually became virtually indistinguishable from them. However, Moses continued to set firm limits on their maximum speeds, again because he thought speeds above 35 or 40 miles per hour were wasteful and unnecessary for urban areas.[92]

Ultimately, many metropolitan neighborhoods through which Moses cut new urban freeways, not only in New York but elsewhere, bore a heavy price for his increasing fixation on traffic service. For better and worse, these developments were a harbinger of things to come for the rest of the nation. In part this was due to Moses's example. But it was also due to the fact that when Franklin D. Roosevelt, the former governor of New York, became president, he brought with him to Washington engineers and planners who had been involved in the creation of the New York parkway system. These men subsequently helped disseminate this model to the rest of the nation through the emerging federal highway program.

Bartholomew's Evolving Plans for Urban Freeways

Harland Bartholomew was also active in the immediate postwar period, preparing plans for Oakland and the East Bay of the San Francisco Bay Area and for Richmond, Virginia, among others. In his plan for Richmond, he emphasized urban planning concerns in addition to traffic service ones, and unsuccessfully attempted to use freeway development as a tool to both halt continued residential decentralization and revitalize the CBD.[93]

In Richmond, and in a later plan for Atlanta, Bartholomew advised routing freeways in order to preserve and not divide neighborhoods. However, this advice was often with respect to "established suburban communities" (that were largely White and more affluent), but not to inner-city "slums" (that were poor and often African American). The latter were to be cleared for freeways, to provide room for the central business district to grow and to delineate and bound Black neighborhoods in order to limit their expansion.[94] After years of controversy over alignments, Bartholomew's recommended expressway system for Richmond was built, but by the state highway department instead of the city and with much more elaborate, higher-speed facilities than had been contemplated in his original plan. Its most negative effects were borne by both the many inner-city minority residents the facilities ultimately displaced and those who remained to live near them.[95]

Most of Bartholomew's earliest postwar plans remained multimodal, again reflecting the broader concerns of his urban clients and a personal outlook that took a holistic set of urban issues into account. His 1947 plan for Alameda County, California proposed the development of a rail transit system using the medians of proposed freeways (see Figure 5.4).[96] The recommended system was not developed until several decades later, while the freeways were soon built. Despite these setbacks, he continued to argue that the only effective way to deal with traffic congestion was through the careful coordination of multimodal transportation planning with land use planning.[97]

The Evolution of the Freeway Plan in Other Cities

In the mid- and late 1940s, other consultants were still preparing freeway plans at the behest of local governments that reflected larger non-transportation concerns, not just the goal of moving as many motor vehicles as quickly as possible. Local leaders were certainly concerned about congestion, but they also worried about slums, uncontrolled decentralization, the decline of CBDs, and the role of transit systems. This "traffic-plus" focus appears in plans prepared by consultants for Detroit (1945, 1949), Cincinnati (1951), and Kansas City (1951), to cite just a few examples.[98] Over time, however, these plans increasingly exhibited tension as the increasing focus on traffic service began to crowd out broader urban and transportation concerns.

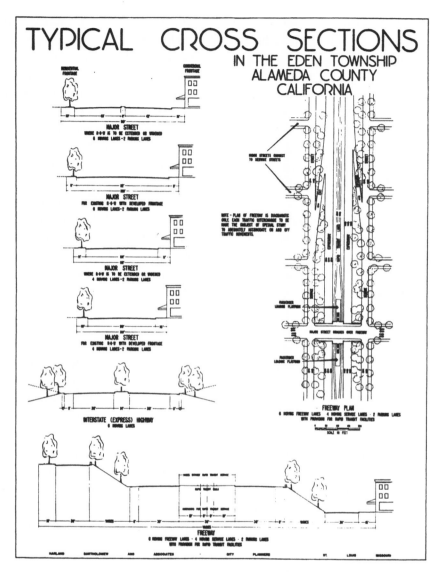

Figure 5.4. Freeway cross-sections from the proposed major-street freeway plan in Eden Township, Alameda County (1947).

Source: Harland Bartholomew and Associates. 1947. "Freeways and Major Streets in Eden Township Alameda County." Prepared for the Board of Supervisors County of Alameda California. St. Louis, MO: Harland Bartholomew and Associates. Plate 9. Permission granted by Barry Hogue for Parsons (inheritor for Harland Bartholomew and Associates).

The 1945 *Detroit Expressway and Transit System* plan—a successor to the widely influential but only partially implemented 1924 plan—and its 1949 follow-up reflect these competing imperatives. When siting the roads, the consultants were torn between addressing congestion by simply following alignments dictated by motorists' desire lines, as captured in origin-destination surveys, and considering roads' broader non-transportation effects, including their impacts on adjacent, often inner-city, neighborhoods.[99] As in Moses's work, slum clearance, primarily in Black neighborhoods, was a major theme of these plans. With chilling optimism, the 1945 Detroit plan embodied the then-prevailing views on routing urban freeways through low-income neighborhoods: "It is fortunate that the general pattern of traffic flow coincides with belts of depressed property cheap enough to acquire for wide traffic arteries."[100] This observation would ultimately prove prescient: the freeways eventually built in the decade following the publication of the 1949 Detroit plan "invariably spared middle-class enclaves . . . [and] uprooted residents of less affluent neighborhoods."[101] As Biles further notes:

> By 1958, construction of the John C. Lodge Freeway resulted in the destruction of 2,200 buildings (residences, shops, and factories) on the Lower West Side and largely African American neighborhoods bordering Highland Park. By the end of the 1950s, bulldozers leveled approximately 2,800 buildings through the black West Side and the northernmost edge of the city's most infamous ghetto, Paradise Valley, to make way for the Edsel B. Ford Expressway.[102]

The 1945 plan expressed frustration with the city's inability to address its mass transit needs due largely to fiscal limitations.[103] The follow-up plan in 1949 wrestled with the interplay between freeways and public transit, as well as the central role of finance. It opened with language that could have easily come from any one of the many multimodal urban transportation plans of the 1930s and early 1940s:

> Whereas highways can be built piecemeal, rapid transit lines cannot be so constructed; each line must be complete at the time the work is undertaken. All the constructive thinking and engineering embodied in the plan herewith submitted will be wasted unless an adequate plan is available for financing both expressways (which afford the rights-of-way for rapid transit) and for the rapid transit lines.[104]

Thus, along with an extensive freeway system, the plan included a proposal for a regional rapid transit system with rail in freeway medians.

In all, the consultants in Detroit and elsewhere understood that what was "best" for motorists was not necessarily what was "best" for the city as a whole, at least as they understood it. In certain cases, the betterment of the city required freeway designs and locations that did not maximize traffic service or provide the highest speeds of travel for motorists. However, also in common with other plans, those elements did not survive the fiscal calculus. The freeway portion alone was projected to cost $228 million ($2.5 billion in 2021$), a sum far beyond the city's ability to pay. Ultimately, as with Bartholomew's plan for the East Bay, the freeway portions were funded while the transit components were not. This was an outcome that was repeated many times over in cities around the U.S.

In sum, in the early postwar years urban concerns were still very much in the minds of city officials and their planners. Cities' physical and human geography, land use patterns, economic development, aesthetics, social and recreational needs, and more were still part and parcel of their plans, as had been the case with plans stretching back to the 1930s. However, these concerns increasingly took a backseat to maximizing auto mobility. This became particularly true once state highway departments took control over urban freeways, a dramatic example of finance leading planning and a story to which we now turn.

Cities Seek a New Source of Revenue

As we have seen, most states adopting motor fuel taxes in the 1920s limited their use to the construction and maintenance of highways *outside* of cities—though the bulk of the taxes were actually paid by urban motorists. The logic behind this geographic transfer was that, thanks to the property tax, urban areas had the population and financial resources to maintain their own streets but sparsely inhabited rural areas did not.[105] Left unspoken was that this system was buttressed by the often-disproportionate power wielded by rural interests in state legislatures. To justify why urban motorists were being forced to pay fuel taxes to cross-subsidize travelers on rural roads and inter-city highways, state highway officials frequently cited benefits to city-dwellers, such as lower prices for goods and reduced travel times for motorists traveling for pleasure.[106] While there was grumbling on the part of urban officials about the rural orientation of the state highway programs, the dependence on urban-generated revenue to finance both urban and rural roads was accepted, if not embraced, by major stakeholder interests through the 1920s.

Cash-Strapped Cities Look to Fuel Taxes to Finance Urban Highways

However, with the Depression and the collapse of property tax revenue, and later with the creation of ever-more-ambitious unfunded freeway plans, officials in many cash-strapped cities and counties around the U.S. cast covetous eyes toward the plentiful motor fuel tax revenues. Thus they, and others representing urban interests, began pushing to end prohibitions against the expenditure of state highway funds in urban areas.

In response, in the early 1930s several states moved to "divert" fuel tax revenues to cities. For example, in California in 1931 the state legislature responded to lobbying by urban interests by expanding the state highway system to pass through cities, which to this time had been impossible due to prohibitions against spending state and federal highway funds in urban areas. This was immensely popular with barely-solvent cities. Two years later, bowing to continuing pressure, the state highway law was amended again to further expand the urban portions of the state highway system and to apportion some fuel tax funds for the construction and maintenance of major urban boulevards and arterials. The legislature required its state highway department, then called the California Division of Highways, to set aside ¼ cent (4.1 cents in 2021$) of the state's three cents per gallon motor fuel tax for the aid of state highways in cities. In 1935 the legislature went still further, raising the sum by an additional ¼ cent.[107]

For the most part, the increasing "urbanization" of state highways during the 1930s was not accompanied by corresponding increases in fuel tax rates. In California, for example, the three cents per gallon motor fuel tax did not change during the 1930s, nor did registration, license, or weight fees. So, by the early 1940s, a highway finance crisis had arisen due to the wartime demand for new and better roadways. With money tight, the mounting expenditure of state fuel tax funds in cities was viewed increasingly warily by many state highway officials.

Moreover, there were others lobbying for a share of the fuel tax funds. Because motor fuel tax revenues had proven so remarkably resilient during the Depression, it was perhaps inevitable that state legislators began to view the proceeds with increasing desire. Since money often proves fungible, even in states with anti-diversion laws that earmarked fuel tax revenues for road expenditures, fuel tax funds eased pressures on shrinking general revenues stretched to the limit by all other non-road needs. Further, outright diversion accelerated as the Depression wore on: in 1932, 16 states diverted $82.8 million ($1.64 billion in 2021$), which rose to $145 million in 1933 ($3.03 billion in 2021$) and $164 million in 1934 ($3.33 billion in 2021$). Unsurprisingly, the petroleum industry and the automobile clubs mobilized in an attempt to stop diversions, achieving considerable success. This included adding anti-diversion amendments to 14 state constitutions by 1942.[108]

Petroleum industry representatives were also increasingly alarmed by the prospect of potential increases to fuel tax rates. With considerable self-interested hyperbole, the American Petroleum Industries Committee (APIC), an oil company–backed lobbying group, proclaimed that "the American petroleum industry has been, and is being, victimized in a manner and to a degree probably unparalleled in recent history."[109] The industry lobbyists argued that every one cent increase in motor fuel taxes (20.3 cents in 2021$) reduced fuel consumption by 5 percent, and the industry histrionically foresaw a day in the future when a 20 cent per gallon tax ($4.05/gallon in 2021$) would mean an end to the use of gasoline as a motor fuel entirely (APIC 1933, 63). (By way of comparison, the total federal fuel tax in 2021 [$0.184/gallon for gasoline and $0.244/gallon for diesel fuel] would be equivalent to about $0.01 per gallon in 1933.)

The reality, of course, was that the enormous popularity of autos and automobile travel (enabled in part by the spending of fuel tax revenues to improve roads) belied doomsday prognostications of a tax-driven slump in fuel consumption. But despite mounting evidence to the contrary, petroleum companies hardened in their opposition to fuel taxes, and they were increasingly joined by other automobile interests. For a time, their lobbying and public relations campaigns got some traction, as during the depths of the Depression between 1932 and 1936 not a single state enacted a motor fuel tax increase. Oil and other automobile interests also lobbied that fuel taxes be the sole province of the states. However, they suffered a defeat on the national level when the federal gasoline tax was imposed in 1932.

A Rural Focus for Urban Roads

In any event, the rural/urban revenue wall was now breached. What was the upshot of state motor fuel tax funds now being spent in cities? Certainly, cities welcomed the additional revenue given their penury and ever-rising demand for more elaborate streets and highways. But the waxing use of state fuel tax revenue for roads in cities had two other important, and not altogether benign, implications. First, some observers, particularly President Roosevelt, had noted that reaping revenue from the increase in land values resulting from highway construction could be a way to finance them. (Specifically, the president was an ardent advocate of purchasing excess right-of-way in advance of construction and selling it later after the land had appreciated.) However, reducing reliance on property and special assessment finance due to an increasing focus on fuel taxes foreclosed an alternate opportunity to re-capture the appreciative effect of highway development on land values. This proved problematic as property values recovered and increased in the postwar era, and land for highways thus became more expensive; insufficient funding for right-of-way acquisition quickly proved the major obstacle in metropol-itan freeway development. This fact was not lost on highway planners at the time. Concerned that the Depression-era shift from property tax finance to fuel tax finance would foreclose the future use of property taxes for urban highways, a Bureau of Public Roads deputy warned in 1937: "Property taxes once gone will be difficult to get back."[110]

Second, and much more importantly, with this shift in the funding burden from the property taxes of cities to the fuel taxes of states came a gradual shift in vision—and the means to enforce that vision—in state after state. At the time, cities were willing to accept this. Freeways in the decade following World War II were universally popular: they were the shiny new technology that would finally do something about managing the auto in cities. Thus, most city leaders gladly welcomed state money to pay for expensive new freeways. But this new money came with strings, lots of them. Thanks to the power of the purse, planning control shifted from direction by urban planners working for municipalities and business groups, to highway engineers employed by state departments of transportation.

State (and later federal) legislation transplanted the established federal-state highway partnership directly into metropolitan freeway development.[111] State officials increasingly took the lead role in freeway planning, construc-tion, maintenance, and operations, while the federal government provided money, expertise, and a regulatory framework. Cities and their planners were largely relegated to the sidelines. This paradigm shift was increasingly evident from the 1940s on, when plans for municipal highway systems began to differ considerably from their earlier predecessors and to increasingly reflect the outlook of state highway departments.

While urban highway planners were still focused on a broad array of eco-nomic, social, and transportation concerns, state highway engineers, by con-trast, were focused on rural road issues revolving around safety and the need to facilitate direct, low-cost, high-speed travel over long distances. Ignoring decades of careful planning at the municipal level, state highway departments eventually used their familiar, tried-and-true rural approach to rural highway planning—but in urban areas. They placed the new facilities where travel desires were strongest, rarely taking into account land use patterns, future development, or even other parts of the transportation system.[112] This shift became increasingly evident with the creation of the Interstate Highway System, as we discuss later.

The traffic problems in cities were perhaps superficially similar to the countryside. Congestion relief, long a central goal of municipal planners, would presumably be fostered by roads that could serve larger numbers of cars and move them at much higher speeds. But the issues facing urban highway planners were very different in important ways.[113] The rural highway problem was largely, well, a highway problem. The urban highway problem was much more, because urban highways profoundly affected cities and their residents in more, and more intense, ways. As we have seen, urban road development is intimately connected with public transit, parking, urban structure, real estate development and local land use patterns, the socioeconomic characteristics of local neighborhoods, environmental hazards, neighborhood character, and a variety of other non-transportation concerns. As we have also seen, many urban planners and engineers were often willing to sacrifice the primacy of traffic service in order to achieve other goals.

State and federal highway engineers, by contrast, had little experience with these kinds of issues. Instead, they brought their rural experience to bear in cities. In terms of routing, as Lovelace[114] observed:

> They (state highway departments) would "consult" and, later, would make environmental impact studies, but these seldom affected the choice of the cheapest alignment that would carry the most traffic. This would eventually result in the preemption of park land (Balboa Park in San Diego, Forest Park in Saint Louis), division of neighborhoods, and destruction of the fabric of historic districts.

This rural orientation also affected the facilities' design. State and federal highway engineers were important partners in the development of freeway standards through organizations like AASHO, whose unique state-federal membership had long placed it at the center of national highway policy.[115] As we have discussed, AASHO played important roles in the professionalization of state highway departments; the creation of new techniques in highway analysis, design, and construction; and, importantly, the establishment of design standards for different classes of roads.[116] These specifications ultimately led to the deployment of an increasingly standardized highway product throughout the United States. AASHO's influence meant that the rural freeway became the prototype for most urban freeways, even including those not on the Interstate System itself. Uniform design standards precluded planning for local context or idiosyncrasies. Design speeds rose from around 40 and 45 miles per hour, to 50 and 55 miles per hour, and still later to 70 and 75 miles per hour. The new facilities grew wider, in the number of lanes (expanding from two in each direction to three, four, or more), in the extent of traffic "weaving" lanes before and after interchanges, and even in the width of the individual lanes. All of this made for greater traffic capacity, but also more disruption when it came time to shoehorn these mammoth new freeways into cities. Touches like elaborate landscaping to mute vehicle noise and capture particulate emissions fell by the wayside, to be replaced by a strictly utilitarian aesthetic. Provision for public transit went from an accommodation of rail and streetcars, to their replacement with CBD-bound express buses, to dropping transit from the plans altogether.

In sum, there was a general trend from plans for cities, to plans for transportation, to plans for cars. Safely providing maximum traffic service at the lowest possible cost was the key objective of the rural highway program, where a focus on these considerations was far less likely to disrupt existing communities. But when these principles were deployed in urban areas, the effects on local communities and the larger metropolitan areas would be profound. Land use concerns were not totally forgotten, but increasingly the only aspect of the urban topography of interest to the engineers designing the new networks was the path of least resistance in terms of cost and political feasibility. In addition to routes through parks, along rail rights-of-way, and adjacent to bodies of water, this largely meant routes through low-income and disproportionately Black areas as well.

The Evolution of the Urban Freeway Plan: The Case of San Francisco

State highway departments increasingly supplanted cities and downtown business groups as the clients for work prepared by both outside and (increasingly) in-house consultants. As a result, the very nature of the freeway plans changed. The transition away from the multimodal, context-sensitive prescriptions for dense systems of smaller, lower-speed facilities that had been produced since the 1930s is perhaps best illustrated by three plans prepared only a few years apart for a single city, San Francisco.

The 1947 *Traffic, Transit and Thoroughfare Improvements for San Francisco* plan[117] was prepared prior to passage of the 1947 Collier-Burns Highway Act that funded a statewide freeway program, which will be discussed later. Since the legislative discussion surrounding the Act was already underway, the plan's authors anticipated that some new state funding for urban freeways would materialize. However, they did not anticipate that the state would essentially take over freeway development, or even try to do so, or that it would have many millions of dollars to spend on new highways. On the other hand, the 1948 follow-up, *A Report to the City Planning Commission on a Transportation Plan for San Francisco*,[118] reflected the radically new fiscal and political circumstances post-Collier-Burns, when the state assumed financial responsibility for urban freeways and took control of freeway planning as a result.

The *Traffic, Transit and Thoroughfare Improvements Plan* of 1947 called for a relatively modest investment of $20 million in highway and $32 million in transit improvements ($243 million and $389 million in 2021$, respectively). The authors did not want freeways penetrating the CBD; in fact, they recognized that such facilities would likely induce even more motorized vehicle traffic that would crowd into the downtown's already congested streets. So, they called for construction of a loop highway just outside the CBD that would connect to the radial freeways proposed in the plan. Mass transit would continue to play a central role in this hilly, densely populated city because of its ability to move large numbers of people more effectively than cars. In fact, transit vehicles and pedestrians were to be given priority over automobiles in the downtown area.

The 1947 plan was embedded within a larger comprehensive planning effort that linked transportation infrastructure with urban land development. Transportation was viewed as an interconnected system with each element (highways, streets, transit, parking, etc.) playing an important role:

> It is the opinion of the City Planning Commission that the problem demands a co-ordinated approach if lasting remedies are to be obtained. Plans for mass transit must be related to plans for freeways; plans for extending pedestrian facilities must be made in conjunction with plans for off-street parking and delivery facilities; plans for improved traffic conditions on the streets must be related to all the above aspects of the overall problem.[119]

Presciently, the plan's authors predicted that the freeway projects would generate substantial opposition from the local neighborhoods, but they argued that the wider public benefits outweighed any negative effects. To finance the system, the authors advocated the use of bonds backed by a combination of property taxes and, perhaps, state motor fuel taxes.

After the passage of the Collier-Burns Highway Act, and its promise of bounteous state funding for urban freeways, San Francisco officials just a year later commissioned a new plan that included many more freeways of the kind envisioned by the state Division of Highways. The 1948 plan[120] was multi-modal like its predecessor, but the highway component was enlarged considerably to include about $111 million of freeway construction (about $1.2 billion in 2021$). The authors claimed that they considered broader land use implications when determining facility siting, but they also conceded that the freeway alignments were based largely on motorists' travel desire lines as developed through an extensive origin-destination survey. Transit was still part of the plan, which proposed to run express buses on the freeways and develop a streetcar subway under Market Street (which would eventually be built in the 1970s).

The planned freeways were developed primarily to provide high-speed access to downtown, which was to be the main beneficiary. The costs of freeway development, particularly in terms of community disruption, would be borne largely by the city's neighborhoods. The facilities proposed in the 1948 plan would feature two lanes in each direction and maximum 50 miles-per-hour design speeds. These were sizable facilities for a densely developed, geographically constrained city of hills that was sure to be disruptive to neighborhoods, though not as disruptive as the even larger and faster Interstate facilities—with 70 miles-per-hour design speeds and three or more lanes in each direction—that would come later.

The 1948 San Francisco plan served as the basis for a similarly themed 1951 follow-up,[121] which was also prepared by the city but this time with much greater involvement from the state Division of Highways. This plan now envisioned a dense network of high-speed traffic arteries deployed across the city, into its heart and along its waterfront—the eventual demolition of which would become a *cause célèbre* a half-century later, as we discuss below. The freeway routes were sited and designed solely to serve motorists. In this compact, transit-friendly city, the transit components of earlier plans were dropped entirely and did not reappear in subsequent plans for years. The stage was now set for the neighborhood versus downtown battles that would characterize the city's later "freeway revolt."[122]

Changing Urban Freeway Planning in Los Angeles

The rapidly evolving character of urban freeway planning in the postwar era can also be seen in the City of Angels. Los Angeles concluded the 1930s with a visionary and ambitious multimodal regional transportation plan, but with money sufficient to start work on only two of its numerous freeway links.[123]

The 1939 Los Angeles Transportation Engineering Board (TEB) plan,[124] which formed the basis for the first metropolitan freeway-only network built in the U.S., was one of the most important early urban freeway plans.[125] Its roots lay in a 1937 study by the Automobile Club of Southern California (ACSC), which argued that the solution to Los Angeles' congestion problems was to be found in a system of limited-access, grade-separated freeways.[126] Such a system would double automobile speeds throughout the region while improving access to both downtown and the suburbs.[127]

City engineer Lloyd Aldrich used the Automobile Club report as the starting point for the 1939 city-sponsored plan. Its centerpiece was an enormous 612-mile freeway system that blanketed the region on a combined grid/ring-radial pattern to facilitate both CBD-to-suburb and suburb-to-suburb travel.[128] The proposed roads were designed for 45-miles-per-hour speeds with limited access. Also, the plan was explicitly multimodal (see Figure 5.5). Aldrich and his coauthors proposed the construction of a rail rapid transit network to operate in both downtown subways and the medians of the many of the proposed freeways outside of downtown. Because of funding uncertainty for the rail component, express buses operating on the new freeways would fill the transit role in the short term. The authors took great care to consider the relationship of the proposed system to adjacent land uses. This was especially true in the downtown area, where the freeways—again, much smaller than today's wider, higher-speed facilities—were tightly integrated with commercial development.

The plan found favor with many constituencies. CBD interests liked it because it promised uncongested downtown access; transit users liked it because it promised to move buses and streetcars off congested surface streets; auto users liked the expansion of highway facilities; land developers liked the proposed increase in developable land; and the state and federal governments liked the lower cost and more practical orientation of the freeways vis-à-vis recreation-oriented parkways.[129]

Popular or not, the financial resources available to Los Angeles in 1939 could not begin to finance a 612-mile freeway and transit system.[130] Los Angeles leveraged state and federal funding for the Arroyo Seco Parkway between downtown and Pasadena 11 miles to the northeast, an important transitional facility linked in design to both the early parkway and the modern freeway.‡ Further, the city proceeded with land acquisition and design for the Hollywood Freeway between downtown Los Angeles and the San Fernando

---

‡ The Arroyo Seco Parkway opened in 1940. It was renamed the Pasadena Freeway in 1954, but then the original name was reinstituted in 2010.

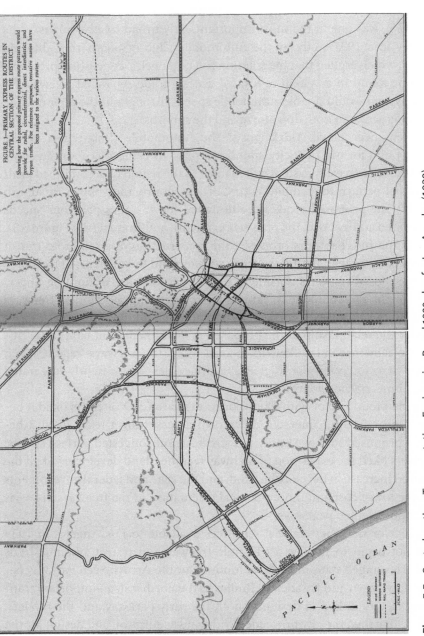

FIGURE 3—PRIMARY EXPRESS ROUTES IN
CENTRAL SECTION OF THE DISTRICT

Showing how the proposed primary express route pattern would
provide for radial, circumferential, direct interdistrict and
bypass traffic. For reference purposes, tentative names have
been assigned to the various routes.

Figure 5.5. Central section, Transportation Engineering Board 1939 plan for Los Angeles.

Source: Transportation Engineering Board. 1939. "A Transit Program for the Los Angeles Metropolitan Area." Los Angeles, CA: City of Los Angeles.
Figure 3, 10–11.

Valley 12 miles to the northwest. But otherwise, progress building a freeway system was slow.

Yet the TEB plan served as the template for postwar development in the region, even as its multimodal components were eventually discarded. During World War II, Los Angeles periodically updated the plan, though with little hope of financing it, at least locally. The follow-up plans fine-tuned the proposal and scaled back its ambitions. The 1941 *Master Plan of Parkways*, prepared by the Los Angeles Department of City Planning, used the TEB plan as a starting point for a more thorough consideration of its highway elements. The report relied on traffic data to justify the key elements of the TEB plan and to insert an additional limited-access facility. The authors asserted that there was relative unanimity among Los Angeles policymakers and interest groups behind the notion that Los Angeles's "unique" low-density, sprawling population pattern; its topography; its "unbearable" traffic; and its "unusually high" rate of automobile ownership required radical, forward-looking, automobile-focused solutions.[131]

Further, the report's authors asserted that no rail rapid transit system could be successful without high fares or a large public subsidy, the latter a rarity in that era. (The need for funding to improve L.A.'s decaying, privately owned rail transit system was acknowledged by the TEB report authors.) The creators of the 1941 plan advocated moving from the then-extensive rail transit network to a system of express buses on highways. The plan included no consideration of how such a system would work, where it would operate, who would run it, or how it would connect with local buses and the remaining streetcar and interurban services.[132]

At about the same time that the city planning department prepared its follow-up to the TEB plan, Los Angeles County's regional planning commission was involved in its own highway planning. Its 1943 report,[133] which also was based on the earlier TEB plan, proposed using motor fuel taxes to provide for what it calculated to be enough road space (8.5 lane miles of pavement for every 1,000 vehicles) to enable the city to retain its character as a decentralized region in "which the single-family dwelling predominates."[134] Unlike the city's plan, the county plan did address the design of the proposed transit system, though it shared with the city's plan a strong private vehicle focus. However, in other respects this plan was a true descendant of the earlier multimodal TEB plan, with its call for a broader consideration of highway planning in relation to the rest of the transportation system and the city as a whole.

Over the next few years, plans continued to appear, sponsored by various local groups. In general, whether sponsored by downtown business interests (who favored designs focused on the CBD) or representatives of suburban governments (who favored less radial and more grid-like networks), the plans were all strongly freeway-focused. While public transit was often mentioned with respect to express buses operating on freeways, it was in all cases—and in contrast with the TEB plan—treated as decidedly subsidiary to the automobile. For example, bus stops were to be located so they wouldn't interfere with the "continuous flow of traffic,"[135] even if doing so greatly interfered with the transit service: "Where buses are to use the freeway, they must be required to leave it for loading and unloading."[136]

By the time the California Legislature funded freeway construction with the passage of the Collier-Burns Act in 1947, freeway planning in Los Angeles had become increasingly, although not yet entirely, single-mode focused and traffic-oriented. Once the state Division of Highways took over the direction of planning, the metamorphosis was complete. The state highway department was unwilling to finance *any* transit infrastructure from motor fuel tax money, including even express buses operating on freeways. In addition, local officials were unable to even get permission from the state to put a local public transit funding plan before the voters.[137] Urban freeway planning in Los Angeles became synonymous with automobile traffic service planning, as transit and land use concerns gradually disappeared from the urban freeway plans with the state takeover.

The Metamorphosis of Urban Freeway Planning in Other States

State highway departments were also the clients for postwar urban freeway plans for places such as Milwaukee, Wisconsin;[138] Boston, Massachusetts (whose plan included freeways that Massachusetts would devote enormous time and resources to tearing down and burying underground a half-century later§);[139] Providence, Rhode Island;[140] Atlanta, Georgia;[141] and Tampa, Florida.[142] The resulting proposals reflected an evolving traffic-first mindset in these cities as well. Common themes included heavy reliance on

---

§ This was the famous Central Artery/Tunnel project, more popularly known as the "Big Dig." The multi-billion-dollar project, which included two tunnels, a bridge, and a greenway established in the former surface-level right-of-way of an interstate freeway, rerouted portions of Interstate 93 into a tunnel underneath central Boston.

origin-destination surveys and motorist desire lines to determine alignments for facilities, a focus on access to downtown, the upscaling of freeway designs to handle more traffic at higher speeds, an interest in using freeways as a tool for slum clearance, and a waning interest in public transit.

Even Harland Bartholomew was not above the shifting winds. He revisited his St. Louis County proposal in 1942[143] while he was serving on President Roosevelt's Interregional Highways Committee that mapped out plans for what would become the Interstate Highway System. Undoubtedly inspired by his committee work, he called for the development of a new class of freeway, which he called "interregional highways," which would connect with the more conventional intraurban freeways as part of an elaborate hierarchy of streets, highways, and freeways. These interregional highways were higher-speed, four-lane (two in each direction), limited-access facilities designed to connect major urban areas to one another.[144] They featured 200-foot rights-of-way, wide medians, no private property access, no intersections at grade, and widely spaced entry and exit points. Interregional highways were designed specifically for higher-speed, longer-distance, interurban traffic. The more conventional freeway, a smaller-scale facility with lower design speeds and rights-of-way no greater than 200 feet in width (which was considerably larger than the roughly 120-foot-wide rights-of-way proposed in many of the early urban freeway plans), was recommended for intraurban traffic between the center of the city and its suburbs. The shift toward ever-larger, more elaborate, and higher-speed urban highways was now evident. During the 1940s, St. Louis made modest progress building some of the highway elements in the plans but was prevented from embarking on more ambitious projects by insufficient local and county fiscal resources.[145]

Philadelphia's 300-mile freeway plan was a product of the heady freeway-building atmosphere of the time.[146] Portland's plan was similarly ambitious, with its call for $275 million (approximately $2.7 billion in 2021$) in local freeway construction.[147] Neither plan paid much attention to transit, the relationship between the roads and adjoining land use, or the needs of the communities through which the enormous new facilities would pass. Neither region's freeway network was fully built because of a combination of cost escalation and growing community opposition to freeway construction beginning in the 1960s.

So, by the mid-1950s, traffic-service concerns reigned supreme in urban freeway planning. At the same time, the intensifying highway finance discussions at the national level prompted the development of ever-more-ambitious metropolitan freeway plans.

Conclusion: Urban Freeway Planning on the Eve of the Interstates

Between the end of World War II and the funding of the Interstate Highway System in 1956, urban freeway plans evolved dramatically. The freeways envisioned in the plans transitioned from modestly scaled, low-speed facilities designed to host multimodal travel, into far larger, utilitarian facilities focused almost solely on the safe, high-speed movement of motor vehicles. With state departments of transportation now funding, and sometimes preparing, plans for metropolitan freeways, the plans shed their focus on transportation as a supporting framework for desired forms of land development, and most lost their multimodal transportation elements as well. State highway engineers, steeped in rural highway planning, typically cared little for such matters. Yet despite this loss of control by cities, the new freeway plans were initially quite popular with local officials, who were happy to have the state and federal governments pay for the facilities, and with motorists, who were eager to travel on them. However, this enthusiasm, particularly in central cities, would eventually wane.

Context-sensitive freeway planning that sought to thread smaller, lower-speed facilities into the urban fabric while minimizing attendant disruption had seen its day. Instead, the new freeways being planned were increasingly similar to the superhighways designed by state highway engineers for high-speed intercity travel, and it is to that story we now turn.

6

Planning and Financing Highways between Cities in the Pre-Interstate Era

Transportation finance has historically disappeared from legislative agendas absent some perceived crisis. With funding in place, roads were (and still are) largely taken for granted by both legislators and the general public. Thus, triage-style financial planning characterized (and today still characterizes) transportation finance. And in the 1930s, the major fiscal crisis was the Great Depression.

It need hardly be said that America's response to the Depression dramatically reoriented politics and policy in many spheres. Highway policy proved no exception. Although plummeting property tax revenue hamstrung cities' efforts to undertake dramatic new initiatives, including those involving urban freeway networks, New Deal policies extended federal support to some urban road-building projects. In terms of highways *between* cities, the new spirit of government activism set off by the New Deal ultimately led to dramatic advances in the quest to create a national highway system.[1]

The Great Depression and the Highway Finance Crisis of the 1930s

Even in the early days of the Great Depression, there was growing support for the notion that highway construction might serve as a jobs program. Thus, despite initial opposition from state highway organizations and the Bureau of Public Roads, the Hoover administration[*] turned to the federal-aid highway program as an economic-recovery and job-creation strategy. This decision was reflected in two pieces of legislation enacted between 1930 and 1932 that had the aim of shoring up states' flagging commitment to road construction by increasing the federal financial commitment to the federal-aid program. The legislation would raise expenditures to $125 million (about $2 billion in

---

[*] Herbert Hoover was president of the U.S. during the first four years of the Great Depression, from 1929 to 1933.

The Drive for Dollars. Jeffrey R. Brown, Eric A. Morris, and Brian D. Taylor, Oxford University Press.
© Oxford University Press 2023. DOI: 10.1093/oso/9780197601518.003.0006

2021$) annually and modify the conditions states had to meet in order to receive federal aid. The Emergency Construction Act of 1930 provided $80 million in federal loans ($1.23 billion in 2021$) to the states to help them meet the 1:1 matching requirement. In order to ensure that the jobs stimulus would be rapid, the Act stipulated that the funds could only be used on projects undertaken within eight months.[2]

Congress expanded this program when it enacted the Emergency Relief and Construction Act of 1932. This legislation made available a further $120 million ($2.3 billion in 2021$) for federal-aid advances to states to help them meet the matching requirements. The law also provided for a significant increase in the mileage of the federal-aid system. Taken together, these two acts were characterized by both Congress and the Hoover administration as jobs bills because of the labor-intensive nature of highway construction, particularly during the initial phases of grading and draining. To protect labor, the 1932 Act also established a federal minimum wage for road construction workers.[3]

New jobs were indeed created as highway construction picked up during the early 1930s, and highway programs enjoyed a relative abundance of resources while many other government services withered. But this raised the question of how to pay for these expenditures, which increasingly strained the federal budget in an era when most viewed budget deficits as an unqualified evil.

The Creation of the Federal Motor Fuel Taxes

At the onset of the Depression, the federal government had no motor fuel taxes. Even after all states had adopted them, the federal government's share of highway expenditures continued to be funded from general revenues. Federal motor fuel taxes were regularly proposed throughout the 1910s and 1920s, but these European-style proposals to tax gasoline and diesel fuel to fund general government expenditures died largely because their sponsors failed to explicitly link the tax revenues to highway spending, raising the ire of motorists and automobile interests.[4] Thus, for a time the federal government did not follow the states and refrained from imposing fuel taxes of its own.

This soon changed amidst the Great Depression. For the fiscal year 1932–1933, Congress faced a budget shortfall of $150 million ($2.92 billion in 2021$).[5] The House Ways and Means and Senate Finance Committees, both responsible for government finance, began to look for possible ways to make up this deficit. Several proposed taxes were floated, but all failed to garner sufficient support. Given the great success that states were having with their motor fuel taxes, and particularly given those levies' resilience as other tax instruments wilted during the Depression, it was only natural that fuel taxes began to look increasingly appealing to federal legislators. Thus, a proposal surfaced calling for a temporary one-year federal fuel tax of one cent per gallon (18 cents/gallon in 2021$) to make up this shortfall (states typically charged 2 cents/gallon at the time).

While many members of Congress have over the years gained some fame for shepherding major legislation or a significant policy change, it is unclear who the "Father" or "Mother" of the federal fuel taxes was. Numerous senators and representatives were quick to champion the idea. The fact that legislators competed to claim credit for introducing the new tax is evidence of both how popular (or at least acceptable) fuel taxes were at the time, and of how much things have changed politically since then. The fuel tax provision of the revenue bill overwhelmingly passed the Senate and House and was signed into law by President Hoover in June of 1932.

The tax produced $125 million sorely needed dollars ($2.5 billion in 2021$) for the U.S. Treasury between June 17, 1932 and June 17, 1933. This was less than had been anticipated but was still a phenomenal amount of money at the time, and it cost the federal government very little effort to collect. While the tax was scheduled to expire after one year, upon assuming office newly elected President Franklin D. Roosevelt had other plans.

With unemployment soaring, there was tremendous pressure on the new president and Congress to enact relief legislation, and thus the first 99 days of the administration and a special session of Congress saw the passage of the so-called alphabet soup programs.[†] Of particular importance for highways was the National Industrial Recovery Act (NIRA), an enormous $3.3 billion ($66.9 billion in 2021$) public works program whose principal goal was to put millions of unemployed Americans back to work—on almost any task.

Of course, a massive new public works program required revenue. New manufacturing sales taxes and a host of excise taxes would pay for part of the cost, but a large share would be borne by federal fuel taxes.[6] The fuel taxes were widely viewed as a gold mine—a near-bottomless well that could and should be tapped by the federal government in the nation's interest. Moreover, since, unlike most states, the federal government did not yet have an anti-diversion policy prohibiting the use of fuel tax revenues for non-highway

---

[†] The alphabet soup programs included a host of programs best known by their acronyms, including the CCC (Civilian Conservation Corps), PWA (Public Works Administration), and TVA (Tennessee Valley Authority), among many others.

purposes, the funds were available for any program. Hence a number of early NIRA financing proposals targeted fuel tax revenues, which would have to rise to meet this new demand.[7] When the NIRA legislation was first proposed in March 1933, the president asked for an increase of 3/4 cent per gallon (15.2 cents per gallon in 2021$) on top of the current one cent per gallon tax (20.2 cents per gallon in 2021$). This would be used to pay the cost of the $3.3 billion ($66.9 billion in 2021$) public works program of dams, bridges, and the like, which included $400 million ($8.1 billion in 2021$) for road construction. Much of the road funding was earmarked to increase safety by improving and eliminating grade-crossing hazards, particularly where roads met railway tracks. (This continued to be a focus of federal funding in subsequent acts.) In order to create jobs, NIRA forbade convict labor, limited workers' workweek to 30 hours, and encouraged manual labor over work by machines. Given the severity of the unemployment problem, this proposal met with broad public support.[8]

The most momentous provision of NIRA, however, was that it temporarily suspended the prohibition against the use of federal highway monies in urban areas. In fact, 25 percent of the NIRA appropriations were ultimately earmarked for urban highways. The prohibition remained part of the legal underpinning of the federal highway program, but in practice this legislation (and legislation that followed) bypassed those rules. Although Depression-era programs had job creation and not highway needs as their focus, in practice, if not in law, the rural-urban wall had been breached at the federal level, and highway finance was irrevocably altered.[9] As a result, state and federal involvement in urban transportation increasingly became both permanent and more expansive, despite the best efforts by rural interests to turn back the clock.[10] Further, the federal-aid program was amended in 1934 and again in 1937 to allow states to use federal funds for new urban extensions of the federal-aid primary system.[11]

The federal fuel tax raised about $63 million in 1932 ($1.2 billion in 2021$), $170 million in 1934 ($3.4 billion in 2021$), and more than $200 million annually after 1937 ($3.7 billion in 2021$).[12] Unsurprisingly, federal officials were unable to wean themselves from this robust revenue-producer as the economic crisis persisted. "Temporary" extensions to the "temporary" federal fuel tax were enacted in 1933, 1935, 1937, and again in 1939. In addition, federal highway taxation further increased in the 1930s when the federal government began to regulate and tax trucking. Each time, Congress maintained that the tax would disappear as soon as the nation's budgetary problems were resolved.[13] However, as the 1930s progressed, congressional assurances about the temporary nature of the tax became fewer and farther between. In the early 1940s, demands for the repeal of the tax finally subsided as the federal government began to contemplate a potentially greater financial commitment to highways as a consequence of the war effort. It was not until the 1980s that demands for devolution and/or the repeal of the federal motor fuel taxes resurfaced in any significant way.

The reaction of the petroleum industry to the federal motor fuel taxes should be easy to guess. Its early acquiescence was a thing of the past, and its opposition was now intense. American Petroleum Institute lobbyists charged that the tax was an onerous burden for taxpayers, that it singled out their industry unjustly, and that it was a violation of federalist principles.[14]

Thanks to the latter argument, and the fact that motor fuel taxes were one of the few reliable sources of state revenue in the persistent economic crisis, state governments became vociferous opponents of the federal tax as well. Throughout the 1930s, state legislators and state highway officials fumed about federal intrusion into motor fuel taxation that state officials asserted properly belonged to them.[15] Many state legislators argued that, having preceded the federal government into the field of motor fuel taxation, they had preempted subsequent federal action. State officials were especially upset because, with the collapse of property tax receipts during the Depression, many states relied upon motor fuel taxes and other motor vehicle fees/taxes for a significant proportion of their budgetary needs. By the late 1930s, motor fuel tax proceeds accounted for nearly 25 percent of all state tax receipts nationwide. In four states, Florida, Nebraska, Georgia, and Tennessee, the taxes accounted for at least half of total state tax revenues.[16] Levying the federal fuel taxes for federal expenditures thus foreclosed the allocation of additional federal tax revenues to the states; it also placed a ceiling on how high states might reasonably be able to increase their own rates before encountering strong motorist opposition, or suffering a decline in total revenue due to the price elasticity of motor fuels demand. However, these protests by states proved unsuccessful.

Diversion and the Federal Fuel Tax

Given its success at securing anti-diversion constitutional amendments in many states, the petroleum industry, allied with the American Automobile Association (AAA), soon turned its efforts to the federal tax. It clamored for an explicit link between federal fuel tax revenues and federal road spending.

The position of the federal government here was paradoxical. The issue of state diversion of motor fuel tax revenues to non-transportation uses was addressed in the federal Hayden-Cartwright Act of 1934, which withheld funds to states that diverted. The Act declared: "It is unfair and unjust to tax motor-vehicle transportation unless the proceeds of such taxation are applied to the construction, improvement, or maintenance of highways."[17] Such explicit indignation by the authors of the federal Act is ironic considering the fact that the federal motor fuel taxes, enacted two years earlier, were adopted to fund jobs programs, many of which had no direct relation to either travel or the federal highway program.[18]

Figure 6.1 charts federal fuel tax and total motor vehicle excise tax proceeds (including taxes on gasoline, diesel fuel, lubricating oil, tires, vehicles, and vehicle parts and accessories). It compares these to the total amount authorized for the federal-aid highway program, including Public Works Administration jobs programs, from 1932 to 1945. During the first decade of the federal tax, total federal highway spending authorizations did not track fuel and transportation excise tax proceeds; authorizations were usually greater than proceeds in the early 1930s and substantially lower in the late 1930s. In 1942, however, they were generally in line. This one-year coincidence proved important in justifying a linkage between the federal tax and federal highway aid in the future, as we discuss below.

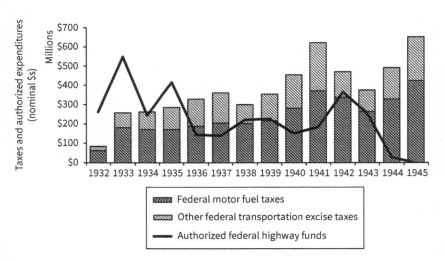

Figure 6.1. Federal fuel and excise tax proceeds and total federal highway aid, 1932–1945.

Data Source: Public Roads Administration, Federal Works Agency, Highway Statistics, Summary to 1945, Table E-3 and p. 57 [unnumbered table], United States Government Printing Office, Washington, D.C., 1947.

Federal Dollars for Urban Roads and the Run-Up to National Highway System Planning

The Hayden-Cartwright Act of 1934 authorized $200 million (equivalent to $4.0 billion in 2021$) in NIRA expenditures for new highway construction as a means of stimulating employment. The Act also expanded the federal-aid highway program, while liberalizing the terms under which states could spend this money. It also created a new secondary highway system of farm-to-market roads and made permanent NIRA's suspension of the prohibition on spending federal money on highways in cities. Finally, in a victory for those who favored a limited network of high-quality intercity roads, the cap on federal spending per mile of highway was lifted entirely.[19]

But perhaps the most important aspect of the Act for the future development of highway systems was the provision that states could spend up to 1.5 percent of their federal highway apportionments on planning, including detailed inventories of roads and their characteristics; surveys of who used particular roads, where they hailed from, and the origin and destination of their trips; traffic counts, including by type and weight of vehicle; studies of what government organs financed and administered particular roads; and engineering studies, such as on how long particular roads might last before maintenance or rebuilding would be needed.[20] This was:

> [t]he start of formal highway planning, although the word "planning" was not used; for Republicans, "planning" had come to represent everything they hated about the Roosevelt Administration, so the word, if not the intent, was left out of [the Act].[21]

Within a few years of the passage of Hayden-Cartwright, 38 states were conducting planning studies under the direction of BPR engineer H. S. Fairbank. These data-gathering exercises were portentous in that they laid the groundwork for more extensive state highway building in the future, and because they provided data that would be used—and perhaps misused—in future Interstate Highway planning.[22]

Congress revisited highway planning when it approved, and the president signed, the Emergency Relief Appropriations Act of 1935. It authorized an additional $400 million (equivalent to $7.9 billion in 2021$) to be split evenly between highway and railroad/highway grade crossing improvements. While these projects were surely needed in transportation terms, the focus of these expenditures was, like the Hayden-Cartwright Act, on stemming the economic crisis gripping the nation by providing jobs.

In combination, the NIRA, federal-aid funding, and the Emergency Relief Appropriations Act directly employed more than 160,000 people to improve over 54,000 miles of roadways and 3,000 railroad/highway grade crossings.[23] NIRA expenditures alone were budgeted at $400 million ($7.9 billion in 2021$).[24] This created a mid-decade boom in highway construction and maintenance. These interventions, intended to be temporary counter-cyclical measures, ultimately became permanent and established the federal government more firmly than ever as a central player—perhaps *the* central player— in highway planning and development.

Roosevelt's Failed Attempt to Shake Up the Federal Highway Program

While Hayden-Cartwright got the states busy with data collection and planning, more direct federal highway planning began with the budget crisis of late 1937.[25] In the fall of that year, President Roosevelt was under enormous pressure to balance a federal budget facing a $1.2 billion ($22.2 billion in 2021$) deficit.[26] When he presented his budget to Congress, the president proposed to eliminate the traditional federal-aid highway program entirely, and to instead fund only highway projects designed specifically as Works Progress Administration jobs programs.[27] Further, Roosevelt asked Congress to rescind previously authorized federal-aid expenditures that had not yet been released to the states.

On one level, Roosevelt sought to gut the regular federal-aid program in order to save his own relief programs from the budget-cutting ax. He believed that they produced more jobs than the traditional federal highway programs, and his administration was focused on kick-starting the economy.[28] At the same time, he had a fundamental problem with the seemingly automatic, out-of-sight manner in which the contract authority provisions enacted in 1922 allowed the traditional federal-aid highway program to operate.

Contract authority gave the states the power to enter into highway construction agreements that obligated the federal government to share in their financing without federal executive branch oversight. Although the system in which states exercised formal authority with federal advice and informal supervision had in many ways been a success, this autonomy was a problem in Roosevelt's view because he wanted to exercise executive branch authority over as many aspects of federal expenditure as possible.[29] In a November 1937 message to Congress, the president wrote about contract authority: "(t)his mandatory provision completely ties the hands of the Executive as to the amount of road funds to be included in the Budget for any fiscal year."[30]

The congressional response to Roosevelt's request for greater executive branch authority was forceful. In the aftermath of Roosevelt's failed Supreme Court–packing scheme,[‡] there was a great deal of concern over the power of the legislative and judicial branches vis-à-vis the executive branch. Most members of Congress, including many of Roosevelt's own Democrats, were wary of increasing the president's powers further.[31] Senator Hayden, one of the coauthors of the Hayden-Cartwright Act, responded to the president's request by noting that tying the hands of the executive was precisely what Congress had intended to do when it had enacted the contract authority provisions.[32]

Roosevelt's assault on the federal-aid program alerted the many members of the Highway Lobby to the possibility of future threats to its very existence. In December 1938, the president of AASHO publicly proclaimed the importance of both federal matching funding for highways and maintaining the existing partnership between the states and the BPR, saying:

> The states must strive to discourage any Federal legislation which would tend to transfer the administration, supervision, and construction of projects from the Bureau of Public Roads and the State highway departments to other Federal governmental agencies and political subdivisions of the States. The importance of administering these projects through the Bureau of Public Roads, keeping them under the direct control of the State highway departments, is paramount.[33]

Congress thus rejected the president's request and instead authorized even larger federal-aid highway appropriations. In the wake of this stinging rebuke, Roosevelt abandoned his efforts to overhaul the contract authority provisions.[§]

[‡] The Supreme Court was hostile to many pieces of Roosevelt's New Deal legislation. In order to protect much of his legislative program from being declared unconstitutional, President Roosevelt proposed adding one additional justice to the Court for each justice over age 70 who refused to retire. This proposal to "pack the court" with additional justices ran into opposition in Congress and among the larger public, and the president ultimately backed down from his proposal. However, the Supreme Court was also more accommodating of the New Deal from that point forward.

[§] Roosevelt was able to eventually convince Congress to reduce federal-aid highway funding by 25 percent, but not until the run-up to World War II in 1940 and 1941 (Gifford 1983).

Toll Roads and Free Roads

The BPR responded to Roosevelt's threat to its independence and authority not only by advocating for a continuance of federal-aid funding. It also began to seek an increased federal role in highway system development in order to build a strong political coalition to defend the BPR program. Specifically, the Bureau sought to preempt future presidential checks on its authority by embracing the concept of a national system of superhighways, or freeways, and also by advocating larger-scale BPR engagement in urban highway development.[34] Both of these notions were quite popular at this time, so adopting these as new BPR missions increased the Bureau's base of political support in Congress and the country at large. Both of these dramatic new turns for the bureau were trumpeted in the landmark publication *Toll Roads and Free Roads*,[35] which was presented to Congress in April 1939.

During the mid-1930s, the U.S. War Department had begun to view the construction of Germany's Autobahn highway system with alarm. Italy's Autostrada had been the world's first modern intercity highway system, but it had not been entirely successful. Germany's system incorporated numerous design improvements over its Italian predecessor and also had greater potential military significance; War Department officials feared that the new Autobahn would aid German troop movement and logistics in time of war—which indeed ultimately proved to be the case. In 1935, the War Department enlisted the BPR in a joint project to study the Autobahn, which resulted in an inspection tour by a group of BPR engineers. They came away highly impressed with the Autobahn's improvements in geometric design and engineering, which permitted uninterrupted travel at astonishing speeds of 75 miles per hour. Thus, the Autobahn helped to generate American interest in creating the country's own intercity, high-speed, limited-access highway network.[36]

The first American experiment with an Autobahn-style intercity highway was the Pennsylvania Turnpike. In 1935, a feasibility study was undertaken for a toll highway to connect Philadelphia and Harrisburg along an abandoned rail right-of-way. It represented a major leap forward in American road-building practices, as it featured top-of-the-line design and engineering never before deployed in American cross-country highways. It was to have four traffic lanes; completely controlled access; no at-grade crossings; no steep grades due to extensive grading and tunneling; sweeping, high-speed curves;

large, legible signage; and minimal roadside clutter. In short, it promised drivers 160 miles of completely uninterrupted, safe, high-speed travel.

In 1937, Pennsylvania officials approved the project, but not without controversy. Many observers (such as BPR Commissioner MacDonald) did not believe that the road would attract enough traffic to pay off its debts through toll revenue. Despite MacDonald's reservations, the federal government, including President Roosevelt himself, enthusiastically backed the project. The Reconstruction Finance Corporation (RFC) and the Public Works Administration advanced funds (with the RFC money to be recouped from future toll revenue) to help pay for it. Ground was broken on October 27, 1938, and it opened to traffic less than two years later on October 1, 1940. While project sponsors forecast that the turnpike would host 1.3 million vehicle trips annually early on, this estimate (viewed as wildly optimistic by skeptics) proved to be much too conservative; early usage of the 160-mile tolled superhighway was 85 percent higher than projected, at 2.4 million vehicle trips per year.[37] As a result, the project was widely viewed as a smashing success.

In response to the progress in constructing turnpikes in Pennsylvania and other states, President Roosevelt and his allies in Congress were keen to see such toll highways scaled up to create a national system. Indeed, Roosevelt summoned MacDonald to his office, presented him with a map of six toll road routes crisscrossing the country, and tasked him with determining their feasibility. Later, Congress passed, and Roosevelt signed, the Federal-Aid Highway Act of 1938. It charged the BPR with preparing a report on the feasibility of a national system of toll roads. The president and Congress obviously had some clearly defined expectations of what such a system might look like, as the act specified that the BPR should investigate:

> . . . the feasibility of building, and cost of, super-highways not exceeding three in number, running in a general direction from the eastern to the western portion of the United States, and not exceeding three in number, running in a general direction from the northern to the southern portion of the United States, including the feasibility of a toll system on such roads.[38]

The BPR reported back in 1939 with *Toll Roads and Free Roads*,[39] an extensively researched advocacy piece that "was a minor sensation in its time."[40] The report, as directed, examined the feasibility of a 14,400-mile system of six transcontinental toll roads (see Figure 6.2).

Figure 6.2. The toll road system from *Toll Roads and Free Roads* (1939).

Source: Bureau of Public Roads. 1939. *Toll Roads and Free Roads*. H. Doc. 272. Washington, D.C.: 76th Congress, 1st session. Plate 9.

For Whom the Road Tolls

In theory, as a finance mechanism, tolls are superior to motor fuel taxes in many ways. They are able to charge users for the costs they impose on the system with great precision, and they are also a better gauge of benefits conferred by that system, as consumers pay tolls when they think that their benefits exceed their costs. So as talk turned to an ambitious national superhighway system in the 1920s and 1930s, many advocated that such roads pay their own way through toll finance. Their arguments would eventually be buttressed by the success of the Pennsylvania Turnpike. Thus, when the president and Congress tasked the BPR with devising the first plan for a potential network of cross-country superhighways, it specifically mandated that the possibility of toll finance be considered.

However, the BPR authors of *Toll Roads and Free Roads* report were highly skeptical of the feasibility of financing its proposed 14,336-mile system from toll revenue. In fact, drawing on extensive travel survey data that had recently been gathered in planning studies (funded in large part by the 1934 Hayden-Cartwright Act), and on the analysis of these data by BPR traffic modeling pioneer Fairbank, the authors of the report concluded that the amount of cross-country auto travel was negligible and thus that toll roads were infeasible because there would be insufficient traffic to make the system self-supporting: "Since a liberal estimate of revenue for the period 1945–1960 is less than 40 percent of a conservative estimate of debt service, maintenance, and operating costs . . . a toll system . . . is not feasible."[41] Barely 20 percent of the proposed road mileage was expected to recoup even half of its projected construction costs from tolls,[42] and only one percent of the system (between Philadelphia and New Haven) was projected to pay its way entirely.[43]

With the benefit of hindsight, the BPR's toll forecasting was almost certainly excessively pessimistic. It relied extensively on traffic forecasts made by Charles Kettering, the head of research for General Motors, who underestimated eventual future motor vehicle travel by nearly two-thirds.[44]

The opening of the Pennsylvania Turnpike in 1940 suggested that the Bureau's traffic forecasts were indeed overly conservative; that highway had an alignment and toll levels nearly identical to what had been forecast, yet it carried more than *six times* more vehicles than the BPR had predicted.[45] In *Toll Roads and Free Roads*, the BPR assumed that travelers would be very sensitive to toll prices; under the best of circumstances, the toll facilities were forecast to carry just one-fourth the traffic of an equivalent free facility.[46] In other words, the Bureau had assumed that travel demand was relatively price elastic, when we know today that this is generally not the case.** The Bureau underestimated motorists' hunger for high-speed travel, and the Turnpike provided this by cutting five to six hours off the truck trip from Philadelphia to Pittsburgh.[47] It thus proved that tolls were a feasible way of financing American highways, and at the same time revealed motorists' powerful latent desire for roads built with the new freeway design principles.

When later asked about the relative success of the Pennsylvania Turnpike, an unpersuaded MacDonald said:

> The Pennsylvania Turnpike . . . may prove to be the first successful modern toll road at other than a bottleneck location. It extends through rugged terrain and offers facilities much superior to those of any of the "free" highways that parallel it. It connects areas having a large traffic movement between them. During its first ten months of operation, however, its revenues averaged only about $220,000 a month, compared with the long-term monthly average of $269,000 that is needed to make the road pay out.

** In the more than eight decades since, repeated travel demand studies have shown travel demand to be relatively inelastic, so that changes in travel behavior tend to be less than proportional to changes in the price of travel (Harvey 1994; Oum, Waters, and Yong 1992; Rodrigue and Notteboom 2013; Small and Winston 1999).

The imposition of tolls on a relatively short route like the Pennsylvania Turnpike, however, is vastly different from the financing of a 30,000 mile network as a toll system.[48]

Backpedaling somewhat on the pessimistic forecasts in *Toll Roads and Free Roads*, MacDonald allowed the possibility of financing limited segments of a national highway system with tolls. But he continued to declare that the construction of a national superhighway system supported solely by tolls was infeasible. While such a conclusion had an obvious factual basis—most of the proposed system would carry a very small traffic load in the early years—it also reflected the desire of Bureau administrators to maintain their considerable oversight powers. Gifford argues that BPR managers felt threatened by a toll-financed national superhighway system because it could be developed without BPR involvement.[49] A successful system of toll roads would not require federal subsidy, which in turn would have dramatically lessened the power and authority of the Bureau. A free road system, on the other hand, would be developed under the existing federal-state partnership favored by the BPR. Whatever the motivation, *Toll Roads and Free Roads*' BPR authors argued that a new highway system represented a critical national need, and they proposed the free road system (to be discussed shortly) as their preferred alternative.

Toll Roads and Free Roads assumed that the network would cost $202,000 per mile, for a total cost of $2.9 billion—both staggering sums for any era, and equivalent to $3.8 million/mile and $54 billion in overall costs in 2021$. In estimating these costs, the Bureau assumed that, like the Pennsylvania Turnpike, the entire system would be built to a uniform high standard—wide rights of way, full access control, grade separation, high design speeds, etc.—whether or not projected demand in a given location warranted such a high-end facility. This marked a key milestone, as it was the first time that the principle of engineering cross-country highways to true freeway standards appeared in federal highway planning.

The Bureau's logic was that to attract sufficient traffic, the tolled facilities must have clear advantages over the surrounding free roads. The toll roads, therefore, were expected to provide safe, continuous operation at 70 miles per hour, over twice the average rural highway speed of the time. But while the toll method of financing was ultimately scuttled by the report, and interest in tolling largely waned until the 1990s,[††] the principle of lofty, expensive, and

---

[††] Portions of the Interstate Highway System would feature tolls on some facilities, most of which were grandfathered into the system. These included sections in Kansas, Massachusetts, West Virginia, Ohio, Indiana, New York, New Jersey, Illinois, Oklahoma, and New Hampshire.

Figure 6.3. The free road system from *Toll Roads and Free Roads* (1939).
Source: Bureau of Public Roads. 1939. *Toll Roads and Free Roads.* H. Doc. 272. Washington, D.C.: 76th Congress, 1st session. Plate 57.

relatively inflexible design standards, deployed regardless of local context, remained long after their original rationale vis-à-vis tolling was gone. These uniform high standards ultimately became a defining feature of the Interstate Highway System. This was another important example of the interplay between finance and planning, with, in this case, the plans for the financing of roads guiding how they were designed and built.

The "Bonus" Free Roads Portion of the Report

Given the Bureau's reservations about a national toll road system, and the BPR's likely diminished role in it, it is not at all surprising that the Bureau included a second "Free Roads" section of the report. It recommended the development of a considerably more ambitious 27,000-mile intercity network of grade-separated, limited-access superhighways built to the same uniform high standards as were proposed for the toll system (see Figure 6.3). In contrast to the pessimistic assessment of the toll road system, this "Master Plan for Free Highway Development"[50] was strongly endorsed by the Bureau and later became a basis for the Interstate Highway System.

How did the BPR find strong justification for a system of free highways, while scuttling the toll road plan? The reason lay in the way the authors of *Toll*

Roads and Free Roads dealt with the question of finance, which was quite obviously of crucial importance if tens of thousands of miles of freeways built to the highest standards were ever to be constructed.

While the section that focused on the tolled system considered finance in depth, there was relatively little discussion about how to pay for the much larger alternate free system, or even what it would cost. There were, at best, only vague allusions to the continuation and perhaps expansion of the existing federal-aid finance system. Thus, while Bureau analysts intensely scrutinized the unloved toll plan on financial grounds, found it lacking, and dismissed it, the BPR's preferred free system was given a pass on the crucial issue of finance, shifting the terms of the debate decidedly in its favor.

The advocacy of an ambitious—in terms of both mileage and design standards—national system of free superhighways was a reflection of the growing disenchantment with both President Roosevelt's jobs-oriented highway program, which had produced limited and often poorly designed and constructed highway mileage,[51] and his focus on tolls as a means to finance a national system of superhighways.[52] Despite its professed collaborative outlook, the BPR sought to maintain its de facto prominent status in highway planning and construction, which it had been reluctantly ceding to other federal agencies with the proliferation of New Deal jobs programs. The free roads proposal not only maintained the Bureau's central role, but significantly increased it.[53] In addition, the BPR further extended its mandate by laying out the routes for the proposed system, a task that had always been left to the states, making the report a striking reversal of MacDonald's traditional policy of federalism and devolution of power.[54]

Toll Roads and Free Roads' Focus on Cities

In a radical departure from decades of federal policy, *Toll Roads and Free Roads* recommended that the proposed new highways penetrate metropolitan areas to serve the CBD in each major city touched by the system. This recommendation for federally funded urban freeways stood in dramatic contrast not only to traditional American intercity highway planning, but also to the intercity freeway networks being developed in Europe, particularly the Autobahn. Although the stricture against any federal spending on urban roads had in practice fallen as a result of the New Deal's initiatives, including urban highways in the official federal-aid network as an integral part of the BPRs mission was another matter entirely.

Why the newfound enthusiasm for urban highway building by the states and federal government after 150 years of active opposition? The new urban thrust in *Toll Roads and Free Roads* was based on extensive travel survey evidence showing that the vast majority of highway traffic—even on rural routes—was to, from, or within metropolitan areas and short-distance in nature.[55] Most trips were less than 10 miles, journeys of under 30 miles accounted for 88 percent of all trips, and only a tiny fraction (1.5%) of trips were over 100 miles, with those over 500 miles contributing less than 0.1 percent.[56] This finding made it starkly clear to federal planners that a massive intercity highway network could only garner sufficient traffic to justify its existence if travel within cities and their suburbs were captured by the system.[57] Thus, the new recommendation for urban highways was not motivated by any particular concern for cities or *intra*city travel, but by the Bureau's desire to attract enough traffic to justify the scale of the *inter*city highways it proposed.[‡‡]

Herein lies a dramatic contrast between metropolitan highway planning, as it had been conducted for decades, and intercity freeway planning. In cities, the chief problems were traffic congestion and haphazard metropolitan street and land development; metropolitan highways were proposed as the means to cope with growing travel demand, the declining relative prominence of CBDs, and undirected growth. For the federal highway program, however, the president, Congress, and the BPR desired an intercity freeway system and the BPR sought a justification for its development. This roundabout logic—constructing a 27,000-mile intercity freeway system that the BPR authors expected would carry mostly intrametropolitan and metropolitan-adjacent traffic—was the essence of *Toll Roads and Free Roads*. And, as we will see, it became the guiding principle in the subsequent development of the Interstate Highway System.

As part of its pivot to prioritizing urban segments of the proposed system, the BPR authors of *Toll Roads and Free Roads* discussed the need to develop an extensive urban right-of-way acquisition program, with a brief allusion to the possible need for the creation of a federal land authority to oversee this.[58] High urban right-of-way costs were indeed a significant problem—as they continue to be today—and there was a clear logic to an expanded right-of-way acquisition program, particularly given the BPR's arguments that urban

---

[‡‡] Gifford (1984, 1991) has argued that the decision to penetrate cities reveals a "primary focus on improving urban highways." We disagree. While *Toll Roads and Free Roads* and its successor *Interregional Highways* devoted considerable attention to the question of urban penetration, both documents were clearly devoted to planning a national, intercity highway network. Both plans recognized that the intercity highways would serve a high proportion of local trips near cities, but the focus throughout was clearly on intercity, not intracity, travel.

land costs often exceeded 80 percent of the total highway construction cost of a given project.[59] Still, the importance of the high-capacity urban segments to validate the need for a national network would, in the minds of the BPR authors, justify their high right-of-way costs. As we will see, the hasty means-justify-the-ends approach to penetrating urban areas importantly shaped the design and character of urban freeways in ways that ran counter to the more context-sensitive (if increasingly traffic service focused) plans and proposals for urban highways we have previously discussed.

Given the nature of travel demand, the Bureau was forced to acknowledge that the intercity highways penetrating to the center of large cities would serve large volumes of intracity traffic. In *Toll Roads and Free Roads*, the Bureau conceded that, in addition to intercity traffic:

> There is usually added to these streams in the outer reaches of the city or its imme-diate suburbs a heavy movement of purely city traffic that mounts to high peaks in the morning and evening rush hours. . . . There are cases in which the daily peak of "in-and-out" city traffic exists without any substantial addition from main rural highways.[60]

In other words, even intercity highways, if built into the heart of cities, would carry mostly intracity traffic.

Given the heavy local traffic projected for urban portions of the system, the Bureau concluded (with no supporting data) that these intracity "movements . . . largely follow the same lines as the traffic entering the city from main rural highways simply because the peripheral city areas and suburbs in which they are generated have developed along such highways." Therefore the "requisite facility" to serve both intercity and intracity travel was "an express highway . . . in all essentials similar to facilities designed to carry external traffic across the city."[61] In other words, similar to the outlook of the state highway engineers discussed in the preceding chapter, the Bureau's highway engineers concluded that roads designed to carry commuters within cities (a topic about which they knew little) should be built with exactly the same guiding principles as those designed to carry trucks between cities and farmers to market (a topic they had studied extensively).

The Bureau's simple, universal descriptions of local traffic in all cities—"It always is largely a movement from the periphery to the center of the city, and is little concerned with intermediate city sections"[62]—lacked the richness, complexity, or supporting travel data found in the major traffic street plans and metropolitan freeway plans described previously. In dramatic contrast to those metropolitan plans, and mirroring events transpiring at the state level,

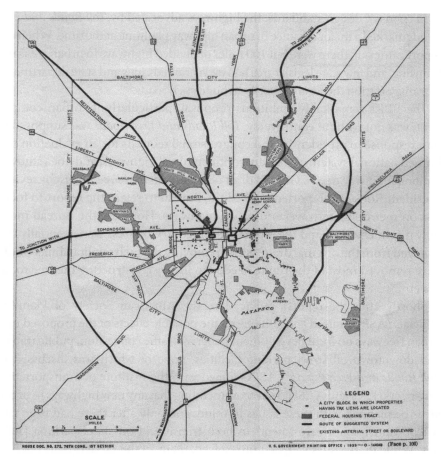

Figure 6.4. The proposed ring-radial plan for Baltimore (1939).
Source: Bureau of Public Roads. 1939. *Toll Roads and Free Roads.* H. Doc. 272. Washington, D.C.: 76th Congress, 1st session. Plate 52.

public transit and non-CBD-bound auto trips were not mentioned. And the urban freeway systems proposed—usually consisting of a radial highway or highways converging on the city center surrounded by a beltway—reflected the Bureau's simplistic conceptions of cities and travel in them. The report included a sample ring-radial plan for Baltimore (see Figure 6.4), which contrasts sharply in detail and nuance with the metropolitan proposals discussed above.§§

§§ In fairness to the Bureau, the report did recommend that cities develop parallel facilities to complement the proposed ring-radial highway systems. But, as the subsequent discussion of freeway finance will show, the structure of state and federal highway programs all but prevented cities from developing such facilities.

In terms of design standards, the highways advocated by *Toll Roads and Free Roads* marked a major advance in urban highway planning at the time. When the report came out, there were but 100 miles of divided highways in urban areas nationwide, and few state legislatures had even granted cities and state departments of transportation the legal authority to build such roads.[63]

The BPR's remarkably ambitious proposal, particularly its urban component, was not without controversy. *Toll Roads and Free Roads* was supposed to be a response to presidential and congressional requests for an evaluation of a limited national system of six transcontinental toll highways, and not a study of national highway needs. Given a draft of *Toll Roads and Free Roads* for review, President Roosevelt reportedly asked the Bureau to revise the report to focus less on metropolitan travel and urban highways. However, the Bureau made only minor changes, and the report submitted to Congress was essentially unchanged from the original draft[64] since removing the metropolitan links would have removed most of the traffic needed to justify constructing the free roads system.

Shortly after the report's publication, the American Society of Planning Officials (ASPO) raised concerns about the possible effects of the proposed new urban freeways on local development patterns, traffic congestion, public transit, and downtown off-street parking facilities, none of which was discussed in *Toll Roads and Free Roads*.[65] ASPO joined with the Institute of Transportation Engineers (ITE) and AASHO in recommending that any new highways in urban areas be planned with these issues in mind, and only after there had been sufficient "anticipatory investment" in both transit and off-street parking facilities. While these issues were left unresolved, many of the same urban concerns resurfaced during the deliberations of the Interregional Highway Committee, which began its work two years later.

The Aftermath of Toll Roads and Free Roads

While the new national highway system proposed in *Toll Roads and Free Roads* quickly became the talk of the town inside of what eventually became the Interstate Highway System's Washington "Beltway," neither Congress nor the president acted swiftly on any of the report's many recommendations.[66] But there was some action on the administrative front; in 1939 the BPR was transferred from the U.S. Department of Agriculture to a new agency, the Public Roads Administration (PRA), which in turn was a division of the newly created Federal Works Administration. The reshuffle made the BPR more central to President Roosevelt's economic recovery initiatives.***

Further, the idea of a national system of limited-access, high-quality freeways both outside cities and within them was now firmly entrenched as part of the national political conversation. It would serve as the inspiration to a group of prominent engineers and planners who revisited the freeway issue during the depths of World War II.

The Federal Highway Program and World War II

Congress dutifully renewed the federal-aid highway program in 1940, although both congressional and presidential attention drifted to increasingly urgent matters overseas. Highway work was overshadowed by heightened concern over national war preparedness, and the military began identifying strategically important highways. The federal government began steering money and other encouragement to the states to improve these roads. Highway construction projects not deemed necessary for rearmament and a potential war effort began to taper off. Materials (such as asphalt and tar for road surfaces and steel for bridges) were apportioned according to a system whereby roads were categorized according to their importance for rearmament, and the availability of materials depended on the road's classification. Further, key workers (such as designers, draftsmen, and inspectors) began to leave highway departments, either because they entered military service or because they moved to jobs more essential for war production.[67]

War, when it came, halted much of the federal-aid highway program; in April 1942, the War Production Board forbade all roadwork except on roads deemed essential to national defense. Road projects had to be submitted to Washington for approval, with their cost and importance to the war effort weighed not only against other road projects, but against all other activities in the economy. But at the same time that roadwork dramatically decreased, the roads took increased pounding due to the decision to permit increasingly heavy trucks to use the highways during the emergency.[68] So rather than focus on the state of the roads at present, Congress and the BPR instead focused on the future. They conducted surveys and engaged in planning to better prepare

---

*** The name PRA was in use until 1949, when it reverted back to the BPR. To try to minimize the confusion we are inflicting on the reader (having already subjected him/her/them to the ORI becoming the OPRI becoming the OPR becoming the OPRRE becoming the BPR), we continue to refer to the agency as the BPR during this period.

the nation for the inevitable economic dislocations and increased travel demand they expected to appear in the postwar period.[69]

It was widely thought that a key to not sliding back into economic depression after the war would be finding employment for the millions of service members and war production workers who would be discharged. One potential strategy for dealing with postwar unemployment was to increase public works spending. There is every indication that the Roosevelt administration intended to use highway construction as a large component of such a program, which surely influenced BPR and congressional highway investigations during the early 1940s.[70] In any event, though there would ultimately be a brief postwar recession, a massive postwar public works program would not be required because the country quickly entered a period of economic prosperity. However, the planning exercises were eventually put to use when the Interstate Highway System was created.

The Interregional Highway Committee

Two years after the publication of *Toll Roads and Free Roads*, President Roosevelt appointed the National Interregional Highway Committee to chart a course for postwar highway development.[71] The goal was to continue examining the feasibility of a national intercity highway system. The committee was headed by none other than Thomas MacDonald and was staffed by BPR Deputy Commissioner H. S. Fairbank and BPR engineers.[72] Roosevelt's appointments to the committee were an interesting mix of "planners, state road engineers, and old-fashioned political appointees."[73] The planners were the by-now-familiar Harland Bartholomew, Frederic Delano (chair of the National Reconstruction Planning Board), and Rexford Tugwell (a nationally known regional planner and former chair of the Resettlement Administration). The road engineers were George Kennedy (a Michigan state highway engineer), Charles Purcell (a California state highway engineer), and, of course, MacDonald. The old-fashioned political appointee was Bibb Graves (appointed to help his ultimately successful campaign for governor of Alabama). The most active planner on the committee was Bartholomew, who, along with highway engineers Kennedy, MacDonald, and Purcell, attended most committee meetings and took an active role in writing the final report.[74]

Staffing a highway planning committee with three of the most prominent urban transportation planners of the era was a noteworthy decision, and the strong presence of urban planners on the committee likely explains its notably more assertive tone with regard to urban highways and city planning than had been the case in *Toll Roads and Free Roads*.

Two years into the work of the committee, Congress again took up the question of national highway planning. It passed, and President Roosevelt signed, the Federal-Aid Highway Amendments of 1943. This paved the way for more federal financial involvement in postwar highway construction by making right-of-way costs eligible for federal reimbursement.[75] More importantly, the Amendments charged the BPR with drafting a follow-on to *Toll Roads and Free Roads*, paying particular attention to interregional highways and the role of highways in national defense.[76] This work was undertaken by the National Interregional Highway Committee. It led to the landmark *Interregional Highways* report, in which urban concerns reached their high-water mark in interstate highway planning.

The *Interregional Highways* Report

Although *Toll Roads and Free Roads* furnished the vision, *Interregional Highways*,[77] published in 1944, became the blueprint for the Interstate Highway System. It recommended a 38,390-mile system of intercity highways to connect nearly every metropolitan area with a population over 100,000 in the country (see Figure 6.5). Though the network would consist of only one percent of U.S. street and highway mileage, it was projected to host 20 percent of its traffic. The proposed system was substantially more ambitious than the 14,000-mile toll and 27,000-mile free highway systems proposed in *Toll Roads and Free Roads*. In addition, because it reiterated and expanded the findings in *Toll Roads and Free Roads* regarding the short distances and urban basis of most rural traffic, it had an even stronger urban component: nearly an eighth (4,470 miles) of the system was to be built within metropolitan areas.[78]

In significant contrast to *Toll Roads and Free Roads*, the system would be grade-separated and limited-access only where traffic levels warranted such treatment. Rural areas would feature 75 miles-per-hour design speeds, urban areas would feature 50 miles-per-hour minimum design speeds, and the number of lanes would be determined by forecast traffic levels. *Interregional Highways* stressed the need for the acquisition and use of new rights-of-way, and where traffic surveys called for more modestly engineered facilities, excess right-of-way would be acquired with an eye toward future functional upgrades.[79] Thus, the system would be designed to meet the projected traffic needs of the nation 20 years in the future.

Figure 6.5. The Interregional Highway System plan (1944).

Source: National Interregional Highway Committee. 1944. *Interregional Highways: Report and Recommendations of the National Interregional Highway Committee.* House Document No. 379. Washington D.C.: U.S. Government Printing Office. Figure 1.

In its call for a comprehensively planned and constructed national highway system designed to meet future traffic needs, the report began by condemning then-current state and federal policy encouraging highway construction and improvement in stages, or phases, which (as we discussed earlier) meant building the basic road up front, with upgrades or expansions to come later as warranted. While construction in stages had been federal policy for many years, it had become a sore point with MacDonald and his fellow BPR engineers. They believed that the practice was one of the principal reasons for the deficient condition of the nation's highways, since most road segments were not engineered with sufficient capacity and safety standards to meet ever-growing travel demand. Instead, roads to meet anticipated future demand would now be built from the outset.

In contrast to the *Toll Roads and Free Roads* report, the Interregional Highways Committee explicitly considered funding. Paying for a 38,390-mile national system of limited-access, high-speed highways was, of course, an enormous hurdle. And though the issue was not addressed in detail, the report proposed the expenditure of $750 million a year ($11.2 billion/year in 2021$), with one-third of that going to urban highways. This money was to be derived primarily from the federal motor fuel taxes. So, while finance was not covered in great depth in *Interregional Highways*, a general concept of fuel tax finance did emerge. This represented a significant break in traditional federal highway finance policy. According to Rose:

> During the afternoon of September 9, at an informal session of the committee, Bibb Graves suggested earmarking federal automotive taxes for highway purposes. Dedication was uncommon at the federal level, argued others, and was "vigorously opposed by . . . powerful influences within the Federal Government." Why not just call attention to the fact that federal automotive excises were about equal to construction costs, suggested Bartholomew. His idea, according to the minutes of the meeting, "appeared to meet with general approval."[80]

"Calling attention" to the rough equivalence of federal automotive taxes with highway construction needs was surely a mild first step. But it proved a significant one on the path to eventually establishing a strict earmarking policy, which, though often explicit at the state level, was not yet federal practice. Thus, the idea that federal motor vehicle excises were simply a general instrument of taxation, which is what they explicitly were when first enacted, faded in favor of the idea that fuel taxes were instead user fees that should benefit the drivers who pay them.

The Urban Focus of Interregional Highways

The drafters of *Interregional Highways*, like those of *Toll Roads and Free Roads*, concluded that the system would host relatively little long-distance, intercity traffic. Instead, they argued that most of the traffic would occur within "zones of influence" around cities, stretching out about 35 miles from large cities and 6 miles from small ones. As a result, the report did not recommend bypass routes around cities, but instead argued for funneling traffic into and out of city centers. This meant the system could not ignore urban concerns in its planning and routing.[81]

Thus, from the outset, the National Interregional Highway Committee members also saw urban highway construction as a way to attract sufficient traffic to justify the system, and in doing so, revitalize cities and shape their future growth.[82] However, unlike *Toll Roads and Free Roads*, the *Interregional Highways* report was much more deferential to cities and planners, particularly regarding the routing, design, and operation of the urban segments. While the rural segments were carefully detailed in the plan, over half of the metropolitan mileage—fully 11.6 percent (4,470 out of the 38,390 miles)—was left to be determined later, because, according to the Committee, "the selection of routes for inclusion in the interregional system within and in the vicinity of cities is properly a matter for local study and determination."[83]

The mixed Committee membership of engineers and planners is reflected in the report's discussion of the urban freeways. On the issue of route selection, for example, the report emphasized the use of traffic data as the primary determinant, but it also stated:

> Because of these two things—the permanency of the highways and the more or less planless form of the cities—the interregional routes must be so located as to conform to the future shape of the cities, insofar as this can be foreseen, as well as to the existing pattern of urban centers.[84]

Interregional Highways was insistent, to the point of redundancy, that the routing, design, and operation of the metropolitan sections be left to local planning authorities and officials, because "[t]he interregional routes, however they are located, will tend to be a powerful influence in shaping the city . . . [but] improperly located, they will become more and more of an encumbrance to the city's functions and an all too durable reminder of planning that was bad."[85] Thus, *Interregional Highways* offered a ringing endorsement of urban planning and the role that other travel modes, such as public transit, should play in metropolitan highway development.

While the focus on urban planning surely reflected the presence of Bartholomew, Delano, and Tugwell on the Committee, these views were frequently shared by highway engineers of the time. State highway departments had little experience in cities, and highway engineers often expressed apprehensiveness about highway developments there.[86] MacDonald expressed this in a 1954 speech following his retirement as Commissioner of the Bureau of Public Roads: "Still, we could plan with much more assurance and comfort if we could clarify and unify somehow the understanding of where we are headed in the forms and ecology of the city organism."[87]

According to *Interregional Highways*, state highway departments would take responsibility over the routes leading to and from cities, but, once the roads reached the cities' edges, authorities that did not yet exist but sound quite similar to modern Metropolitan Planning Organizations (MPOs) would take the lead role. "A metropolitan authority would avoid obvious mistakes in the location of the interregional routes and thus prevent distortions in the development of the area."[88]

The Committee was particularly eager to use urban highway siting to remove and redevelop poor districts near the CBD, which reflected prevailing (and since abandoned) views that replacing blighted center-city properties—which of course disproportionately housed and employed people of color and the poor—with freeways would help to revitalize these neighborhoods.[89]

While many highway engineers of the era professed their lack of expertise on the form and function of cities, they were nonetheless confident in the ability of their new freeways to remake cities for the better. They argued that, planned wisely, freeways could guide the future development of the city along the "desired lines" of urban revitalization and controlled, guided suburban decentralization long favored by urban transportation planners. In an early 1944 speech, the rural highway engineer MacDonald claimed:

> The interregional system of highways has potential for beneficial effects upon urban areas beyond any tools that have as yet been devised if the use is designed and directed by superior intelligence. But the same tool may be used to produce disappointing, if not actually bad, effects. [But] if the plan is given effect, values in decadent areas will be progressively restored and those in the central business district will be preserved by the conversion of all urban land to its best use. Destructive and uneconomic decentralization will be checked and nucleated.[90]

While such claims of "superior intelligence" directing urban freeway development reflect both hubris and naïveté on the part of MacDonald and a generation of urban freeway builders that would follow him, such comments cast the gradual "urbanization" of intercity highways in sharp relief. Initially conceived to attract sufficient traffic to justify their construction, urban freeways were now envisioned as substantially more than mere traffic conduits (see Figure 6.6).

In sum, *Interregional Highways* was explicit in its concern for urban issues being part of urban freeway development. It called for close cooperation between state engineers and local officials and planners in making urban route location decisions, and it emphasized the need to integrate transportation and land use in one overall metropolitan planning process.[91] This was a dramatic turn of events for a federal government with an almost exclusively rural focus prior to the Great Depression. However, this new urban outlook would ultimately prove ephemeral.

Figure 6.6. Elevated urban Interregional Highway section, circa 1944.

Source: National Interregional Highway Committee. 1944. *Interregional Highways: Report and Recommendations of the National Interregional Highway Committee.* House Document No. 379. Washington D.C.: U.S. Government Printing Office. Plate VIII.

The Interstate Highway System Comes into Being—on Paper

Interregional Highways served as a starting point for Congress when it debated renewal of the federal highway program in 1944. The legislation it crafted and then adopted over the course of nine months of political wrangling, which was ultimately titled the Federal-Aid Highway Act of 1944, fell somewhat short of what was proposed by *Interregional Highways.* It focused on the existing federal-aid system, to which it made several changes. First, in addition to the primary system, the Act formally established a federal secondary highway system, including popular rural farm-to-market roads and feeder roads. Also, it authorized the creation of a category of federal-aid roads in urban areas, the "urban extensions" of the federal primary system. This was an important development, since in contrast to the temporary Depression-era job-creation urban road measures it made urban highways permanently eligible for federal-aid funding. Funding for urban extensions was to be allocated to places with more than 5,000 people on the basis of population. This regular federal-aid program, dubbed the "ABC" program, now contained three sets of highways: primary highways, the secondary system, and the urban extensions, which were to receive 45 percent, 30 percent, and

25 percent, respectively, of the $500 million/year ($7.72 billion in 2021$) in federal-aid appropriations. But despite the new focus on urban highways, no one either in Congress or the administration emerged as a vocal public champion of *Interregional Highways'* recommended approach to urban freeway planning, and it was not seriously discussed.[92]

The absence of a legislative endorsement of the report's urban freeway planning recommendations did not necessarily reflect disagreement with them. In fact, there were no lengthy congressional hearings on the report's recommendations where any such disagreements might have been aired. The executive and legislative branches of government during the mid-1940s were overwhelmingly focused on war-related events, and they had little time for serious discussion of significant new domestic policy initiatives.

Of greater import was that the Act created, but failed to fund, a new and separate national freeway network: the National System of Interstate Highways.[†††] Compared with what was proposed in *Toll Roads and Free Roads*, it was to be an even larger 40,000-mile national system of limited-access, uniformly high-quality, high-speed highways intended to meet the traffic needs of Americans 20 years hence.[93]

Uniform design standards were at odds with the nuanced proposals in *Interregional Highways* to tailor the roads to local demands and conditions, and to defer to metropolitan planners on the location and design of the urban segments. It was, however, consistent with the logic espoused in *Toll Roads and Free Roads* and was justified by the fact that highway engineering studies had for years shown that uniform design standards had markedly improved safety. The Act directed the BPR to work with AASHO in developing the design standards for the Interstate system and, in doing so, continued the long-running state-federal highway partnership. Thus, by default it made state highway departments the principal players in urban freeway development, which was already the case in many states because of state control over fuel tax revenue, as discussed earlier. The absence of debate over this approach to urban highway planning, combined with general satisfaction with the federal highway program as it was then constituted, meant that no real alternatives to the rural-focused, state-federal highway model for freeway development in America's cities were considered.

[†††] *Interregional Highways* was linked to President Roosevelt and the New Deal, and both had lost a great deal of their earlier luster in certain quarters on Capitol Hill. Giving more attention to the commission's report might have provided Roosevelt with a potential credit-claiming opportunity that few legislators seemed eager to grant. When Congress eventually endorsed the planned new national highway system, congressional leaders moved quickly to change its name from the "Interregional Highway System," due to its close association with the president's initiative (Lovelace 1993; Weingroff 2000).

In addition to making no mention of the need for the federal government and state highway departments to cooperate with local entities in urban freeway planning, the Act also failed to include any of the other numerous recommendations about urban freeway planning contained in *Interregional Highways*. In fact, urban freeway planning was not even addressed.

The commitment to limited access throughout the system was an outgrowth of the concern that the new highways would suffer development encroachment. As has been noted, highway engineers were keen to avoid the problem of residences and businesses flocking to the sides of highways. This generated unpredictable vehicle movements that disrupted the free flow of vehicles, sapped the roads of much of their traffic-movement capability,[94] and precluded further widening. Also, because the Act called for a system that would accommodate projected traffic two decades in the future, the inevitable result was plans for very large freeways with wide rights-of-way.[95]

The Interstate routes were to be selected by the states in conjunction with the Bureau of Public Roads on the basis of four criteria that were assigned specific weightings: (1) national defense (30%); (2) road network integration (30%); (3) population (20%); and (4) the needs of industry and agriculture (20%). These criteria were very broadly defined, and a great deal of subjectivity entered into the route-designation process. The desire for geopolitical equity and widespread congressional support was a paramount concern, as portions of the proposed system bisected over 400 of the 435 House districts. In addition to uniform design, limited access, and explicit provisions for advance right-of-way purchase, physical restrictions were placed on the size and weight of vehicles that could use the roads, and advertising along routes was to be strictly controlled as well.[96]

Not surprisingly, President Roosevelt regarded the new highway legislation as, first and foremost, a jobs bill, saying that the new highway programs would serve "as a means of utilizing productively during the postwar readjustment period a substantial share of the manpower and industrial capacity then available."[97] But, of course, any short-term stimulus would ultimately pale next to the legislation's long-term impacts on transportation and urbanization.

The Aftermath of the Federal-Aid Highway Act of 1944: Setting the Stage for the Interstate System

At the request of the BPR, AASHO staff went to work on developing specific design standards for the new freeways. The trend toward more consistent and universal roadway design standards to increase driver familiarity and safety continued, though it was agreed that there would not be total uniformity throughout the system and that context would matter. But where Interstates were built in similar environments (in terms of things like population density, topography, and traffic volumes), they were to be built to similar standards. The first standards were published in August 1945. Interstates would be designed to accommodate projected traffic levels far in the future, defined as the 30th highest hour of traffic volume forecast for 20 years from the date of construction.[98] Put another way, over the course of a year two decades in the future, travelers on a given stretch of Interstate Highways would be expected to experience traffic delays due to capacity constraints during just 29 (0.3%) of the 8,766 hours during that year.

States differed in terms of how elaborate they wished the Interstate standards to be. In order to reach concord, the AASHO committee developed a set of absolute "minimum" standards and a separate set of "desirable" standards. For example, rural highways on flat ground had a 60 miles-per-hour minimum design speed and a 70 miles-per-hour desirable speed.[99] On their face, many standards adopted in 1945 appear similar to those contemplated in the metropolitan highway plans discussed in previous chapters. In urban areas, the new roads would have 12-foot lanes, 12-foot medians, and 10-foot shoulders.[100] The initial stipulated desirable urban design speed—50 miles per hour—was faster than most earlier plans for cities had contemplated, but not dramatically so.

The BPR also worked to develop the routing for the new system. The states were invited to delineate the paths the Interstate Highways would take within their borders. They presented requests that totaled 45,070 miles; this was ultimately pared down by the BPR to 37,681 miles. This included 2,882 miles of urban freeways; 2,319 miles of bypass routes around cities were, for a time, excised from the system pending future consideration. By the end of 1947, all states and the federal government had agreed to these route maps.[101]

New plans and high design standards notwithstanding, Congress failed to appropriate any additional money for the Interstate Highway System in 1944. Thus, its construction proceeded at a snail's pace for better than a decade. Years of Depression-related, and then war-related, federal budget deficits dampened congressional enthusiasm for expensive new programs, especially as it became clear that the economy would not slide back into depression after the war. So, while individual members of Congress, and most of their constituents, wanted these new roads, they were loath to levy new taxes to pay for them. In 1944, Congress did allocate a total of $1.67 billion (about $25.1 billion in 2021$) over three years for the regular federal-aid highway program,[102] but most of these funds went to non-Interstate segments.

Although the nation was not yet ready to fund the Interstates, the potential to do so was clearly there. By the end of World War II, America had settled on a taxation instrument for road finance, the motor fuel tax, that generated abundant revenue. That revenue was dedicated by custom, and increasingly by law, to exclusively fund road construction and maintenance. Given the chorus of demands for improved highways, so long as diversion of fuel tax funds to non-road uses was not widespread, the broad swath of American public opinion and even many (though not all) auto-related interest groups supported the highway finance system based on this user fee.

Lashed to ever-burgeoning vehicle travel, this robust source of income permitted—indeed, in a way almost demanded—the funding of road construction projects that grew progressively more ambitious as the twentieth century wore on. These projects established the technical, engineering, political, administrative, and economic framework for the eventual realization of dramatic new highway plans, to be constructed by the states but with substantial federal involvement. The road network called for in these plans grew fantastically elaborate, in terms of both its extent and its design standards. In short, a tax instrument that could generate terrific amounts of revenue; a requirement that that revenue be focused exclusively on roads; rapidly growing ambitions for an elaborate, federally directed national highway system; and the fall of the prohibition on spending fuel tax revenue in urban areas set the stage for the mass production of the most monumental superhighway system the world has even seen.

Still, to get the Interstate System off the drawing board, a grand fiscal bargain had to be struck. A dozen years in the making, it fast-tracked highway construction. It largely cut cities, city planners and engineers, and the vision so clearly and insistently articulated in decades of city plans as well as *Interregional Highways*, out of urban freeway planning. And it changed American cities and travel in them for generations. It is to the story of these developments, which ultimately led to the momentous events of 1956, that we now turn.

7

Financing Freeways in the Postwar Era

During the 1940s, one state took a series of steps that foreshadowed subsequent federal highway finance developments: California. In the decade following World War II, the Golden State led the nation in constructing an elaborate state freeway network both between and within cities.[1] The fiscal and administrative program it built to do so became a template for the rest of the country—most importantly, for the U.S. Interstate Highway System.[2]

California Resumes Highway Planning after Wartime Neglect

World War II put unprecedented strain on highways around the U.S., including in California. The state was a major defense production center and military gateway to the Pacific Theater, and its roads and bridges were heavily worn by truck transport of heavy military materiel and other goods. As in most states, labor and resources had been diverted away from highway maintenance and construction to address pressing wartime needs.[3] Studies conducted during the war concluded that revenue from the motor fuel taxes (which had not been raised in the state since 1927) and other motor vehicle taxes (which were first and last set in 1937) were not sufficient to cover the estimated $635 million ($9.5 billion in 2021$) in road repairs, upgrades, and new construction projected to be needed over a ten-year period.[4] Existing tax revenue was projected to cover just 39 percent of this cost.[5]

Following the war, the California Division of Highways produced a report that identified urban highways as an area of "need" requiring $386 million (about $5.8 billion in 2021$). As in other states, this attention by the state highway department to urban roads was relatively new.[6] This proposed expansion of the state's mandate was not happenstance; it was the result of a sustained lobbying campaign by California's cities, which argued that most fuel tax revenues were paid by urban drivers who should reap some of their benefits. Further, they stressed their penury due to the aforementioned precipitous, Depression-induced decline in property tax revenue. For example, Los Angeles' funding for streets had dropped 90 percent between 1929 and

The Drive for Dollars. Jeffrey R. Brown, Eric A. Morris, and Brian D. Taylor, Oxford University Press.
© Oxford University Press 2023. DOI: 10.1093/oso/9780197601518.003.0007

1935.[7] The Automobile Club of Southern California and the California State Automobile Association also called for state-financed urban highways.[8]

The state legislature did not initially act on these calls. Legislators eyed new taxes warily, and some argued that the "needs" of the highway system had been exaggerated. Many legislators, particularly those representing rural areas, argued that urban highways were not a state issue.[9] Instead, they insisted that the state should continue to focus on intercity and rural travel.

The Collier Committee Identifies California's Highway Needs and Proposes a Way to Pay for Them

Following the war, numerous states conducted new studies of their highway needs in the late 1940s. Notwithstanding the fact that the BPR had gathered much data in the prewar period, such studies were difficult and laborious to perform. They were also subject to much guesswork since they involved understanding the condition of the current road network, determining future travel demand (a process that, at the time, consisted largely of projecting past growth rates of population, vehicle ownership, etc., into the future), assigning demand to the existing highway network, and computing the cost of future actions to remediate the resulting deficiencies.[10]

In June 1945, California's State Senate created a committee to investigate state highway needs. It was chaired by Senator Randolph Collier, a senior legislator and expert on highway issues, and it soon became known as the "Collier Committee." Its mission was to (1) determine the proper size, location, and cost of the state road system; (2) equitably apportion the costs of creating and maintaining such a system; and (3) determine which levels of government were best suited to administer the system.[11]

The Committee tasked the state's Division of Highways with producing a new deficiency report. The resulting 1946 report advocated a ten-year, $1.2 billion ($17.6 billion in 2021$) highway modernization and expansion program, which was nearly double the estimate completed just three years prior.[12] The reason for the increase was the report's call for substantially more spending on urban highways.[13] It justified this newfound urban focus on the grounds that all roads in the state were part of an interconnected network,[14] which of course had also been the case during the many years when urban highway expenditures had been prohibited.

Two other factors may have motivated this move into cities.[15] First, the chronic problem of traffic congestion increased rapidly in booming postwar urban California, and cities' plans for addressing it now centered on freeways. For example, as noted earlier, Los Angeles had published a 612-mile freeway plan in 1939 and had updated it in 1941, but it had no means to fund it.[16] Second, the cities were becoming increasingly powerful actors in the rapidly urbanizing Golden State. Ultimately, the cities' wishes prevailed over rural opposition and in 1947 the Collier Committee included a recommendation for urban highways as an integral part of the state highway program.

A subsequent committee estimate of highway needs extended the time horizon three years to 1959, and more than doubled the projected cost to a staggering $2.8 billion ($40.2 billion in 2021$). However, the committee calculated that, at the current rates of taxation of fuel, trucks, and vehicle registration, all levels of government would raise only $1.33 billion (about $19.1 billion in 2021$) over that period.

To close the gap, the committee recommended large increases in all motor vehicle taxes and fees.[17] As Collier himself put it:

In order to recommend the proper allocation of this burden, the proposed projects are being analyzed to determine the "purpose," the responsibility for the "cost caused," the relative "need," the comparative "use," the recipient of the benefits, and finally the "ability" and "willingness" of the various groups of taxpayers to bear this tremendous expense.[18]

Committee consultant Bertram Lindman proposed that the burden should be apportioned based on the benefits principle, applied to three groups: property owners, highway users, and the public and government.[19] Since the local streets gave property its value, Lindman argued that they should be supported solely by property owners. He also argued that highway users were the main beneficiaries of the state highway system, and that they should bear the entire responsibility of paying for it. Major county roads and city streets fell between these cases and should thus be financed jointly by property owners and road users. In sum, Lindman argued that 73.2 percent of the program cost should be borne by highway users through motor vehicle taxes, 22.8 percent by property owners primarily through property taxes, and 4 percent by the federal government through the federal-aid highway program.[20]

Breaking down the motorists' share, Lindman focused on raising taxes on those who imposed the most costs on the highway system. Accordingly, he proposed three basic changes in tax rates:

1. Increasing the state's gasoline tax from 3 cents per gallon to either 4 or 4.5 cents (from $0.43/gallon to $0.57 or $0.65 in 2021$);

2. Taxing diesel fuel at a rate 50 percent higher than gasoline. This was based on the logic that the typical diesel engine, more common in trucks than cars, moved 57 percent more ton-miles per gallon of fuel than the typical gasoline engine, and a higher diesel tax would offset this advantage;[21]

3. For heavy trucks and other commercial vehicles, repeal of the state's gross-receipts tax (based on a trucking firm's annual revenue) and fees based on the weight of empty trucks. Charging based on the weight of trucks when not fully laden encouraged loading as much weight onto trucks as possible, which increased road damage since road wear is caused primarily by the amount of weight borne per axle.[22] The fees to be eliminated would be replaced with a ton-mile tax based on the weight of trucks when fully laden and their distance traveled.

Increasing the motor fuel tax rate had considerable appeal in terms of revenue-raising potential.[23] As we have noted, the Great Depression had for the most part not dampened Americans' driving, with vehicle miles traveled rising 69 percent nationwide between 1929 and 1941.[24] The 3 cent per gallon state motor fuel tax brought in over $78 million in 1946 (approximately $1.1 billion in 2021$). The proposed increase to 4 or even 4.5 cents on gasoline was steep, but would still leave California's fuel tax rates near the national average.[25]

The proposals to raise diesel taxes and impose weight-based mileage taxes on trucks were more radical, though they were logically consistent with the costs-imposed principle. With the obvious exception of the trucking industry and its legislative allies, nearly everyone agreed that trucks did not pay their fair share based on the damage they inflicted on roads.[26] Higher truck taxes and the weight-based mileage tax system were thus seen by many as fair and economically efficient.[27] The new system would be more costly for virtually every trucker, due not only to the higher tax burden but also to the expense of more onerous record-keeping. Two members of the committee voted against the proposal, ostensibly due to the latter reason.[28]

The California Legislature Meets to Act on State Highway Needs

In early 1947, the Collier Committee submitted its reports to a special session of the legislature convened by Governor (and later U.S. Supreme Court Chief Justice) Earl Warren. The legislators faced two important questions.

The first was whether freeway construction should immediately commence or be delayed until postwar economic conditions were more favorable. The general consensus was that 1947 was a bad time to embark on the program since wages and prices would likely fall during the postwar economic adjustment.[29] But the legislature ultimately decided that the highway needs were too pressing to delay. Ultimately, those who advocated delay were wrong; costs increased steadily in the late 1940s and the early 1950s, were mostly flat during the mid-1950s, and then began to rise again at the end of the decade.[30]

The second question revolved around the time horizon for highway planning, an issue that was being debated not only in California, but nationwide.[31] Some maintained that forecasting highway needs decades into the future was unavoidably speculative and would inevitably result in costly mistakes; this proved correct, for example because the long-range forecasts seriously overestimated actual population growth through 1980.[32] Focusing on the short term resulted in less spending today to meet uncertain future needs, which permitted lower taxes on fuel. This course of action was, unsurprisingly, preferred by the petroleum industry. However, in the end, long-term planning, as advocated by Collier and the Division of Highways, won out. The result was a far more ambitious and expensive plan than the skeptics wanted.

Collier Committee members and other supportive legislators offered several arguments to justify a long-term outlook. One was that deferring road maintenance was penny wise but pound foolish. Resurfacing a road that was beginning to show wear cost far less over the long run than rebuilding it later when it was broken down and would need major repairs. Another argument was that highways were essential for economic growth, which all wanted after the Depression and the war. Another argument was that reducing traffic congestion saved time and vehicle operating costs, which helped all Californians. Also, proponents of more long-range, expansive planning noted that new roads would raise property values.[33]

However, the most potent argument in favor of spending more now concerned safety.[34] As motor vehicle travel had surged, so had crash fatalities, injuries, and property damage. Highway supporters argued (correctly) that new roads with the most up-to-date designs could help to stem the carnage, noting that new facilities like the Arroyo Seco Parkway in Los Angeles and the San Francisco–Oakland Bay Bridge had one-third to one-half the fatality rates of the average state highway.[35] As Governor Warren put it: "I refuse to believe, that with people dying on our congested highways, as they are today, the Legislators will go home from this session without taking proper steps to end the slaughter."[36] This argument proved more viscerally powerful than recourse to dry statistics about vehicle operating costs or pavement damage.[37]

Warren and other proponents of safer highways, in California and elsewhere, were encouraged by the Automotive Safety Foundation (ASF), a lobbying, educational, planning, and public relations organization primarily funded by the automobile-related industries. This group agitated for higher design standards, particularly on the most heavily used and dangerous highways, often as determined by ASF-sponsored planning studies.[38]

The Fate of Senate Bill 5

The omnibus highway Senate Bill 5 (SB 5), authored by Collier, passed the State Senate in March 1947 and it was then sent to the State Assembly. The bill featured an accelerated and expanded program of right-of-way acquisition and highway construction, which would be paid for largely as Lindman recommended but with somewhat higher tax rates:

1. Increase the gasoline tax from 3 to 5 cents per gallon;
2. Increase the diesel tax from 3 to 7.5 cents per gallon;
3. Increase the vehicle registration fee from $3 to $6;
4. Repeal the gross-receipts tax on for-hire vehicles;
5. Replace the unladen truck weight fees with a vehicle-mileage tax of 5.6 to 14.6 mills* per ton-mile on trucks with gross (truck + cargo) weights over 14,000 pounds;
6. Create a special trust fund dedicated to highway spending that would receive the net proceeds of the gasoline, diesel, and vehicle-mileage taxes.

The proposed tax increases were large, although the fact that they were perceived as user fees made the proposal more politically appealing than a general tax hike.[39] However, their size spelled trouble in the more populist Assembly. Further, legislative staff economist Richard Zettel estimated that the taxes proposed would only cover $2.1 billion of the projected $2.8 billion ($25.6 billion out of $34.1 billion in 2021$) 10-year needs. The remaining $700 million ($8.5 billion in 2021$) would have to come from local and county property taxes.[40]

Although anti-diversion sentiment was as old as fuel taxes themselves, and although anti-diversion amendments had been added to numerous state

---

* One mill is equal to a $1 tax on every $1,000 of assessed value.

constitutions, including California's, the trust fund to formally sequester highway revenue was a new innovation.

Had SB 5 become law, it might have remedied some of the structural weaknesses that plague highway finance to the present day, particularly inadequate incentives to reduce truck weights per axle.[41] However, the tax increases and shift in the cost burden were so substantial that they generated intense hostility from the petroleum industry and the automobile clubs, which opposed the fuel tax increases, and the trucking industry, which opposed the higher diesel tax and the new ton-mile taxes.[42] The events that followed illustrate the tenacity (and in this case also the effectiveness) with which "winners" in any public finance arrangement, no matter how philosophically unjustified it might be, will fight to retain their privileges.

The Assembly Committee on Revenue and Taxation initiated the chamber's consideration of SB 5. Here its opponents made their stand. Truckers protested that their industry was in a dire financial condition and that higher taxes might be its ruin.[43] They also maintained that the proposed system's record-keeping burden was unreasonable.[44] They further argued that, given trucking's critical economic role, raising taxes on it would hurt all Californians.[45] In addition, the truckers claimed that recent developments in gasoline engines had eroded diesel's efficiency advantage, and thus they objected to the differential tax for diesel on fairness grounds.[46] Arguments that the new taxes would result in a boon to truckers in the form of better roads fell on deaf ears. Truckers wanted new and better highways—they just wanted others to pay for them. However, they offered few ideas on how to do so.

Automobile club opposition to SB 5 was also formidable, despite the fact that a great deal of the tax revenue ($1.1 billion, or $13 billion in 2021$) would fund the urban roads for which they had long lobbied. Further, fierce opposition came from the petroleum industry, which had a considerable presence in mid-century California and did not accept the proposition that new roads would lead to greater demand for fuel.[47] Like the trucking industry, they claimed the tax increases were too onerous and that their industry was being unfairly singled out.[48] The industry and its supporters in the Assembly privately conceded that some fuel tax increase was needed; however, they drew a proverbial "line in the sand" at one cent per gallon (equivalent to 12.2 cents in 2021$).[49]

When SB 5 was discussed by the committee, the press was filled with accounts of the supposedly nefarious activities of its opponents, particularly the petroleum companies and truckers. Governor Warren singled out the lobbying by oil companies for blistering attacks.[50] Ultimately the lobbyists opposed to the legislation won out and the bill was forwarded to the Assembly stripped of its revenue-raising provisions. Senator Collier characterized the committee's actions as "childish and disgraceful" and Governor Warren stated that "he had never seen a time when the lobbyists were any more active, any more ruthless or when they had a greater disregard for the truth and welfare of the people."[51] In the end, the Assembly returned the bill to the Senate minus the new tax provisions.[52]

Legislative Compromise Produces the Collier-Burns Highway Act

The Senate was in no hurry to consider the amended bill gutted of its carefully crafted financial elements. But there was constant pressure from the newspapers, the automobile clubs, and Governor Warren to produce some sort of legislation.[53] In response, a committee of five members from each house was formed to produce a compromise.[54] It deadlocked, unsurprisingly, on the issue of finance, particularly the size of the fuel tax increase. The senators scaled back their proposal to 1.5 additional cents per gallon ($0.18/ gallon in 2021$), while the Assembly members would concede no more than a half cent ($0.06/gallon in 2021$).[55]

Finally, in a last-ditch effort to pass a bill before the end of the special session, Assemblyman Michael Burns introduced a compromise which dropped some of the prior bill's more innovative features. In a victory for the trucking industry, increases in both the gasoline and diesel taxes were limited to 1.5 additional cents ($0.18/gallon, to $0.55/gallon total in 2021$). Further, the ton-mile tax was jettisoned and unladen-weight fees were retained (albeit increased), along with the gross receipts tax. Annual vehicle registration fees were raised from $3 to $6 (from $36 to $72 in 2021$), and new driver's license fees of $2 ($24 in 2021$) for originals and $1 ($12 in 2021$) for renewals were included.[56] In short, there were across-the-board tax and fee increases, but all were less obviously related to the costs imposed by drivers (and particularly truckers) and were lower than those proposed under SB 5. All said, the finance mechanisms would raise highway revenue by nearly 66 percent.[57]

Perhaps most consequentially, the gasoline tax, diesel tax, and gross receipts tax revenues would be deposited in a new Highway Users Tax Fund, to be used exclusively for road construction and maintenance.[58] One other interesting provision of the law was that the survey of state roads it mandated was to be conducted by engineers from outside the state to avoid any local favoritism or political hijacking of the process.[59]

The compromise satisfied the petroleum and trucking industries as well as the auto clubs. This, combined with the intense public pressure for improved roads, worked in the bill's favor as it passed in both houses and was signed into law by the governor.[60]

The Legacy of the Collier-Burns Highway Act

The 1947 Collier-Burns Highway Act, as it became known, involved three key political compromises that made passage possible. First, the sequestering of fuel and other motor-vehicle-tax revenue in the California Highway Users Tax Fund ensured dedicated, bounteous, and steady road-construction funding for decades to come. The fund operated off-budget, without legislative and interest group interference, which proved an enormous benefit to long-term planning. California was the first state to establish such a trust fund.[61] It ultimately allowed the undertaking of a host of new highway projects, including 330 route miles of new freeways by 1956.[62]

Second, Collier-Burns's increases in motor vehicle taxes were limited to levels that could be tolerated by the powerful highway lobby, particularly the trucking industry. These interests killed the most innovative and equity-driven aspects of the legislation, including the weight-mileage tax and the disproportionate diesel tax increases. The trucking industry lobbyists successfully argued that what was good for the trucking industry benefited everyone else as well, an argument they continue to make (often successfully) to the present day.

Third, Collier-Burns made urban freeways an integral part of the state highway system. This was necessary to assure urban voters and legislators that their money would not be siphoned away to pay for exclusively rural roads.[63] California's cities, particularly in the Los Angeles and San Francisco areas, thus finally secured long-desired state funds for their ambitious freeway plans. But the money did not come without strings. These included ceding control over urban freeways to state elected officials, the Division of Highways, and state highway engineers.[64] The Division of Highways was thus thrust into urban environments where it had little prior experience and where its principles for constructing rural highways would clash inharmoniously with their new urban context.

These three characteristics of Collier-Burns would have enormous impacts on cities in California, and, ultimately, the nation.

National Developments during the Truman Years (1945–1952)

Due to a glut of household savings and the end of wartime rationing, vehicle production rose from just 70,000 in 1945 to 2.6 million in 1946 to 3.5 million in 1947 to 3.9 million in 1948.[65] Of course, this was matched by a concomitant surge in miles driven. Traffic volumes rebounded dramatically in the immediate postwar period, reaching 1941 levels by 1946 and the prewar trend line by 1948. Widespread suburbanization, in part a result of society's response to the postwar housing crisis, also led to more driving as people traveled greater distances to reach jobs and other destinations. All of this meant that total vehicle miles traveled grew more than 40 percent between 1945 and 1947.[66] Traffic surged disproportionately in the more industrialized states and, in particular, in and near large cities.[67]

Other states, including Connecticut, Massachusetts, Michigan, North Carolina, Oregon, and Washington, followed California's path in conducting studies that found that substantial highway improvements were needed. But, as in California, available funding proved inadequate, particularly in light of postwar inflation in highway construction costs, which by 1948 were double what they had been before the war. Similar to the situation after World War I, shortages of labor (particularly skilled labor) and materials quickly developed as states raced to construct the elaborate highways they had long planned but had been unable to construct during the war. This meant that highway projects nationwide competed with one another, and with other construction needs such as housing. In response to rising prices, states began rejecting projects where the low construction bid was deemed too high. For this reason, they were able to spend only 36 percent of their federal allotments in 1946. The situation began to ease in subsequent years, but still states spent only 62 percent of their allotments in 1947 and 79 percent in 1948. Only in 1949 did the states reach prewar construction levels.[68]

States attempted to address revenue shortfalls with higher fuel taxes, borrowing (particularly to fund toll roads), increases in toll rates, or some combination of the three. State highway expenditures rose from $362 million in 1944 ($5.6 billion in 2021$) to $2.5 billion in 1951 ($26.3 billion in 2021$).[69] Also, states turned, hats in hand, to Washington, D.C., but the federal government was slow to respond. Part of this was because the new U.S. president, Harry Truman, was wary of expanding the federal government's financial role in highways, a position that stood in stark contrast to both his predecessor, Roosevelt, and his successor, Eisenhower.[70]

But the pressure on Congress and the Truman administration from automobile clubs, trucking interests, state highway officials, and the public to spend more federal money on roads eventually grew too strong to resist. Federal action came about in part because of increasing perceptions of a highway infrastructure crisis due to years of wartime neglect, as well in part to persistent fears about the nation sliding back into a postwar economic depression.[71] But the Keynesian public works rationale, that the highway program would be a necessary source of jobs, largely though not completely disappeared when a relatively minor postwar recession faded and the United States entered a period of economic growth and prosperity. The boom was due in large part to the substantial household savings that had piled up during the war, which were now being spent on goods of all sorts, including automobiles.[72]

Most observers inside and outside Congress came to see the postwar highway situation as critical, and as was the case in California and most other states, highways and their finance were constantly on the legislative agenda. But despite all of the talk, widely agreed-upon highway needs were not met by a concomitant federal financial commitment. Congress' first postwar highway legislation, the Federal-Aid Highway Act of 1948, actually *reduced* combined federal highway assistance between 1949 and 1951. This led to a drop in expenditures from $440 million in 1949 ($4.8 billion in 2021$) to $427 million in 1951 ($4.4 billion in 2021$). While federal support grew over the next several years to over $750 million (about $7.4 billion in 2021$), the growth in real dollars per vehicle-mile-traveled was much flatter.

Nearly 95 percent of this money was budgeted for work on the federal-aid system; no money was explicitly budgeted for the Interstate System, which by and large continued to exist solely on maps in the Bureau of Public Roads' offices.[73] Legislation proposed in 1950 that would have dedicated some funding specifically to the Interstates was ultimately unsuccessful. State officials were permitted under the legislation to use some of their federal-aid apportionments on Interstates, including in urban areas, but given the high costs of these facilities, and states' obligations to match federal funding for them on a 1:1 basis, few states were inclined to do so.

This cut in federal-aid funding, of course, occurred despite surging driving, worsening congestion, and deteriorating highway conditions. But other issues loomed larger in the minds of congressional leaders and President Truman. Widespread fears of escalating postwar inflation and rising budget deficits moved big new spending programs to the back burner.[74] Truman was particularly concerned about the effect an expanded federal highway program might have on a budget stretched thin by still large, albeit contracting, defense expenditures—concerns that would be shared by his successor, Dwight Eisenhower.

At this point, federal taxes on motor vehicles, including gasoline and diesel taxes, were still not earmarked for street and highway expenditures. So, unlike most state legislatures, Congress had yet to be convinced that the federal motor fuel taxes should be legally regarded as a user fee. Occasional proposals to dedicate the vehicle tax proceeds to highway construction did appear, including one in 1948 that drew on the design of existing state highway trust funds. But this proposal went nowhere.[75]

Shortly after passage of the 1948 Federal-Aid Highway Act, the BPR, at Truman's request, commissioned a study of the condition of the nation's bridges and highways. This came against the backdrop of the rapidly heating-up Cold War, and specifically focused on whether the nation's highways were up to national defense needs. The picture painted by the Bureau was not pretty, although given the virtual cessation of highway construction during the war it was not unexpected. The report found that nearly 95 percent of the nation's highway mileage needed modernization or repair. It estimated that a 20-year modernization program would cost $11.2 billion ($120.1 billion in 2021$) to correct highway-system deficiencies to meet current needs, 47 percent of which were in urban areas. This would require $500 million ($5.4 billion in 2021$) in annual appropriations, amounting to a nearly sevenfold increase in spending. Note that this estimate was just for maintenance and repair, and did not include building new roads, Interstate Highways or otherwise. To pay for the needed modernization, the report suggested letting states borrow against future federal highway aid. It also recommended dedicating money specifically to the Interstates and raising the federal match for Interstate spending.[76]

The BPR's report stimulated some action in Congress, but not nearly at the level that highway proponents would have liked. Geopolitical tensions, notably the start of the Korean War, put a damper on congressional enthusiasm for expanded domestic federal-aid program expenditures. The 1950 Federal-Aid Highway Act increased funding for highways modestly, to roughly $567 million (about $6.3 billion in 2021$) annually for fiscal years 1952 and 1953. But $500 million per year of this was budgeted for the regular federal-aid system; once again, the Interstate program was not singled out for special funding treatment. So, fully six years after its adoption, progress on the Interstate System was still at a crawl.

The 1948 reduction in the size of the federal-aid program, coupled with increasing pressure from rapidly growing traffic, led many states to again consider highway tolls. Though *Toll Roads and Free Roads* had dampened federal enthusiasm for tolling, many states embraced it. So the late 1940s and early

1950s were a golden age of toll roads. Pennsylvania extended its Turnpike soon after the war, and Maine, New Hampshire, and New Jersey built new toll facilities. Ultimately, nearly 3,000 miles of these highways were built in states from New York to Colorado.[77] Following the example of the hugely successful Pennsylvania Turnpike, these facilities embraced many of the design features associated with modern Interstate Highways, offering higher speeds and fewer crashes than the federal ABC system of free primary, secondary, and "urban extension" highways. This ensured their popularity with toll-paying motorists, resulting in abundant revenue for the states and turnpike authorities. These successes helped to spread the turnpike model, as revenue spun off by successful toll roads was used to build new ones.[78]

The toll roads were of import for the Interstate System in two ways. First, nearly all were built on planned Interstate routes, and so in a way the tollways represented a substantial step forward in the funding and construction of that system. Second, for many motorists the toll roads were their first introduction to high-quality highways offering uninterrupted (save stopping at toll booths), high-speed, high-safety, low-stress travel, raising motorist expectations for highway performance. Many toll road design features—limited access, forgiving road geometries, wide rights-of-way, center dividers, rest areas, and landscaping—set standards that the Interstate builders would dutifully follow.[79]

Eyeing the success of the toll roads, and contrary to the conclusions in *Toll Roads and Free Roads*, some began to argue that much if not all of the Interstate system should be financed by tolls, and that such roads could be subsidized or even owned by the federal government. A 1955 follow-up to *Toll Roads and Free Roads* showed dramatic changes since 1938; the mileage of roads projected to be able to support themselves with tolls had expanded to 6,700 as opposed to a few hundred in the earlier report, even with a 50 percent increase in the revenue required to be classed as self-sustaining.

Legislation was introduced in Congress to permit federal spending on toll roads, though the BPR objected. One argument against toll roads was that the tollbooths would have to be spaced far apart to keep both toll-collecting costs and motorist delays down, but that the wide interchange spacing would prevent the roads from being used by short-distance, local traffic. Thus, the Bureau argued, parallel free roads would have to be built alongside the toll roads to serve local traffic needs. Further, the Bureau simply did not want to burden motorists with tolls. A 1955 report to Congress recommended against the use of toll roads in the Interstate System, except for grandfathering in toll roads that were already built, that ran on routes that had been designated for Interstates, and that met Interstate standards.[80]

Eventually, the toll road boom dissipated when federal-aid expenditures began to increase in the 1950s,[81] but many of these toll roads (such as the New Jersey Turnpike, the Garden State Parkway, and the Tri-State Tollway) continue to operate today, with many grandfathered into the Interstate System.[82,†]

During this period, a pro-highway lobbying movement began to take shape, with the curiously perfunctory name "Project Adequate Roads." This was a coalition of trucking, petroleum, and tire industry interests; automobile clubs; and state highway officials who wanted new highways—but without paying higher taxes for them.[83] Not only did this transparently parochial movement oppose all new motor vehicle taxes, it advocated for the repeal of existing federal taxes.

How were "adequate" roads to be funded without federal fuel taxes? The movement's leaders wanted the federal government to pay for roads from general tax revenue instead. To justify a move from quasi-user-fee finance to general-fund finance, Project Adequate Roads leaders promoted a new rationale for the Interstate System: defense. Given the onset of the Cold War, the adequate roaders asserted that new, improved highways would speed the movement of soldiers and defense-related vehicles and equipment, and facilitate the evacuation of cities in case of nuclear attack. Both were viewed as public goods that justified an expanded federal highway system funded from general federal revenues.

Though well-organized, Project Adequate Roads proved unable to stop a federal motor fuel tax increase in 1951 that was enacted primarily as a deficit reduction measure, with funds being apportioned to the general fund and not earmarked for highways.[84] This failure to either increase highway spending or reduce highway taxes led to the short-lived coalition's collapse, although the diversity of interests, with their competing agendas, likely doomed it anyway. For example, automobile clubs and railroad interests argued that user fees, if needed, should primarily fall on the trucking industry on the grounds that heavy trucks inflicted the vast majority of damage on the roads—a position that was, as we have seen, vigorously opposed by the trucking lobby.

By the time of the 1951 federal fuel tax increase, state highway officials and the automobile clubs had changed their tactics. They noted that the federal fuel tax raised $1 billion annually (about $10.5 billion in 2021$) and that

---

† State officials where this happened later protested that their highways were paid for by revenue from their motorists, while other states received Interstates almost completely paid for by federal money (USDOT, FHWA 1977).

federal excise taxes on autos, trucks, oil, greases, and tires raised another billion. At the same time, only $500 million was disbursed to the states by the federal-aid program, resulting in a case of the very "diversion" that the federal government had discouraged the states from doing.[85] Instead of advocating for the repeal of the federal motor fuel taxes, they lobbied for the dedication of these tax revenues for roads, along the lines of the trust fund model.[86] It was a prescient idea that would eventually prove powerful.

By the early 1950s, progress on building new Interstate Highways was halting and piecemeal at best. Fewer than 5,000 of the more than 30,000 miles of Interstate routes officially selected by the Bureau of Public Roads in 1947 were in operation, and most of these were previously constructed turnpikes grandfathered into the system.[87] Spending growth was glacial. Thus, many members of Congress agreed that dedicated funds would be needed to construct the Interstates in earnest.

Progress would soon be made. With the Federal-Aid Highway Act of 1952, the last piece of highway legislation enacted during the Truman years, the Interstate System and the issues associated with its construction and financing finally moved to center stage on the nation's highway policy agenda. In a significant departure from earlier highway acts, Congress allocated $25 million (about $247 million in 2021$) in each of fiscal years 1954 and 1955 specifically for the Interstate System. The Interstate funds were to be divided among the states according to land area, population, and rural road mileage, similar to the formula already in place for the federal primary system. The federal-state matching ratio was set at the same 1:1 level that existed for the regular federal-aid program.[88] This marked a definite break in the federal-aid tradition, in that the Interstate System was for the first time singled out for special financial treatment by Congress. Interstate proponents were hopeful that this would be but the first step toward a much more dramatic federal financial commitment.

However, although Interstate funding was established in principle, there was little progress in practice. A $25 million apportionment was but a tiny drop in the very large bucket. Moreover, it was unclear from where even these meager resources would come. In 1953, Congress again considered charging tolls on certain federal-aid highways, specifically segments of the Interstate System.[89] A Senate proposal for Interstate tolling did not advance very far, particularly because of reluctance from legislators outside the Northeast for whom tolling was unfamiliar. Many tolling opponents argued that tolls on highways represented a form of double taxation on motorists who already paid fuel taxes.[90] But if not tolls, then what? This question remained unanswered as President Eisenhower took office in January 1953.

Financing the Interstate Highway System (1954–1956)

While today's urban freeways have more than their share of critics, the national highway policy debates of the 1940s and 1950s took the desirability of the Interstates, including those in urban areas, for granted. Sentiment for improving highways was bipartisan and almost universal. Despite this, inflation-adjusted federal spending on highways per vehicle-mile of travel was essentially flat from the late 1940s into the mid-1950s (see Figure 7.1).

Eisenhower took office facing intense lobbying by auto clubs, the trucking industry, and other affected interests; rapid postwar growth in motorization; and a report that estimated that completing the Interstate System to standards capable of meeting future traffic demand would cost a staggering $216 billion in 1954 dollars over 30 years (about $2.2 trillion in 2021$, not even counting inflation's effect on nominal 1954 dollars over this time period). Thus, the new administration and Congress began in 1954 to seriously debate highway finance in general and the expensive new Interstate Highway System in particular.[91]

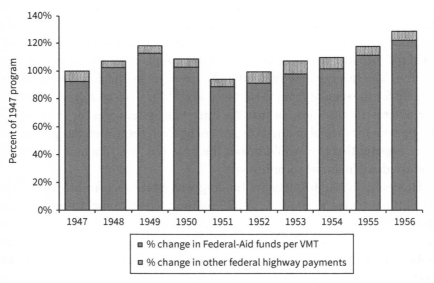

Figure 7.1. Growth of the federal highway program, 1945–1956.

Data Sources: U.S. Department of Transportation, Federal Highway Administration, Highway Statistics Summary to 1965, Table FA-205, United States Government Printing Office, Washington, D.C., 1967; U.S. Department of Transportation, Federal Highway Administration, Highway Statistics Summary to 1985, Table VM-201, United States Government Printing Office, Washington, D.C., 1967; U.S. Bureau of Labor Statistics, Consumer Price Index.

Note: VMT is vehicle miles of travel.

The debates spilled into 1955, when several highway finance proposals were introduced in Congress. In a by-now-familiar refrain, the petroleum, trucking, tire, and automobile industries combined to help defeat them all. However, just a year later, in 1956, similar legislation sailed through Congress and was signed into law by Eisenhower with little opposition.

What explains this abrupt about-face? A confluence of fiscal-political factors came together that decisively, and largely inadvertently, funded the Interstate system, influenced the design of rural and urban freeways, and changed travel and life in America and its cities.

Prelude to a Finance Revolution: The Early Eisenhower Years and the Clay Committee

Popular accounts often label Dwight Eisenhower as the creator of the Interstate System; indeed, its official title is the "Dwight D. Eisenhower National System of Interstate and Defense Highways." As we have noted, accounts often trace Eisenhower's concern with the poor state of the nation's roads back to his participation as a young officer in the cross-country Army truck convoy in 1919, when it took 62 days for the troops to travel from coast to coast.[92] But, in reality, Eisenhower did not "create" the system, which had been formally adopted more than a decade earlier in 1944. Nor did he approve of many of its proposed characteristics. If the system has a presidential father, that title belongs to Franklin Roosevelt. However, it was on Eisenhower's watch that the country finally figured out how to pay for this expansive freeway system, allowing construction to actually take off.

Shortly after Eisenhower took office, the issue of financing the Interstate System came to dominate discussions about federal highway aid. Pressure to increase funding mounted, and Congress did not disappoint. The Federal-Aid Highway Act of 1954 provided what was, in comparison to prior appropriations, a staggering level of spending: $875 million ($8.5 billion in 2021$) in each of fiscal years 1956 and 1957, with $175 million each year ($1.7 billion in 2021$) assigned specifically to Interstate Highway construction. But, as before, the money came from the Treasury's general fund. There were also changes in the manner by which Interstate funds were appropriated and in the share of federal involvement. Dropping state land area and rural highway mileage limits from the funding allocation formula, the Interstate funds were now allocated solely according to the ratio of each state's population to the national total—a clear victory for the larger-population states, which also tended to have the most motor vehicles and the heaviest traffic congestion.[93]

In order to provide an additional incentive for states to undertake Interstate construction projects, the federal-state matching ratio was raised 50 percent from 1:1 to 3:2.[94]

In principle, Eisenhower was committed to the Interstates and generally favored these actions, although he still had serious misgivings about both the increased federal financing role and the expensive urban segments.[95] These misgivings were largely driven by his fears that an expanded federal highway program might push the budget into deficit. Indeed, one important reason for the twists and turns of federal highway finance debates in the 1950s was the need to maintain a balanced budget. In the end, however, Eisenhower agreed that the 3:2 matching ratio kept the states financially committed to the program but did not transform it into a completely federal obligation. He was subsequently quoted in *Congress and the Nation* as saying that the legislation "keeps in the states, as I deeply believe it should, primary responsibility for highway construction. At the same time, it recognizes the responsible relationship of the federal government to the development of a sound, nationwide highway system."[96]

Eisenhower would likely have preferred a much smaller, purely interregional system whose urban segments were limited to spur routes.[97] Such a system would have been less extensive, less invasive, and much less expensive than what was ultimately built. Nevertheless, in the end the president signed off on the bills funding an interconnected national system containing extensive urban mileage. Whether Eisenhower fully understood the scope, scale, and reach of the proposed Interstate System has been the subject of some debate. Specifically, was he duped into signing the 1956 legislation, as Rose seems to suggest, or had he had a genuine change of heart?[98]

The available evidence suggests the former; the president appears to have been misled by his advisors, and perhaps by his own inattention to policy details, into agreeing to a massive, expensive rural and urban federal highway program. As we have noted, Eisenhower reportedly later responded with shock and dismay when he discovered that a Washington traffic jam in which he found himself was due to urban Interstate construction, which he had not realized would be part of the program.[99] However, the president's aides made it clear to him that the 1956 legislation would never have passed without including these sections, which ensured the support of urban representatives, as we shall see shortly.

Shortly after the president signed the Federal-Aid Highway Act of 1954, his administration, facing a rising public and congressional clamor for better roads, went to work to develop a proposal to pay for a further large-scale modernization of the nation's highways. The outlines of the proposal were first publicized in Vice President Richard Nixon's speech to the National Governors' Conference on July 12, 1954, which he delivered on behalf of the temporarily ailing president. Nixon announced that the president would propose a $50 billion (a staggering $486 billion in 2021$) joint federal-state program to modernize the nation's highways by 1970.[100] Nixon read Eisenhower's message:

> It [the current highway system] is obsolete because in large part it just happened. It was governed in the beginning by terrain, existing Indian trails, cattle trails, arbitrary section lines. It was designed largely for local movement at low speeds of 1 or 2 horsepower. It has been adjusted, it is true, at intervals to meet metropolitan traffic gluts, transcontinental movement, and increased horsepower. But it has never been completely overhauled or planned to satisfy the needs ten years ahead.
>
> We live in a dramatic age of technical revolution through atomic power, and we should recognize the fact that the pace is far faster than the simpler revolutions of the past. It was a very long generation from the Watt steam engine to a practical locomotive. It was less than nine years from the atomic bomb to the launching of an atomic-powered submarine. We have seen a revolutionary increase in opportunity, comfort, leisure, and productivity of the individual. . . . [Top priority must be given to transportation and other necessities because] America is in an era when defensive and productive strength require the absolute best that we can have. [America needs] a grand plan for a properly articulated [highway] system that solves the problems of speedy, safe transcontinental travel—intercity transportation—access highways—and farm-to-farm movement—metropolitan area congestion—bottlenecks—and parking. . . . [The president's $50 billion, ten-year proposal] will pay off in economic growth . . . and we shall only have made a good start in the highways the country will need for a population of 200 million people.[101]

Nixon was vague as far as the funding was concerned, although toll financing was mentioned as one possibility.[102] The reality was that the administration had yet to take a firm position on either the specifics of the modernization program or its crucial financing provisions. The one thing the administration was sure of was that it would not allow the budget to be "broken" by the highway program.[103]

The Clay Committee Crafts a New Interstate Plan

In order to flesh out the proposal, the soldier-president tapped another old soldier. This was retired General Lucius Clay, who was also then a member of the board of directors for General Motors. Clay was appointed to chair a new national highway advisory committee, which was dubbed the "Clay Committee." At about the same time, the National Governors' Conference appointed a committee of state highway officials to develop a program of its own.[104]

The governors' committee published its findings first, on December 3, 1954. The study envisioned a massive 30-year $101 billion ($982 billion in 2021$) program to be financed by existing state and federal levies on gasoline, diesel, and other motor-vehicle-related products, which might be raised slightly over time. The federal contribution was to be $30 billion ($292 billion in 2021$) over the first ten years, of which nearly $23 billion ($224 billion in 2021$) would be dedicated to construction of the Interstates. The amount to be allocated for urban freeways was not specified. However, the governors' proposal, which called for a radical expansion of the financial commitment to the national highway program, elicited very little congressional reaction, other than a few stray remarks to the effect that the program was simply one long wish list and could not be taken very seriously.[105]

In contrast, the Clay Committee report, which was submitted to Eisenhower in January 1955 as *A 10-Year National Highway Program: A Report to the President*[106] received a much more serious hearing. In addition to Clay, the other committee members included Stephen Bechtel of the Bechtel Corporation, David Beck of the Teamsters Union, S. Sloan Colt of the Bankers Trust Co. of New York, and William Roberts of the Allis Chalmers Manufacturing Company based in Milwaukee. The committee received staff assistance from the Governors' Conference Committee and from an interagency team made up of representatives of the Departments of Defense, Treasury, Commerce, and Agriculture. The committee also held public hearings in Washington, D.C., and took testimony from 22 different organizations involved in highway issues.[107] It focused on all of the components of the federal highway system but paid specific attention to the Interstate System.

The Clay Committee, bowing to Cold War fears, administration pressure, and an emerging postwar congressional tradition, played up the defense aspect of the Interstate System:

> From the standpoint of civil defense, the capacity of the interstate highways to transport urban populations in an emergency is of utmost importance. Large-scale evacuation of cities would be needed in the event of A-bomb or H-bomb attack. The Federal Civil Defense Administrator has said the withdrawal task is the biggest problem ever faced in the world. It has been determined as a matter of federal policy that at least 70 million people would have to be evacuated from target areas

in case of actual or threatened enemy attack. No urban area in the country today has highway facilities equal to this task. The rapid improvement of the complete 40,000 mile interstate system, including the necessary urban connections thereto, is therefore vital as a civil defense measure.[108]

Having justified the Interstate System, at least in its own eyes, on national defense grounds, the Committee next turned to an assessment of the actual problems facing the current highway system. The first was the growth in vehicle traffic. With 58 million automobiles in the U.S. in 1954, the nation's highways were deemed to be terribly clogged, and an additional 23 million vehicles were forecast by 1965. Without highway modernization this would, in the committee's collective opinion, lead to catastrophe in terms of motorist time loss, vehicle operating expenses, and lost economic growth.

Second, as had been the case in California's highway finance debate, the committee highlighted safety. Safety problems were evident from high crash rates on the existing federal-aid highways. The committee predicted (correctly) that these rates would be cut drastically when existing roads were replaced with new ones designed to Interstate standards. The committee noted that "[the] death rate on high-type, heavily traveled arteries with modern design, including control of access, is only a fourth to a half as high as it is on less adequate highways."[109] The Committee cited no specific sources to support its assertions, but instead stated generally that most Americans were fed up with traffic fatalities (which had escalated to upwards of 40,000 annually) and would be willing to pay for safer new highways.

Relying on the testimony of witnesses and the results of state-level highway needs surveys, the Committee concluded that the nation required a ten-year highway program totaling $101 billion (about $989 billion in 2021$); this was the same amount recommended in the Governors' Commission report, but to be spent over just ten years instead of 30. The Committee recommended that $37 billion of the total cost ($362 billion in 2021$) was needed for urban areas. The needs of the Interstate System alone were estimated to be $23 billion ($225 billion in 2021$), nearly evenly split between urban and rural areas. The Committee urged that the federal government assume a remarkable 90 percent of the cost of the development of the Interstate System because it wished to keep the state contributions at current levels in light of state budgetary constraints.[110] This was a sharp break from the long-standing 1:1 federal-state financial partnership, or even the 3:2 federal-state split more recently adopted in an effort to fast-track Interstate construction. This shift to a 9:1 federal match stretched the logic of the 10 percent state share from being a "match" to more of a "co-payment" by states. Despite its important future impacts (discussed below), the significance of this shift was not widely noted and was accepted at the time, as evidenced by the fact that the recommendation was subsequently adopted by Congress in 1956 with virtually no debate.

Before unveiling its own finance recommendations, the Clay Committee discounted the long-debated toll option. Making arguments similar to those in *Toll Roads and Free Roads*[111] a decade and a half earlier, the Committee concluded that only 10 to 20 percent of Interstate System mileage was potentially self-supporting through tolls.[112] Its report stated:

> While toll financing on a sound financial basis can meet the needs of a limited portion of the system, it cannot support the cost for the system as a whole. . . . Our committee feels strongly that the Federal Government should not enter into toll-road construction nor provide funds for deficit financing of otherwise non-self-supporting projects.[113]

Instead, the Committee favored the creation of a Federal Highway Corporation that would issue $20 billion ($195 billion in 2021$) worth of 30-year, 3 percent interest rate bonds to finance the federal share of the crash ten-year construction program. The bonds would be retired through the allocation of federal gasoline, diesel, and excise tax proceeds, though those funds would not be strictly earmarked. Should these revenues fall short, the Corporation would receive the right to withdraw up to $5 billion ($49 billion in 2021$) from the federal Treasury for debt service.

Eisenhower forwarded the study to Congress, along with his endorsement, on February 22, 1955.

Congressional Disagreement and Inaction in 1955

The Clay Committee's recommendations were well received in Congress, where there was near-unanimous agreement on the need to expand the highway program.[114] Secretary of the Treasury George Humphrey gave voice to this sentiment when he told House members bluntly, "Everyone wants roads—more and better roads."[115] Congressman John J. Dempsey of New Mexico agreed that he "would vote for any bill at this time that will give us roads."[116] Roads, it would seem, had come to rival Marilyn Monroe and Elvis Presley in popularity.

However, though sentiment in favor of a big highway bill was palpable, it was not strong enough to lead to consensus on finance, despite some congressional support for the financing provisions of the Clay proposal.[117] The chief opponent of the Clay Committee plan was conservative Democratic Senator Harry F. Byrd, Sr., of Virginia, who objected to two features of the proposal: the high interest costs (estimated to be nearly $12 billion [$117 billion in 2021$] over the 30-year life of the bonds) and the lack of congressional oversight of a program that would be placed off-budget and under the control of the proposed Federal Highway Corporation.[118] Eventually, even General Clay himself, in testimony before the Public Works Committees of both houses, expressed reservations about his committee's bond-financing scheme.[119] In the end, Byrd's view prevailed and the financing features of the administration proposal were soundly defeated in both houses.

Congress soon turned to consider alternatives to the Clay Committee proposal. After an intensive study by his Roads Subcommittee of the Committee of Public Works, Senator Albert Gore, Sr., of Tennessee prepared the first bill. Gore confessed that, at the start of the process, he had opposed active federal involvement and felt that highways should be left up to the states, but as a result of his subcommittee's study he had turned 180 degrees.[120] The bill that emerged from committee extended the traditional federal-aid program, although the level of aid was significantly increased. The bill proposed that from fiscal year 1957 through fiscal year 1961, $900 million annually (about $8.8 billion per year in 2021$) would be expended on the regular federal-aid system, while a total of $6.75 billion (about $66 billion in 2021$), in escalating apportionments, would be allocated for the Interstate System.[121] The Senate quickly passed the Gore bill.

However, while the Gore proposal laid out a general vision of the size of the program, including a possible one cent increase in the federal motor fuel taxes to pay for it, it contained no finance provisions since responsibility for initiating these lay with the House of Representatives. Accordingly, Representative George Fallon of Maryland, a key member of the House Public Works Committee, introduced a revenue proposal that contained a $0.01 increase in the federal gasoline tax, to $0.04 per gallon (equivalent to a $0.10/gallon increase to $0.37/gallon in 2021$; the actual 2021 federal gas tax is $0.184/gallon), plus dramatic increases in truck taxes, a $0.06 per gallon tax on diesel (equivalent to a $0.59/gallon tax in 2021$; the actual federal diesel fuel tax is $0.244/gallon in 2021), and a tax of $0.50 per pound ($4.89/pound in 2021$) on large truck tires. Fallon's idea was to make all motorists pay more, but most of all truckers whose heavy vehicles imposed the most damage on roads—a familiar equity argument that had been beaten back by trucking interests before, for example in California. Thus the bill would have relied upon user financing and the costs-imposed principle, as well as an unofficial trust fund of sorts, to pay for a proposed 13-year, $36 billion (about $353 billion in 2021$) program for Interstate and other federal-aid highways.[122]

In late July, however, the Fallon bill was soundly rejected by the House on non-partisan lines by a 123–292 vote, largely due to a highly effective lobbying effort waged by the trucking industry, the intercity bus industry, the Teamsters, and the tire industry (all of which would, ironically, later become members of the so-called Highway Lobby). Operators of heavy vehicles protested against both the large diesel tax and heavy vehicle tax increases proposed in the bill.[123] The American Trucking Association (ATA) argued that trucking, which represented less than 3 percent of vehicles, would pay 45 percent of all new taxes under the proposal, an increase "to a confiscatory, ruinous and unjustified level" which would damage the economy and cost nearly 7 million jobs.[124] Many believed the intense hostility from the trucking industry was a major factor in scuttling the bill. House Majority Leader John W. McCormack (D-MA) stated, "I have a sneaky idea that the truckers of the country played an important part in what happened."[125] The comparatively disorganized private-sector proponents of the bill were unable to mount an effective defense due to internal dissension among them over the cost of the program.

Immediately following the defeat of the Fallon proposal, President Eisenhower publicly pleaded with Congress not to let the controversy over financing delay the construction of badly needed roads.[126] Nevertheless, 1955 closed without the passage of a new highway bill.

The Yellow Book and the Success of the 1956 Interstate Legislation

Remarkably, given a decade of failed attempts, 1956 saw the fiscal logjam broken and the passage of an Interstate funding plan by overwhelming majorities in both houses of Congress. There was little opposition to the 1956 funding scheme, even from interest groups that just a year before had been determined opponents of a very similar proposal. The dramatic shift in sentiment in the course of one year requires explanation, and several closely related hypotheses for why it took place have been offered.

First, between the end of the 1955 and the beginning of the 1956 legislative sessions, the BPR issued a report designating the urban routes of the Interstate Highway System. Recall that the 1944 *Interregional Highways* report had offered an extended, even passionate argument for leaving the routing of the urban portions of the Interstate System to local planners,

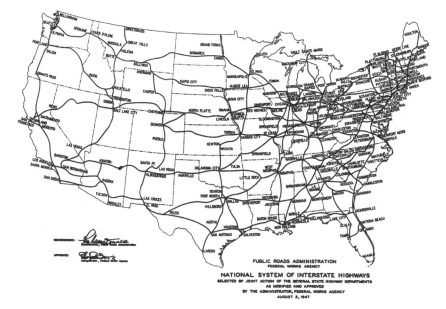

Figure 7.2. Interstate highway system map from the *Yellow Book* (1955).

Source: Bureau of Public Roads. 1955. "General Location of National System of Interstate Highways." Washington, D.C.: U.S. Department of Commerce.

engineers, and public officials. In 1947 the BPR had published a report detailing the general location of rural routes but had left the designation of most urban route locations to some future time due to the need for more sophisticated urban traffic studies. Now, in the wake of the failed congressional action in 1955, the BPR took a page from the book of California, where experience had shown that bringing the urban lobby onboard by including metropolitan freeways as an integral part of the highway program was essential for its passage. Thus, the BPR hastily published a report entitled *General Location of National System of Interstate Highways*,[127] which quickly became known as the *Yellow Book*. It designated the approximate routes the urban Interstates would take (see Figure 7.2, Figure 7.3, Figure 7.4, and Figure 7.5).

The BPR made sure the maps of the urban routes were widely distributed among members of Congress and other interested parties. The release of this publication proved a watershed because it changed perceptions of the Interstate System in the minds of many from being primarily a rural program to an explicitly urban one, too.[128] The fact that the Interstate Highways, with all routes now designated, would serve so many congressional districts (400 out of 435) merely increased their appeal.[129]

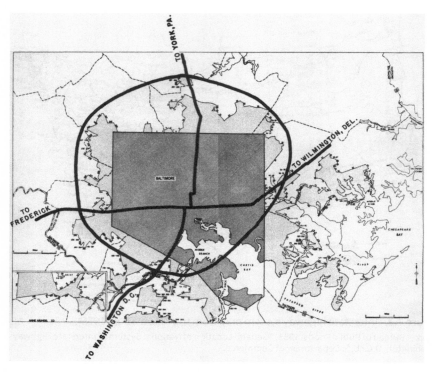

Figure 7.3. The *Yellow Book* urban Interstate System for Baltimore (1955).
Source: Bureau of Public Roads. 1955. "General Location of National System of Interstate Highways." Washington, D.C.: U.S. Department of Commerce.

The report consisted of little more than crude sketch maps of the general lo-cation of the urban segments in 100 urban areas that legislators could show to one another and their constituents. These routes were hastily "planned" over a period of only nine months, with only limited local consultation and little sensitivity to highly complex urban dynamics in terms of land use, economic development, traffic patterns, transit service, etc.—a process that the authors of *Interregional Highways* had specifically warned against. However, as ques-tionable as the *Yellow Book* was as a planning document, it was highly effec-tive as a public relations exercise, and it helped to quickly create a powerful urban constituency of mayors, business leaders, and other local interests in favor of adopting a federal highway financing bill. Needless to say, this hur-ried and limited planning process had enormous implications for the future of American cities.

Second, the interval between the failed legislation of 1955 and the suc-cessful legislation in 1956 gave some time for the natural proponents of the

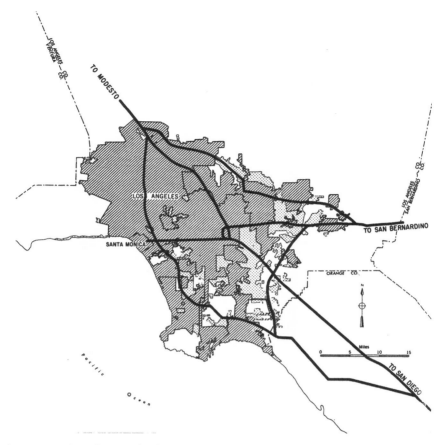

Figure 7.4. The *Yellow Book* urban Interstate System for Los Angeles (1955).
Source: Bureau of Public Roads. 1955. "General Location of National System of Interstate Highways."
Washington, D.C.: U.S. Department of Commerce.

Interstate System, most notably the construction industry, to rally public
and congressional support.[130] Further, many of the opponents of the failed
1955 legislation were mollified because the motor fuel tax rates in the 1956
legislation were somewhat reduced from the earlier proposals,[131] while still
providing benefits to affected interest groups (motorists, the auto clubs, and
the like).

Third, as in California, dramatically scaling back proposals to tax heavy
vehicles in line with the road damage they caused was essential to molli-
fying opposition from the trucking lobby. The new legislation stipulated that
tax rates should be roughly in line with benefits received by each road-user
class. A study performed a few years later showed that motorists paid close
to the benefits they received, while truckers paid more than the benefits they

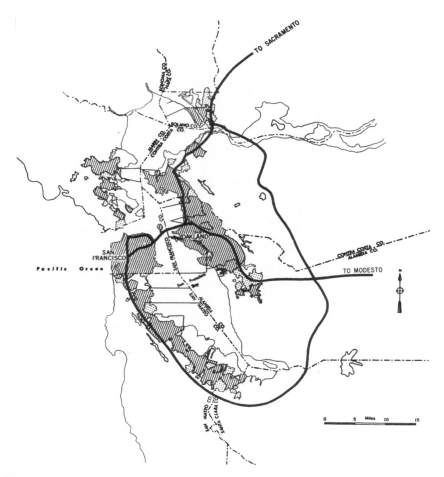

Figure 7.5. The *Yellow Book* urban Interstate System for San Francisco (1955).
Source: Bureau of Public Roads. 1955. "General Location of National System of Interstate Highways." Washington, D.C.: U.S. Department of Commerce.

received. Hence taxing by benefits received and not costs imposed was the desired outcome for the trucking industry.[132]

Fourth, the acquiescence of organized labor was secured by provisions in the legislation that guaranteed Interstate construction workers the "prevailing wage" as outlined in the Davis-Bacon Act of 1935. Opponents of this provision argued it was unfair in that it raised wages in low-cost rural areas to levels established by unions in large cities. However, the new legislation not only used this standard, but also applied it to the Interstates even though they were state, and not federal, projects. The provision was bitterly fought by AASHO and the road-building associations, who argued that these Interstate wage levels would come to be applied to all road construction, raising construction costs nationwide by between 15 and 40 percent. But ultimately the provision was included in the legislation as the price of labor support.[133]

Another innovation was that the new legislation appropriated the funding for the entire project at once, unlike the federal-aid program that needed continual renewal. Also, it was to be completed according to a single nationwide 13-year timetable and not left to be dragged out as the states pursued their own agendas.[134]

Finally, Congress would establish an off-budget trust fund, as California had done nearly a decade earlier.[135] This account would sequester most motor vehicle tax revenue, including the fuel taxes, though a few sources of revenue, such as a 10 percent excise tax on vehicles, would still go to the general fund.[136] The trust fund appeased those fearful of diversion, particularly automakers and other members of the Highway Lobby.

Spurred by these developments, in early 1956 the House of Representatives took up the highway legislation. Two finance bills, HR 8836 by George Fallon and HR 9075 by Hale Boggs, were assigned to the House Ways and Means Committee in early February; the Fallon Bill was also assigned to the House Committee on Public Works, which looked at the non-finance portions of the bill.

The two highway bills were eventually combined as HR 10660, the Highway Revenue Act of 1956. The Fallon bill was essentially the same as what had been introduced in 1955. The Boggs bill, whose tax rates ultimately prevailed, raised gasoline and diesel taxes to 3 cents per gallon each ($0.29/gallon in 2021$), but there was no diesel fuel differential, a significant victory for the trucking industry. The Boggs bill also increased excise taxes on trucks, buses, and trailers from 8 to 10 percent and raised taxes on tires by 60 percent. Congressman Boggs estimated that his proposal would, in conjunction with existing taxes, raise $34 billion (about $332 billion in 2021$) over 15 years.[137]

In addition to placating the nascent Highway Lobby, the proposed Highway Trust Fund helped secure Eisenhower administration support by alleviating concerns over the Interstates' budgetary effects.[138] The administration, led by Treasury Secretary Humphrey, was not enthusiastic about the Treasury losing highway tax revenues to the new trust fund.[139] But with highways expected to be self-supporting from revenue tied to the level of vehicle travel, the trust fund would protect the Treasury from being raided to pay for highways in the future. This "firewall" between the trust fund and the rest of the Treasury would not be breached for nearly a half century.

The House Ways and Means Committee heard witness testimony, made very few changes to the proposed legislation, and forwarded HR 10660 to the Senate Finance Committee for its consideration in mid-May 1956. While senators supported most of the House provisions, Finance Committee Chairman Byrd was concerned about the possibility of deficits in the proposed Highway Trust Fund during the first few years of the program.[140] To guard against these, the Senate added the "Byrd Amendment" which mandated that total highway tax receipts must either match or exceed total expenditures in any given year of the program.[141] Other than this alteration, there was little controversy about this substantial tax increase among senators or affected interest groups, an almost unimaginable turn of events from the perspective of the hyper-partisan politics of the twenty-first century. Throughout the proceedings, trucking, automobile club, and petroleum industry interests lobbied for lower tax rates, but given that they had already won important concessions, they ultimately accepted the increases called for in the House bill once it was clear that the revenues would be dedicated exclusively to highways.

The Senate passed its bill on May 29, 1956, and a House-Senate conference committee ironed out the relatively minor differences between the two bills. The House quickly accepted the Byrd Amendment. The House passed the final bill overwhelmingly, 388 to 19, while the Senate passed the legislation on a voice vote.[142] The Highway Act of 1956 legislation, consisting of the Federal-Aid Highway Act of 1956 (Title I) and the Highway Revenue Act of 1956 (Title II), was signed into law by President Eisenhower on June 29, 1956.

Preparing to Undertake the Largest Public Works Program in History

So, after a dozen years of false starts and failed attempts to fund the Interstate Highway System since its adoption back in 1944, the 1956 legislation finally set the stage for the mass production of highways on a national scale. It authorized a mammoth road-building program funded by $31 billion (about $303 billion in 2021$) in state and federal funds over a period of 13 years. This made it arguably the largest public works project not only in American history, but in the history of the world. Construction of the Interstate System was scheduled to be completed in 16 years, by 1972—a target that would be missed by about two decades.[143] We turn to the short-lived era of breakneck Interstate construction, and its long-term consequences, next.

PART IV

THE FREEWAY ERA AND ITS ENDURING LEGACY

8

The Rise of the Freeway Era

With the passage of the landmark Federal-Aid Highway Act of 1956, it appeared to nearly everyone at the time that the United States had at last discovered an economically efficient and politically effective method of financing new highways, both rural and urban. The federal government had followed the lead of California, and then other states, in establishing a trust fund to serve as a repository for motor fuel taxes and related highway-user revenues. Money was disbursed from both federal and state trust funds to state highway departments for road design, construction, operations, and maintenance. This involved a relatively low level of legislative involvement and interference, which made representatives from other sectors of government green with envy. By and large, the trust funds were out of sight, and elected officials' concerns over their operation were out of mind, for a time anyway. However, the effect of the trust funds was anything but invisible, as the amount of revenue moving through them was substantial and growing, and this money needed to be spent as it rolled in. This set the stage for the mass production of freeways, both between cities and within them.[1]

With the launch of this national freeway construction juggernaut, the conflicts between urban and rural highway-planning principles, and between financial imperatives and planning ones, finally came to a head. Put simply, finance now trumped planning, as authority over highways in and between cities was jointly vested in Washington and the state capitals and their highway departments. This was due not to any reasoned calculus about the appropriate roles of various levels of government in the production of freeways, but to the politics of finance and the power that control over the purse strings entailed. As the saying goes, he who has the gold makes the rules, and thanks to the enormous revenue generation of state, and now federal, motor fuel taxes, those rules would *not* be made by cities, their neighborhoods, or their planners.

Since the states and the federal government were now the driving force behind the freeways generally, and the Interstates (including their urban extensions) in particular, planning customs and tenets forged by state

The Drive for Dollars. Jeffrey R. Brown, Eric A. Morris, and Brian D. Taylor, Oxford University Press.
© Oxford University Press 2023. DOI: 10.1093/oso/9780197601518.003.0008

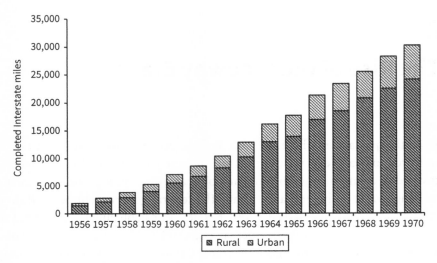

Figure 8.1. Completed miles of fully access-controlled divided highways on the Interstate System, 1956–1970.

Data Sources: U.S. Department of Commerce, Bureau of Public Roads, Highway Statistics 1956–1964, Table INT-11, United States Government Printing Office, Washington D.C., 1958–1966; U.S. Department of Transportation, Federal Highway Administration, Highway Statistics 1965–70, Table INT-11, U.S. Government Printing Office, Washington D.C.

highway departments during decades of almost-exclusively rural highway construction now manifested themselves in cities. Precepts developed to move growing numbers of private and commercial vehicles at very high speeds across vast open spaces were now applied in densely developed urban areas across the country. This model led to some important successes, as the capacity of cities to host burgeoning private and commercial vehicle travel increased substantially, particularly for longer trips. But there were numerous problematic outcomes as well.

Figure 8.1 shows that less than 2,000 miles of the Interstate Highway System were completed and opened to traffic between the system's adoption in 1944 and the year 1956—just over 150 miles per year.* But just four years after the Federal Highway Act legislation in 1956, the nation was home to more than 7,000 miles of Interstates; in 1965, the mileage exceeded 17,000; and, by 1970, the U.S. was blanketed with over 30,000 miles of Interstate Highways. To give an example of how the accelerated Interstate planning and construction process worked, we again turn to the story of California.

---

* Completed miles consisted of four or more traffic lanes of divided highways with full access control.

California Leads in Metropolitan Freeway Development

California embraced metropolitan freeway development early on and with exceptional abandon because of its size, its explosive post–World War II growth, its rapid urbanization, its substantial state commitment to postwar highway finance, and because, more than any other state, it went all in on freeway development. Its experience exemplified trends that soon manifested themselves nationally, since not only the finance system developed by the Collier-Burns Act, but the template for freeway planning and construction developed by the California Division of Highways was eventually adopted by most other states.[2]

Planning the California Freeway System

Following the funding of the Interstate System, the California Legislature in 1957 instructed the state Division of Highways to prepare a comprehensive plan "for the ultimate freeway and expressway system of the entire State."[3] It returned in 1958 with an ambitious 12,241-mile plan, titled simply *The California Freeway System*.[4] The plan called for an enormous system to be built both between and within metropolitan areas in networks far denser than those proposed by national highway planners.

In cities, freeways were roughly platted on a four-mile by four-mile grid, which was a substantial departure from the ring-radial networks based on the existing patterns of roads and rail lines leading to and from city centers favored by most early metropolitan highway planners. The plan also differed even from the skeletal ring-radial networks produced by the Bureau of Public Roads for the *Yellow Book* (see Figure 8.2 and Figure 8.3). But state freeway planners in 1958 argued that the proportion of trips to and from city centers was dwindling. Metropolitan freeway networks, they concluded, should be modeled after urban street grids to better distribute traffic around the region rather than funneling trips downtown.[5,†]

Such a position typifies the contrast between state and local approaches to planning freeways for cities. The early metropolitan highway plans were motivated, in large part, by the desire to stem the decline of CBDs and inner-ring

---

† It is possible that blanketing California's metropolitan areas with freeways constructed on a four-mile grid would have ultimately resulted in smaller, less invasive facilities than those eventually built. But as we discuss later, a majority of the proposed links in the California Freeway System plan would never be built, leaving behind a sparser network of very high-capacity, traffic-concentrating facilities.

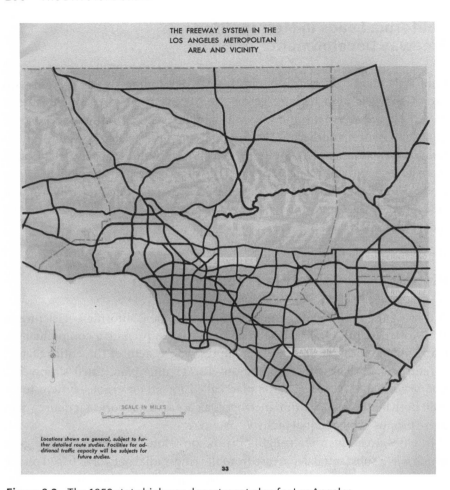

Figure 8.2. The 1958 state highway department plan for Los Angeles.

Source: California Division of Highways. 1958. The California Freeway System: A Report to the Joint Interim Committee on Highway Problems of the California Legislature in Conformity with Senate Concurrent Resolution No. 26, 1957 Legislature. Map, p. 33.

areas vis-à-vis the suburbs. California's state highway engineers, at least early on, had little patience for such efforts at social engineering. The task of the state highway planner, in their view, was to accommodate, not manipulate, travel demand. Said Edward Telford, California State Division of Highways District Engineer for Los Angeles, in a 1961 speech: "We cannot classify today's travel and transportation patterns as perverse or irrational and dismiss them as something that should be changed or modified by edict of some all-powerful agency."[6]

Metropolitan land use was mentioned in the 1958 plan, but only to note that land development adjacent to highways interfered with through traffic,

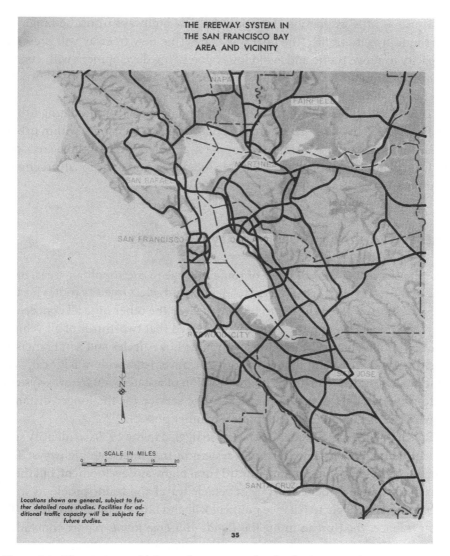

THE FREEWAY SYSTEM IN
THE SAN FRANCISCO BAY
AREA AND VICINITY

SCALE IN MILES
0   5   10   15   20

Locations shown are general, subject to further detailed route studies. Facilities for additional traffic capacity will be subjects for
future studies.

35

Figure 8.3. The 1958 state highway department plan for the San Francisco Bay Area.
Source: California Division of Highways. 1958. The California Freeway System: A Report to the Joint Interim Committee on Highway Problems of the California Legislature in Conformity with Senate Concurrent Resolution No. 26, 1957 Legislature. Map, p. 35.

reflecting past experience that highways on the outskirts of cities often attracted traffic-generating commercial development that atrophied the roads' performance.[7] This outcome was abhorred by the state highway engineers behind the California plan; given their rural, intercity ethos, they saw the primary purpose of urban freeways as accommodating traffic at speeds as high as possible. So their approach was to integrate freeways with adjacent land use as little as possible, isolating the new highways from the tangle of surrounding city traffic. The goal was that "[t]he new freeway will preserve capacity to move traffic and avoid low-value string development with consequent deterioration of public investment in highways."[8] This approach would later characterize Interstate Highways nationwide.

This disdain for freeway-adjacent development and accommodating urban traffic resulted in plans that limited the number of interchanges within urban areas to discourage use by intrametropolitan travelers. This would be resisted by local planners and officials, who often fought for, and occasionally secured, additional interchanges to serve intracity travel.

Intracity Demand for Intercity Highways

Despite the major commitment of route mileage to metropolitan areas, only one of the ten explicit criteria used to identify and select freeway routes for the 1958 California plan referred to intracity travel; the other nine all concerned intercity travel. Though the plan acknowledged that two-thirds of all vehicle travel in California at the time was within the Los Angeles and San Francisco metropolitan areas, and that a "majority of travel [statewide was] local,"[9] its authors concluded that "the primary function of a state-wide freeway system is to provide relatively rapid through-traffic service for the longer distance trips in the most direct and economical manner possible."[10]

Recall that federal BPR engineers had struggled in the 1930s to identify sufficient demand to justify a national system of free interstate highways. The Bureau had a strong orientation toward rural highway development, but there was indisputable evidence that most vehicle travel and traffic problems were urban. In its struggle to balance political will and bureaucratic tradition with the evidence, the Bureau in its *Toll Roads and Free Roads* report concluded that a national freeway network connecting city centers was the answer.

Twenty years later, the California Division of Highways similarly struggled to justify the extensive statewide freeway system called for by state legislators. The resulting plan focused on the need for improved recreational and commercial intercity travel, presumably because the average lengths of these trips (15.5 miles and 8.5 miles, respectively) were the longest of all measured trip types. The plan, however, presented no data showing that intercity recreational and commercial travel constituted a significant proportion of vehicle travel, or that such travel warranted special attention. In fact, it ignored data from numerous traffic studies over the previous two decades, including *Toll Roads and Free Roads* and *Interregional Highways*, which had clearly revealed the relatively small role played by long-distance, intercity trips.

The incompatibility between data showing that most travel was both urban and local, and the Division of Highways' rural highway orientation toward "rapid through-traffic service for longer distance trips,"[11] helps to explain why the 1958 plan for California substantially *over*estimated the future role of freeways in rural areas and *under*estimated their impact in urban areas.

The Grand Ambitions of the California Highway Plan

Like so many plans before it, the 1958 California plan was silent on the cost of the freeway system, saying only that it "is economically feasible and can be accomplished within the framework of present highway user finances within a reasonable period of years."[12] In hindsight, such a conclusion was naïve, and wrong, but at the time it probably appeared reasonable given the torrent of incoming highway-user tax revenue. Given the bounteous funding appropriated by Collier-Burns, and the copious federal revenue appropriated in 1956 (and increased in 1961), inflation-adjusted revenues for state highways in California rose over 400 percent between 1947 and 1966 to a 2021 equivalent of nearly $6.3 billion per year.[13] Figure 8.4 shows all funds available to the state from 1947 to 1966 for highway construction, and the share attributable to the state fuel taxes.

This fiscal windfall came not just because of higher fuel and related tax rates, but also because of average annual increases in fuel consumption in excess of 5 percent. This extraordinary growth in highway revenues radically changed highway-planning practice. No longer were scarce resources allocated incrementally to projects based on existing demand. Instead, new, large-scale freeway plans that appeared fanciful in the late 1940s were not only possible but often appeared conservative just a decade later. So when motor fuel taxes were extended and other highway user tax revenues were modestly increased with the passage of the Federal Aid Highway Act of 1961, freeway funding appeared set. So widespread was the belief that freeways were adequately funded that *all* the revenues from the only state highway tax increase in California during the 1960s (which raised the state motor fuel tax by one cent per gallon and most other vehicle fees by about 15 percent) went to cities and counties for roads, and *none* to the state highway program.[14]

A financial evaluation of the California plan was prepared for the state legislature. It set the cost of completing the system by 1980 at $10.5 billion; about two-thirds of the projected costs were for urban freeways and one-third for rural ones.[15] The evaluation concluded that the entire freeway system could be built with funds from existing highway revenue programs, assuming little

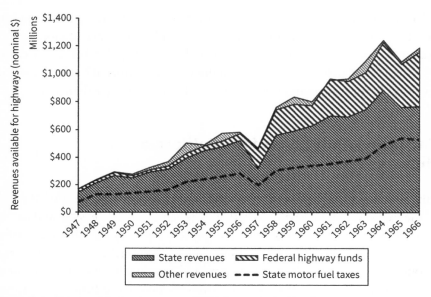

Figure 8.4. State and federal revenues for highways in California, 1947–1966.

Data Sources: Public Roads Administration, Public Works Agency, Highways Statistics 1947, Table SF-1, United States Government Printing Office, 1949; U.S. Department of Commerce, Bureau of Public Roads, Highway Statistics 1948–1964, Table SF-1, United States Government Printing Office, Washington D.C., 1950–1968; U.S. Department of Transportation, Federal Highway Administration, Bureau of Public Roads, Highway Statistics 1965–1966, Table SF-1, United States Government Printing Office, Washington D.C.

cost escalation over the 21-year life of the program.[16,‡] In 1958 dollars, $10.5 billion was a staggering sum for a public works project in a single state, equivalent to $96.0 billion in 2021. To soften the impact on the reader, the evaluation presented several indexed measures of the total system cost, such as cost per vehicle per year and cost per vehicle-mile traveled: "In terms of cost per mile of travel, the average is well under one-half cent per vehicle-mile. Reducing billions to these more meaningful terms, then, the program cost no longer appears to be fantastic."[17]

But "fantastic" accurately describes the scope and scale of the proposal. At 12,241 miles, the California Freeway System was to be over a quarter the size of the entire Interstate Highway System. It would be the largest public works project ever undertaken by a single agency. To put the enormity of this plan in some perspective, if the Interstate Highway System were proportional in extent to the proposed California Freeway System plan, it would have been 283,935 miles in length, rather than the 48,191 miles ultimately built.

---

‡ The report concluded, however, that subsequent tax increases would likely be required to cover the effects of inflation.

Table 8.1 1959 California Freeway Plan Projections versus Actual Outcomes

	Actual in 1957[a]	Projected for 1980[a]	Projected Change	Actual in 1980	Actual Change
Population	13 M	31 M	+ 139%	23.8 M[b]	+ 83%
Registered vehicles	7 M	17 M	+ 141%	17.6 M[c]	+ 143%
Vehicle miles traveled	65 B	200 B	+ 208%	155.9 B[d]	+ 140%

Sources: [a] California Division of Highways 1958, p. 15; [b] USA Facts, 2022; [c] U.S. Department of Transportation, Federal Highway Administration, Highway Statistics 1980, Table MV-1; [d] U.S. Department of Transportation, Federal Highway Administration, Highway Statistics 1980, Table VM-2.
Notes: Data in millions (M); billions (B).

The plan projected extraordinary growth in population and travel for the state, even more, as it turned out, than the large-scale growth that actually occurred (see Table 8.1).

In spite of its ambition, or perhaps because of it, the plan met with almost universal legislative support. Most of the debate was about whether its growth projections were too conservative. After officials added an additional 171 miles, the plan was adopted almost unanimously by both houses of the state legislature in 1959.[18]

A Torrent of Freeway Construction

In the late 1950s, popular and political support for freeways was at an all-time high.[19] Further, it appeared that the federal-state financial program was sufficient to complete both the national Interstate System and the considerably more ambitious California Freeway System by 1980.[20]

In California, more miles of freeways were opened between 1957 and 1959 than had been built to 1956, and then more miles of freeways were opened between 1960 and 1964 than had been built to 1959.[21] The freeway system in California grew by over 150 miles per year; nationally, freeway growth was over 2,500 miles per year. Freeway development continued to expand in the 1960s, reaching a peak nationally in 1966 and in California in 1967. In those years, 3,606 miles of freeways opened across the nation and 271 miles opened in California. To put this figure in perspective, the number of new freeway miles opened to traffic in the U.S. in 1966 alone was greater than the driving distance from the Canadian border crossing just north of Blaine, Washington, in the far northwest (111 miles north of Seattle) to Key West, Florida, in the far southeast (166 miles south of Miami), a distance of 3,559 miles, which is the longest one-way driving trip one can make in the continental United States.

The Impact of the Trust Fund

As we have seen, an explicit link between motor vehicle tax revenue and highway finance had been the norm at the state level for decades. But the adoption of this system of trust fund finance at the federal level was both new and crucial. The notion that the motor fuel and related taxes were user fees whose proceeds should be expended for the benefits of travelers would prove an ironclad basis of federal highway finance for four decades. As we will see, only in the 1990s would this logic begin to fray, and not until the later years of the following decade would it unravel at the federal level.

But the linkage between motor vehicle revenue and freeway construction engendered problems. One ironically arose from its very success. As Table 8.2 shows, as a means of raising revenue the 1956 legislation was a triumph, generating over $28 billion in its first decade to support over $20 billion in construction expenditures. In nominal terms, federal highway expenditures grew rapidly prior to the 1960s, as shown in Figure 8.5, and steadily thereafter until the 1970s.

Although the fuel tax increases and the Highway Trust Fund put the Interstate System on firm financial footing, they also meant that there was pressure to spend rising revenues as quickly as they came in. According to a former chief engineer at the California Division of Highways: "In the late 1950s we couldn't build freeways fast enough. The money was piling up faster than we could spend it."[22]

This meant that Interstate construction often took place with terrific haste, something which, as we will outline below, was facilitated by the limited planning regulations of the day. The crash building program did not allow Interstate builders time to evaluate their own work and learn from their mistakes, which would have been the case had the system been rolled out more slowly and evolved more incrementally.

The new, laser focus on freeway construction was exacerbated by the 9:1 federal-state matching ratio on Interstate projects. This proved a powerful incentive to states to commit to the Interstate program. In fact, it was an incentive so radical that it dramatically altered the planning calculus of state highway departments.[23] Financing a metropolitan freeway without federal matching dollars was now 900 percent more expensive than building a comparable Interstate freeway. This strongly discouraged states and cities from developing companion facilities to the Interstates, which might have distributed urban traffic rather than concentrating it.[24]

Table 8.2 Vehicle Miles Traveled (VMT), Fuel Consumption, Federal Highway Trust Fund (HTF) Receipts, and Interstate Expenditures (1953–1966)

Year	Vehicle Miles of Travel (M)[a]	Fuel Consumption (M gallons)[b]	HTF Revenues from Federal Motor Fuel Taxes ($M)[c]	Total HTF Revenues ($M)[c]	Interstate Expenditures ($M)[d]
1953	544,433	42,746	n.a.	n.a.	$6
1954	561,963	44,366	n.a.	n.a.	$18
1955	605,646	47,732	n.a.	n.a.	$38
1956	631,161	50,216	n.a.	n.a.	$89
1957	645,004	51,866	$1,326	$1,482	$439
1958	664,653	53,420	$1,608	$2,044	$1,254
1959	700,480	56,334	$1,657	$2,087	$1,838
1960	718,762	57,880	$2,044	$2,536	$1,601
1961	737,421	59,306	$2,361	$2,799	$1,797
1962	766,734	61,697	$2,374	$2,956	$1,983
1963	805,249	64,516	$2,462	$3,293	$2,430
1964	846,298	67,901	$2,643	$3,539	$2,904
1965	887,812	71,104	$2,736	$3,669	$2,815
1966	925,899	74,664	$2,846	$3,924	$3,054
	Totals		$22,057	$28,329	$20,116

Sources: U.S. Department of Transportation, Federal Highway Administration, Highway Statistics Summary to 1995. [a] Table VM-201A; [b] Table MF-221; Table [c]FE-201; [d] Table FA-203.
Note: Figures are in nominal dollars and not adjusted for inflation.

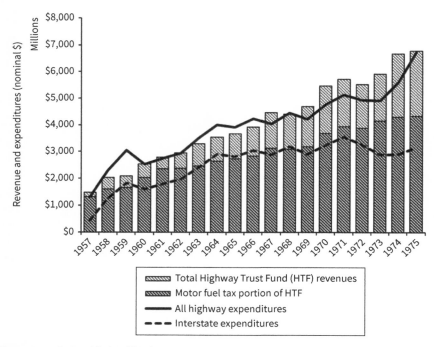

Figure 8.5. Annual federal highway revenues and expenditures, 1957–1975.
Data Source: U.S. Department of Transportation, Federal Highway Administration, Highway Statistics Summary to 1975, Table FA-205, Table FE-201, United States Government Printing Office, Washington, D.C.

Sparse Networks and Elaborate Engineering

The planning and engineering imperatives created by the 1956 Act were further distorted by the mileage limit of the Interstate System. Since the original BPR studies for "a very limited mileage of super-service highways," the Interstates had been planned as a fixed system with a cap on total extent.[25] While this was perhaps a sensible plan for developing an intercity super-highway network, inside of heavily trafficked metropolitan areas strictly limiting Interstate mileage resulted in relatively sparse networks of freeways. This ultimately concentrated traffic into a handful of increasingly congested and polluted corridors.

Further questionable incentives derived from the fact that while Interstate mileage was capped, expenditures were not. Beginning in 1960, all Interstate funds were apportioned to states on the basis of each state's estimated cost to complete the remaining parts of their system. In concert, the 9:1 matching ratio, the fixed system mileage, and the absence of a cost ceiling had signifi-cant effects on the freeways built. Since states paid only one-tenth of the bill, and since the miles of Interstate they could construct were strictly limited, there were strong incentives to design each mile of Interstate highway with as much capacity and as many bells and whistles as possible—more lanes, more elaborate traffic "weaving" sections, and bigger interchanges. This served to further drive up costs and promote the construction of mega-facilities that further encouraged the concentration of very large volumes of urban traffic, thereby increasing the health hazards for those living, working, and playing near them (see Figure 8.6).

In addition to these incentives, the fact that state highway engineers, and not urban planners, designed and built the metropolitan freeways helped lead to ever-more-elaborate engineering and designs. First, the BPR encour-aged states to adopt uniform standards for highways, as safety research at the time showed that consistent signage, lane striping, and roadway geometry all reduced crashes. As we have seen, the safety benefits of divided, limited-access, grade-separated highways had been touted by freeway backers for many years. By the 1950s, the desirability of uniform design standards was a deeply inculcated, and not unreasonable, belief among highway-engineering

Figure 8.6. The Interchange of the 57 and 91 freeways in Orange County, California.
Copyright (2015) California Department of Transportation, all rights reserved.

professionals. Thus consistent design standards were the norm for all Interstate facilities.[26]

The safety arguments for uniform design standards turned out to be well justified, as freeways are the safest roadways per vehicle mile of travel. In 1950, there were about ten deaths per 100 million freeway miles of travel; by 1965, the fatality rate had been cut in half, to five per 100 million; and, by 1980, it was halved again, to about two and a half per 100 million.[27] Freeways' safety advantages over urban arterials and local streets (on a per-vehicle-mile-traveled basis) remain considerable to the present day. These improvements were surely commendable, but they significantly increased the size, cost, and disruption to the city that freeways brought.

Recall that the earliest urban freeway plans had 35- to 45-miles-per-hour design speeds, while later plans upped these design speeds to 45 to 55-miles per hour. In contrast, nearly all freeways on the Interstate System, both rural and urban, were built for high speeds: 50 miles per hour in mountainous terrain, 60 miles per hour in rolling hills, and 70 miles per hour on flat terrain.[28] The need for, or even desirability of, moving vehicles at nearly one-and-a-quarter miles per minute through densely developed urban areas received little scrutiny at the time amidst the widely lauded shift toward design uniformity.

Because these new standards required substantially larger rights-of-way to accommodate sweeping, high-speed curves, wide lanes, and long acceleration and deceleration sections on entry and exit ramps, it often proved more difficult to shoehorn these new freeways into already built-up areas without substantial displacement of residences and businesses. As we will see, these displacements disproportionately affected poor, Black, and other minority communities, ultimately helping to erode popular support for urban freeways.

The 1956 Act stipulated that Interstate highways would have minimum lane widths of 12 feet to accommodate large trucks, road shoulders at least 10 feet wide, and complete grade separation with no intersections or railroad crossings. These already lofty design standards grew only more extravagant over time. In addition to more forgiving road geometries, lane widths were increased to 12.5 feet in order to comfortably host large trucks. In concert, these changes meant that Interstate Highways typically required a minimum of 160-foot-wide rights-of-way in urban areas, roughly twice the width of major boulevards and often more.[29] Further, at the insistence of many city officials, over- and underpasses grew more frequent to minimize the considerable traffic flow disruptions that freeways inflicted on urban street systems. Interchanges also became more elaborate and frequent to move vehicles on and off freeways with minimal disruption and impacts to surface streets.

Table 8.3 Examples of the Upscaling of Freeway Design Standards

Design Feature	1955 Minimum	1985 Minimum	Difference
Left freeway shoulder width	2 feet	10 feet	+ 400%
Right freeway shoulder width	8 feet	30 feet	+ 275%
Urban freeway curve radius	1,100 feet	3,000 feet	+ 173%
Rural freeway curve Radius	2,200 feet	5,000 feet	+ 127%
Left bridge shoulder width	2 feet	5 feet	+ 150%
Right bridge shoulder width	8 feet	10 feet	+25%

Source: Charles Pivetti, Highway System Engineer, California Department of Transportation (authors' interview, 1992).

Table 8.3 shows additional increases in minimum design standards for California Interstates between 1955 and 1985.

Obviously, these ever-more-elaborate designs increased freeways' footprints and made them more invasive. The earlier municipal highway plans would of course have required some displacement of existing homes and businesses. But the scale of property condemnation and building removal was a function of both the sheer mass of the urban freeways and their design speeds, and these increased substantially as the Interstate era wore on. At its peak in the 1960s, federal highway construction involved the razing of over 60,000 housing units and the displacement of up to 200,000 people per year, and in many cities the freeways disproportionately traversed and displaced poor and Black neighborhoods.[30] Once built, the hulking, noisy, and pollution-generating urban freeways would continue to profoundly disrupt adjacent neighborhoods in perpetuity.

Many highway engineers and urban planners were aware of these potential impacts at the time, though their cautionary words were generally lost amidst the widespread enthusiasm for the new Interstate program. None other than legendary highway builder Robert Moses predicted in 1954 that urban Interstates would be "the hardest to locate, the most difficult to clear, the most expensive to acquire and build, and the most controversial."[31] Moses's prescience in this regard is a topic of the next chapter.

The Consequences of Interstates for Rural Areas

The binge of freeway construction began to link U.S. regions, states, and cities to one another via superhighways plied by fast-moving cars and trucks. While the most significant economic benefits of the intercity freeways would be due to the cheaper, faster, and more reliable movement of goods and labor around the country, they also had the effect of creating rural and small-town economic winners and losers, just as the railroads had a century earlier.

While the access advantages of new freeways relative to their social and environmental costs were greater in suburbs than in central cities, they were greater still in rural areas. This is because travel distances were often substantial and travel speeds slow on previous generations of rural highways. Further, relatively few of those residing in the countryside lived directly adjacent to freeways, and those freeways were, in any case, less heavily trafficked and polluting than their urban counterparts. While there was occasional opposition to proposed rural freeway routes through particular farms, or historic or scenic areas, complaints from rural interests were more often that the proposed freeway would pass too far away as opposed to too near. So while the residents of many urban neighborhoods ultimately fought freeways planned through their communities, many of those living in small towns and rural areas welcomed the new freeways and the much higher levels of access they brought.

Freeways between cities were often so successful at attracting high-speed traffic that they economically benefited the small cities and towns that they skirted. But at the same time, they economically harmed places further from them. Many small towns that were left off the Interstate Highway System experienced significant decline, as the economic activities that were dependent upon serving highway travelers (gas stations, motels, diners, and the like) relocated to the newer Interstate interchanges. Chandra and Thompson studied the long-term economic impacts of rural Interstate construction, focusing on differences between counties that hosted the new rural Interstates versus adjacent counties that did not.[32] They found that the Interstates indeed increased economic activity in counties they directly traversed, but that this came at the expense of adjacent counties which lost activity, leaving the net level of economic activity across Interstate and non-Interstate counties largely unchanged. Such findings were echoed by Forkenbrock and Foster in their earlier study of Midwestern highway development,[33] and by Michaels,[34] who found that retail sales increased 7 to 10 percent in rural counties that received freeways versus those that did not.

These impacts can be seen in many parts of the country, including along the iconic U.S. Route 66 in the American Southwest. Running from Chicago to Los Angeles, Route 66 was established in 1926, though AASHTO decertified it in 1985, many years after most of its traffic had diverted to freeways like Interstate 40, which roughly paralleled Route 66 from Albuquerque, New Mexico, west to Barstow, California. Small communities on Route 66 like

Peach Springs, Arizona, which had enjoyed economic prosperity as a gateway to the Grand Canyon during the pre-Interstate era, went into serious decline as a result of being left off the newer highway system.[35]

The idea that the Interstate Highways created rural winners and losers is widely held, and would come as no surprise to the merchants and residents of Peach Springs—or its fictional doppelgänger Radiator Springs, which is the setting for the popular 2006 Disney Pixar film *Cars*. Like its real-world counterpart, Radiator Springs was sent into an economic tailspin when the new Interstate freeway passed it by.

The Decline and Fall of the Freeway Era

While enormously consequential, the freeway-building boom proved to be short-lived. Eighty percent of the current California freeway system, and 81 percent of all freeways nationally, were built between 1956 and 1974.[36] While most of the planned Interstate System was eventually completed, construction from 1974 until 1992 (when the Interstate construction era essentially ended) was both piecemeal and, near the end, glacial. In California, much of the outsized freeway ambitions went unrealized: to the relief of many urbanists, more than half of the 12,241-mile California Freeway System plan remains unbuilt.[37] Thus, the era of freeway mass production ended as abruptly in the 1970s as it began in the 1950s. We turn now to the reasons behind the freeways' rapid fall from grace.

9
The Fall of the Freeway Era

The vast and growing new networks of freeways quickly transformed cities and travel in them. And they soon generated considerable controversy thanks to mounting concerns over the displacement they caused; their disproportionate routing through poor and Black neighborhoods, parks, and waterfronts; the lack of public input on their routing and design; and their outsized footprints. As a result, the extraordinary bipartisan political consensus that had emerged around freeway development proved both short-lived and an exception to the century-old rule of ad hoc U.S. transportation planning and finance.

But even more importantly, the smoothly running highway finance machine that was in high gear in the early 1960s began to sputter just a few years later. Conventional wisdom holds that rising political opposition to urban freeways cut their development short; that's true, but only part of the story. Ultimately, urban freeways were stopped more by the fiscal well running dry than by the public backlash. It is to this story that we now turn.

Steamrolling Freeways through Cities

The grandiose freeway-building ambitions of the 1950s were made possible in part by the limited regulations governing freeway planning and construction in that era. To illustrate, Los Angeles' Harbor Freeway connects the Arroyo Seco Parkway/Pasadena Freeway in downtown Los Angeles with the Port of Los Angeles in San Pedro, 23 miles to the south. South of downtown, the route bisects historically African American neighborhoods, skirting Exposition Park (home to the Los Angeles Memorial Coliseum and many of the region's major museums) and the University of Southern California, which sit just to the west, and Central Avenue a little over a mile to the east, which at the time was widely considered the cultural heart of Black Los Angeles.

Work on the Harbor Freeway began in the 1940s, and the main portion of the freeway opened to traffic in 1952.[1] Its swift completion was in large part due to the brief period between detailed planning and engineering for the project and the start of construction. Building the Harbor Freeway required substantial clearing and relocation of homes and businesses. Once the routing

The Drive for Dollars. Jeffrey R. Brown, Eric A. Morris, and Brian D. Taylor, Oxford University Press.
© Oxford University Press 2023. DOI: 10.1093/oso/9780197601518.003.0009

and design of the freeway were finalized, the Division of Highways prepared and filed a condemnation resolution with the court to allow the state to take private property in the freeway's path and compensate the owners through the powers of eminent domain. With minimal notice and virtually no public debate, the condemnation resolution for the Harbor Freeway was approved by the court *the day after it was filed by the state*. The following day—just two days after the condemnation resolution was initially filed—every piece of private property on what was about to become the Harbor Freeway right-of-way was posted with a 15-day notice to vacate. So less than three weeks after filing the condemnation resolution with the court, the Division of Highways began clearing condemned properties in these primarily African American neighborhoods in preparation for construction.[2]

Freeway Routing and Race

The story of the steamrolling of the Harbor Freeway through Black neighborhoods in Los Angeles is, unfortunately, an oft-repeated one, as the relatively high financial and political cost of urban freeways influenced the timing and location of their construction in socially consequential ways. As chronicled in earlier chapters, urban planners, whether working for municipalities, downtown business associations, states, or the federal government, had for decades viewed highway construction as a tool for urban renewal that could be used to raze and redevelop "slums." It was commonplace to view slum clearance as an effective way to address persistent poverty and inequality; to profess that replacing buildings, particularly decrepit ones, with freeways would help to revitalize poor neighborhoods; and to argue that freeways could and should be used to "delineate" (i.e., segregate) poor and minority neighborhoods from wealthier and whiter districts. Such efforts were justly derided later as "poor removal" and "Negro removal" by critics of urban renewal.[3]

There is today a substantial literature on the heavy prices paid by poor, and in particular Black, communities in the construction of urban freeways, most of which are case studies of freeways being unsuccessfully opposed in Black neighborhoods and/or freeways that were rerouted from White areas to Black ones. The cities that have been profiled include Baltimore, Birmingham, Camden, Detroit, Houston, Kansas City, Los Angeles, Memphis, Miami, Milwaukee, Minneapolis-Saint Paul, Montgomery, Nashville, New Orleans, New York, Oakland, Pittsburgh, and Washington, D.C., among others.[4] In their case study of the construction of Interstate 94, which displaced fully one-seventh of Saint Paul's African American population, Rose and Mohl quote a critic of the highway as saying "very few blacks lived in Minnesota, but the road builders found them."[5]

While most research on racial and economic bias in freeway routing consists of qualitative case studies, Brinkman and Lin presented multi-city statistical evidence.[6] Looking at a sample of 64 U.S. metropolitan areas, they compared the original planned routing of freeways as outlined in the *Yellow Book* (discussed in Chapter 7) with where the freeways were eventually built. Interestingly, the *Yellow Book* routes did not place a disproportionate share of freeways in Black areas when statistically controlling for other factors. But as the freeway era progressed, the highways became more and more likely to be moved to areas with more residents who were Black or who had lower educational levels. Controlling for things like population density, education, and income, by 1966 a census tract that was all-Black in 1950 was more than six percentage points more likely than an all-White neighborhood to have a freeway built in it. Similarly, by 1967 a census tract with a one standard deviation increase in the share of college graduates in 1950 was 3.7 percentage points less likely to receive a freeway.

In addition to both explicit racism and the implicit racism associated with slum clearance, financial and political incentives contributed to racially biased shifts in freeway routing. State highway engineers were, perhaps ironically, not as interested as urban planners were in the opportunity for slum clearance that freeways presented. But they were certainly cognizant of the fact that differences in land values meant that right-of-way acquisition costs were lower in poor and minority areas.

The political costs tended to be lower as well. Residents of low-income, Black, and other disadvantaged neighborhoods more often lacked the resources and connections to mount effective political opposition to locally unpopular routes. All of this meant that freeway builders tended to start first with the "low-hanging fruit" (freeways that required little or no displacement of existing homes or businesses) and then continue along the path of least resistance (proceeding to build in areas where both land costs and political influence were low). This meant cutting routes through lower-income and Black areas, as well as along coastlines, rivers, and rail routes, and through parks and open spaces.[7] Freeway building also migrated to newly developing suburban areas that typically required relatively less displacement of existing homes and businesses.

Routes requiring substantial displacement on more expensive land were not only costly but often entailed coping with well-organized and well-financed opposition, thus posing much greater challenges to the freeway builders.

Difficult routes such as these were more likely to be moved down project priority lists, rerouted, or canceled altogether.[8] All of this suggests that freeway builders' responses to financial and political incentives, in addition to their hubris and explicit or implicit racial animus, combined to locate freeways disproportionately in non-White, poor, industrial, and open-space areas.

By the time the more costly and politically fraught routes were ready for construction, the freeway-building program was losing steam for reasons we will soon discuss. Thus many of the routes through better-heeled areas were shelved, never to be constructed. For example, in contrast to the Harbor Freeway in Los Angeles cited above, the Beverly Hills Freeway, which appeared in local and later state freeway plans for decades, was never built. The omission of this and many other planned freeway routes was ultimately due more to fiscal incentives than organized opposition; this is demonstrated by the fact that many freeways slated to run through areas with high land costs, for example in California, were dropped and never built, even where there was little formal political protest against them.[9]

A Poor Fit from the Start: Freeways' Impacts on Cities

Having largely abandoned context-driven transportation planning that was congruent with social and land-use considerations, state highway departments built freeways that often cut against the urban grain, working against rather than with existing land uses. This meant that some neighborhoods were burdened with large, noisy, polluting facilities that often divided and always altered them.[10] This was particularly the case for inner-city areas, since, in addition to the factors just outlined, the ring-radial urban freeway networks of the *Yellow Book* had the effect of increasing the density of freeways, and their concomitant disruption, where the radial routes converged on the city center.

Further, while early freeway plans assumed that radial networks would save CBDs by funneling traffic into them, the radial routes proved to be equally effective (if not more so) at funneling people *out* of CBDs. This contributed importantly to suburban sprawl. Baum-Snow found that each highway running through a city center was associated with an 18 percent center city population decline;[11] thus, the Interstates may be responsible for roughly one-third of the decline in the share of the urban population living in central cities between 1950 and 1990 (though it should be noted that some, such as Cox, Gordon, and Redfearn,[12] contested this conclusion). Brinkman and Lin argued that freeways provide both access benefits (largely in the form of faster travel) and offsetting disamenities, such as consuming land and impeding cross-street traffic.[13] However, since central cities had relatively high accessibility by foot and public transit even before the arrival of the freeways, the accessibility benefits associated with new freeways there were proportionately smaller; further, the hoped-for congestion-reduction benefits largely failed to materialize in the face of rapidly increasing vehicle travel. This meant that, in central areas, access benefits were often outweighed by the disamenities of freeways. In contrast, for outlying areas the accessibility benefits were relatively large and mostly outweighed the disamenities. This contributed to central neighborhoods seeing large declines in population and income in the freeway era, particularly in places very close to freeways. At the same time, outlying suburban and exurban areas saw the mirror image, with net population growth that was particularly high in places nearest the freeways. Thus, though there have been many factors behind American suburbanization, such as rising incomes, White flight, cultural preferences for more space and bucolic living, national housing policies favoring home ownership and large property lots, high levels of auto ownership, and high suburban amenity levels (such as better parks and schools), there is almost certainly truth to the assertion that freeways accelerated suburban sprawl. And despite some heartening regeneration of many U.S. central cities since the 1990s, sprawling growth at the metropolitan fringe remains the dominant theme of U.S. urbanization,[14] a pattern that appeared to intensify during the COVID-19 pandemic.

The sparse networks of high-capacity, high-speed freeways that were ultimately built led to heavy concentrations of development and traffic near their interchanges. In addition, the abandonment of plans for multimodal highways integrated with public transit privileged private vehicles over all other means of travel. This often resulted in suburban development that could best be characterized as "dumb sprawl," which entails suburban office and commercial centers built at densities too high to be effectively served exclusively by automobiles, but too low to be effectively served by public transit, biking, or walking (see Figure 9.1). In a surprise that Interstate planners did not anticipate, these concentrations of suburban development arose along the circumferential ring routes that were intended to carry intercity traffic *around* center cities.[15] Often, and ironically, this development generated chronic traffic congestion on routes specifically designed to bypass city traffic.

Thus serious equity and environmental issues that reverberate to the present day were raised by the combined effects of (1) the aim of planners to use urban freeways for "slum clearance" of poor, Black, and other disadvantaged neighborhoods; (2) financial and political incentives that made it cheaper and easier to build freeways along the path of least resistance (such

Figure 9.1. Tysons Corner outside of Washington, D.C. (2010).
Photo by La Citta Vita. https://creativecommons.org/licenses/by-sa/2.0/legalcode

as through parks, along waterfronts and rail lines, and through low-income, minority neighborhoods); (3) ring-radial networks that concentrated freeway building near center cities, accelerating White flight and suburban expansion; and (4) the oversized footprint of, and concentration of traffic on, urban freeways.[16]

The Rise of Freeway Revolts

Beginning in the 1960s, the broad consensus of support that freeways enjoyed in the 1950s began to evaporate, as popular opposition to the social and economic displacement that accompanied freeway construction culminated in a series of "freeway revolts." One of the earliest grassroots revolts against a slated freeway project took place in San Francisco in the late 1950s.[17] Protests in other cities quickly followed.[18] Organized opposition to freeway projects occurred in Atlanta, Baltimore, Boston, Charleston, Cleveland, Detroit, Honolulu, Indianapolis, Los Angeles, Memphis, Nashville, Newark, New Orleans, New York, Philadelphia, Pittsburgh, Portland, Reno, Richmond, San Antonio, Seattle, and Washington, D.C., among other places.[19]

The reasons behind these revolts varied. To be sure, many opponents of metropolitan freeway projects were motivated by self-interest, as most who fought freeways in their own communities doubtless did not swear off driving on freeways that bisected others' communities. But self-interest does not necessarily imply shortsightedness, and popular and political discomfort with urban freeway displacement only grew with time.

The protests were often associated with larger 1960s counterculture movements.* Some freeway revolts were associated with the rising environmental movement, whose leaders were mostly White and often relatively well-educated and affluent. Their efforts frequently centered on opposing proposals for freeways along waterfronts or through parklands. Other freeway revolts, often associated with civil rights protests and the Black empowerment movement, opposed construction through minority neighborhoods. These efforts typically garnered less mainstream attention and were often less successful.[20] Several authors have attributed racial uprisings in the 1960s at least in part to urban freeway construction.[21] Biles, Mohl, and Rose concluded that urban freeways "widened and accentuated the split between a suburban white middle class and an urban black working class. They also made living in walled-off downtown communities much more difficult."[22] The social and environmental movements behind the freeway revolts were sometimes in league but sometimes at odds, such as when debates took place over whether a freeway would be routed through a park *or* a Black neighborhood.[23]

Mohl compared and contrasted two freeway revolts in Tennessee, one successful and one not.[24] The successful case was the opposition to the routing of Interstate 40 through Overton Park in midtown Memphis; the second, unsuccessful effort opposed the construction of the same Interstate 40 through the Black neighborhood of North Nashville, 200 miles to the east. In Memphis, sustained community opposition for 25 years ultimately led to a U.S. Supreme Court decision establishing judicial review over freeway routing; this forced the abandonment of the routing proposed by the state highway department in favor of a circumferential bypass route. In Nashville, by contrast, city and state highway officials shifted the route north to pass through the mostly Black area. This shift eventually

[demolished] more than 620 black homes, twenty-seven apartment houses, and six black churches. It dead-ended fifty local streets, disrupted traffic flow, and brought noise and air pollution to the community. It separated children from their playgrounds and schools, parishioners from their churches, and businesses

---

* On the other hand, Avila (2014) saw them as more protracted, isolated struggles not necessarily linked to larger social movements.

2

from their customers. Three key black community institutions—Fisk University, Meharry Medical College, and Tennessee A. & I. University (later Tennessee State University)—were walled off from each other and from the larger black community by the six-lane expressway and its access roads.[25]

In Nashville, the anti-freeway I-40 Steering Committee consisted of a coalition of Black professionals opposed to the new freeway. They were later than their Memphis counterparts to commence their opposition to the proposed I-40 routing, in part because the state highway department had, by all indications, actively worked to keep its revised routing plans under wraps. The committee, with the support of the NAACP Legal Defense and Education Fund, pursued legal action alleging racial discrimination in the routing decision-making, particularly due to a lack of public notice of the routing plans. The plaintiffs lost in Tennessee court, and again on an appeal to the U.S. Circuit Court of Appeals, in part because state officials had such a poor public notice and participation record in other places as well.[26] In contrast to the Memphis case, the Supreme Court declined in 1967 to hear a further appeal. It was several more years before claims of discriminatory racial impacts in freeway routing decisions led to changes in federal highway policy.[27]

As the revolts spread, the objectives of freeway opponents diversified to protect many cultural assets—parks and open space, historic areas, churches, schools, and neighborhoods—from freeway bulldozers. While the earliest grassroots revolts attracted a great deal of media attention, most were ultimately unsuccessful in stopping freeway construction, particularly in poor and minority neighborhoods. Over time, however, opposition to particular urban freeway segments increasingly attracted the support of local elected officials, and the number of successful construction delays and route deletions began to mount. New York Senator Daniel Patrick Moynihan became a vocal and widely recognized critic of urban freeways, and several influential urban writers—most notably Lewis Mumford, Jane Jacobs, and Herbert Gans—joined the fray.[28] By the early 1970s, states around the U.S. were dropping controversial route segments from their freeway plans.

The Tank Runs Dry: Finance and the End of the Freeway Era

However, it is unlikely that the deletion of particularly unpopular projects—such as the Lower Manhattan Expressway in New York, the Vieux Carré Expressway in New Orleans, or the Beverly Hills Freeway in Los Angeles—by themselves significantly reduced the total freeway mileage eventually constructed. Instead, we argue that the system was doomed primarily due to the collapse of a finance system that only a few years before had been a phenomenal money-spinner.

Evidence for the contention that money and not individual freeway revolts doomed Interstate construction comes from the fact that, in many places, locally popular freeway routes with little political opposition were never built anyway, due not to public protest but simply to a lack of funding. For example, while several controversial freeway segments were deleted from the *California Freeway System* plan between 1959 and 1975, only 7 percent of the unconstructed freeway routes that remained in the plan in 1975 were actually built by 1990, suggesting that lagging revenues and rising costs, more than protests against individual proposed highways, were most directly responsible for the decline in urban freeway construction.[29]

Further, new freeway construction began to plummet in the mid-1960s, before the freeway revolt movement was in full swing. As Figure 9.2 shows, in California freeway construction peaked in 1967, but then began to fall

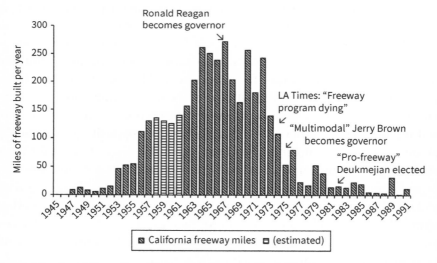

Figure 9.2. Centerline miles of freeway constructed in California, 1945-1991.

Data Sources: Zettel, Richard, and Paul Shuldiner (1950). "Freeway Location Conflicts in California," Institute of Transportation and Traffic Engineering, University of California, Berkeley, p. 13; California Department of Public Works (1963 to 1973). "Statistical Reports of the Department of Public Works Pertaining to the Division of Highways," Table "State Highway Mileage by Type." Annual Report, Business and Transportation Agency. Sacramento: California Department of Public Works; California Department of Transportation (1974 to 1983). "State Highway Program: Financial Statements and Statistical Reports," Table "State Highway Mileage by Type." Caltrans. Sacramento: California Department of Transportation; California Department of Transportation (1983 to 1991). "Annual Financial Statement and Miscellaneous Statistical Reports," Table "State Highway Mileage by Type." Caltrans. Sacramento: California Department of Transportation.

Note: Mileage from 1958–1961 estimated.

precipitously under ostensibly pro-freeway Governor Ronald Reagan. Indeed, by the time anti-freeway crusader Jerry Brown became governor (for his first term) in 1975, the freeway program had already been in steep decline for years. After Brown, the election of avowedly pro-freeway Republican George Deukmejian in 1982 had virtually no effect on freeway construction, as the fiscal cupboard was by that time nearly bare.

We argue there were two more consequential impacts of the freeway revolts than the deletion or rerouting of particular segments. The first was their contribution to bringing about new environmental review and public participation standards for transportation planning. The second was their contribution, in concert with general enmity to taxes and waxing support for funding mass transit, to depressing popular support for the tax increases needed to keep freeway finance on course.

The Rising Costs of Freeway Development

A principal cause of declining freeway development was the dramatic rise in construction and maintenance costs during the 1960s, 1970s, and 1980s. Between 1960 and 1990, freeway development costs nationwide grew faster than the general rate of inflation, particularly in urban areas. The rapid cost escalation had four principal causes: (1) increasing construction and maintenance unit costs; (2) the significant upscaling of freeway designs; (3) rising urban land values that significantly increased right-of-way costs; and (4) new environmental and community planning regulations.

Increasing Construction and Maintenance Costs

The Federal Highway Administration has compiled and published indices of highway construction, maintenance, and operation costs intermittently for over 50 years. Indices for construction, and for maintenance and operations, are based on average contractor bid prices for a typical highway project.[30] These indices reflect unit cost changes in construction, maintenance, and operating costs only; they do not reflect per-mile cost increases due to facility upscaling, increased right-of way costs, increased project planning and engineering costs, or increased environmental mitigation costs, all of which have contributed to rising freeway costs as well. But even for the restricted set of costs that these indices do monitor, they reveal a significant escalation in prices, particularly in the 1970s and 1980s.

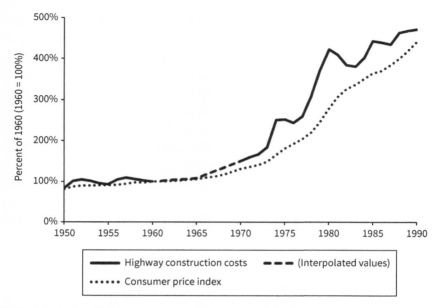

Figure 9.3. Indexed highway construction costs and inflation, 1950–1990.

Data Source: U.S. Department of Commerce, Bureau of Public Roads, Highway Statistics, 1960, Table PT-1, United States Government Printing Office, Washington, D.C., 1962; U.S. Department of Transportation, Federal Highway Administration, Highway Statistics, 2003. Table PT-1, https://www.fhwa.dot.gov/policyinformation/statistics.cfm; U.S. Department of Transportation, Federal Highway Administration, National Highway Construction Cost Index (NHCCI) 2.0, 2019, https://www.fhwa.dot.gov/policy/otps/nhcci/pt1.cfm; U.S. Bureau of Labor Statistics, Consumer Price Index. https://www.bls.gov/cpi/.

Note: Values from 1961–1964 and 1966–1969 are interpolated to account for missing data.

Figure 9.3 shows that highway construction unit costs were essentially flat during the 1950s. These largely inflation-free cost trends were what informed the financial planning for freeways in the 1950s and led analysts to assume little or no escalation in construction costs between 1959 and 1980.[31] However, between 1960 and 1990, highway construction unit costs rose significantly, often faster than the general rate of inflation as measured by the U.S. Consumer Price Index. Between 1975 and 1980, the escalation in unit costs was especially dramatic.

The reasons for the rapid increase in highway construction unit costs were largely the same as for the increases in all construction costs during this era: (1) high levels of demand for construction services; (2) strong demand for construction materials and equipment; and (3) high levels of industry unionization contributing to rapidly climbing compensation rates. Yet the sharp growth of construction unit costs was only part of the picture: for example, only 26 percent of the increase in California freeway construction costs during the 1960s was due to increasing construction costs generally.[32] The remainder was due to specific characteristics of freeways and their rights-of-way, which we will discuss shortly.

There was a similar, albeit less volatile, increase in highway maintenance and operating costs between 1960 and 1990.[33] National maintenance and operating costs rose faster than the general rate of inflation, especially during the late 1970s and early 1980s. In fact, throughout the 1980s, maintenance and operating costs increased faster than highway construction costs. These increases are particularly important because maintenance costs have constituted a growing proportion of total highway costs over time, as the focus of the highway program shifted from building new freeways to maintaining existing ones. And as freeways built in the 1940s, 1950s, and 1960s reached the ends of their design lives, freeway maintenance increasingly entailed reconstructing road beds and bridges in addition to resurfacing pavements and restriping lanes.[34]

Due in large part to inflation, nominal growth in highway spending masked the fact that real spending peaked in 1971 and then began declining as the highway program gradually lost steam. Viewed in terms of spending per vehicle-mile of travel, disbursements started declining even earlier, steadily dropping after 1961.[35]

The Upscaling of Freeway Designs

As we have noted, highway engineers created increasingly large and elaborate freeways as the freeway-building era wore on. While there are no comprehensive nationwide data on the role of design upscaling on rising freeway construction costs, a 1970 California study found that nearly half (46%) of increased freeway development costs in California during the 1960s were due to the increasing scale and complexity of freeways.[36]

Much of this was the result of the lack of per-mile cost controls on an Interstate system fixed in mileage but not in cost. It also resulted from the lobbying of local officials who regularly pressured state highway department engineers to increase the number of interchanges in urban areas in order to better integrate freeways with local street systems and to distribute surface street traffic more evenly. Freeway engineers, concerned that frequent traffic weaving on freeways caused by numerous on- and off-ramps would both compromise safety and impede traffic flows, tended to resist such calls, but not always successfully. Relatedly, urban officials also tended to push for more freeway over- and under-crossings to allow a freer flow of surface street traffic across freeway rights-of-way. State highway engineers typically, albeit reluctantly, obliged, which substantially increased project costs as well.[37]

The slowing pace of new freeway development after the mid-1960s further encouraged the upscaling of freeway designs. As it became apparent that ambitious urban freeway plans might never be completed, state highway officials attempted to accommodate growing traffic demand by designing more and more capacity into the declining number of new routes being built. While the total (centerline) miles of Interstate freeways changed little between 1980 and 2015, the number of lane miles (six lanes on a one-mile stretch of freeway is six lane miles) more than doubled.[38] But more lanes, more elaborate interchanges, and separated weaving sections all increased right-of-way requirements, and, of course, costs.[39]

Rising Right-of-Way Costs

From the outset, the highway problem in cities was largely a right-of-way problem. Virtually every early urban traffic study and transportation plan addressed the difficulty and expense of constructing or expanding urban roads in congested areas.[40] As early as 1932, studies showed that up to 94 percent of the cost of street widening was due to the purchase of additional right-of-way.[41]

Part of the problem is that urban land is inherently valuable, but another problem is that freeways, particularly on the suburban fringe, make adjacent land more accessible. This encourages development, which in turn attracts traffic, which then raises land values, and so on. Eventually, the adjacent development reaches a point where the freeway becomes chronically congested. Widening freeways to accommodate more demand, however, has now become extremely expensive because the adjacent right-of-way is occupied by development, requiring expensive, time-consuming, and often hotly contested displacement of homes and businesses. Freeways, in other words, became victims of their own success, particularly in suburban and exurban areas.

For this reason, as a cost-containment strategy, early metropolitan freeway plans repeatedly stressed the importance of advanced right-of-way acquisition to minimize the amount of subsequent displacement required.[42] But highway planners and engineers soon discovered that even in not-yet-built urban-adjacent areas, the mere existence of freeway *plans* contributed to rising land values and, hence, right-of-way costs.

In an earlier era of road finance, this was less of a problem. Recall that in the first decades of the twentieth century, metropolitan highways and arterials were financed largely with property taxes and special assessments. Thus, funds for highway construction were augmented when property values rose. But with the transition to fuel taxes and other vehicle-user fees, highway finance became divorced from adjacent land values. When freeways increased land values, the additional property tax receipts typically went into local or county coffers to be used for other purposes.

High right-of-way costs were primarily a problem in urban, suburban, and urban-adjacent areas, where they frequently represented over half of total project costs. However, in rural areas, right-of-way costs were normally less than 10 percent.[43] Thus, rising right-of-way costs hit urbanized states particularly hard. Because more substantial portions of their highway systems were located in cities, these states had to devote much larger shares of their freeway budgets to right-of-way acquisition. Figure 9.4 shows that in the relatively urban states of California and New Jersey, right-of-way expenditures mostly exceeded the national average from 1950 through 1990, sometimes substantially.[†] In one year in California, 1974, fully 69 percent of state right-of-way acquisition expenditures were in the Los Angeles, San Diego, and San Francisco metropolitan areas—areas that collectively account for about 5 percent of the state's land area.[44]

Despite concerted efforts to secure rights-of-way in advance of construction, these costs grew much faster than revenues. A study of rising freeway construction costs in California during the 1960s found that right-of-way unit costs were increasing 7 percent per annum statewide, and even faster in urban areas. Fully 26 percent of all freeway development cost increases in California were due to rising right-of-way costs,[45] and fragmentary evidence suggests similar experiences in metropolitan areas around the U.S.

Figure 9.4 also shows that freeway right-of-way expenditures peaked nationally between 1960 and 1965, when better than $1 out of every $5 of freeway costs went to right-of-way acquisition, while right-of-way expenses were closer to $1 in $10 after 1975. Does this suggest that acquiring land for freeway rights-of-way became less expensive over time? Quite the opposite, in fact. As funds began to run short in the late 1960s, state highway officials chose to spend them to construct freeways on rights-of-way already in hand, and cut back on purchasing additional land for planned freeways that might never be built. In other words, the first casualty in response to rising costs and tightening budgets was advance right-of-way acquisition, as state highway

[†] The greater variability of right-of-way expenditures in New Jersey reflects the fact that individual projects have greater effect on statewide averages in smaller states than in larger ones like California.

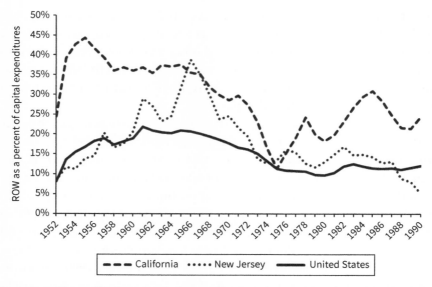

Figure 9.4. Share of highway capital expenditures spent on right-of-way (ROW) acquisition, 1952–1990.

Data Sources: U.S. Department of Commerce, Bureau of Public Roads, Highway Statistics 1952–1959, Supplement 1 to Table SF-4, United States Government Printing Office, Washington D.C., 1954–1961; U.S. Department of Transportation, Federal Highway Administration, Highway Statistics 1960–1964, Table SF-4C, United States Government Printing Office, Washington, D.C., 1962–1966; U.S. Department of Transportation, Federal Highway Administration, Highway Statistics 1965–1991, Table SF-4C, United States Government Printing Office, Washington, D.C.

departments around the U.S. abandoned these cost-containment strategies. This ensured that ambitious plans for many urban freeway networks would never be fully realized.

New Environmental and Community-Participation Regulations

The haste with which the urban Interstates were planned and built contributed to an environmental and planning process backlash that helped to revolutionize urban planning in the U.S. New development projects (not just transportation facilities, but other land uses as well) became far more procedurally complex, participatory, context-sensitive, aligned with some kinds of stakeholder concerns and input, and, arguably, greener. Many of these shifts were in direct response to the damage and displacement caused by urban freeway construction; collectively, they made it far more difficult to construct new transportation infrastructure.

The Federal Highway Act of 1958 required state highway departments to hold public hearings for Interstate Highway projects. In 1962, Congress authorized the use of Interstate funds to assist with the relocation of families (including renters) and businesses affected by Interstate highway construction, and began requiring multimodal (autos, public transit, etc.) transportation planning in urban areas. In 1964, the Bureau of Public Roads issued a directive requiring the evaluation of 20 social, economic, and environmental factors for all reasonable alternative highway alignments. In 1965, Congress allowed the use of Interstate funds for scenic enhancements, as well as spot safety improvements. In 1966, legislation required better soil-erosion control in Interstate construction, as well as the preservation of parklands. In 1968, legislation allowed the use of Interstate funding for park-and-ride facilities, and increased funding for relocation assistance and replacement housing construction as well. In 1970, legislation was passed permitting the use of federal highway funds for the construction of "last resort housing" for those displaced by highway construction who were unable to find suitable replacement housing.‡ In addition, funds could now be used for bus lanes and highway-adjacent transit stops and stations, as well as for highway traffic-control devices (like freeway ramp meters). And in 1973, Congress began permitting the substitution of expenditures on public transit projects instead of certain urban Interstate routes. In concert, these various new requirements and expansions of the scope of Interstate projects demanded more spending. Along with the general upscaling of Interstate highway design standards, such expanded planning procedures, mitigation measures, and "mission creep" were estimated to more than double the cost to complete the Interstate system.[46]

To give an example of this dramatic transformation, consider Los Angeles' east-west Century Freeway, which bisects the Harbor Freeway (discussed above) eight miles south of downtown L.A. (see Figure 9.5). In stark contrast with the clearing of land to construct the Harbor Freeway, which took place at lightning speed and with virtually no public input, acquiring and clearing the land for the Century Freeway took nearly 20 years. Land acquisition was nearly finished in 1972 when a coalition of area residents, environmentalists, and civil rights organizations filed suit against the state for failing to comply with environmental and relocation laws and regulations, many of which had recently been enacted.[47] After nearly ten years of litigation, the parties agreed to a consent decree in 1981 whereby Caltrans (the new, more multimodal name

---

‡ In the fiscal year 1975 alone, the Federal-Aid highway program relocated 21,162 people from 8,605 dwelling units; 44 percent were homeowners, 56 percent were tenants, and 24 percent were people of color. In addition, 2,186 businesses, 116 farms, and 103 nonprofit organizations were displaced and relocated as well (USDOT, FHWA 1977).

Figure 9.5. The Harbor Freeway and Century Freeway interchange, Los Angeles (2009).
Credit: Photo by Remi Jouan. https://en.wikipedia.org/wiki/Judge_Harry_Pregerson_Interchange#/
media/File:Los_Angeles_-_Echangeur_autoroute_110_105.JPG License: https://creativecommons.
org/licenses/by-sa/3.0/legalcode.

for the California Division of Highways) would, among many other things, implement a $300 million ($902 million in 2021$) program to rebuild and/ or relocate over half of the residential dwellings cleared for freeway construction, and to provide displaced residents with 3,700 homes and apartments.[48] Such tenant relocation assistance went well beyond what was then required by state eminent domain law, but it was especially important in areas—like the Century Freeway corridor—where large numbers of lower-income renters, who were disproportionately Black and Hispanic, were displaced, but only their landlords received any compensation for property taken.

The consent decree resulted in another major source of cost escalation. In response to pressure from public transit advocates, Caltrans agreed to allow the construction of a transit line down the Century Freeway median.[49,§] While somewhat in keeping with the earlier "transit in highway medians" plans of the 1940s, the light rail line eventually built was both highly costly ($718 million, about $1.2 billion in 2021$) and disappointing in terms of patronage (with an average of just 30,839 weekday riders in 2018).[50] The prolonged litigation surrounding the Century Freeway, including the delays, legal costs,

§ As chronicled by Garrett (2006, 508–509), the transit portion of the consent decree evolved from a busway to even-more-expensive light rail.

additional relocation expenses, and added design requirements, are estimated to have increased the project cost nearly fivefold, from $502 million in 1977 to $2.5 billion in 1993;[51] this increase was equivalent to rising from $2.2 billion to $4.59 billion in 2021$. In terms of inflation-adjusted construction cost per centerline mile, the cost more than doubled from $116 million per mile to $244 million per mile in 2021$. Mandates like relocation assistance and sound walls did add to project costs and helped to mitigate the impact of the new freeway on the many Black and Hispanic residents displaced by, or still adjacent to, the new freeway. But most of the cost escalation attributable to the new environmental requirements adopted during the 1970s was actually due to construction delays. Increasingly extensive environmental documentation and approval processes, plus the extremely lengthy litigation, considerably increased the time required to plan, design, and build the new freeway. These delays proved especially costly during a period of high inflation.[52] Similar stories of cost escalation amidst protracted controversies over urban freeway development were told many times over in metropolitan areas around the nation.

A recent study of infrastructure costs by Brooks and Liscow concluded that the most significant contributor to rising Interstate construction costs was the increase in "citizen voice," which they define as increased citizen participation in decision-making, as well as the associated rise in environmental mitigation expenditures.[53] They argued that these contributed to both mitigation costs and the upscaling of freeway designs.

A Cost-Revenue Squeeze

As a result of all of these factors, it cost about *three times as much* to construct a mile of highway in the 1980s than in the early 1960s, even after controlling for inflation.[54] During the 1960s, per-mile capital outlays for state-administered highways** nationwide increased an average of 11.6 percent per year, which was 4.8 times the average annual inflation rate of 2.4 percent.[55] In the 1970s, partly because of the much higher rates of inflation, costs rose even faster. Freeway construction expenditures went from $263,000 per mile in 1970 ($1.82 million/mile in 2021$) to $564,000 in 1977 ($2.52 million/mile

---

** These data are for state administered highways broadly, and not just freeways. These include state primary highways, state secondary highways (including urban extensions), and county roads under state jurisdiction.

in 2021$); thus, the average annual increase of 16.3 percent was well ahead of the average 1970s inflation rate of 8.7 percent.[56]

Even after inflation began to ease in the 1980s, freeway costs, particularly in urban areas, stayed high. Figure 9.6 displays separately (due to data incompatibility) the trend of capital expenditures per new mile of urban Interstate freeway. They show that—controlling for the effects of inflation—per-mile urban freeway capital expenditures doubled between 1960 and 1975, and doubled again between 1980 and 2010. In addition to the numerous cost-escalation factors discussed above, these extraordinary cost increases were due to the fact that the very few urban freeway miles added since the 1970s were often expensive projects to close gaps or rebuild key links in existing metropolitan freeway networks.[57]

While Costs Rise, Revenues Stagnate

The increasing costs of freeway development would not necessarily have been a problem for freeway builders if revenues had grown proportionally. But revenues for urban freeway development lagged behind increasing costs after the mid-1960s for three principal reasons: (1) fuel taxes are generally not indexed to rising costs; (2) more urbanized states like California and Texas did not receive back highway funding commensurate with the federal highway tax revenues they generated; and (3) increasing vehicle fuel efficiency caused fuel tax revenues to lag behind the growth in vehicle travel.

Fuel Tax Rates Rarely Rise with Inflation

Most taxes, such as those on income, property, and sales, generate increasing revenues during periods of high inflation. This is not the case, however, for most fuel excise taxes because revenues increase or decrease only with the volume of fuel sold and not its price. So, to keep pace with rising costs and/or increasing fuel efficiency, per-gallon fuel tax rates must be increased periodically. Between 1951 and 1961, federal highway user fees were increased four separate times, including three increases to the federal motor fuel taxes in 1951, 1956, and 1959. All of these increases were enacted during times of relatively low inflation. After 1959, however, the federal motor fuel taxes would not change for nearly a quarter of a century, until the taxes on both gasoline and diesel fuel were finally increased by a nickel by Congress and President Reagan in 1983.[58]

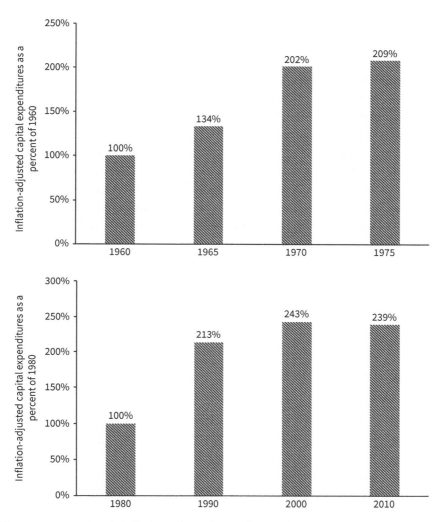

Figure 9.6. Increases in inflation-adjusted capital expenditures per mile of completed urban freeway, 1960–2010.

Source: U.S. Department of Commerce, Bureau of Public Roads, Highway Statistics, 1960–1964, Table INT-11; Table SF-11, United States Government Printing Office, Washington D.C.,1962–1966; U.S. Department of Transportation, Federal Highway Administration, Highway Statistics, 1965–1979, Table INT-11, Table SF-11, United States Government Printing Office, Washington, D.C.; U.S. Department of Transportation, Federal Highway Administration, Highway Statistics 1980–2010, Table HM-20; Table SF-12, United States Government Printing Office, Washington, D.C.

Notes: Freeway mileage is based on a four-year running average (e.g., 1960–1964) calculated for Urban Interstates, divided highways, four or more lanes, with full access-control. Capital outlays by State Highway Departments calculated for all Urban Interstates. These two periods are shown in separate figures because the manner by which the data were collected and reported by the U.S. Federal Highway Administration changed beginning in 1980. In addition, the sample year data presented in these two figures mask considerable year-to-year variation in per-mile expenditures.

Similarly, in most states periodic increases in motor fuel tax rates were the norm from the initiation of the first state fuel taxes in 1919 through the early 1960s. But, as with the federal fuel taxes, the appetite for increased highway-user fees at the state level withered beginning in the 1960s. Between 1930 and 1959, the inflation-adjusted average state motor fuels tax per gallon remained relatively constant at about $0.53 per gallon in 2021$. By comparison, from 1960 to 1989, the average state motor fuel tax rate *declined* by 43.9 percent in real terms, from $0.52 per gallon to an average of $0.30 per gallon in 2021$.

The result of having very few fuel tax rate increases in an era of rapidly increasing costs is shown in Figure 9.7, which compares the growth in highway construction costs shown in Figure 9.3 with the much slower growth of average state and federal fuel tax levies over the same period. This resulted in a widening cost/revenue gap.

This figure shows how rapid inflation in the 1970s caused the per-gallon tax to essentially fail as a reliable means for financing highways. Without

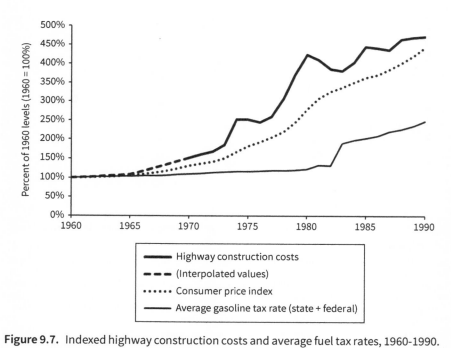

Figure 9.7. Indexed highway construction costs and average fuel tax rates, 1960-1990.

Data Sources: U.S. Department of Transportation, Federal Highway Administration, Highway Statistics, Summary to 1985, Summary to 1995; 2000, Table MF-205; Highway Statistics 2019, Table FE-101A; Highway Statistics, 1992, Table PT-1; United States Government Printing Office, Washington, D.C. https://www.fhwa.dot.gov/policyinformation/statistics.cfm; U.S. Department of Transportation, Federal Highway Administration, National Highway Construction Cost Index 2.0, 2019, Table PT-1, October 2019. https://www.fhwa.dot.gov/policy/otps/nhcci/pt1.cfm.

Note: Construction costs from 1961–1964 and 1966–1969 are interpolated.

some mechanism to index revenues to rising costs—such as a special sales tax on fuel or a per-gallon tax rate indexed to consumer or highway construction prices—it would have taken regular, substantial, and politically painful increases in fuel taxes throughout the 1970s and beyond to maintain the 1960s pace of new freeway construction. This did not happen.

Bias of the Federal Highway Program in Favor of Rural States

Throughout the twentieth century, federal motor vehicle taxes were collected disproportionally in urban areas but were expended disproportionally in rural areas. Throughout the Interstate era, relatively urbanized states with high levels of vehicle use—such as California and Texas—contributed considerably more in federal highway user revenues than they received in federal highway appropriations. Texas was by far the largest "donor" state to the federal highway program; by 2000, the state had received about $0.84 in federal highway appropriations for every $1.00 in federal highway taxes paid by the state's highway users, a differential that amounted to $5.4 billion (equivalent to $8.4 billion in 2021$).[59] On the other hand, largely rural "donee" states like Alaska and Montana received far more in federal highway funds than the federal fuel taxes their residents paid. Between the inception of the Highway Trust Fund in 1956 and the de facto end of the Interstate era in 1991, drivers in Montana paid $1.1 billion ($2.2 billion in 2021$) into the fund, while the state received $2.8 billion ($5.4 billion in 2021$) in appropriations over the same period.[60] This urban-state-to-rural-state bias in the program meant that more urban states, which typically had more expensive freeways to build, had less federal money to build them than if funds had been returned in a more geographically uniform way. This donor/donee question became a major issue in post-Interstate federal legislation, as we discuss in the next chapter.

The Vehicle Travel/Fuel Use Gap

Vehicle travel in the U.S. increased sixfold over the last half of the twentieth century, due both to population growth and per capita increases in motor vehicle ownership and use. Figure 9.8 shows total vehicle travel and vehicle travel per capita from 1945 to 1990, indexed to 1945. It demonstrates that, with the exception of two fuel supply shocks during the 1970s, personal

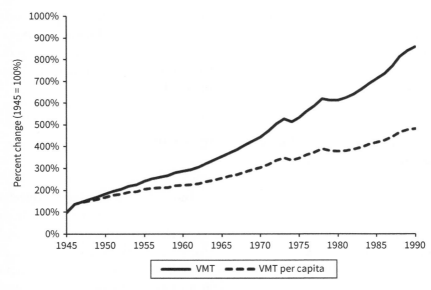

Figure 9.8. Percentage growth in U.S. annual vehicle miles traveled (VMT), total and per capita, 1945–1990.

Data sources: U.S. Department of Transportation, Federal Highway Administration, Highway Statistics Summary to 1995, Table VM-201, U.S. Government Printing Office, Washington D.C.; U.S. Census, 2021. National Intercensal Tables, Historical National Population Estimates: July 1, 1900, to July 1, 1999.

and commercial vehicle travel—overall and per capita—increased year over year.

But the rising trend in vehicle travel diverged sharply from the trends in motor fuel consumption over the same period. During the 1950s, when state and federal Interstate financing commenced, motor fuel consumption increased nationally at an annual rate of just under 5 percent.[61] But in 1973, the first global oil shock, caused by the Yom Kippur War in the Middle East, occurred. This spurred fuel shortages and curbed vehicle travel. Six years later, in 1979, the Iranian Revolution resulted in a second global oil shock, again causing fuel shortages and reduced vehicle travel. These two reductions in driving and fuel consumption of course caused motor fuel tax revenues to fall as well.

More importantly, the longer-term effects of the two 1970s fuel shortages were to spur interest in vehicle fuel efficiency, which had in any event been rising thanks to the national environmental movement emerging beginning in the 1960s. The first major policy push on vehicle fuel efficiency came with the Energy Policy and Conservation Act of 1975, which required yearly increases in the fuel efficiency of each automobile company's fleet of new passenger cars sold. These were regulated by the Corporate Average Fuel Efficiency (CAFE) Standards, which mandated an increase from 14.2 miles per gallon in 1974 to

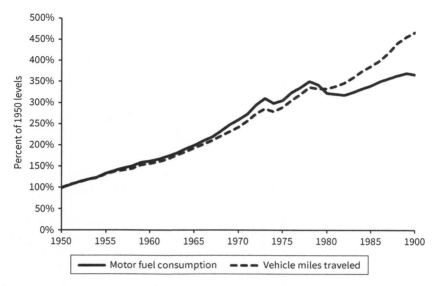

Figure 9.9. Increases in motor fuel consumption and vehicle miles traveled, 1950–1990.
Data Source: U.S. Department of Transportation, Federal Highway Administration, Highway Statistics Summary to 1995, Table VM-201A; U.S. Government Printing Office, Washington, D.C., 1997.

27.5 miles per gallon by 1985. This standard was relaxed slightly between 1986 and 1989, but returned to 1985 levels of 27.5 miles per gallon in 1990.[62]

As a result of this legislation, a widening gap emerged between vehicle travel and fuel use in the 1980s as vehicles became more fuel efficient. Figure 9.9 shows that while the growth in vehicle travel and motor fuel consumption largely tracked one another from 1950 through the late 1970s, after that time a gap began to grow.

While the pace of vehicle fuel-efficiency improvements has been far too slow for many, this widening gap between fuel use and vehicle travel has been good news for natural resources and the environment. But it has not been such good news for a highway finance system fueled by fuel consumption. This vehicle travel/fuel use gap means that even if there were no inflation in freeway construction, operations, or maintenance costs, the motor fuel taxes would not have tracked the use of and wear and tear on streets, roads, and freeways since about 1980.

The Fiscal Squeeze Chokes Off the Highway Program

Given these dynamics—rising construction costs, upscaling of freeway designs, rapidly rising right-of-way costs, a gradually increasing maintenance

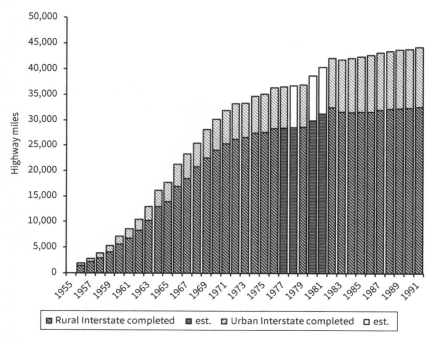

Figure 9.10. Completed miles of Interstates up to the nominal end of the Interstate era, 1955–1991.

Source: U.S. Department of Commerce, Bureau of Public Roads, Highway Statistics 1956–1964, Table INT-11; United States Government Printing Office, Washington, D.C., 1958–1966; U.S. Department of Transportation, Federal Highway Administration, Bureau of Public Roads, Highway Statistics, 1965–1979, Table INT-11, United States Government Printing Office, Washington, D.C., 1967–1981; U.S. Department of Transportation, Federal Highway Administration, Highway Statistics 1982–1991, Table HM-55, Highway Statistics Summary to 1995, Table HM-215, United States Government Printing Office, Washington, D.C.

Note: Missing data from 1977, 1978, 1980, and 1981 are estimated.

load, expanding environmental mitigation costs, revenue sources indexed to neither rising costs nor increasing road use, urbanized states fiscally hamstrung by their status as fuel tax "donors," and improving vehicle fuel economy—it should come as no surprise that the Interstate Highway construction program simply ran out of gas. As Figure 9.10 shows, the finance model that launched an era of mass production of freeways in the late 1950s and early 1960s began to atrophy in the mid-1960s. Freeway proponents sought increased revenues to complete the ambitious and once-popular plans for urban freeways, but with little success. In addition to the inherent structural problems with per-gallon motor fuel taxes, a rising anti-tax sentiment beginning in the 1970s and the growing hostility toward urban freeways combined to undermine the political will to increase revenues.

All of this led to a collapse in freeway building in the late 1960s and early 1970s. As a result, another two decades were required to (mostly) complete the Interstate system.

The Transition to the Post–Freeway Era

The outsized burden of urban freeway construction on poor and Black neighborhoods, freeway revolts, and, most decisively, the collapse of freeway finance had the proximal effect of stopping numerous freeway projects, as well as the ultimate effect of weakening federal-state dominance in metropolitan transportation development. These factors first slowed and then stalled the short-lived freeway juggernaut—to the relief of the many urban freeway critics, but to the chagrin of freeway supporters. In the next chapter we examine the emergence of an alternative metropolitan transportation-planning model, which was in no small part a reaction against the mass production of freeways.

10

Turning Back the Clock

Finance and Planning in the Post-Freeway Era

In many respects, the U.S. transportation-planning process has come full circle. It has gone from mostly local, to national, and back to mostly local again; from multi-modalism to a myopic focus on autos and freeways, and back to multimodalism; and from relative penury, to wealth, and back to penury. This is nowhere more evident than in the federal surface-transportation program and its formerly ironclad partnerships with state departments of transportation. These partnerships have eroded considerably since the 1990s amidst a return to more regional control of metropolitan planning. But also, much of the dramatic shift in transportation planning and policy has to do with the decisive role played by finance. The return to more local, multimodal, and modestly funded highway programs has to do with the continued atrophy of the transportation finance system, particularly at the federal level. So, while federally funded freeways continue to play an outsized role in travel in the twenty-first century, the era of Interstate Highway construction has long since ended. We now consider the current, post-Interstate era, beginning with the resurgence of interest in public transit.

The Revival of Public Transit

In the late nineteenth and early twentieth centuries, public transit was the workhorse of urban transportation. But outside of a brief respite during World War II, per capita transit patronage went on a long, secular decline from the 1920s to the 1970s as private vehicles rose to dominate travel in increasingly dispersed metropolitan areas. During the height of the freeway-building era, between 1945 and 1975, transit systems experienced a collective patronage free-fall as ridership plummeted from 167 annual transit trips per capita to 33 (Figure 10.1).

But context is critical. Public transit systems are good at moving large numbers of people in the same direction at the same time. They thrive in urban environments where trip origins and destinations cluster, particularly in city

The Drive for Dollars. Jeffrey R. Brown, Eric A. Morris, and Brian D. Taylor, Oxford University Press.
© Oxford University Press 2023. DOI: 10.1093/oso/9780197601518.003.0010

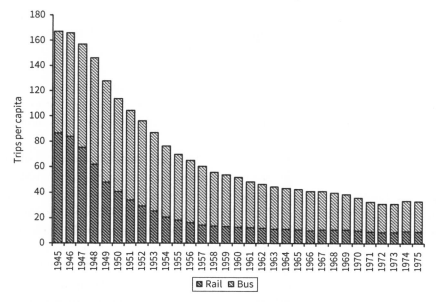

Figure 10.1. Per capita annual U.S. public transit ridership, 1945–1975.
Data Source: American Public Transit Association, APTA 2020 Fact Book, Appendix A, Table 1, Washington D.C; U.S. Census, National Intercensal Tables, 1900–1999.

centers, so that travelers can easily walk from their origin to a transit stop or station, and from another stop or station to their destination. In part for this reason, prior to the COVID-19 pandemic, the greater New York metropolitan area was home to about 6 percent of the U.S. population but around 40 percent of the nation's transit trips. Indeed, overall transit use varies enormously from city to city. In September 2019, the largest (New York) and second largest (Los Angeles) urbanized areas in the U.S. averaged 229 and 42 annual transit trips per capita, respectively, while the 12th (Phoenix) and 13th (San Francisco) largest urbanized areas averaged 16 and 125 annual transit trips per capita.[1]

Given its inherently local character, federal involvement in public transit was slow in coming and grew only gradually. The Urban Mass Transportation Act of 1964 authorized $375 million ($3.2 billion in 2021$) in matching grants to help cities and states revive their often-failing private transit systems. The money was to be used for "the acquisition, construction, reconstruction, and improvement of facilities and equipment for . . . mass transportation service in urban areas."[2] These early grants were more about urban development than transportation; it wasn't until 1968 that federal transit programs were shifted from the Department of Housing and Urban Development to the Department of Transportation.

From this tentative start, federal support for urban public transit grew substantially over time. Subsequent legislation in 1974 and 1978 expanded the scope of eligible expenditures to include operating costs (such as wages) in addition to capital spending (for vehicles, stations, facilities, etc.). Local matching requirements were gradually reduced as well. The net effect of these laws, as well as subsequent federal acts in 1982, 1987, 1991, and 1998, was to substantially increase the federal role in public transit, particularly its financing.[3]

While early federal subsidies for public transit ostensibly aimed to simply return formerly private, for-profit systems to economic self-sufficiency, this goal has long since been abandoned. Today, virtually all public transit service in the U.S. is publicly owned and heavily subsidized.[*] Nationwide, farebox revenues cover barely a third of operating costs, and essentially none of the capital costs. While they can be applied to both capital and operating expenses, federal transit subsidies explicitly favor the former, which has helped to create a heavily capitalized industry that tends to emphasize new equipment and politically visible new rail and rapid bus projects over maintenance and more cost-effective local bus services.[4] This capital-project, construction-focused mindset is little different from that of the freeway-building era, and here, too, fiscal stability has long proved elusive.

Since the 1960s, public transit subsidies have risen dramatically. Between 1988 (the earliest year for which complete national subsidy data are available) and 2018, total (capital plus operating) federal subsidies for transit grew from $3.4 billion ($7.7 billion in 2021$) to $12.6 billion ($13.1 billion in 2021$). In addition to federal support, transit systems depend on substantial local and (often) state subsidies as well, particularly in the largest cities. Total (federal, state, and local) capital and operating subsidies increased from a little over $12.3 billion in 1988 ($27.9 billion in 2021$) to $46.6 billion in 2018 ($49.2 billion in 2021$), which constitutes an inflation-adjusted increase of 44.8 percent from $3.21 per unlinked passenger trip in 1988 to $4.94 in 2018.[5,†]

Despite these substantial public investments, however, subsidy growth has not been matched by ridership growth. Although absolute ridership reached its nadir in the early 1970s and had been generally steady until falling steeply during the COVID-19 pandemic, transit use per capita and particularly per vehicle revenue hour have continued to erode in recent decades (see Figure 10.2). Overall, transit carries a very small share of U.S. travel: according to

---

[*] Though they are public entities, smaller transit systems often contract with private transportation companies to operate their service.
[†] A "linked" transit trip, which entails a transfer among two vehicles, is counted as two "unlinked" trips in transit patronage data.

the National Household Travel Survey, public transit carried just 2.5 percent of all person trips in 2017, compared to over 82 percent of all trips in private vehicles, a ratio of 33:1.[6]

So while expanding freeway investment and capacity in the 1950s and 1960s facilitated an explosion of motor vehicle travel, subsequent increases in public transit subsidies and capacity in the 1990s and the following decade— though admittedly nowhere near the scale of freeway expenditures a half-century earlier—have engendered a far more tepid response from travelers, largely because most of urban America is designed around autos and freeways that reward driving and punish its absence.

Although federal and state highway accounts were not initially tapped to provide transit subsidies, the increasing public commitment to transit at a time when freeway finances were in a free-fall constituted an opportunity cost that almost certainly inhibited efforts to enhance freeway revenues. Starting with the 1982 Surface Transportation Act, this modal competition for federal transportation funding became explicit as public transit began to draw revenue directly from the Highway Trust Fund. This competition—sometimes

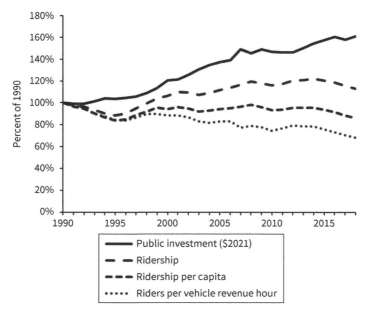

Figure 10.2. Trends in U.S. inflation-adjusted capital and operating transit subsidies and ridership, 1990–2018.

Data Source: APTA 2020 Factbook, Appendix A, Tables 1, 13, 62, and 68.

Note: Public Investment = Operations and maintenance expenditures + 10-year moving average of capital expenses.

covert and sometimes overt—between highway and transit spending defines U.S. urban transportation policy to the present day, as more than 27 percent of all public surface transportation expenditures go to public transit, compared to 29 percent for local streets and roads and 44 percent for highways (see Table 10.1). During the pandemic in 2020 and 2021, federal transit subsidies increased substantially via three federal COVID-19 relief bills, as ridership (and associated fare revenues) fell by more than half. As of this writing in mid-2022, transit ridership has recovered much more slowly than travel by other modes, though transit subsidies remain, for the most part, robust.

This enthusiastic embrace of public transit investment in metropolitan areas has not, for the most part, spread to smaller cities and towns, where transit has traditionally played a much smaller role. But with the shift away from freeways and toward new transit investments in most large metropolitan areas over the last quarter of the twentieth century, a philosophical divide emerged between some public officials (often representing rural and outlying suburban areas) who favored a new round of investment in freeways and other auto-related infrastructure, and others (often from central cities and inner-ring suburbs) who argued for transportation dollars to be spent to reinvigorate deteriorating public transit systems to provide greener, less invasive alternatives to driving. This divide between accommodating increased motor vehicle travel on the one hand and investing in alternatives to motor vehicle travel on the other, has only intensified over time and in many ways defines U.S. urban transportation policy debates to the present day. The return of multimodalism also signals a return to the outlook of the early, pre-freeway metropolitan transportation planners whose work we have discussed above.

A Gradual (Re)Turn to Metropolitan Planning

The last third of the twentieth century also saw a rise in metropolitan transportation planning. As with transit, this shift was instigated in no small part by the federal government. In 1961, the BPR established an Office of Planning for the first time, and the Federal Housing Act of that year authorized grants to urban areas to conduct traffic studies to aid regional transportation planning. The following year, the Federal-Aid Highway Act of 1962 gave a significant boost to metropolitan transportation planning by mandating that transportation projects in urbanized areas receiving federal funding must "be based on a continuing, comprehensive transportation planning process carried out cooperatively by states and local communities." The goal was to address the problem of often uncoordinated and sometimes contradictory transportation

Table 10.1 Government Expenditures on Surface Transportation, 2014

	Capital ($M)	% of Government Spending	Maintenance and Operations ($M)	% of Government Spending	Total ($M)	% of Government Spending	Spending per Passenger Mile (Transit) or Vehicle Mile (Streets/Highways)
Public transit	$18,466[a]	15%	$44,425[b]	46%	$52,891	29%	$1.05[c]
Local streets/county roads	30,412[d]	25%	28,680[d]	30%	59,092	27%	$0.02[e]
State/federal highways	75,011[d]	60%	22,762[d]	24%	97,774	44%	$0.03[e]
Total	$123,889	100%	$95,867	100%	$219,757	100%	

Sources: [a] APTA 2019 Factbook, Table 62; [b] APTA 2019 Factbook, Table 68; [c] Calculated from APTA 2019 Factbook, Table 3; [d] U.S. Department of Transportation, Federal Highway Administration, Highway Statistics 2015, Table HF-2; [e] Calculated from U.S. Department of Transportation, Federal Highway Administration, Highway Statistics 2015, Table VM-202.

Note: Data in millions (M).

plans and projects.[7] This continuing, comprehensive, and cooperative requirement gave rise to what became known as the "3C Process," which beginning in
the 1970s was carried out by newly established metropolitan planning organizations (MPOs).

While the 3C process mandated ongoing and coordinated multimodal
transportation planning, the MPOs that have conducted this planning are not
the independent regional governments, led by directly elected officials, found
in many other countries. Instead, as Sciara and Handy have noted, "[u]nder
the 3-C framework, regional transportation planning is embedded in, not independent of, other levels of government, as evidenced by MPOs' structure
and the decidedly intergovernmental environment in which they operate."[8]
Most MPOs in the U.S. are governed by locally elected officials who serve on
the MPO boards in addition to their primary roles as city council members,
county supervisors, and the like. Still, the mandated 3C process for MPOs
represents yet another way in which transportation policymaking has come
full circle, returning to the early auto era when urban planning was closely
tied to transportation planning.

Transportation Planning Goes Green

Beginning in the 1960s, mounting concern about environmental quality, especially pollution from photochemical smog, led to federal and some state legislation to reduce motor vehicle emissions, set and attain air quality standards,
and increase environmental planning and public participation. Here again,
California was a trendsetter, with the first vehicle emissions regulations placed
on new cars in 1961. Several other states and the federal government followed
suit by 1964. The first national Clean Air Act in 1963 focused primarily on
research and monitoring, while the Motor Vehicle Pollution Control Act of
1965 authorized federal emission standards and controls on motor vehicles.
The subsequent Clean Air Act of 1970 substantially increased those air quality
standards and regulations and included provisions for citizen lawsuits for
noncompliance.[9]

California was also the first state to establish an air quality regulatory
agency, the California Air Resources Board, in 1967. Shortly thereafter, in
1969, the U.S. created the Environmental Protection Agency as part of the
National Environmental Protection Act (NEPA). Among its many effects,
NEPA mandated public participation in government decision-making. Also,
decision-making now had to consider economic, environmental, and social
impacts, and chronicle them in "environmental impact statements" as part of

the 3C planning process.[10] NEPA also required consideration of alternative courses of action for highway and other major transportation projects, as well as the involvement of other affected government agencies and the public in decision-making.[11] This made building freeways (as well as many other infrastructure projects, including transit) far more complex.

In yet another return to the ideas of the past, this new concern about the environmental impacts of transportation impacts hearkened back to the days when planners were at their wits' end in confronting horse pollution in American cities.

The End of the Interstate Program and the Weakening Federal-State Partnership

The final federal-aid highway act—the Surface Transportation and Uniform Relocation Assistance Act of 1987—marked the last time where the Interstate Highway System was the centerpiece of federal surface transportation legislation. Indeed, the Interstate era essentially closed with the passage of the Intermodal Surface Transportation Efficiency Act of 1991 (ISTEA).‡ ISTEA represented a significant turn away from a primary focus on highway and freeway construction and toward intermodal and locally directed transportation planning. Among other things, it combined highway and public transit programs into a single bill, and, as we have noted, substantially increased the role and authority of MPOs vis-à-vis state departments of transportation.[12]

While this shift toward a more comprehensive, inclusive, multimodal, and context-sensitive approach to transportation was long overdue, the absence of any galvanizing objective—like blanketing the nation in superhighways— decisively, albeit gradually, diminished the focus, funding, and influence of federal transportation policy. This reduced federal role has been especially pronounced in cities. It has meant that the consensus that emerged around state- and federally directed freeway development proved to be both short-lived—a little over four decades—and an exception to a centuries-old rule of mostly local and ad hoc urban transportation planning and finance.

ISTEA and its alphabet soup successors—the 1998 Transportation Equity Act for the 21st Century (TEA-21), the 2005 Safe, Accountable, Flexible, Efficient Transportation Equity Act: A Legacy for Users (SAFETEA-LU),

‡ The official end of the Interstate Highway program occurred with the passage of the National Highway System Designation Act in 1995, when the Interstate System was rolled into what became known as the National Highway System.

the 2012 Moving Ahead for Progress in the 21st Century Act (MAP-21), and the 2015 Fixing America's Surface Transportation Act (FAST)—were all vigorously debated efforts to correct the mistakes of the Interstate-freeway-building era. But their collective lack of any galvanizing transportation policy objectives likely explains why, despite intense lobbying from various interests, the buying power of federal transportation revenues has continued to erode for decades. As in a prior era, local funding for local transportation projects, especially in cities, has to a large extent become the new normal.

Coming Full Circle

Regional transportation plans and proposals today—like many of the big-city highway and transit plans crafted before the Interstate era—reflect a wide array of urban concerns, including promoting economic development and social equity, linking housing and employment, reducing greenhouse gas emissions, protecting public health, improving public transit service, encouraging walking and bicycling, and managing traffic congestion. In another return to the thinking of the past, elected officials today often justify their support for large transportation projects in terms of the jobs created by such projects, as was the case with Roosevelt's highway policy during the Great Depression.[13]

The devolution of power to more local levels of government has been accompanied by a shift in outlook: from embracing to tolerating increased auto use, from circumventing stakeholder objections to facilitating stakeholder input, from aiding suburban expansion to encouraging less auto-dependent forms of development, from constructing new highway facilities to mitigating the effects of existing facilities, and from focusing on freeway networks to focusing on multimodal planning with an emphasis on developing public transit.[14]

Worthy though these goals surely are, with the loss of a singular focus on completing the Interstate Highway System, parochial interests—which were always present but were more constrained—dominate transportation policy today more than during the Interstate era. Just as in the pre-Interstate era, when state and county highway building proceeded piecemeal without coordinated national direction, today's devolution of control has brought with it more decision-making at the regional and community levels—for better and for worse.

As the Interstate program began winding down in the 1980s, members of Congress increasingly "earmarked" federal transportation funds for popular projects in their home states and districts. This practice increased

dramatically with each successive piece of surface transportation legislation between the 1980s and the first decade of the twenty-first century. There
were 11 earmarks for "demonstration," "priority," or "high-priority" projects
in the Surface Transportation Assistance Act of 1982, a figure that grew to a
mind-boggling 5,700 earmarks in 2005's SAFETEA-LU (see Figure 10.3).[15] By
2006, earmarked outlays accounted for fully 13 percent of U.S. Department of
Transportation expenditures.[16] Earmarked rail transit projects proved especially popular with elected officials.

By the middle of the decade, earmarks were so widely viewed as having spiraled out of control that Alaska's infamous "Bridge to Nowhere"—a proposed
$400 million ($496 million in 2021$) bridge to replace ferry service between
Ketchikan, Alaska (population 8,288), and a nearby island that was home to
the Ketchikan airport and 50 residents—became a *cause célèbre* in the 2008
presidential election. Bipartisan embarrassment over widespread perceptions
of wasteful earmarking finally led Congress to eschew all legislative earmarks
in 2012's MAP-21 reauthorization bill.

But while earmarks were eliminated from MAP-21 and the 2015 FAST
Act, the parochial focus of elected officials was not.[17] Some observers argued
that the absence of earmarks (which often grease the legislative skids) helps
to explain why the latter reauthorization was years overdue, was only a two-
year bill, and contained no meaningful revenue enhancements. In an explicit

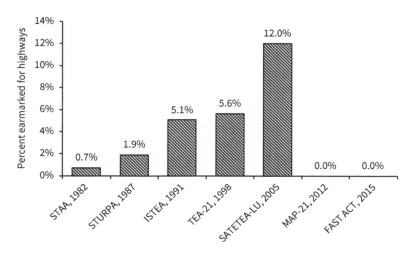

Figure 10.3. Percent of highway authorizations earmarked for specific projects in
recent U.S. surface transportation bills.

Data Source: Gian-Claudia Sciara, Financing congressional earmarks: Implications for transport policy
and planning, Transportation Research Part A: Policy and Practice 46 (8), 1328–1342, 1329, Table 1.

acknowledgment that transportation earmarks would increase the odds of congressional approval of a new surface transportation bill, House Democrats announced in early 2021 that they intended to abandon the decade-long ban on earmarks.[18]

Is it possible the pendulum may have swung too far? Has an era of comprehensive, top-down, centrally directed freeway planning given way to an era of piecemeal, excessively localized planning that lacks coordination, direction, or vision? Or does the shift in focus to regions and communities enable more effective, participatory, context-sensitive planning? One could surely argue that most travel *is* local, that transportation needs and aspirations vary substantially from place to place, and that increased local and regional control over transportation policy, planning, and finance is likely to lead to more experimentation and context-appropriate outcomes than would be the case with a nationwide one-size-fits all policy, like driving freeways through urban neighborhoods.

Finally, the calculus of fiscal politics has not lost its power, though the modern situation is in many ways the mirror image of that faced by the freeway builders in the middle third of the previous century. In one more return to the past, the Interstate era of fantastic financial largesse has given way to one of comparative poverty, as cities and regions scramble to cobble together funds for projects much as they did in the 1920s, 1930s, and 1940s.

Interstates 2.0?

While the near-completion of the Interstate Highway System in the early 1990s prompted significant transportation policy changes over the succeeding three decades, the national system of freeways remains a massive piece of heavily used infrastructure, and an aging one at that. As of this writing, even the newest segments of the Interstate System are over 30 years old, while the oldest segments have been operating for better than eight decades. Whether and how to rebuild, restructure, or retire various segments of the system remain unsettled questions.

Every four years or so, the American Society of Civil Engineers (ASCE) issues a "report card" on the state of 18 different components of America's infrastructure, including bridges and highways. The grades are consistently low, and the corresponding calls for more investment in maintenance, rehabilitation, and reconstruction are typically urgent. The first report card on the state of the nation's roads—a C+—was the high-water mark. Indeed, in the years since, America's roads have garnered grades of D+ (once), D (4 times), and D– (twice).[19]

Admittedly, civil engineers have an interest in increased infrastructure spending, and may be inclined toward calls for more, well, civil engineering. While some experts do not see the state of transportation infrastructure in as dire terms as does the ASCE,[20] concern over the nation's roads and bridges has grown over time. On August 1, 2007, the 40-year-old Interstate 35W bridge across the Mississippi River in Minneapolis, Minnesota, suddenly collapsed, killing 13 people and injuring another 145. The horrific spectacle of the bridge's catastrophic failure dominated the news for days and brought warnings from organizations like the ASCE into the limelight.[21] Subsequent analyses of the collapse suggested that a design flaw, more than poor maintenance, was the ultimate cause of the tragedy.[22] But since then, concerns over repairing the nation's "crumbling" roads, bridges, and other infrastructure have become part of the American zeitgeist.

Since that Interstate Highway bridge collapse in Minnesota, each of the three succeeding presidential administrations—Obama, Trump, and Biden—has called for significant new investments in highways and other infrastructure; one of Biden's primary campaign themes was "Build Back Better." While Barack Obama, elected in 2008, and Donald Trump, elected in 2016, shared little in common politically, each proposed but failed to enact major transportation infrastructure legislation. Obama's plan centered on building high-speed intercity passenger rail and rebuilding roads and bridges, while Trump's proposal also emphasized highway reconstruction as well as privatization. But neither president garnered enough congressional support to raise revenues to put their proposals into action. Indeed, "Infrastructure Week" became something of a running joke about the lack of policy progress on this ostensible priority during the Trump years.[23]

In 2015, Congress directed the Transportation Research Board of the National Academies of Science, Engineering, and Medicine to examine what would be needed to upgrade and restore the aging Interstate Highway System. The Academies reported back in 2019 with *Renewing the National Commitment to the Interstate Highway System*.[24] It presented a sobering picture of the state of the Interstates and an urgent call for substantial reinvestment. The authors found that most of the system had exceeded its design life: one-third of the system's bridges were over a half-century old. Many of the system's more than 15,000 interchanges needed to be reconfigured and reconstructed; merely resurfacing roadways would no longer be sufficient because most are sitting on underlying structures that are breaking down and need to be rebuilt. The authors also found that the rate of road deterioration is accelerating as automobile and truck use continues to grow.

The authors calculated that current capital spending on the Interstates, between $20 billion and $25 billion annually, is at least 50 percent below what would be needed to make meaningful progress on the maintenance backlog and reconstruct the Interstate System. They concluded that at least $30 billion per year for 20 years would be needed for both deferred and future maintenance. Another $15 to $40 billion per year over the same period would be needed to renew, expand, and modernize the system. This would include additional intercity routes;[§] interchange reconfiguration and reconstruction; greater resiliency to extreme weather events due to climate change; additional special-purpose and managed lanes;[**] expanded capacity (particularly in urban areas); and selective remediation of the "economic, social, and environmental disruption caused by highway segments that communities find overly intrusive and are not deemed vital to network and intermodal traffic,"[25] which presumably would entail the removal of some urban freeways.

The Waning Power of Federal Fuel Taxes

While there is bipartisan support for investing in and improving the aging Interstate System, it should come as little surprise that, two years after the delivery of this report to Congress, there was no agreement on how to pay for it. In response to the erosion of the buying power of motor fuel taxes, the report concluded that fuel tax levies needed to be raised and indexed to changes in inflation and fuel efficiency, and, with the rise of electric and alternative fuel vehicles, electronic tolling should be introduced as well.

But the fuel taxes that were raised so frequently in the late 1940s, 1950s, and early 1960s have proven heavy political lifts in the twenty-first century. As noted above, while the federal gas tax doubled between 1956 and 1959, it remained unchanged for nearly a quarter century after that, despite rapidly escalating costs in the 1960s and 1970s. Finally, in 1983, it was more than doubled (to $0.09/gallon, equivalent to $0.24/gallon in 2021$) in the face of looming financial shortfalls. Notably, $0.01/gallon of the nickel increase in 1983 was earmarked for public transit, which was a significant step in the shift away from an exclusive focus on highways. The tax was bumped

§ Due to high rates of population growth in the South and West, more than 37 urbanized areas with populations greater than 50,000 are more than 25 miles from the nearest Interstate Highway.
** Such lanes include those reserved for carpools, buses, or trucks, or for drivers willing to pay tolls that vary with congestion levels in order to keep traffic flowing in the toll lanes.

another \$0.051/gallon in 1990 (equivalent to \$0.10/gallon in 2021\$), but this time the diversion from the Highway Trust Fund was even greater; half of the increased revenues went to the general fund for "deficit reduction."[26] The Trust Fund firewall[††] was shattered completely in 1993, when the federal gas tax was increased by \$0.043/gallon to \$0.184/gallon (an \$0.08/gallon increase to \$0.34/gallon in 2021\$), with *all* of the increase going to the general fund. In 1997, however, the \$0.043/gallon gas tax increase from four years earlier was returned to the Trust Fund.

Also, the diesel fuel tax rate was increased above the gasoline tax rate, to \$0.244/gallon, in 1993 (equivalent to \$0.45/gallon in 2021\$). This finally responded to the fact that heavy vehicles like trucks, which typically run on diesel fuel, cause disproportionate damage to roads, a fact that has been repeatedly shown by extensive research and numerous highway cost-allocation studies.[27] Thus higher taxes on trucks are a more equitable, albeit imperfect, way to address this problem under the costs-imposed principle. As we have seen, the trucking industry had for decades bitterly, and successfully, opposed such differential rates. But in 1993, its efforts finally fell short.

MAP-21, passed in 2012, broke from a nearly three-quarters of a century precedent by shifting the federal surface transportation program away from reliance on user-fees. Far from transferring transportation tax revenue *to* the general fund, \$18.8 billion, or almost a fifth of the 2012 bill's \$105 billion authorization (\$121 billion in 2021\$), was funded *from* general fund revenues.[28] This was largely the result of a failure to raise fuel taxes once more. Similarly, the five-year FAST Act of 2015 also left untouched federal motor fuel tax rates, whose revenues were clearly inadequate to fund the \$305 billion bill (\$341 billion in 2021\$).[29] Thus, as of 2022, 1997 marked the last time the federal fuel tax rate was increased.

Increasing general fund transfers to the federal surface transportation program have been necessary in large part because, given the paucity of rate increases, fuel tax revenues have fallen ever further behind rising costs. While inflation rates were considerably lower in the 1990s (3.1%/year) and in the first decade (2.5%/year) and the second decade (1.9%/year) of the twenty-first century than they were in the 1970s (7.3%/year) and 1980s (5.8%/year), time has still continued to weaken the buying power of the unchanging federal fuel tax.[30] Over the 28 years between the last federal fuel tax increase in 1993 and 2021, even the relatively modest levels of inflation reduced the buying power of the \$0.184/gallon federal fuel tax by 47 percent, to a 2021 equivalent of

---

[††] The firewall refers to the separation of federal surface transportation revenues and expenditures into trust funds separate from other parts of the federal budget.

0.10/gallon. This buying power was reduced even more with the steep rise in inflation in 2022.

Other factors also sap the fuel taxes' vitality. Admittedly, recent years have seen rising numbers of larger, heavier, and more powerful vehicles (such as SUVs and light trucks) that are less fuel-efficient than the typical sedan. They have also seen overall increases in vehicle travel, notwithstanding a dip in the mid-2010s. While these trends taken in isolation have augmented fuel tax revenue, they are more than outweighed by countervailing factors. First, as electrification (and to a lesser extent, the use of natural gas and hydrogen) to power vehicles has gained steam, fewer drivers rely on motor fuels and pay motor fuel taxes at all. In addition, motor vehicles that do run on gasoline and diesel have continued to become more efficient with the tightening of the CAFE standards. In 2012, as part of global agreements to mitigate climate change, the Obama administration announced dramatically higher average fuel economy standards of 54.5 miles per gallon for the 2025 model year. This change in policy was intended to push automakers not only to develop more fuel-efficient internal combustion engines, but also to accelerate the development and sales of electric and hydrogen fuel-cell vehicles.[31] While, in 2018, the Trump administration moved to roll back the 2012 increases (in order to "Make Cars Great Again"), this move did little to restore the vitality of the fuel tax. Even with the change, vehicle fuel efficiency continued to improve, albeit at a slower rate than would have occurred with the earlier mandated adjustments.[32] However, almost immediately after taking office in early 2021, the Biden administration announced both a U.S. return to the Paris climate accords and a return to Obama-era CAFE standards. In sum, electrification and tightening fuel-economy standards have been inexorably leading to less fuel consumed (and revenue collected) per vehicle mile driven. While vehicles that burn less fuel are surely good for the environment, they are increasingly problematic for transportation finance.

The erosion of state and federal user-fee finance in the twenty-first century has been substantial. Over 60 percent of all highway funding came from motor fuel taxes, registration fees, weight fees, tolls, and driver's license fees in 1994; this share had dropped below 40 percent by 2017.[33] While the fuel tax remains an important source of revenue, Figure 10.4 shows that the inflation-adjusted fuel tax revenue collected per vehicle mile of travel since 1980 has been less than half the levels collected during the heyday of freeway construction in the 1960s (when such taxes accounted for 84% of all highway revenues). For example, the current average motor fuel tax rate (states plus federal) of 46 cents per gallon would have to be more than doubled to

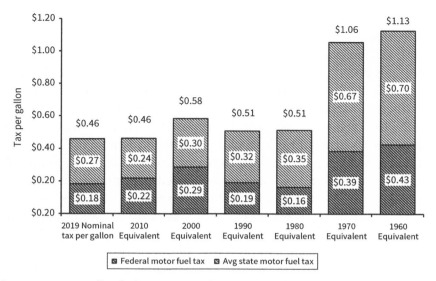

Figure 10.4. Per-gallon fuel taxes required in 2019 to restore inflation-adjusted revenues per vehicle-mile of travel to the level of prior decades.

Data Sources: U.S. Department of Transportation, Federal Highway Administration, Highway Statistics, Washington D.C.; Summary to 1995, Table FE-201; Highway Statistics 2014, Table FE-201; Highway Statistics 2015–2019, Table FE-9. U.S. Department of Transportation, Federal Highway Administration, Highway Statistics Summary to 1995, Table MF-201, Highway Statistics 1996–2019, Table MF-1. U.S. Department of Transportation, Federal Highway Administration, Highway Statistics 2019, Table MF-202. U.S. Department of Transportation, Federal Highway Administration, Highway Statistics Summary to 1985, Table VM-201A; Highway Statistics 2019, VM-202.

$1.13 per gallon to generate the same real revenue per vehicle mile as in 1960. Revenues from fuel taxes increased between 1985 and 2000, when federal taxes were increased gradually from 9 cents to 18.4 cents per gallon, but have been eroded by inflation and greater fuel economy since then. Even though inflation-adjusted fuel tax revenues have been relatively flat since the 1980s, the federal share of the fuel tax fell in the first two decades of the twenty-first century, while the average state share has recently been increasing (which we discuss further below).

By 2010, three separate bipartisan commissions had conducted studies of transportation finance in the U.S. All three concluded with calls for fuel tax increases to rebuild aging bridges and highways and increase road and public transit capacity in the near term, and a shift to mileage-based user fees over the longer run.[34],[‡‡] But these calls all fell on deaf ears. Federal officials, on both sides of the political aisle, have proven loath to increase fuel taxes, and

‡‡ Mileage-based user fees (MBUFs) refer to the electronic tolling of vehicle travel.

have looked—mostly in vain—to other finance mechanisms, before resorting to borrowing and general tax revenues.

With the fuel tax withering, federal transportation finance is more unsettled and uncertain in the early 2020s than at any point since the Great Depression. The solutions adopted to date have failed to address the fuel tax's key structural weaknesses. Absent the sort of compelling vision associated with the federal highway program in the postwar era, urban transportation policy—particularly at the federal level—has muddled through.

But after many years of calls for increased federal investment to improve crumbling infrastructure—calls that foundered over disagreements about who should pay it—Congress finally broke through in the fall of 2021 with a simple, if unsettling, solution: just shift previously allocated funds, apply some budgetary gimmicks, and borrow the rest. Soon after taking office, the new Biden administration advanced a broad infrastructure bill. In addition to funding many initiatives like increasing broadband access and cleaning up drinking water, it promised to pay for a rebuilding of America's roads and bridges. After months of tortured negotiations between Democrats and Republicans, and among the progressive, liberal, and moderate wings of the Democratic Party, a major infrastructure bill finally passed both houses of Congress and went to the president's desk for signature in November 2021. The bill designated about $1 trillion in myriad infrastructure expenditures over ten years, including $110 billion for roads and bridges, $66 billion for passenger and freight rail, $39 billion for public transit, and $11 billion for transportation safety, including for pedestrians and cyclists.[35]

However, to fulfill a campaign pledge not to raise taxes on households making under $400,000, the Biden administration opposed raising motor fuel taxes to pay for this investment. This opposition met with broad support from Republicans generally averse to tax increases. So while it took years for the executive and legislative branches to negotiate a package of tax increases to finance the Interstate Highway System, it took even longer for Congress to pass a $1 trillion infrastructure package in 2021 that raised no new revenues, relying instead on existing revenue sources, "budgetary gimmicks" such as clawbacks of funding previously allocated for other purposes, and borrowing. Nonpartisan analyses estimated that the bill would add at least $250 billion to the federal budget deficit over a decade.[36]

Given the enduring political resistance to raising federal motor fuel tax rates and an ever-increasing reliance on general fund revenues for transportation expenditures, some now argue for abandoning the user-fee logic of highway finance entirely in favor of general revenue funding.[37] Once more, this would represent a full circle return to the early days.

Donors Become Donees Too

Further, fuel tax "donor" states have argued with increasing vigor, and success, against transfers to "donee" states in the post-Interstate surface transportation bills. By 2019, the total amount of appropriations received in federal taxes by highway users in Texas, historically the largest donor state, was nearly equal to taxes paid since 1956, and California, long a major donor, had gotten back slightly more than its highway users had paid in that time.[38]

How has this "rebalancing" occurred? Some of it has been due to the establishment of a guaranteed "floor," which mandates that a certain share of revenues collected in a state must be returned to it. MAP-21, for example, set this floor at 95 percent. But the most important source of rebalancing has come from increasing general fund contributions to the Trust Fund. As noted earlier, beginning in 2008, fuel tax revenues no longer covered federal surface transportation program obligations, and $8 billion ($9.9 billion in 2021$) was transferred from the general fund to the Highway Account of the Trust Fund to cover the shortfall. While this was touted as "stimulus" spending in response to the onset of the Great Recession in 2008, general fund transfers became necessary again in 2009 ($7 billion, or $8.7 billion in 2021$), and in 2010, when $14.7 billion ($17.7 billion in 2021$) was transferred to the Highway Account and another $4.8 billion ($5.8 billion in 2021$) to the Mass Transit Account of the Trust Fund. Through 2018, $114.7 billion in general fund money ($121.1 billion in 2021$) had been transferred to the Highway Account and $28.9 billion ($30.5 billion in 2021$) to the Mass Transit Account.[39] As a result, nearly all states have in recent years become "donees," so that, between 1956 and 2019, U.S. highway users had received $1.20 in federal highway appropriations for every dollar paid in user fees (including fuel taxes) they paid into the Highway Trust Fund.[40] The level of "donee" status among states figures to rise even further with the 2021 passage of the substantially general-fund dependent federal infrastructure bill.

So where is transportation finance headed? Many successors to the federal fuel tax have been auditioned, but none has yet managed to capture the leading role.

A Halting Renaissance of State Fuel Taxes

In spite of federal inaction on fuel taxes, numerous states have raised theirs for transportation expenditures, particularly in recent years, as evidence of voter hostility toward transportation tax increases has waned.[41] In response to rapidly increasing highway construction costs, some states restructured motor fuel taxes to try to keep pace with financial needs. Between 1977 and 1985, 11 states and the District of Columbia each adopted some form of variable rate mechanism for their state/district motor fuel taxes.[42] Eight of these jurisdictions replaced their per-gallon fuel tax with a sales tax earmarked for highway expenditures; two states indexed the per-gallon tax to the combined U.S. Highway Construction and Maintenance Cost Indices; one state linked its per-gallon tax to the Consumer Price Index; and one state adjusted its per-gallon tax based on a combination of fuel prices and the highway cost index.[43]

There have been two major problems with indexed taxation. First, rising energy costs both increased fuel prices and helped to drive up construction and maintenance costs. This increased fuel taxes indexed to these costs, which then drove up prices at the pump still further. Second, when fuel prices fell, fuel tax revenues would fall as well, just at the time when cheap fuel encouraged more driving and wear and tear on roads.[44] In short, indexing fuel taxes is procyclical, amplifying price swings, when ideally it would work to counter them in order to keep revenues more stable.

Further, for the most part these indexed fuel tax systems proved unpopular with both motorists and voters. Despite the revenue advantages of indexed levies, four of the 12 jurisdictions—Arizona, Indiana, New Mexico, and Washington—subsequently repealed them and returned to a standard per-gallon tax.[45] The unpopularity of "automatic tax increases" discouraged many other states from adopting indexed fuel taxes, so that by the early 2010s just five states still did so.[46]

The sales tax on motor fuels has proven somewhat more politically palatable. By 2010 seven states had either extended their general retail sales taxes to fuel or had added a dedicated fuel sales tax. However, not all states dedicate these sales tax revenues to transportation. In addition, revenues from these sources have proven volatile as fuel prices tend to fluctuate substantially, while increases in road construction and maintenance costs tend to rise and fall more gradually.[47] Further, sales taxes based on the price of fuel also amplify swings in prices at the pump.

While increasing the per gallon levy has proven an impossibly heavy political lift at the federal level for more than a quarter century, it has proven the most popular way to overcome the structural weaknesses of the tax at the state level. Between 2000 and 2019, 36 states and the District of Columbia increased their gas tax, and 39 states and the district increased their diesel tax, with the average state gas tax increasing 44 percent ($0.086/gallon) and the average diesel tax increasing 47 percent ($0.094/gallon). Such averages are deceiving, as the changes to the levies varied widely from state to state: Pennsylvania's gas tax increased \$0.317/gallon and its diesel tax a whopping \$0.433/gallon. Five other states increased their gas tax,[§§] and seven their diesel tax,[***] by more than \$0.20/gallon; 16 more states increased their gas tax, their diesel tax, or both by at least \$0.10/gallon. All but three of those increases took place between 2010 and 2019. Contrast these substantial increases with the ten states that did not change their gas tax, and the nine states that did not change their diesel tax, between 2000 and 2019,[†††] and with the four more states that actually *reduced* their gas tax and the two that reduced their diesel tax over the same period.[48,‡‡‡]

That most states have increased their fuel taxes, many substantially, while the federal tax has remained frozen, is another telltale sign of the gradually declining federal role in surface transportation. While by no means a minor player today, federal influence in surface transportation since the de facto close of the Interstate Highway program in 1991 has fallen mightily since its heyday. This is largely because the relative amount and influence of federal matching funds has gradually waned. Finance, once again, is leading policy and planning.

A Return to General Revenue Finance

The rising reliance on general fund transfers into the federal transportation trust funds does have some clear advantages. First, at least some of the benefits of the transportation system (including its use for national defense, police/fire access, access to education, etc.) redound to all of society regardless of use of the transportation system. Thus, it may be fair that all taxpayers contribute something for the upkeep of that system. Because income taxes (at least at the federal level and in some states) are progressive, and property taxes are somewhat so, paying for transportation from these revenue sources may be fair under the ability-to-pay principle. Also, critics might contend that there is no compelling reason for transportation to have its own protected revenue stream while many other worthy government programs, from foreign aid to education, must continually fight for revenue. Perhaps, then, it would be

---

[§§] California, Florida, Illinois, New Jersey, and Washington.
[***] Connecticut, Georgia, Illinois, Indiana, New Jersey, Ohio, and Washington.
[†††] Hawai'i raised gas and diesel taxes one cent from 2007 to 2015 but then returned them to the 2000 level; Colorado raised its diesel tax for one year and then returned it to the previous level.
[‡‡‡] New York reduced its gas and diesel taxes in 2001; since then, they have risen gradually but not to the previous levels.

easier and fairer to dedicate the "right" amount of revenue to transportation if it were made part of the regular annual or biennial appropriations processes.

However, the use of general funds also comes with obvious drawbacks. First, taxing those who do not drive or take transit, or do so very little, in order to subsidize the behavior of those who travel a lot is unfair under the user-pays principle. Second, unlike fuel taxes or tolls, general fund finance does not send signals to travelers to change their behavior in ways that would be beneficial for the environment and transportation system—primarily by driving cleaner, more fuel-efficient vehicles, driving more selectively, or, in the case of tolling, shifting driving to routes and times where there is less demand. And third, as is the case with the 2021 infrastructure bill, most of the federal transportation expenditures simply add to the national debt; although interest rates were low at the time of the bill's passage, the servicing of the new debt threatens to become more expensive as interest rates rise, as they did in 2022.

Rising Debt Finance

Public borrowing for transportation projects (beyond federal general fund debt discussed above) has grown substantially in recent decades. In the first decade of the twenty-first century, total state and local debt obligations for highways increased a whopping 120 percent in inflation-adjusted terms, from $96.2 billion in 2000 ($143.5 billion in 2021$) to $212 billion in 2010 ($256 billion in 2021$).[49]

This has often been referred to as "innovative finance," but the process of government borrowing to fund pressing present needs is in fact an ancient one. Governments have long borrowed money to pay for big-ticket projects. Common examples of bond-financed projects are schools, dams, and sewage treatment plants, which are often paid for by bonds because they require large lump-sum payments up front to build them and they then generate a steady stream of benefits over many years or even generations. Transportation projects often fit this bill. Typically, the heaviest reliance on bonds comes in wartime when the present benefits of victory are deemed so worthwhile that part of the cost is billed to future generations. In many cases, debt finance has been highly successful, but in others the results have not justified the expense.

While bonds have an important and long-established role in public finance, they are not a revenue *source*, they are instead a finance *technique*, because, in the end, bonds must be repaid with interest from some revenue source. While there can be strong justifications for borrowing money to pay for expensive projects that will provide many years of benefits, there is less

justification for borrowing money to pay for ongoing operations or maintenance expenditures, or for adopting excessive payback periods for projects
to make them less costly early on but highly onerous later. Doing so simply
puts off the uncomfortable task of raising revenues or cutting expenditures by
saddling future generations (who will also have to pay for their own operating
and maintenance costs) with debt service. While equity issues are raised by
this practice, enjoying transportation benefits now and worrying about how
to pay for them later is politically tempting and thus common.

Importantly, the cost of borrowing varies substantially over time and interest rates were at or near historic lows for much of the first two decades of the
twenty-first century. In the 1980s, the benchmark prime interest rate varied
from 7.5 percent to a remarkable 21.5 percent, and in the 1990s the range was
from 6.0 percent to 10.0 percent. But in the following decade, rates were lower,
ranging from 3.25 to 9.5 percent, and in the 2010s much lower still, ranging
from 3.25 to 5.5 percent.[50] Given this extended period of relatively low interest
rates (which ended in 2022), and large transportation infrastructure maintenance and reconstruction backlogs, proponents of increased transportation
spending argued in both the Great Recession and its aftermath (from 2008 to
2013), and again in the COVID-19 pandemic-induced recession of 2020, that
increased borrowing at low rates would be a wise way to both reduce transportation infrastructure backlogs and increase employment. Such arguments
echo those made in the Great Depression nine decades ago when New Deal
programs funded road construction and maintenance.

Conversely, though, deficit hawks can point to even earlier in the twentieth
century, when many states nearly drowned in debt thanks to their support for
road construction through costly bond finance, until the arrival of fuel taxes
ameliorated the problem. In all, increasing reliance on debt is another way in
which transportation planning and finance have returned to the methods of
the past, perhaps for better *and* for worse.

Local Option Taxes

Perhaps the most significant new fiscal development in transportation during
the last four decades is the rise of voter-approved local option taxes (LOTs) for
transportation, which are normally collected by localities, usually counties.
These new taxes have proven popular with public officials and voters.

LOTs typically increase the local sales tax, which is levied on most (though
not all) consumer purchases. The first LOT for transportation in the U.S. was
enacted when Santa Clara County voters in California's Silicon Valley raised

their sales tax in 1976. Forty-two years later, in 2018 alone, voters in 34 states considered 512 separate ballot measures to fund transportation projects, and collectively approved about $40 billion ($42 billion in 2021$) in LOT increases to fund them.[51] In 2017, 24 California counties, home to 88 percent of the state's population, had active LOT measures (all of which were sales tax levies) that collectively generated $4 billion per year ($4.5 billion in 2021$) for transportation projects and services.[52] Most of these measures were approved by at least two-thirds voter majorities, as required by California law. In most cases, LOTs "sunset," meaning they need to be periodically renewed by the voters.[53]

When LOTs increase sales taxes, the increases are small in percentage rate terms, but can raise considerable amounts of revenue since they are levied on so many transactions. And they are often less visible than other types of taxes. People typically pay property taxes once or twice per year in lump sums and reconcile their income taxes once per year. Both involve large and very visible sums of money, but sales taxes are paid a few cents at a time over hundreds or even thousands of transactions per year, meaning that most people are unaware of their annual sales tax bill.[54] This may be a key reason LOTs are popular with voters.

LOT revenues are usually dedicated to specific road and/or transit spending proposals specified in the ballot measure. Such project lists have raised concerns about whether they preempt local, regional, state, and federal transportation planning. While the proposed projects are typically drawn from local transportation project wish lists, the ballot measures themselves are crafted to increase the odds of passage by offering something for every voter constituency—expanded highways, new transit service, bike lanes, and so on. The projects are typically spread geographically across the taxing jurisdiction to be sure every area gets its "fair share." While such heterogeneous project lists reflect the increasing political sophistication of measure sponsors, political sophistication is not the same as effective planning. As a result, politically popular but likely ineffective projects often find their way onto these lists.[55]

LOTs are not user fees and thus are more properly considered as subsidies to transportation. This represents another return to the past. Sales tax finance of transportation is a relatively recent development, but as we have shown, the basic concept that the general taxpayer should finance transportation systems hearkens back to the era when state legislatures funded rural highways from general funds, and back even further to the days when the entire community turned out to do mandatory road work. Then as now, such a system was seen as unfair in that it does not discriminate between those who use the transportation system very little and those who use it a great deal. Also, it does not encourage travelers to use transportation systems judiciously. Finally, because those with lower incomes tend to spend more of their money on purchases subject to sales taxes, sales taxes are regressive and unfair under the ability-to-pay principle.

Reviving User-Fee Finance: A Return to Tolls?

Highway finance has seen yet another return to the strategies of the past. Harkening back to the age of the turnpikes of the 1940s and early 1950s, and before that to the turnpike era of the 1830s, recent years have seen a revival of interest in toll finance. Bucking the countervailing trends just discussed, this represents a movement toward new forms of user-fee finance.

In the past, the failure of toll finance to gain widespread adoption was in large part due to the difficulty, disruption, and high cost of collecting tolls. As we discussed, toll collectors are expensive to pay, toll booths are expensive to build, paying tolls slows travelers, and "leakage" (by drivers circumventing toll booths and (in the early days) some toll collectors pilfering part of what is collected) have long combined to make toll roads logistically difficult. However, the rise in information and communications technologies has made toll payment far easier. Tolls can now be paid by various means without needing to stop and pay cash to a toll collector. We are witnessing a rapid expansion of electronic payment mechanisms across many sectors, and transponder, smart card, and smart phone payment media that remotely deduct payments as travelers pass through transit fare gates or under payment gantries are becoming increasingly widespread. Many toll roads give discounts to those who pay electronically, and an increasing number of toll facilities are eliminating toll booths and cash payments entirely, for example by billing those without onboard transponders by taking a picture of their license plate and allowing them to pay via a website. These developments could usher in a new era of more efficient versions of the age-old toll road.

A Return to User-Fee Finance: Mileage-Based User Fees?

Not only has electronic toll payment made tolls less burdensome and expensive to collect, it has also greatly expanded the potential extent of roadway tolling. This would address the twin problems of increasing vehicle fuel efficiency and the rising number of vehicles on the road that burn neither gasoline nor diesel fuel. Gas-electric hybrids, fully electric vehicles, vehicles that run on natural gas, and those powered by hydrogen fuel cells have all been made available to consumers in recent years, and their popularity is growing. Tesla, a relatively new automaker, has considerably increased the cache of battery electric vehicles, adding to their popularity.§§§ As we have outlined, these vehicles all pay less in fuel taxes or none at all, which will further erode the ability of traditional motor fuel tax revenues to keep pace with the wear and tear of increasing vehicle travel.

To address these challenges, mileage-based user fees (MBUFs) are being developed and tested around the world, including in several U.S. states. The endgame would be to eventually replace the motor fuel taxes with them. Such systems record and report vehicle travel via telemetry systems built into vehicles or drivers' smartphones; these are linked to both global positioning satellite systems and accounting systems. They can bill travelers for road use via user accounts linked to checking or credit accounts, or, for unbanked drivers, special debit accounts.

Oregon, which was the first state to introduce the motor fuel tax in 1919, was also the first to successfully test MBUFs. Its OReGO program became the first to allow drivers to opt out of paying motor fuel taxes and into paying for road use directly in a proof-of-concept pilot test. A total of 1,300 drivers opted into the pilot study, which charged them 1.5 cents per mile regardless of driving location or vehicle type.[56] Subsequently, California conducted a field test of MBUFs where 5,400 participants received simulated monthly bills and paid for their more than 37 million vehicle miles of travel between 2016 and 2017. At the conclusion of the trial, 73 percent of participants reported that they now viewed MBUFs as fairer than fuel taxes.[57]

Following these two pilot tests, 14 Western states began collaborating on the development of an integrated multi-state MBUF system. In the Northeast, 17 states and the District of Columbia pursued a similar collaboration. These efforts were supported by the 2015 FAST Act, which provided up to $20 million per year ($23 million in 2021$) for grants to states developing MBUFs.[58]

The Tantalizing Promise of Marginal Social Cost Road Pricing

Recall that a major advantage of fuel taxes is that they encourage drivers to change their behavior in ways that will bring about socially desirable

---

§§§ In 2021, the market valuation of Tesla was roughly equal to that of the next nine largest automakers (Toyota, Volkswagen, Nissan, Hyundai, General Motors, Ford, Fiat/Chrysler, Peugeot, and Honda) *combined*.

outcomes. Heavier vehicles do disproportionate damage to roads and tend to consume more fuel, so shifting to lighter and more fuel-efficient vehicles reduces road maintenance expenses. Similarly, gas guzzlers emit more pollutants and greenhouse gases, so shifting to more fuel-efficient, gas/electric hybrid, electric, or hydrogen fuel-cell vehicles benefits the environment. But the MBUFs being tested typically charge a flat per-mile fee regardless of vehicle weight or fuel efficiency. While this has been done to test the concept and avoid thorny debates over how toll rates might vary across types of vehicles and trips, flat per-mile fees lack some of the behavioral incentives of fuel taxes. As a result, these pilot MBUF programs risk locking in expectations that MBUFs will remain flat per-mile charges.

However, MBUF technology has the potential to greatly enhance incentives for judicious use of the transportation system. Transportation economists have long argued that fuel taxes, despite their many merits, are a "second best" method for pricing motor vehicle travel. Ideally, each traveler would be charged for the marginal social cost their trip imposes on society—which includes delays imposed on others, pavement damage, the consumption of non-renewable energy resources, the emission of noise and air pollution, and so on. To date, road pricing that reflects such costs has been clumsy and imperfect (in the case of tolling individual facilities) or practically impossible (in the case of charging for all driving). However, this is changing with the development of electronic tolling and MBUFs.

These new tolling technologies have moved marginal social cost road pricing from a theoretical ideal to a practical possibility. For example, variable prices could be configured to encourage reduced axle loads on commercial vehicles, which could greatly extend the service life of roads and dramatically reduce maintenance costs.[59] A turn to variable road pricing could also encourage travelers to use transportation systems in places and at times when excess capacity exists, and would signal drivers to be more judicious in their consumption of roads (and transit seats) in congested places and at times of peak demand. Such changes could dramatically reduce congestion delays, increase economic efficiency, reduce emissions, and decrease exposure to pollutants among those who live and work near (formerly) congested freeways. Such residents and workers are more likely low-income and Black or Hispanic,[60] while the toll-paying drivers are more likely higher-income and White.[61] These advantages have increased interest in new forms of electronic tolling among many observers, including elected officials.[62]

There have been promising experiments with variable road pricing in the U.S. In 1995, a four-lane, privately financed, electronic-toll facility opened in the median of the State Route 91 freeway in metropolitan Los Angeles.

Users of the 18-mile facility can bypass congestion on the adjacent free lanes and save up to 50 minutes per trip. Evaluations have found that the facility increased traffic throughput and decreased congestion on both the toll facility *and* the adjacent free lanes, at least initially.[63] Over time, however, increased demand has led to more severe congestion in the adjacent free lanes, which has meant that the peak toll price has had to be raised regularly to keep the toll facility's traffic free-flowing.

In 1998, underutilized high-occupancy vehicle (carpool) lanes in San Diego, California were converted to allow single-occupant vehicles to pay a toll to use the lanes and bypass congestion on the adjacent unrestricted lanes. The San Diego facility was the first to set tolls that change every few minutes based on congestion levels. In addition to these facilities, tolls on bridges in the New York City area and in southwestern Florida vary throughout the day to encourage travelers to use them at less-congested times.[64] The move toward managed toll lanes continues, albeit far slower than proponents would like, with recent pilots and projects in Atlanta, Chicago, Dallas, Denver, Houston, Indianapolis, Los Angeles, Miami, Minneapolis, Orlando, San Diego, San Francisco, Seattle, and Washington, D.C.[65]

Collectively, these congestion-priced facilities have worked well in practice. Traffic flow is increased, delay and emissions are reduced, and the people who voluntarily pay tolls to bypass congestion report high levels of satisfaction. Even the travelers in congested, adjacent free facilities are generally satisfied with the congestion-priced facilities, because they tend to experience improved traffic flow in the free lanes and because the tolled lanes give them the option to buy out of congestion if they wish to do so.[66]

Despite the success and local popularity of these congestion-pricing experiments, in the U.S. they have been mostly limited to projects that feature congestion-priced lanes operating in parallel with unpriced lanes, and in most cases high-occupancy vehicles pay a reduced toll or no toll at all. Other forms of congestion pricing, such as cordoned zones where motorists pay for the use of *all* streets and highways in congested central areas, have been deployed in London, Stockholm, and Singapore. But they have not yet been tested in the U.S., notwithstanding plans for such a system that have been developed for Manhattan. This is likely because most elected officials remain wary of political backlash against tolling by drivers angry about paying for something that was formerly "free" (at least from the driver's perspective). Further, cordon tolls may be a difficult sell because drivers cannot see the congestion relief they are experiencing the way they can with managed lanes that run directly adjacent to congested, unpriced lanes. With respect to partisan politics, many

Republicans are wary of any government schemes to raise revenues and influence individual behavior, while many Democrats are wary of any new charges that might disproportionately burden low-income households. However, research, along with a growing number of applications, suggests that using prices to influence driver behavior could bring about dramatic economic efficiency and environmental justice benefits,[67] and that variable pricing would likely be more progressive than the fuel and sales taxes they could replace.[68] But most travelers, and the officials they elect, simply cannot believe that variable pricing could meaningfully reduce traffic delays, and do believe it would make most travelers worse off in the process—despite mounting evidence that it can and would not.[69]

So marginal social cost road pricing holds great promise. But the visceral negative reactions against it, despite promising pilot programs, means its expansion is likely to be both halting and gradual.[70] In sum, as it has throughout U.S. history, road pricing continues to flit in the wings of transportation finance. It remains to be seen whether it will ever be allowed to take center stage.

Conclusion

Whether we migrate further away from user-fee finance, or back toward technology-enabled applications of it, the story of this chapter, and this book, is that the means of raising, collecting, and spending revenues for transportation systems will importantly influence their planning, construction, operation, and use. With the rise over the past four decades of transportation LOTs—which do little to incentivize efficient use of transportation systems—metropolitan transportation planning has frequently been preempted by politically crafted lists of projects designed to appeal to the needed number of voters. But appealing to a cross section of voters may be at odds with building cost-effective projects, decreasing congestion, or reducing transportation's impacts on the environment.

On the other hand, variable road pricing is slowly expanding, and has the potential to substantially increase the efficiency and effectiveness of road systems, as well as to encourage travel by other modes, such as walking, biking, and public transit, in areas where the demand for roads consistently exceeds their supply. Enthusiasts argue that if the endless, and largely futile, efforts to increase road and freeway capacity to satisfy the demand for vehicle travel were to be replaced by congestion-free priced roads, planning to meet future travel needs would require substantial recalibration. The breathless race to get out in front of ever-congesting roads—a race that led the U.S. to mass produce high-speed metropolitan freeways—might finally come to an end.

Then again, as this book has shown, "solutions" to the congestion problem have come and gone for centuries, and none to date has ever fully achieved this elusive goal.

11

Conclusion

Groping for a Post-Freeway Consensus

This is a book about money. Not the money of personal or corporate wealth, or the dark money of graft, corruption, or political influence, but the vast amounts of money that governments raise and spend on transportation; money that must be collected from the people, through fees, taxes, bonds, assessments, and the like. Money matters in transportation because the manner by which we collect revenue *for* transportation and the manner by which we expend revenues *on* transportation importantly shape *how* we travel and live. The influence that money has on transportation systems and travel has played out vividly in the story of American freeway development and its enduring legacy.

This is also a book about plans. Plans for urban streets, rural roads, metropolitan expressways, and interregional highways. Plans that were developed during the infancy and adolescence of the city planning and civil engineering professions. Plans that were sometimes visionary and offered inspiring views about the future of cities and the travel in and between them. Plans that were largely crafted by powerful and influential men (and they were almost all men in that era) and which reflected a faith in the ability of science and engineering to solve transportation, and societal, problems. Plans that ultimately made freeways the backbone of virtually every metropolitan transportation system in the U.S., engendering a cascade of intended and unintended consequences—ranging from the beneficial to the malign—that manifest to the present day.

And finally, this is a book about lessons learned. What better way to understand the vexing transportation challenges we face today, and how to best address them, than by looking carefully at how we tried to solve similar problems in the not-so-distant past? Our story helps us understand how we got to the current state of play, and why so many widely touted silver bullets—better pavement; traffic laws and signalization; road hierarchies and street system rationalization; segregation of pedestrians, public transit, and cars; and, ultimately, freeways—all turned out to be not so silver after all.

The Drive for Dollars. Jeffrey R. Brown, Eric A. Morris, and Brian D. Taylor, Oxford University Press.
© Oxford University Press 2023. DOI: 10.1093/oso/9780197601518.003.0011

Cities and their transportation systems are messy and complex. We have sought to make sense of that messiness and complexity. The story of freeway development during the past century was one of ever-grander plans to accommodate and then tame the automobile, and the political deals crafted to pay for them. We have highlighted those financial deals as the key to understanding transportation in America yesterday, today, and tomorrow. To understand transportation, we have to follow the money.

The Roads Not Taken

We have shown how both urban transportation planners and rural highway engineers worked during the second quarter of the twentieth century to develop a new kind of road—the freeway—to address pressing transportation problems. Outside of cities, the problems were rural isolation and poverty, farmers stuck in the mud, the monopoly practices of railroads, slow travel speeds, and untenable rates of crashes, injuries, and fatalities. In cities, safety was also a concern, but the primary issue was burgeoning motor vehicle use and the chronic and worsening congestion that kept traffic, and public transit, moving at a crawl. Related challenges included channeling mass suburbanization and stemming the decline of the central cities. Viewed from a distance, the proposed solutions to these two sets of problems, one rural and one urban, looked similar. But up close, the freeways conceived to address rural problems and those to address urban ones differed dramatically.

In comparison with rural freeways, the freeways proposed early on for cities tended to be smaller, on substantially narrower rights-of-way, with lower design speeds and simpler interchanges, and configured in denser networks closely tied to existing boulevards and arterials. While the proposed urban freeways often differed substantially from one another, many were adapted to their urban context, were explicitly linked to adjacent land uses, and were to be multimodal facilities with separate rights-of-way for trucks, buses, and trains.

The political economy of highway finance importantly determined that this vision for urban freeways was mostly not realized. Cash-strapped cities turned to state and federal governments, and their respective highway departments, for access to the spigot of road funding that was the motor fuel taxes. But that funding came at a steep price; it required cities and suburbs to mostly give up control over the design, scaling, and routing of freeways.

Federal and state transportation planners and engineers who were focused on rural areas needed to increase the number of vehicles traveling on their proposed freeways in order to justify their construction costs. This meant not only building them into urban areas, but also maximizing the volume of traffic by directing them into city centers to capture suburb-to-downtown daily commuters. The combination of caps on total Interstate system mileage and the (at first) seemingly limitless funds further encouraged construction of a smaller number of very high-capacity, invasive facilities in urban areas. In addition, growing concerns over safety dictated the design of wide, limited-access roads that could handle travel at higher speeds. Some planners certainly objected early on to these behemoths, perhaps still preferring the context-sensitive compact designs of an earlier era. But many others bought into the vision—of federal administrators, state highway engineers, local business leaders, and politicians at all levels—that their proposed roads were the ultimate "cure" for all the maladies that beset urban transportation.

The result was that rural superhighways—built to accommodate the highest possible vehicle speeds, to interact as little as possible with adjacent land uses, and to be configured in sparse networks of very high-capacity roads—became the urban freeways of today. And because it was an article of faith among most transportation engineers of the day that inconsistent roadway designs were (with some justification) important causes of crashes and deaths, uniform design standards ensured that a freeway stretching across the plains of Kansas differed as little as possible from one that plowed its way through the very heart of New Orleans.

Context Matters

Given this, it should come as no surprise that rural freeways met so many of their objectives. Outside of cities they were (and still are) fast and relatively safe; they effectively connected farms to cities, and cities to one another; they helped to reduce rural isolation; and they weakened the railroads' stranglehold on intercity goods and passenger movements. While they tended to create winners and losers among the small towns that were located near or far from them, we argue that on balance the benefits of rural, intercity freeways have far outweighed their costs.

In the suburbs, where the plurality of Americans reside, freeways have presented more of a mixed blessing. Most suburbanites get around in cars, and freeways enable drivers to travel relatively quickly and safely to both central cities and other suburbs. But the freeways built in most suburbs were large, noisy, and polluting, and far too many of them either cut through housing and recreational areas or attracted such development to their vicinity after they were built—though the latter is as much a failure of land use planning as transportation system design.* The result is that the typical suburbanite is happy to live within shouting distance of a freeway interchange, but would prefer to be not too close to the freeway itself.

But in older and more densely developed urban areas, where access by foot and public transit were already comparatively high, the big, high-speed, high-capacity rural-style freeways were, and remain, a problematic fit. The wide rights-of-way and broad, sweeping curves meant to host fast-moving traffic required far more displacement of homes and businesses than would have been the case for the smaller, slower facilities envisaged by the early freeway planners. The denser networks of smaller facilities in the early urban freeway plans would have dispersed traffic, rather than concentrating it on just a few freeways so large that they flood surface streets around them with traffic at interchanges, and substantially inhibit the movement of traffic on the perpendicular streets that dead end, rather than pass under or over them. And rather than including and speeding the movement of buses and streetcars, as was envisaged in many of the early urban freeway plans, public transit was almost entirely excluded from the urban freeways. An engineering mindset that prioritized maximizing traffic flow per mile of road, largely for cost-effectiveness reasons, underlay all of these developments.

The much smaller footprints of the freeways planned for many U.S. cities would likely have done far less damage to built-up urban areas broadly, and poor, Black, and other minority communities in particular. Much less displacement of homes and businesses would have been required, and they would have showered those nearby with less noise and air pollution. As a result, freeways would also likely have been a far less attractive tool for the tragically misguided slum clearance efforts of the 1950s and 1960s. Context, in other words, matters, and when it comes to freeways, one size most decidedly does not fit all.

While arguments about what might have been are necessarily speculative, they are not without evidentiary support. In the 1970s, in Portland, Oregon, the 30-year-old Willamette River-side freeway was razed, with most of the traffic rerouted onto a new Interstate freeway built mostly through an industrial area. Similarly, a protracted legal battle eventually resulted in the replacement of the decrepit West Side Elevated Highway in Manhattan with a boulevard in the 1980s. And, most famously, the elevated Central Artery

---

* The eldest of this book's authors grew up 400 meters from the roar of a 10-lane Interstate suburban freeway. While his family gladly drove on the freeway to all manner of destinations, his middle school directly abutted the noisy, polluting, hulking road and he had to run the dark, deafening gauntlet on the surface street underneath it on his bicycle twice each school day during high school.

freeway in Boston was demolished and replaced with a large, complex, and enormously expensive tunnel system in a 16-year-long project known colloquially as the "Big Dig."[1] While the share of urban freeway mileage removed through 2021 remains quite small, the freeways that have been torn down almost always cut through and diminished the appeal of places like waterfronts and densely populated, often Black and poor, communities. It is widely agreed that conditions have improved, sometimes dramatically, in the communities where freeways have been removed.[2]

The Congress for New Urbanism (CNU), an urban planning and design advocacy organization that champions walkable urbanism, identified 15 freeway teardown projects completed or underway through 2021, 11 of which were in the U.S.[3] Four more cities—Detroit; New Haven, Connecticut; Somerville, Massachusetts; and Syracuse, New York—have committed to removing an urban freeway, ten more urban freeway removals have been proposed, and an additional 19 are under consideration.[4] In some cases the removed freeway was moved underground; in others it was rerouted away from scenic and residential areas and through industrial areas; and in a few cases a freeway stub end was not replaced by a grade-separated roadway at all.[5] The former freeway rights-of-way have in many cases been replaced by wide, divided boulevards, sometimes with light-rail transit or exclusive bus lanes, and often with bike lanes and widened sidewalks. While they typically lack the partial or full grade-separation of the early urban freeway plans, in many other ways they bear considerable resemblance to them (see Figure 11.1).

Most recently, the freeway teardown movement has broadened to include efforts to remove freeways cut through Black and other minority urban neighborhoods, some of which were unsuccessfully opposed by the same neighborhoods when they were built decades ago. The rerouting of I-880 around mostly African American West Oakland, following the collapse of the Cypress Freeway during the 1989 Loma Prieta Earthquake, is a notable example. The former path of the double-decked highway has been replaced by Mandela Parkway, which is a four-lane boulevard with a wide green bikeway in the median.[6] These efforts to remove or replace freeways that are viewed as particularly damaging to Black communities, such the Chairborne Expressway (I-10) through the Tremé, Tulane/Gravier, and 7th Ward neighborhoods in New Orleans, are now being championed at the national level by the Congressional Black Caucus Foundation.[7] Shortly after taking office in 2021, the Biden administration signaled a significant shift in federal policy regarding urban freeways when it issued a memorandum on *Redressing Our Nation's and the Federal Government's History of Discriminatory Housing Practices and Policies*. It acknowledged: "Many urban interstate highways were

Figure 11.1. A wide multimodal facility (separate ways for cars, transit, bikes, and pedestrians) replaced the double-deck Embarcadero Freeway in San Francisco.
DTM Media/ShutterStock.com. License: standard image license, https://www.shutterstock.com/license.

deliberately built to pass through Black neighborhoods, often requiring the destruction of housing and other local institutions. To this day, many Black neighborhoods are disconnected from access to high-quality housing, jobs, public transit, and other resources."[8] At this writing, the Biden administration has proposed $20 billion in federal funding to help reconnect neighborhoods divided by highways.[9]

Building New Freeways Has Fallen Out of Favor; Driving on Them Has Not

Whether one loves or loathes them, freeways are undeniably defining and even dominating pieces of infrastructure that profoundly shape American urban life. They have exerted enormous influence, permitting the automobile to achieve much of its promise and popularity. While the freeway city has in many ways proven a Faustian bargain, freeways' central role in metropolitan and rural mobility endures.

All but the most avid freeway enthusiasts are probably relieved that California never fully implemented its wildly ambitious *California Freeway System* plan to blanket all of California's metropolitan areas in a four-mile-by-four-mile grid of freeways. But if we assume a linear relationship between the size of the freeway system proposed and freeways' projected share of vehicle travel,[†] it is possible to adjust the California Division of Highways' 1958 freeway travel projections to account for the fact that less than half the planned freeway system was ultimately completed by the time most new freeway construction ended in 1980. The adjusted projections for 1980 freeway traffic shares in that 1958 plan show that the California Division of Highways *overestimated* the role of freeways in rural areas by about 33 percent, but *underestimated* the role of freeways in metropolitan areas by about 81 percent.[‡] In other words, the role of freeways in California's metropolitan areas in 1980 was nearly double what was anticipated by state highway planners in the 1950s (see Table 11.1).

Today, rural freeways and expressways account for about 2 percent of all rural road lane miles nationwide, and about 4–5 percent in California. Urban freeways and expressways account for about 6 percent of urban road lane miles in the U.S. and 8 percent in California. Figure 11.2 shows that shares of road capacity have not changed much since 1980, the first year for which comparative federal data were available. Further, since not all freeways are part of the Interstate system, the urban Interstates' share of all urban roads is even smaller. At the nominal end of the Interstate era in 1992, freeways in urbanized areas with 200,000 or more residents accounted for just 2.9 percent of all roadway center-line miles,[§] which decreased to just 2.7 percent by 2019.[10]

But while freeway capacity has not changed much since 1980, the share of vehicle travel on freeways and expressways is very substantial, and increasing. Figure 11.3 shows that the share of rural vehicle travel on rural Interstates increased from 20.1 percent in 1980 to 26.6 percent in 2019, and from 20.3 percent to 30.4 percent over the same period in California. Nationwide, the share of urban vehicle travel on all urban freeways and expressways is higher than

---

[†] This is probably a conservative assumption given that the freeways built, especially in rural areas, were in the corridors with the highest travel demand (Schaeffer 1992).

[‡] This is done simply by multiplying the projected freeway traffic share for 1980 by the proportion of the system actually completed in 1980:

(projected traffic share) * (proportion of system completed) = adjusted traffic share projection
- High rural estimate: (75%) * (44%) = 33%
- Low rural estimate: (60%) * (44%) = 26%
- Composite rural estimate: (33%) + (26%) / 2 = **30%**
- High urban estimate: (62%) * (46%) = 29%
- Low urban estimate: (52%) * (46%) = 24%
- Composite urban estimate: (29%) + (24%) / 2 = **26%**

(actual 1980 traffic share) / (adjusted traffic share projection) = percent of over- or underestimation of freeway traffic share
- Rural freeways: (20%) / (30%) = −**33%**
- Urban freeways: (47%) / (26%) = +**81%**

[§] As a reminder, a mile of freeway with three lanes of traffic in each direction would count as one center-line mile and six lane miles.

Table 11.1 Actual versus Projected Traffic Shares in California

	Projected for 1980[a]	Actual in 1980	Percent Difference
Percent of planned rural system completed	100%	44.0%	−56%
Percent of rural travel on rural freeways	60% to 75%	20.3%[b]	−66% to −73%
Percent of planned urban system completed	100%	46.0%	−54%
Percent of urban travel on urban freeways	52% to 62%	47.0%[b]	−10% to −24%

Sources: [a] California Division of Highways, The California Freeway System: Report to the Joint Interim Committee on Highway Problems, 1958, p. 26; [b] USDOT, FHWA Highway Statistics 1980, Table VM-2.

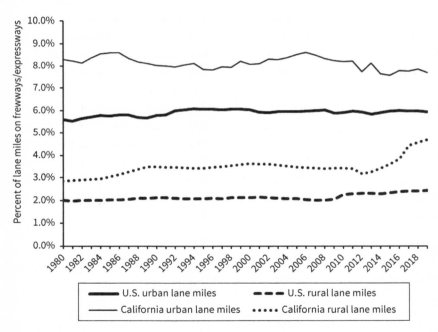

Figure 11.2. Urban and rural freeways and expressways in California and the U.S. as a share of total (urban and rural) road capacity, 1980–2019.

Data Sources: U.S. Department of Transportation, Federal Highway Administration, Highway Statistics 2019, Table HM-260; Highway Statistics, 1980–2019, Table HM-60, U.S. Government Printing Office, Washington D.C.

Note: The data presented for California rural lane miles are a five-year rolling average to account for apparent anomalies in the data reported for some years.

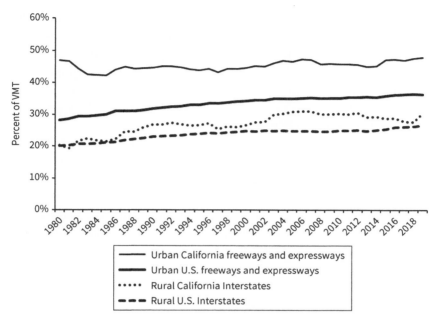

Figure 11.3. Share of all rural and urban vehicle travel on rural and urban freeways, 1980–2019.

Data Sources: U.S. Department of Transportation, Federal Highway Administration, Highway Statistics 2019, Table VM-202; Highway Statistics 1980–2019, Table VM-2; U.S. Government Printing Office, Washington, D.C.

for all freeways, increasing from 28.2 percent in 1980 to 36.5 percent in 2019. While the share of vehicle travel on urban freeways and expressways in California has not changed much since 1980, their absolute role in the Golden State is enormous: just under half of all vehicle miles of travel in California's cities are on the one-half of the planned California Freeway System that eventually got built.

Thus, the focus on rural and intercity travel in the freeway plans in the 1940s and 1950s underestimated the enormous impacts that freeways would have on cities and travel in them. Further, while many would argue that moving vehicles should not be the sole, or even primary, purpose of transportation policy, it is without question that freeways are car-moving machines par excellence.

Still, given their high cost to, and significant disruption of, urban neighborhoods, it is perhaps unsurprising that there has been relatively little appetite to meaningfully add to the existing urban freeway networks—and indeed there have been growing efforts to subtract from them, as noted above. It's been better than a half-century since urban freeway revolts helped to roil and then capsize the freeway consensus, a similar amount of time since highway revenue sources began their long atrophy at the very time that highway costs experienced a sustained rise, and more than a quarter century since the first post-Interstate surface transportation legislation made metropolitan transportation planning and multimodalism official federal urban transportation policy. But while *building* new urban freeways has largely fallen out of favor, *driving* on them is more popular than ever.

Because new urban freeway construction has essentially ended while urban freeway use is still growing, the density of vehicular traffic continues to climb, making traffic delays increasingly common. Between 1980 and 2015, travel on urban freeways increased 230 percent.[11] So while they have long since fallen out of fashion among urban transportation planners, the fact that nearly four out of ten vehicle miles of urban travel nationwide in the late 2010s were on freeways suggests that, as travelers, Americans highly value them.

Freeways, for Better and Worse

Both the benefits and costs of urban freeways and the larger Interstate Highway System are obvious and substantial. In many ways, the freeway has dramatically improved our quality of life—though this is rarely acknowledged in transportation policy and planning circles today. There have been numerous attempts to quantify the benefits over the years, though many of these studies have looked at the economic effects of highway or infrastructure investment more broadly. Overall, these studies have collectively concluded that the construction of the Interstate System has had very positive effects on the U.S. economy.[12] This is due to the fact that:

> [Interstate] construction created a new national system. Where a few new major roads might have had only modest effects, an entire system created a variety of efficient connections that previously did not exist. This resulted in an economy wide return on investment in roads that was very high in the immediate decades after World War II, but that declined in later decades.[13]

The principal way that freeways generally, and the Interstates in particular, affect the economy is by reducing the friction of distance for both producers and consumers. The Interstates did this most dramatically in rural areas, more modestly but still importantly in suburbs, and less still in urban areas where origins and destinations are in closest proximity and where travel by means other than driving is more common. Even in cities, though, freeways have made it easier for producers to draw on larger numbers of suppliers and to increase the geographic scale of their markets; they have allowed firms to draw on larger pools of workers, and workers to choose among larger numbers of jobs; and their faster travel speeds have allowed suppliers, producers, distributors, and retailers to lower inventories.[14]

For example, Keeler and Ying examined the effect of federal-aid highway expenditures on trucking.[15] They found that freeway investments (including in the Interstates) between 1950 and 1973 substantially reduced the industry's costs; had these investments not been made, trucking costs would have been 19 percent higher. They concluded that the cost-savings benefits to the trucking industry during that 23-year span alone equaled at least one-third of all Federal-Aid highway expenditures.

In a comprehensive analysis for the U.S. Federal Highway Administration, Nadiri and Mamuneas found that the significant increases in investment in national highway capital (dedicated primarily, albeit not exclusively, to the Interstates) up through the 1970s accounted for an astounding share of U.S. productivity growth:[16] 32 percent of growth between 1952 and 1963, 25 percent between 1964 and 1972, and 23 percent between 1973 and 1979. They estimated that between 1980 and 1989, when the Interstate System grew only modestly, increases in highway capital stock were still responsible for 7 percent of U.S. productivity increases. These are remarkable returns on public investment. Focusing on cities, Duranton and Turner also found clear economic benefits from highway spending; they estimated that a 10 percent increase in a city's highway stock caused a roughly 1.5 percent increase in jobs over a 20-year period.[17]

Cox and Love also attempted to calculate freeway benefits versus their costs.[18] Though they are admittedly ardent pro-freeway advocates, their estimates, even if generous, offer evidence for freeways' positive contributions to American life. They estimated that the Interstates cut intercity travel times by 20 to 30 percent, resulting in time savings of between 75 and 125 billion hours from the system's beginnings through 1996, the year of their study. This translated to approximately a full week of time saved for every American alive in the 1990s. Cox and Love also found substantial reductions in vehicle operating costs, which, combined with the time savings, resulted in a dollar savings of roughly $1.55 trillion (in 2021$). They also calculated that truck travel was 17 percent cheaper on Interstates compared to alternate roads, with $0.23 of savings on goods movement for each dollar invested in freeways. This equates to approximately $1.66 trillion (2021$) in reduced product prices due to faster and more inexpensive goods movement, the fostering of logistics innovations like just-in-time delivery, and expanded competition. In all, they calculated that through 1996 the Interstates have returned $6 for each $1 invested.

Allen and Arkolakis calculated that removing the Interstates entirely would reduce total U.S. welfare by between 1.1 and 1.4 percent.[19] Since they determined that the system costs about $100 billion annually ($128.0 billion in 2021$) for maintenance and depreciation over time, and since the U.S. GDP in 2007 was $14.25 trillion ($18.41 trillion in 2021$), the system is estimated to generate between $150 and $200 billion ($192.1 and $256.1 billion in 2021$) in surplus welfare, suggesting an overall return on investment of at least 50 percent in any given year, or an annualized return of at least 9 percent.

In addition, the highway engineers who designed the modern freeway were right about safety; the Interstates are far safer than alternate roads. In 2019, there were 0.46 deaths per 100 million miles of urban Interstate travel versus 1.1 for arterial streets, 0.88 for collectors, and 0.69 for local streets (and the disparities are even greater for rural roads).[20] Cox and Love calculated that for the period from 1957 to 1996, the Interstate Highway System saved $368 billion ($623.5 billion in 2021$) in costs from fatalities, injuries, and property damage and saved the lives of at least 187,000 people.[21]

The system has also benefited users by increasing mobility, reducing travel time, lowering vehicle operating costs, and contributing to economic growth. Cox and Love summed these total benefits to roughly between $2.1 trillion and $2.5 trillion in 1995 (or $3.7 to $4.4 trillion in 2021$). Also, there were many benefits for which Cox and Love could not compute monetary returns, such as better accessibility for emergency vehicles, better access to healthcare, improved quality of life (for example, due to greater options in residential location choice), and expanded employment opportunities.

However, it is admittedly difficult to know how travel behavior and land use would have evolved in an alternate world without Interstates. The challenge of such analyses is that freeways, particularly in cities, enabled both sprawling suburban development and a heavy reliance on driving that likely would not have occurred to the same extent in the absence of freeway development. But given the dramatic growth of auto ownership during the first half of the twentieth century, prior to the mass production of freeways, it is highly likely that "freeway-less" American cities would still be dominated by private vehicle travel, if somewhat less so. For example, Kopecky and Suen attributed 60 percent of suburbanization between 1940 and 1970 to factors broader than the construction of the highway network, including the falling real cost of automobiles, rising postwar incomes, a change in the relative cost of traveling by car versus by public transportation, and urban population growth generally.[22]

In the absence of metropolitan freeways, however, U.S. cities might well be more compact and walking- and transit-friendly than today. The experience of countries like Australia and Canada, which, while considerably less populous than the U.S., developed and urbanized over roughly the same time frame and are also quite spacious and wealthy, shows that large cities in these countries are indeed more compact and see less driving and more transit use. But autos and trucks in those places remain, by far, the primary means of conveyance.

It's important to distinguish the benefits and costs of metropolitan freeways, which are both substantial, from the benefits and costs of driving, which are both gargantuan. It's relatively cheap to drive in the U.S. because drivers are mostly shielded from the substantial public costs of auto dependence—delay imposed on others, noise, crashes, air pollution, and greenhouse gas emissions. Such policy choices to keep the cost of driving low help to explain urban freeways' continued popularity among drivers, but it is these auto-friendly policies—and not necessarily the freeways themselves—that are responsible for so many of the external costs of auto dependence.

Further, while there is wide agreement on the positive economic effects of the Interstate System, particularly during the third quarter of the twentieth century, economists have debated whether additional construction of Interstate freeways in later years brought similarly high levels of economic benefit. On the one hand, a widely debated study by Aschauer argued that declining levels of public infrastructure investment in the U.S. contributed to lagging economic productivity growth since the 1970s, suggesting that increasing levels of highway (and other infrastructure) investment would, in recent decades, have returned the sorts of economic productivity growth seen in the post–World War II era.[23]

Other studies in the 1990s and the following decade, however, have suggested that the big contribution of Interstate investment to productivity was due to the initial creation of a national, interconnected highway network, and that subsequent investments have resulted in declining rates of productivity improvement. Some studies have concluded that continued highway investment would bring modest economic returns, while others have found that returns would be negligible altogether.[24] Duranton and Turner, calculating motorists' time and monetary costs, concluded that more highways were built between 1983 and 2003 than was socially optimal.[25] It is worth noting, however, that some of the measured declines in the productivity of the Interstate Highway System are due to increasing congestion and delays on the system, which presumably could be addressed by intelligently managing traffic on them, such as through road pricing.

On the other hand, it is equally important to acknowledge freeways' considerable costs. Perhaps the most pernicious are the health effects of the vehicle emissions that highways generate and concentrate. People who live near freeways are exposed to far more vehicular emissions than those who live farther from them.[26] Research has found that proximity to major roads increases mortality by 3.8 to 6.5 percent for persons over 75 who spend twice as much time downwind of them.[27] Proximity to major roads raises the risk of cardiopulmonary disease,[28] decreases lung function in teenagers,[29] leads to higher mortality in those who suffer from acute myocardial infarction,[30] and increases the odds of premature birth and low birth weights.[31]

Noise, particularly from heavy truck traffic, is also an important problem for those living near freeways. Singh et al. reviewed recent literature and found that road traffic noise is linked to a variety of health and psychological problems, including irritation, annoyance, hypertension, hearing loss, sleep disturbance, cardiovascular disease, risk of stroke, and diabetes.[32] Nelson reviewed the literature on highway noise and hedonic pricing—that is to say, the impact road noise has on property values—and finds an average "noise depreciation index" of a 0.55 percent reduction in home values per additional decibel of noise.[33] Further, Bateman et al. found a reduction in property values of 0.2 percent per decibel,[34] and Kim et al. found that a one percent increase in noise levels (in decibels) is associated with about a 1.3 percent decrease in land prices.[35] Andersson et al. also reported that property prices fall in response to roadway noise.[36]

Highways also consume land that could be put to other purposes. Brinkman and Lin estimated that, in Chicago, freeways consume 0.5 percent of the land in total and 2 percent of the land within five miles of the city center, although they did not find that this crowded out housing.[37] Further, using travel data from Detroit collected before and after the construction of the Interstates, they found a substantial time penalty for motorists who must cross freeways. They calculated this to be a problem particularly in central areas since these tend to have high freeway density due to the radial layout typical of American highway systems.

Finally, few among us find highways to be aesthetically pleasing; indeed, Bateman et al. found that views of roads decrease property prices.[38]

Because of these impacts of freeways, and because who lives near freeways is not random, the many costs of freeway adjacency are disproportionately borne by poor, Black, and other non-White households.[39] To analyze the effects of freeway-adjacent costs on the population, Manville and Goldman examined census block groups collectively intersected by and adjacent to freeways in the ten most traffic-congested urbanized areas in the U.S.[40] They found that freeway-proximate block groups are

> substantially poorer than their [Urbanized Areas] at large, and much poorer than places without freeways. Across the freeway-dominated [block groups], poverty averages 20 percent, compared to 13 percent in areas without freeways. In New York, the poverty rate in freeway-dominated places is almost double that in places without freeways, and in Atlanta, Boston, and Seattle it is at least twice as large. In total, freeway-dominated areas appear to be locations of concentrated disadvantage. They are 0.4 percent of the land area in these [Urbanized Areas], and hold 1.6 percent of the total population, but almost 4 percent of the poor.[41]

Similarly, freeway-dominated block groups are more likely populated by Black and other non-White residents in eight of the ten urbanized areas analyzed. Collectively, these freeway-dominated block groups were 20 percent Black, while block groups away from freeways were 16 percent Black. Similarly, the freeway-dominated block groups across the ten Urbanized Areas were 62 percent non-White, compared to 49 percent in block groups away from freeways.

Since living or working near a freeway *interchange* conveys substantial access benefits but living or working near a *freeway* entails outsized health and travel costs, the net effect may be ambiguous. Scholars have attempted to net out the effects of the disamenities and accessibility benefits of freeways using the hedonic technique. The body of evidence on this topic is large enough that papers have been published that synthesized and reviewed the work of others.[42] To cite some representative studies, Seo found that, on balance, freeways do not affect nearby property values for better or worse.[43] Bowes and Ihlanfeldt found no effect of living within a mile of a highway on residential property prices, but that living at least one but no more than three miles from a highway is associated with higher prices.[44] They also found no links between location near a highway and either crime or retail density. Ryan found that highway proximity decreases office rents but has no effect on the value of industrial properties.[45] Kim et al. found no relationship between distances to highways and residential property prices.[46] Freeways move a lot of "eyes" past adjacent land parcels, so commercial property owners—of movie theaters, restaurants, or car dealers, for example—may value the visibility of freeway adjacency. Indeed, Andersson et al. found evidence that property prices are actually higher near highway entrances when controlling for road noise, though the effect is relatively weak.[47] Li and Saphores found that increases in total freeway traffic have only small effects on the price of nearby housing, but that increases in truck traffic have a larger, negative impact.[48] They also reported that greater distance to the nearest highway on- or off-ramp is associated with lower property prices. In sum, these studies have collectively found relatively weak associations between freeway proximity and real estate prices, suggesting that the costs and benefits of highway proximity are either poorly understood by consumers, are relatively modest, and/or that the access benefits and pollution and disruption costs are largely offsetting.

Finally, as noted above, freeways are more of a mixed blessing, as opposed to an unambiguous curse, in suburban areas. In outlying areas, their benefits have often outweighed their costs; in fact, many outlying suburban areas would never have developed without freeway access. Using population growth as a measure of the attraction/repulsion of freeways, Brinkman and Lin found evidence that the costs of freeways are higher in urban areas than in suburban or rural areas.[49] They concluded that in central cities freeway proximity has been associated with population loss, but in outlying areas it has been associated with growth.

It is also worth noting that many of the benefits of freeway access are spatially dispersed, such as facilitating economic activity across a region, while the costs tend to be spatially concentrated on those who live, work, study, and play near freeways. This leads us to suggest that these dispersed benefits may have been achieved at lower cost in urban areas through smaller, slower multi-modal freeways configured in denser networks, as envisioned by many urban transportation planners a century ago.

What Have We Learned?

The state of metropolitan transportation planning in the U.S. today—which has provided levels of mobility unmatched in human history but with enormous environmental challenges, persistent inequities, chronic congestion, ambiguous intergovernmental authority, unstable finance systems, a small role for analysis in decision-making, and a central role for fiscal politics—is not so different from the situation faced by the first generation of urban transportation planners a century ago. Despite the many similarities, we have much better information today, including the opportunity to learn from our mistakes. So, with the benefit of hindsight, what have we learned?

First, and perhaps foremost, it is clearer than ever that the geopolitics of transportation finance are firmly established at all levels of government and are likely to remain so far into the future. Public investment in transportation systems will continue to be determined more by political struggles over the spatial distribution of resources, and decisions on how to apportion the costs of transportation in the most politically acceptable manner, as opposed to being determined by factors such as transportation system use and effectiveness, fostering and channeling growth, environmental quality, social equity, economic effectiveness, or any of the other broader concerns held by the early municipal transportation planners. Thus, we must be sure that decisions over how to raise and expend revenue will promote and not detract from efforts to attain important transportation, land use, economic, social, cultural, and environmental goals.

In line with the thinking of the Interstate era, the emphasis on flashy transportation capital investments over spending on operations and maintenance also shows little sign of abating. While the overcapitalization of transportation systems is clearly economically inefficient, it is politically popular and is likely to remain so. This means that transportation investments will continue to emphasize projects over programs, lines and modes over integrated systems, and expenditures over savings. In light of the freeway-building experience, we would be wise to seriously reflect on whether we can continue to afford this focus on high-profile infrastructure spending (such as on high-speed rail) over improved operations and prudent maintenance.

We also must address substantial institutional challenges in the post-freeway-construction era. The appropriate federal role in U.S. surface transportation is more hotly debated than ever. On one hand, the federal government has become a principal financier of new, entirely locally serving light rail transit lines, while on the other, it has been unable to develop any sort of a consistent program to manage dramatic increases in goods movement. The latter is a particular problem because many of the benefits of global trade and goods movement accrue nationally and not to the localities that host ports, airports, rail yards, and warehousing centers. So the movement of goods is a place where federal policy and planning, and involvement in local projects and facilities, are justified—but where national leadership has been in short supply.

At the local level, metropolitan planning organizations (MPOs) have had their power, authority, and (thanks often to local option taxes [LOTs]) financial heft expanded. But most MPOs are composed of and constrained by boards of locally elected officials. They have no elected leader, and most people have never heard of them. To avoid the mistakes of the freeway era, it is crucial that we ensure that the federal role is bounded where deserved, but also active enough to motivate coordination when no other body can do so. We must also ensure that MPOs and other local and regional organs plan carefully, function effectively, and avoid political logrolling (for example, by putting regional concerns over those of individual municipalities)—a very tall order given how most are structured.

We have learned that there was much wisdom in the outlook of the early transportation planners. In creating urban transportation systems today, we overlook context at our peril. Freeways have proven to have dramatic effects on the metropolitan areas that host them, from the geography of residential settlement, to regional economic competitiveness, to serious issues of equity. We must never again plan and construct transportation systems in isolation from the broader urban systems in which they function. This means a focus on accessibility over mobility, on multimodal transportation over planning exclusively for autos, on studying the dynamic interplay between freeways and land use as opposed to taking urban form as a given, and on acknowledging transportation infrastructure's costs as well as its benefits.

This then leads to one key lesson from the Interstate era we have learned well—but perhaps *too* well. As we have shown, the experience of creating the Interstates was a major contributor to the modern planning paradigm that takes community concerns into account when creating all manner of infrastructure, not just freeways. Certainly, we must never return to an era when freeways were bulldozed with astonishing speed through neighborhoods, whatever the cost to the people who lived near them. We must always take community concerns seriously and give all of those affected a meaningful voice in planning processes.

However, it is possible that the new planning system may have resulted in too great a swing, with paralysis replacing hyperactivity. One problem is that while communities that are to host new infrastructure have been given very considerable power to block such investments, potential beneficiaries, often from throughout the region, do not have a comparable voice in the planning process. The benefits to individual users from throughout the region may be too small to motivate them to attend public meetings or write letters to elected officials. The potential beneficiaries may not even know they are potential beneficiaries. And many of them might receive rewards far in the future; in fact, infrastructure investments may have dramatic benefits to people who are not yet even born. Along with substantial costs, the national Interstate Highway System has delivered substantial economic returns, though many observers today are loath to acknowledge them. Thus we must take care that the "community" in "community participation" is not too narrowly defined, and that small groups of citizens, no matter how highly motivated, do not have an outsized voice in blocking projects that may deliver substantial benefits to the community at large.

But regardless of who makes metropolitan transportation policy or how, they will have to reckon with urban freeways. All policymakers—whether at MPOs; local, state, or federal departments of transportation; or elected bodies—will have no choice but to adapt to the travel and land-use patterns that metropolitan freeway networks have bequeathed. Though the era of freeway mass production has long since ended, we live today in cities and suburbs laced with freeways and dominated by freeway travel. This is a hand which we have no choice but to play.

Finance, Freeways, and the Future

It is remarkable that an ephemeral financial commitment made over the space of less than two decades more than a half-century ago has had such a lasting influence on American cities—and it is an influence that appears likely to be felt for decades to come. Given this, we now return to the journey of the time traveler we visited at the start of this book. Setting the controls of her time machine to 2050, what kind of transportation and transportation finance system is she likely to find?

Predicting the future is a dangerous game, and if the authors of this book were clairvoyant we'd be fabulously wealthy sports gamblers or hedge fund traders, rather than humble transportation academics. Further, history has shown a stubborn ability to surprise. Many of the seemingly most fanciful futuristic ideas, the source of comedy in *The Jetsons* or *Back to the Future*, often have a way of becoming reality.[50]

In the realm of transportation, though we have been promised flying cars and jetpacks for decades, dogged enthusiasts are still today continuing to develop these technologies and maintain they will soon be science fact, not science fiction.[51] Elon Musk and various firms are developing a "hyperloop" technology they promise will soon carry travelers in underground vacuum tubes at speeds of 750 miles per hour. Perhaps, though we are generally skeptical of such grandiose claims.

Our skepticism is supported by the fact that the history of futurism is rife with predictions that never came true. Despite thousands of years of effort, we cannot transform base metals into gold. Mass famine never struck the world in the 1960s as many had predicted, and the world's oil supply has yet to be depleted; we are now highly likely to shift away from fossil fuels in order to slow climate change, and not because we have run out of oil. The world's computer systems did not fall prey to the "Millennium Bug" on January 1, 2000, and we did not have lunar colonies, missions to Jupiter, and killer computers named HAL by the year 2001. So to avoid the perils of overly speculative prognostication, we will confine ourselves to considering three developments we see as highly likely, and two others often talked about that are in our view more uncertain to shape cities and travel in them in the near future.

First, while freeways have proven most problematic in central cities, only 28 percent of U.S. adults live in urban neighborhoods, while over three-quarters (77%) live in suburban and rural areas where the vast majority of travel is by car or truck.[52] Such car-friendly environments are likely to host high levels of driving for years to come, so continuing to reduce the environmental footprint of cars and trucks is essential. Thus, the first major development is the likely electrification of the vehicle fleet.

Developments are moving rapidly as we write. Although today fully electric vehicles still comprise only a tiny fraction of overall vehicle sales, over the medium term the conversion of the vehicle fleet to electricity looks increasingly inevitable. Giddy investors have bid the stock of electric vehicle manufacturer Tesla up to stratospheric heights, and Tesla is not alone, as all major vehicle manufacturers are investing heavily in electric vehicle (EV) technology (and some in hydrogen fuel-cell technology as well). Improvements in batteries continue to decrease their cost and charging time, and increase their range, the three major problems currently hindering the adoption of EVs. Many nations are debating, and some are implementing, plans to phase out gasoline and diesel vehicles entirely, with mandates that often specify that all new vehicles sold run on alternate sources of power by the years 2025, 2030, 2035, or 2040, including California in the U.S. Further, the 2021 federal infrastructure bill supports vehicle electrification, including networks of EV charging stations. Given the pressing problem of climate change, the electrification of much of the vehicle fleet now seems a question not of if, but of when.

While the shift to EVs looks increasingly certain, the effect of this shift on transportation finance is ever more unsettled. With battling climate change and dramatically reducing emissions and noise becoming urgent imperatives, and EVs promising to help significantly with all three, a switch away from gasoline and diesel propulsion systems will substantially reduce fuel tax revenues. Mileage-based user fees broadly, and congestion and emissions pricing in particular, are promising solutions to gradually sunsetting fuel taxes, but it remains to be seen whether there is the political will to maintain a system of user-fee finance, or whether we will continue to slide toward more use of sales tax and general fund finance. We would argue that this question is enormously consequential for the future of travel and cities, but for now it is a can that most elected officials seem eager to keep kicking down the road.

Second, since the inception of the Internet, futurists have argued that this revolutionary technology would render much physical travel obsolete. The possibilities for working, shopping, enjoying entertainment, socializing, and even receiving medical care at home have long been touted as, among other things, a balm for our overtaxed transportation systems. However, the "death of distance"** promised by the Internet had been slow in coming. Although the share of those working and shopping from home has been gradually rising for decades, it was from a very low base. As a result, many transportation scholars had concluded that face-to-face contact could never be substantially replaced, and that the Internet would never dramatically decrease travel—and in some ways might even increase it.[53]

As we write, the world is still in the grip of the COVID-19 pandemic. While "Zoom fatigue" certainly set in during the second and third years after the outbreak, one dramatic lesson from the pandemic is that information and communications technologies *can* substitute for physical travel to an extent most of us never thought possible. During the summer of 2020, an astonishing 42 percent of Americans were working from home and, despite the fact all would agree that the situation had its drawbacks, it is remarkable how well the economy and society continued to function without physical proximity, allowing us to avoid both economic collapse and the horrific death toll that would likely have resulted had so many not been able to shelter at home. Advocates of the death of distance now argue they have been vindicated: we were not working, shopping, socializing, and recreating online not because the technology did not permit it, but because we had been too stubborn to try.

While many jobs cannot be done remotely, as many as half can. For the latter, surveys consistently show that workers want to work from home "more" after the pandemic than before. They cite benefits such as a quieter work environment with fewer distractions, the ability to dress more casually, a better work-life balance, and—most consequentially for our story—freedom from the grind of the daily commute.[54] Firms, too, may reap advantages from more remote working: improved worker morale; less need for costly office space; possibly increased productivity; and potentially the ability to hire workers worldwide, including in places with lower costs of living (and thus perhaps lower wages).

Online shopping has many advantages over the brick-and-mortar sort, including easy price comparison and handy product reviews, and in terms of transportation it can improve efficiency by replacing many individual auto

---

** The term refers to the gradual weakening of physical distance as a barrier to the exchange of information, innovation, capital, services, and goods.

trips to and from stores with more efficient deliveries from larger vehicles that move from house to house.

While we are not certain what the world will look like post-pandemic, it *is* certain that it will never be the same. Proponents of physical proximity may be right that human beings will always crave the presence of other humans and that innovation comes from serendipitous social interactions, but it seems highly likely that having experienced the possibilities, we will shift more of our lives online permanently. How *much* more is the question that, as of this writing, we cannot yet answer. Although estimates vary widely, surveys of employers and employees alike suggest that many workers will continue to work from home, at least part of the time, well into the future.[55] Indeed, by the third year of the pandemic, so-called "hybrid work," where some work time is spent in the office and some is spent at home, had become a common, and popular, arrangement. The effects of shifting work venues on traffic congestion may be substantially positive, though some, or perhaps all, of reduced daily commutes may be offset by more non-work travel and/or by workers living farther from their jobs.

Third, we think it unlikely that we will see a public undertaking in the transportation realm as audacious and enormous as the Interstate Highway System anytime soon. As we discussed in these closing chapters, citizen voice in transportation decision-making has increased substantially since the heyday of mass freeway construction. This has entailed far more consideration of environmental impacts and, more recently, recognition of the disproportionate harms caused by urban freeway development in low-income, Black, and other minority communities. This increased attention to the equity implications of transportation investments is long overdue and a welcome change.

The collective effect of these changes is that communities are now much less likely to be steamrolled by highway builders' bulldozers, and all new transportation projects, highways or otherwise, are more likely to include mitigations to reduce their negative impacts. Along with this, transportation project planning and development have become more deliberative and time-consuming, and the unit costs of transportation projects have increased dramatically. For example, a 2021 study of public transit capital projects in the U.S. found that inflation-adjusted construction costs per mile ranged from 50 to 250 percent higher than similar projects in other countries, even though the international projects entailed, on average, more tunneling, more stations, and more construction in crowded historic centers.[56]

Given this, we do not foresee major, transformative new transportation investments—in a new, bigger Interstate system, a national high-speed rail network, all new metro systems in our biggest cities, or in Hyperloops, etc.—in the years ahead. Perhaps this is for the better, as the biggest, shiniest projects are often not the most cost-effective ones. And while there is often talk of project "streamlining" in order to build new projects faster and cheaper, the power of communities and other interests to shape, and veto, projects is now well established, and unlikely to be relinquished.

We turn now to two other future developments that we see as less certain— the first because we believe its effects are likely exaggerated, and the second because its realization remains in doubt.

First, some readers may already wonder why we have not put self-driving vehicles on our list of likely transformative transportation changes. While vehicle automation is progressing apace, and we fully expect that it will continue to do so, we see so-called full Level 5 automation and its potentially transformative effects as still many years off, at best. At Level 5, vehicles are entirely autonomous and require no input, or even back up, from human drivers. In what will likely be a protracted interim, we see the increasing levels of automation playing more of an incremental role in the evolution of motor vehicles and driving. Rear-end collisions will become rarer, parallel parking easier, and so on, but drivers will still be involved at some level.

In particular, we would argue that most of the transformative (and dystopian) changes that some transportation futurists fear with vehicle automation—such vehicles clogging roads by driving in circles empty rather than paying to park, or hosting sleeping passengers for 100-mile one-way commutes—are simply part and parcel of the many decades of efforts to make driving easier and cheaper, which have invariably encouraged more driving and will likely continue to do so with or without human drivers. However, were we to intelligently manage human-driven vehicles, through pricing or some other means, such management would mostly apply to auto-driven vehicles as well, which would address many of the concerns raised by worried futurists.[57]

The intelligent management of motor vehicle traffic is our second, more uncertain future for cities and travel in them. A major theme of this book is how transportation planners' and engineers' struggles to accommodate swelling numbers of cars and trucks led to ever-greater investments in road infrastructure, culminating in freeway networks. But, after better than a century of effort, planners and engineers are *still* struggling with how best to accommodate cars and trucks in cities. During that time, we have learned that adding more traffic lanes, grade-separated intersections, and parking all make driving easier and faster in the short term, but this often encourages more driving to the point that congestion returns. This in turn regularly prompts a new round of calls for urban road-capacity enhancements, or a tack toward investments in alternatives to driving, like public transit. While critics argue that the return of congestion proves that road improvements are ultimately fruitless, such improvements do enable more travelers to reach more destinations than before. And while public transit continues to play a central role in large cities where substantial shares of the land were developed prior to the automobile era—like Boston, Chicago, Philadelphia, San Francisco, and especially New York—its role remains decidedly modest across most of the U.S.

As we have seen, traffic congestion has been a vexing problem, defying "permanent" solutions for centuries. But while urban traffic congestion has proven both chronic and vexing, it is also nonlinear, where adding just a few vehicles to a road network operating at capacity can have a disproportionate effect on increasing traffic delays. Conversely, if only some people replace only a few of their social, recreational, household maintenance, shopping, and, especially, work trips by car or truck with travel by another mode, or "travel" of the virtual sort, the strain on the transportation system in general and our congested highways in particular could be relieved considerably. Information and communications technology advancements offer us an alternative to investing ever more in road and/or transit capacity, neither of which have had lasting effects on traffic congestion and emissions. Further, charging drivers directly to access popular roads and scarce parking has demonstrated the potential to shift driving behavior enough to, at last, broker a lasting truce between cars and cities. So, it's entirely possible that driving in U.S. cities in 2050 will be easier, more convenient, more expensive, and rarer than today. The newly uncongested urban streets would be more pleasant places to walk, bike, shop, and socialize, and would enable buses to operate more quickly and frequently as well. And the revenues generated by road and parking pricing could fund improved walking, biking, transit and, where warranted, road infrastructure, as well as programs to subsidize lower-income residents.

But it's also entirely possible, and perhaps even more likely, that widespread road and parking pricing will prove just too viscerally unpopular politically. Instead, the shift away from user-fee finance discussed in the previous chapter may accelerate, so that most transportation investments will be funded primarily by general instruments of taxation, like sales and income taxes, which are disconnected from travel. So, in 2050, it is perhaps likely that transportation planners and engineers will still be debating how best to accommodate (probably safer, less polluting) cars in cities, whether road improvements are warranted, and how much to fund investments in other transportation modes in an attempt to lure recalcitrant drivers out of their cars—just as they do today. Given this, we offer one final prediction: thousands of years of transportation history strongly suggest that whether our time traveler sets her machine for

2050, or 2080, or 2110, it is likely that people will *still* be complaining about congestion.

Last Words

It is extraordinary from the perspective of the twenty-first century that any government would go all in on an undertaking as audacious as the American freeway system. Given its vast scale, such a commitment could perhaps only have been made in an era very different from our own. The decade of the 1950s was a time of dizzying optimism about the promise of technology, a comparative lack of cynicism about the efficacy of government, a relatively high degree of bipartisan consensus about the tasks facing the nation, widespread acceptance of tax increases when these were seen as necessary, planning processes that often excluded dissenting voices, and a willingness to believe that high-speed, high-capacity superhighways could somehow be shoehorned into already built-up urban areas in order to finally solve the problem of chronic traffic congestion. This constellation of factors is unlikely to repeat itself. But regardless, a bell once sounded cannot be unrung, and freeways built by state highway departments between the 1950s and 1980s will continue to play an outsized role in metropolitan life in the U.S. for many years to come, their existence providing testimony to the power of public finance to remake our society, for good and for ill.

Notes

Chapter 1

1. Bruegmann 2006; Jackson 1987; McShane 1994; Morris 2006.
2. McShane 1994; McShane and Tarr 1997; Morris 2006, 2007; Tarr 1996.
3. McShane 1994; McShane and Tarr 1997; Morris 2006, 2007; Tarr 1996.
4. McShane 1994; McShane and Tarr 1997; Morris 2006, 2007; Tarr 1996.
5. Roberts and Steadman 2000; U.S. Census Bureau 2019a, 2019b.
6. Bruegmann 2006; Jackson 1987.
7. Bruegmann 2006; Jackson 1987.
8. Jackson 1987.
9. Bottles 1987; Jones 1985.
10. Gordon 2016; Jackson 1987.
11. Morris 2006.
12. McShane 1994.
13. Gordon 2016.
14. Duany, Plater-Zyberk, and Speck 2010; Kay 1998.
15. Lewis 1997.
16. Glaeser and Kohlhase 2004; PB Consult Inc 2007.
17. Cox and Love 1996.
18. Burby 1971; Hebert 1972; Kay 1998; Leavitt 1970; Lupo, Colcord, and Fowler 1971; Mowbray 1969.
19. Jones 1989.
20. USDOT, FHWA n.d.a. *Highway Statistics 2019*, Tables HM-60, VM-2.
21. Jones 2008.
22. Lewis 1997; McNichol 2006; Swift 2011.
23. Rose 1979, 1990; Seely 1987.
24. Mowbray 1969.
25. Leavitt 1970.
26. Hebert 1972.
27. Kelley 1971.
28. Kay 1998.
29. See, for example, Burby 1971; Gutfreund 2004; Hebert 1972; Lupo, Colcord, and Fowler 1971.
30. USDOT, FHWA 1977.
31. Brodsly 1981.
32. Dunn 1998.
33. Cox and Love 1996.
34. Bullard, Johnson, and Torres 2004.
35. Rose and Mohl 2012.
36. Avila 2014.

37. Ingram 2014.
38. Foster 1981; Schwartz 1976.
39. Schwartz 1976, 512.
40. DiMento and Ellis 2013.
41. Lindbloom 1995.
42. Lewis 1997.
43. Lewis 1997.
44. See, for example, Baumbach and Borah 1981; Lewis 1997; Mohl 2004.

Chapter 2

1. Pant and Fumo 2005.
2. McShane 1975; Morris 2006.
3. McShane 1975; Morris 2006.
4. McShane 1975; Morris 2006.
5. McShane 1975.
6. Morris 2006; Norton 2008.
7. McShane 1975; Morris 2006; Petroski 2016.
8. McShane 1994, 63.
9. Petroski 2016.
10. McShane 1994.
11. Bramlett 1982; Zettel 1946.
12. Duffy 1968, 1974, 1990; McShane 1994; Morris 2006.
13. Chudacoff and Smith 2005; McShane 1975, 1994; McShane and Tarr 1997; Morris 2006; Norton 2008.
14. McShane 1975, 1994; Morris 2006.
15. USDOT, FHWA 1977.
16. Chudacoff and Smith 2005; McShane 1994; Morris 2006; Petroski 2016.
17. Higgens-Evanston 2002.
18. McShane 1994.
19. McShane 1994.
20. Blanchard 1919.
21. Jones 1985.
22. USDOT, FHWA 1977; Vance, Jr. 1990.
23. USDOT, FHWA 1977.
24. Burch 1962; USDOT, FHWA 1977; Vance, Jr. 1990.
25. Burch 1962.
26. USDOT, FHWA 1977.
27. USDOT, FHWA 1977; Vance, Jr. 1990.
28. USDOT, FHWA 1977; Vance, Jr. 1990.
29. Seely 1987; Vance, Jr. 1990.
30. USDOT, FHWA 1977.
31. USDOT, FHWA 1977; Vance, Jr. 1990.
32. USDOT, FHWA 1977; Vance, Jr. 1990.
33. USDOT, FHWA 1977; Vance, Jr. 1990.
34. Holt 1923; Zettel 1946.

35. USDOT, FHWA 1977; Vance, Jr. 1990.
36. Agg and Brindley 1927.
37. Burnham 1961; Holt 1923.
38. USDOT, FHWA 1977; Vance, Jr. 1990.
39. Gordon 2016.
40. USDOT, FHWA 1977.

Chapter 3

1. USDOT, FHWA 1977.
2. Portions of this chapter are adapted from Brown, Jeffrey R. 2006. "From Traffic Regulation to Limited Ways: The Effort to Build a Science of Transportation Planning." *Journal of Planning History* 5 (1): 3–34.
3. Burnham and Bennett 1909.
4. Burnham and Bennett 1909; Hines 1979; Jacobs, Macdonald, and Rofe 2002.
5. Hines 1979.
6. Burnham and Bennett 1909.
7. Hines 1979; Burnham and Bennett 1909; Southworth and Ben-Joseph 2003.
8. Peterson 2003; Schultz 1989; Scott 1995.
9. Peterson 2003; Scott 1995.
10. Alchon 1985; Brown 2006; Peterson 2003.
11. Peterson 2003; Scott 1995.
12. Creese 1994; Unwin 1994.
13. Robinson 1916.
14. Robinson 1916.
15. Robinson 1916.
16. Creese 1994; Jacobs, Macdonald, and Rofe 2002; Southworth and Ben-Joseph 2003.
17. Scott 1995.
18. McShane 1999; St. Clair 1986.
19. Olmsted 1911.
20. Bartholomew 1921.
21. City Plan Commission of Saint Louis 1912.
22. City Plan Commission of Saint Louis 1912; Heathcott and Murphy 2005.
23. City Plan Commission of Saint Louis 1912.
24. USDOT 1997, Table VM-200.
25. Jones 1985; Gordon 2016.
26. McShane 1999.
27. Bottles 1987; McClintock 1925.
28. McShane 1999, 381.
29. Longstreth 1997, 1999; Wachs 1984.
30. Bartholomew 1917; Olmsted, Bartholomew, and Cheney 1924.
31. Bottles 1987; Heathcott and Murphy 2005; St. Clair 1986; Wachs 1984.
32. Eno Center for Transportation 2021a.
33. Bottles 1987; Brown 2005; McShane 1999.
34. Norton 2008.
35. Bartholomew 1924; McClintock 1925.

36. Cook 1989.
37. Heathcott 2005.
38. Heathcott 2005.
39. Cook 1989.
40. Cook 1989.
41. EWGCOG 2017; Jackson 2021.
42. Heathcott 2005.
43. Bartholomew 1924; Knowles 1925; McClintock 1927.
44. McClintock 1926.
45. USDOT, FHWA 1977.
46. McClintock 1926, 1927.
47. McClintock 1926.
48. McClintock 1926, 1927.
49. Jacobs 1993; Jacobs, Macdonald, and Rofe 2002; Marshall 2005; Southworth and Ben-Joseph 2003.
50. Altshuler 1965a; Levin and Abend 1971.
51. Bartholomew 1917; Cheney 1921.
52. McClintock 1925.
53. USDOT, FHWA 1977.
54. McClintock 1926.
55. McClintock 1926, 1931.
56. McClintock 1931.
57. McShane 1999.
58. Roberts and Steadman 2000.
59. McClintock 1926.
60. Gladwell 2019; Seo 2019; Sorin 2020.
61. Bartholomew 1924; Cheney 1921; McClintock 1925.
62. Bartholomew 1917; Cheney 1921.
63. Harland Bartholomew and Associates 1927.
64. Bartholomew 1924; Bottles 1987.
65. Bartholomew 1924.
66. Hill 1917; McClintock 1925, 1926.
67. McClintock 1925; Olmsted, Bartholomew, and Cheney 1924.
68. Cheney 1921; Olmsted, Bartholomew, and Cheney 1924.
69. Bartholomew 1924; Harland Bartholomew and Associates 1927.
70. Creese 1994; Bartholomew 1917; Olmsted, Bartholomew, and Cheney 1924; Robinson 1916; Unwin 1994.
71. Jacobs 1993; Jacobs, Macdonald, and Rofe 2002; Marshall 2005; Southworth and Ben-Joseph 2003.
72. Bartholomew 1924; Olmsted, Bartholomew, and Cheney 1924; Sheridan 1927.
73. McClintock 1925.
74. Marshall 2005.
75. Unwin 1994.
76. Harland Bartholomew and Associates 1928a; McClintock 1925.
77. Peterson 2003; Scott 1995; Southworth and Ben-Joseph 2003.
78. Bartholomew 1917, 1921; Cheney 1921; Olmsted, Bartholomew, and Cheney 1924.
79. Bartholomew 1917; Cheney 1928.

80. Cheney 1921; Olmsted, Bartholomew, and Cheney 1924.
81. Bartholomew 1917.
82. Bartholomew 1917; Lovelace 1993.
83. Lovelace 1993.
84. Bartholomew 1917, 12.
85. Bartholomew 1917.
86. Bartholomew 1917.
87. Lovelace 1993.
88. Bartholomew 1921; Olmsted 1911.
89. Bartholomew 1921.
90. Bartholomew 1921.
91. Olmsted, Bartholomew, and Cheney 1924.
92. McClintock 1931; Foster 1981.
93. LATC 1922, 1.
94. Bottles 1987; Foster 1981.
95. LATC 1922.
96. Olmsted, Bartholomew, and Cheney 1924.
97. Harland Bartholomew and Associates 1927.
98. Olmsted, Bartholomew, and Cheney 1924.
99. Bottles 1987; Foster 1981.
100. Olmsted, Bartholomew, and Cheney 1924.
101. Olmsted, Bartholomew, and Cheney 1924.
102. Olmsted, Bartholomew, and Cheney 1924.
103. Foster 1981; Wachs 1984.
104. Bottles 1987.
105. Bottles 1987.
106. Harland Bartholomew and Associates 1928b; Cheney 1928.
107. Chicago Plan Commission 1925; Harland Bartholomew and Associates 1928a; Nolen 1926, 1930.
108. Harland Bartholomew and Associates 1927.
109. Harland Bartholomew and Associates 1927.
110. Harland Bartholomew and Associates 1928a.
111. McShane 1994.
112. Wachs 1984.
113. Snell 2009.
114. Jones 1989.
115. USDOT, FHWA 1977.
116. Snell 2009.
117. Snell 2009.
118. USDOT, FHWA 1997. *Highway Statistics, Summary to 1995*, Table HF-210.
119. Jones 1989.
120. Highway Research Board 1925, 239.

Chapter 4

1. USDOT, FHWA 1977.

2. USDOT, FHWA 1977.
3. USDOT, FHWA 1977.
4. McShane 1994; USDOT, FHWA 1977; Vance, Jr. 1990.
5. Lewis 1997; McShane 1994; Vance, Jr. 1990.
6. USDOT, FHWA 1977.
7. Hilles 1958, as cited in Vance, Jr. 1990.
8. Lewis 1997; McShane 1994; Seely 1987; Swift 2011; USDOT, FHWA 1977; Vance, Jr. 1990.
9. Lewis 1997; McShane 1994; Seely 1987; Vance, Jr. 1990.
10. Seely 1987; USDOT, FHWA 1977; Vance, Jr. 1990.
11. Lewis 1997; Seely 1987; USDOT, FHWA 1977.
12. USDOT, FHWA 1977.
13. Ingram 2014, 131-2.
14. Ingram 2014.
15. Seely 1987; Swift 2011.
16. Seely 1987; Swift 2011; USDOT, FHWA 1977.
17. USDOT, FHWA 1977.
18. USDOT, FHWA 1977; Vance, Jr. 1990.
19. USDOT, FHWA 1977.
20. USDOT, FHWA 1977.
21. Swift 2011; USDOT, FHWA 1977.
22. Melluso 2020.
23. Seely 1987.
24. USDOT, FHWA 1977.
25. McShane 1994; Seely 1987; Swift 2011; Vance, Jr. 1990.
26. Agg and Brindley 1927.
27. Swift 2011, 15.
28. Seely 1987; USDOT, FHWA 1977.
29. Lewis 1997; Seely 1987; Swift 2011; USDOT, FHWA 1977; Vance, Jr. 1990.
30. Lewis 1997; USDOT, FHWA 1977.
31. USDOT, FHWA 1977.
32. Seely 1987; USDOT, FHWA 1977.
33. USDOT, FHWA 1977.
34. Seely 1987; USDOT, FHWA 1977.
35. Seely 1987; USDOT, FHWA 1977.
36. Seely 1987; USDOT, FHWA 1977.
37. Seely 1987; USDOT, FHWA 1977.
38. Seely 1987.
39. Agg and Brindley 1927; Holt 1923.
40. Highway Education Board 1929; Seely 1987; USDOT, FHWA 1977; Vance, Jr. 1990.
41. USDOT, FHWA 1977.
42. USDOT, FHWA 1977.
43. Vance, Jr. 1990.
44. Seely 1987; Swift 2011; Vance, Jr. 1990.
45. Lewis 1997; Seely 1987; Swift 2011; USDOT, FHWA 1977; Vance, Jr. 1990.
46. Seely 1987; USDOT, FHWA 1977.
47. Seely 1987; Swift 2011.
48. Seely 1987; Swift 2011; USDOT, FHWA 1977.

49. Brown 1998; USDOT, FHWA 1977.
50. USDOT, FHWA 1977.
51. Vance, Jr. 1990.
52. Seely 1987; USDOT, FHWA 1977; Vance, Jr. 1990.
53. Brown 2003; Seely 1987; Swift 2011; USDOT, FHWA 1977; Vance, Jr. 1990.
54. Jones 2008; Seely 1987; Swift 2011; USDOT, FHWA 1977; Vance, Jr. 1990.
55. Swift 2011; USDOT, FHWA 1977; Vance, Jr. 1990.
56. Lewis 1997; Seely 1987.
57. USDOT, FHWA 1977.
58. USDOT, FHWA 1977.
59. Seely 1987; Swift 2011.
60. USDOT, FHWA 1977.
61. USDOT, FHWA 1977.
62. USDOT, FHWA 1977.
63. Lewis 1997; Seely 1987; Swift 2011; USDOT, FHWA 1977; Vance, Jr. 1990.
64. USDOT, FHWA 1977.
65. Lewis 1997; Swift 2011; USDOT, FHWA 1977.
66. Lewis 1997; Swift 2011; USDOT, FHWA 1977.
67. Lewis 1997; Swift 2011; USDOT, FHWA 1977.
68. Seely 1987; USDOT, FHWA 1977.
69. USDOT, FHWA 1977.
70. Swift 2011; Vance, Jr. 1990.
71. Lewis 1997.
72. Lewis 1997; Seely 1987; Swift 2011; USDOT, FHWA 1977.
73. Seely 1987; Swift 2011; USDOT, FHWA 1977.
74. Lewis 1997; Seely 1987; Swift 2011.
75. Seely 1987.
76. Lewis 1997; Seely 1987; Swift 2011.
77. Lewis 1997; Seely 1987; Swift 2011; USDOT, FHWA 1977.
78. USDOT, FHWA 1977.
79. USDOT, FHWA 1977.
80. Seely 1987.
81. Seely 1987.
82. Seely 1987; Swift 2011.
83. Agg and Brindley 1927.
84. USDOT, FHWA 1977.
85. CBO 1978; Paxson 1946.
86. Jones 2008; Lewis 1997; Seely 1987; Swift 2011; USDOT, FHWA 1977; Vance, Jr. 1990.
87. Vance, Jr. 1990.
88. Seely 1987; USDOT, FHWA 1977.
89. USDOT, FHWA 1977.
90. Swift 2011.
91. Seely 1987.
92. Lewis 1997; Seely 1987.
93. USDOT, FHWA 1977.
94. Seely 1987; Vance, Jr. 1990.
95. USDOT, FHWA 1977.

96. Burnham 1961.
97. Zettel 1946.
98. Brown et al. 1999; Zettel 1946.
99. USDOT, FHWA 1977.
100. USDOT, FHWA 1977.
101. Zettel 1946.
102. USDOT, FHWA 1977.
103. Burnham 1961; USDOT, FHWA 1977.
104. Bramlett 1982.
105. Crawford 1939.
106. USDOT, FHWA 1977.
107. Burnham 1961; Higgens-Evanston 2002.
108. Crawford 1932.
109. Crawford 1932, 1939.
110. Zettel 1946.
111. Burnham 1961.
112. USDOT, FHWA 1977.
113. Seely 1987; USDOT, FHWA 1977.
114. Burnham 1961.
115. Purcell 1940; Schwartz 1976; Fein 2008.
116. Fein 2008.
117. Seely 1987.
118. FWA, PRA 1949.
119. Seely 1987; Swift 2011; Vance, Jr. 1990.
120. Lewis 1997; Seely 1987; Swift 2011; USDOT, FHWA 1977; Vance, Jr. 1990.
121. Swift 2011.
122. Lewis 1997; Vance, Jr. 1990.
123. Vance, Jr. 1990.
124. Swift 2011.
125. Seely 1987.
126. Seely 1987.
127. APTA 2019.
128. USDOT, FHWA 1977.
129. USDOT 1967b, Table MV-201.
130. USDOT 1967b, Table VM-201.
131. USDOT, FHWA 1977; USDOT, FHWA 1997, Table MF-203.
132. USDOT 1967b, Table SF-201.

Chapter 5

1. Portions of this chapter are adapted from Brown, Jeffrey R. 2005. "A Tale of Two Visions: Harland Bartholomew, Robert Moses, and the Development of the American Freeway," *Journal of Planning History* 4 (1): 3–32.
2. McShane 1994; Orlin 1992.
3. Orlin 1992; USDOT, FHWA 1977.
4. Ellis 1990; Orlin 1992.

5. Brown 2005.
6. Vance 1988.
7. McClintock 1937.
8. Orlin 1992.
9. Caro 1974.
10. Brown 2005; Caro 1974; Orlin 1992.
11. Bassett 1930, 95.
12. Ellis 1990; Swan 1931.
13. De Leuw 1939; McClintock 1932; Whitten 1930.
14. Harland Bartholomew and Associates 1928a, 1930; McClintock 1937.
15. Taylor 2000.
16. Harland Bartholomew and Associates 1930; TEB 1939.
17. Commonwealth Club of California 1946; Rapid Transit Commission 1924; TEB 1939.
18. Rapid Transit Commission 1924, 11.
19. Rapid Transit Commission 1924.
20. Rapid Transit Commission 1924.
21. Rapid Transit Commission 1924, 7.
22. Rapid Transit Commission 1924.
23. Rapid Transit Commission 1924.
24. Brown 2005.
25. Foster 1981.
26. Bottles 1987.
27. Brown 2005; Harland Bartholomew and Associates 1927, 1928a.
28. Caro 1974.
29. Harland Bartholomew and Associates 1930.
30. Caro 1974; Lovelace 1993.
31. Harland Bartholomew and Associates 1927, 1928a, 1930.
32. Bartholomew 1917; Harland Bartholomew and Associates 1928a; Olmsted, Bartholomew, and Cheney 1924.
33. Lovelace 1993.
34. Harland Bartholomew and Associates 1927, 1928a.
35. Harland Bartholomew and Associates 1930.
36. Harland Bartholomew and Associates 1930.
37. Lovelace 1993.
38. Harland Bartholomew and Associates 1930.
39. Harland Bartholomew and Associates 1930.
40. Caro 1974; Moses 1970.
41. Moses 1951, 1.
42. Moses 1970.
43. Moses 1938, 1970.
44. Johnson 1995.
45. Regional Plan Association 1929.
46. Caro 1974; Moses 1970.
47. Brown 2005; Caro 1974.
48. Caro 1974.
49. Jones 2008.
50. The American City 1933.

51. Caro 1974; Moses 1938, 1970.
52. Moses 1938.
53. Moses 1970.
54. Moses 1939.
55. Moses 1939.
56. Brown 2005.
57. Whitten 1932, 24.
58. Young 1928.
59. McClintock 1932.
60. De Leuw 1939.
61. Chicago Plan Commission 1943.
62. Whitten 1930.
63. McClintock 1937.
64. Jones 2008.
65. USDOT, FHWA 1977.
66. USDOT, FHWA 1997.
67. USDOT, FHWA 1997, Table VM-201.
68. Longstreth 1997.
69. Moses 1943.
70. Brown 2005.
71. Moses 1944.
72. Moses 1944.
73. Moses 1944, 9.
74. Leavitt 1970.
75. Moses 1944; Taylor 2000.
76. Mohl 2012a, 298.
77. Swift 2011.
78. Mohl 2004.
79. Lieb 2011, 52.
80. Moses 1946.
81. Baumbach and Borah 1981; DiMento and Ellis 2013; Lewis 1997.
82. Moses 1946.
83. Moses 1970.
84. Moses 1946.
85. Moses 1970.
86. Moses and Andrews & Clark Consulting Engineers 1949.
87. Altshuler 1965b; Baldwin 1963; Jacobs 1961; Rose and Mohl 2012.
88. Mohl 2012a.
89. Moses 1970.
90. Brown 2005; Moses 1970.
91. Moses 1941.
92. Moses 1953.
93. Silver 1984.
94. Bayor 1996; Connerly 2002; Silver 1984.
95. Silver 1984.
96. Harland Bartholomew and Associates 1947.
97. Harland Bartholomew and Associates 1954.

98. Andrews 1945; City Plan Commission (Cincinnati) 1951; City Plan Commission (Kansas City MO) 1951; Rapid Transit Commission 1949.
99. Rapid Transit Commission 1949.
100. Andrews 1945, 8.
101. Biles 2014, 850.
102. Biles 2014, 850.
103. Rapid Transit Commission 1949.
104. Rapid Transit Commission 1949, I–II.
105. Holt 1923; Jones 2008; FWA, PRA 1949; Zettel 1946.
106. FWA, PRA 1949.
107. Jones 1989.
108. Purcell 1940; Schwartz 1976; USDOT, FHWA 1977.
109. APIC 1933, 61.
110. Fairbank 1937.
111. Brown 2005; Taylor 2000.
112. Altshuler 1965a; Brown 2005.
113. Brown 2005.
114. Lovelace 1993, 135.
115. Seely 1987.
116. Seely 1987.
117. Technical Committee of the Council 1947.
118. De Leuw Cather and Company, and Ladislas Segoe and Associates 1948.
119. Technical Committee of the Council 1947, 1.
120. De Leuw Cather and Company and Ladislas Segoe and Associates 1948.
121. Department of City Planning, City and County of San Francisco 1951.
122. Mohl 2004.
123. Brown 2005; TEB 1939.
124. TEB 1939.
125. Foster 1981; Taylor 2000.
126. ACSC 1937.
127. ACSC 1937; Foster 1981.
128. TEB 1939.
129. Jones 1989; Taylor 2000.
130. Brown 2005; Taylor 2000.
131. Los Angeles Department of City Planning 1941, 13.
132. Foster 1981; Jones 1985.
133. Los Angeles County Regional Planning Commission 1943.
134. Los Angeles County Regional Planning Commission 1943, i.
135. Los Angeles County Regional Planning Commission 1943, 19.
136. Los Angeles County Regional Planning Commission 1943, 17, emphasis in the original.
137. Adler 1987.
138. Ammann and Whitney and Cherniack 1952.
139. Joint Board for the Metropolitan Master Highway Plan 1948.
140. Maguire, Charles and Associates 1947.
141. H.W. Lochner and Company and De Leuw, Cather & Company 1946.
142. State Road Department of Florida 1947.
143. Harland Bartholomew and Associates 1942.

144. Harland Bartholomew and Associates 1942.
145. Lovelace 1993.
146. City of Philadelphia Traffic and Transportation Board 1955.
147. Oregon State Highway Department 1955.

Chapter 6

1. Portions of this chapter are adapted from Taylor, Brian D. 2000. "When Finance Leads Planning: Urban Planning, Highway Planning, and Metropolitan Freeways in California," *Journal of Planning Education and Research* 20 (2): 196–214.
2. Gifford 1983; USDOT, FHWA 1977.
3. Gifford 1983; USDOT, FHWA 1977.
4. Agg and Brindley 1927.
5. U.S. Congress 1932.
6. Crawford 1939.
7. U.S. Congress 1932.
8. USDOT, FHWA 1977.
9. USDOT, FHWA 1977.
10. Gifford 1983.
11. Gifford 1984; Schwartz 1976.
12. Crawford 1939.
13. U.S. Congress 1932, 1937.
14. APIC 1933.
15. Brown 1998.
16. Crawford 1939.
17. CBO 1978, 4.
18. Schwartz 1976
19. USDOT, FHWA 1977.
20. USDOT, FHWA 1977.
21. Weingroff 2017c, 1.
22. USDOT, FHWA 1977.
23. USDOT, FHWA 1977.
24. U.S. Congress 1932.
25. Gifford 1983.
26. Gifford 1983; U.S. Congress 1937.
27. Gifford 1983.
28. Gifford 1983.
29. Gifford 1983.
30. Committee on Roads 1937, 6.
31. U.S. Congress 1937.
32. USDOT, FHWA 1984.
33. Purcell 1939, 2.
34. Gifford 1983.
35. BPR 1939.
36. Jones 2008; Weingroff 2017c.
37. Pennsylvania Turnpike Commission 2021.

38. BPR 1939, 1.
39. BPR 1939.
40. Gifford 1991, 8.
41. BPR 1939, 86; Gifford 1983.
42. Schwartz 1976.
43. BPR 1939; USDOT, FHWA 1977.
44. Gifford 1983.
45. Gifford 1983.
46. BPR 1939.
47. USDOT, FHWA 1977.
48. MacDonald 1941, 248.
49. Gifford 1983.
50. BPR 1939.
51. Rose 1990.
52. USDOT, FHWA 1977.
53. Seely 1987.
54. Jones 2008.
55. Fairbank 1937.
56. BPR 1939.
57. Jones 2008; Swift 2011.
58. BPR 1939.
59. Gifford 1983.
60. BPR 1939, 93.
61. BPR 1939, 93.
62. BPR 1939, 93.
63. Jones 2008.
64. Gifford 1991.
65. Jones 2008.
66. Gifford 1983; Rose 1990; Seely 1987.
67. USDOT, FHWA 1977; Zettel 1946.
68. USDOT, FHWA 1977.
69. Rose 1990; Schwartz 1976.
70. Rose 1990; Schwartz 1976.
71. National Interregional Highway Committee 1944.
72. USDOT, FHWA 1977.
73. Rose 1979, 19.
74. Rose 1979.
75. CBO 1978.
76. Rose 1979; USDOT, FHWA 1977.
77. National Interregional Highway Committee 1944.
78. USDOT, FHWA 1977.
79. Jones 1985; Jones 2008.
80. Rose 1990, 20.
81. USDOT, FHWA 1977.
82. Rose 1990; Schwartz 1976.
83. National Interregional Highway Committee 1944, 56.
84. National Interregional Highway Committee 1944, 53.

85. National Interregional Highway Committee 1944, 71.
86. Fairbank 1937; Purcell 1940.
87. MacDonald 1954, 15–16.
88. National Interregional Highway Committee 1944, 56.
89. Altshuler 1965b.
90. Weingroff 2017b, 1.
91. National Interregional Highway Committee 1944.
92. Lovelace 1993; Weingroff 2000.
93. U.S. Congress 1944.
94. Rose 1990.
95. Gifford 1983.
96. Burch 1962; Gifford 1983; Rose 1990.
97. National Interregional Highway Committee 1944, iv.
98. AASHO 1945.
99. USDOT, FHWA 1977.
100. AASHO 1945.
101. USDOT, FHWA 1977.
102. CBO 1978.

Chapter 7

1. Brown et al. 1999; Jones 2008.
2. Portions of this chapter are adapted from two articles: Morris, Eric A., Jeffrey R. Brown, and Brian D. Taylor. 2016. "Negotiating a Financial Package for Freeways: How California's Collier–Burns Highway Act Helped Pave the Way for the Era of the American Interstate Highway." *Transportation Research Record* 2552 (1): 16–22, and Taylor, Brian D. 2000. "When Finance Leads Planning: Urban Planning, Highway Planning, and Metropolitan Freeways in California," *Journal of Planning Education and Research* 20 (2): 196–214.
3. Zettel 1946.
4. California State Division of Highways 1943; Lindman 1946.
5. Price 1949.
6. Brown, Morris, and Taylor 2009; Jones 1989.
7. Jones 1989.
8. Zettel 1946.
9. California Legislature 1945; Jones 1989.
10. USDOT, FHWA 1977.
11. Collier 1949; Price 1949.
12. Brown 1998.
13. Lindman 1946.
14. Kennedy 1946; Price 1949; Zettel 1958.
15. Price 1949.
16. Jones and Taylor 1987; Los Angeles Department of City Planning 1941; TEB 1939.
17. Lindman 1946.
18. Collier 1949, 12–13.
19. Lindman 1946.
20. Lindman 1946.

21. Lindman 1946.
22. Small, Winston, and Evans 1991.
23. Zettel 1946.
24. USDOT 1967b, Table VM-201.
25. Lindman 1946.
26. California Legislature 1947b; Price 1949.
27. Zettel 1946.
28. California Legislature 1947b.
29. Price 1949.
30. Engineering News Record 1960; U.S. Congress 1960.
31. USDOT, FHWA 1977.
32. Taylor 1992.
33. Collier 1949.
34. California Legislature 1945.
35. California Legislature 1947b.
36. Vail 1955, 77.
37. Mitchell 2006.
38. USDOT, FHWA 1977.
39. Price 1949.
40. Zettel 1958.
41. Small, Winston, and Evans 1989.
42. Mitchell 2006.
43. California Legislature 1947a, 1947b.
44. Zettel 1958.
45. California Legislature 1947a.
46. California Legislature 1947a.
47. Mitchell 2006.
48. California Legislature 1947a.
49. Price 1949; Mitchell 2006.
50. Mitchell 2006.
51. Vail 1955, 67.
52. California Legislature 1947b; Price 1949.
53. Mitchell 2006.
54. California Legislature 1947a.
55. Price 1949.
56. California Legislature 1947a, 1947b.
57. Taylor 1992.
58. Jones 1989.
59. USDOT, FHWA 1977.
60. California Legislature 1947a, 1947b.
61. Price 1949.
62. Taylor 1992.
63. Mitchell 2006.
64. Eno Center for Transportation 2014.
65. USDOT, FHWA 1977.
66. USDOT 1967b, Table VM-201.
67. USDOT, FHWA 1977.

68. USDOT, FHWA 1977.
69. USDOT, FHWA 1977.
70. McCullough 1992.
71. Gifford 1983; Rose 1990; Schwartz 1976.
72. USDOT, FHWA 1977.
73. CBO 1978.
74. U.S. Congress 1948.
75. U.S. Congress 1948.
76. U.S. Congress 1948, 1949; USDOT, FHWA 1977.
77. Rose 1990.
78. Burch 1962; Rose 1990; USDOT, FHWA 1977.
79. USDOT, FHWA 1977.
80. USDOT, FHWA 1977.
81. Rose 1990.
82. USDOT, FHWA 1977
83. Rose 1990.
84. Rose 1990; U.S. Congress 1951.
85. USDOT, FHWA 1977.
86. Rose 1990.
87. Rose 1990.
88. Schwartz 1976.
89. U.S. Congress 1955.
90. Schwartz 1976.
91. USDOT, FHWA 1977.
92. Davies 2002; Swift 2011; Karnes 2009.
93. Gifford 1983.
94. USDOT, FHWA 1977.
95. Rose 1990.
96. CQ Press 1965, 1:530.
97. Rose 1990; Schwartz 1976.
98. Rose 1990.
99. Lewis 1997.
100. President's Advisory Committee on a National Highway Program 1955.
101. President's Advisory Committee on a National Highway Program 1955, 1.
102. President's Advisory Committee on a National Highway Program 1955.
103. Rose 1990.
104. Rose 1990.
105. U.S. Congress 1955.
106. President's Advisory Committee on a National Highway Program 1955.
107. President's Advisory Committee on a National Highway Program 1955; Rose 1990; Schwartz 1976.
108. President's Advisory Committee on a National Highway Program 1955, 7.
109. President's Advisory Committee on a National Highway Program 1955, 11.
110. President's Advisory Committee on a National Highway Program 1955; Rose 1990.
111. BPR 1939.
112. President's Advisory Committee on a National Highway Program 1955; Rose 1990; Schwartz 1976.

113. President's Advisory Committee on a National Highway Program 1955, 16.
114. Schwartz 1976; Rose 1990.
115. U.S. House of Representatives, Public Works Committee 1955, 1189.
116. U.S. House of Representatives, Public Works Committee 1955, 1106.
117. U.S. Congress 1955.
118. U.S. Senate Public Works Committee 1955; Schwartz 1976; Rose 1990.
119. U.S. Congress 1955.
120. USDOT, FHWA 1977.
121. U.S. Congress 1955, 1956.
122. USDOT, FHWA 1977.
123. Weingroff 2017d; Morris et al. 2016; Schwartz 1976; Rose 1990.
124. Weingroff 2017d.
125. As quoted in Weingroff 2017d, 8.
126. CQ Press 1965.
127. BPR 1955.
128. Schwartz 1976.
129. Burch 1962.
130. Schwartz 1976.
131. Schwartz 1976.
132. USDOT, FHWA 1977.
133. USDOT, FHWA 1977.
134. USDOT, FHWA 1977.
135. Burch 1962; Lewis 1997; Mitchell 2006; U.S. Congress 1955; Rose 1990; Schwartz 1976; U.S. House of Representatives, Committee on Ways and Means 1956; U.S. Senate Finance Committee 1956; Weingroff 1996.
136. USDOT, FHWA 1977.
137. U.S. House of Representatives, Committee on Ways and Means 1956.
138. Rose 1990; Schwartz 1976.
139. U.S. House of Representatives, Committee on Ways and Means 1956.
140. U.S. Senate Finance Committee 1956; U.S. Congress 1956.
141. U.S. Senate Finance Committee 1956.
142. Weingroff 1996.
143. U.S. Congress 1956.

Chapter 8

1. Portions of this chapter are adapted from Taylor, Brian D. 1995. "Public Perceptions, Fiscal Realities, and Freeway Planning: The California Case," *Journal of the American Planning Association* 61 (1): 43–56.
2. Jones 1989.
3. Metropolitan Transportation Engineering Board 1958, 13.
4. California Division of Highways 1958.
5. Jones 1989.
6. Quoted in Jones 1989, 243.
7. USDOT, FHWA 1977.
8. California Division of Highways 1958, 20.

9. California Division of Highways 1958, 8–10.
10. California Division of Highways 1958, 22.
11. California Division of Highways 1958, 22.
12. California Division of Highways 1958, 32.
13. FWA, PRA 1948, Table SF-1; USDOT [1966 Highway Statistics], n.d., Table SF-1.
14. Zettel and Senate Transportation Committee 1980.
15. Zettel 1958.
16. Zettel 1958.
17. Zettel 1958, I–13.
18. Jones 1989.
19. BPR 1967; Zettel and Shuldiner 1959.
20. CQ Press 1965; Zettel and Shuldiner 1959.
21. California Department of Public Works, and Business and Transportation Agency 1973; Jones 1989; Zettel and Shuldiner 1959.
22. Schaeffer 1992.
23. Altshuler 1965a.
24. Gifford 1984.
25. MacDonald 1936.
26. Gifford 1984.
27. Pivetti 1992.
28. USDOT, FHWA 1977.
29. Schaeffer 1992.
30. Mohl 2004.
31. Quoted in Mohl 2004, 678.
32. Chandra and Thompson 2000.
33. Forkenbrock and Foster 1990.
34. Michaels 2008.
35. Milowski 2018.
36. California Department of Public Works, and Business and Transportation Agency 1973; California Department of Transportation 1983; Jones 1989; Zettel and Shuldiner 1959.
37. California Department of Public Works, and Business and Transportation Agency 1973; California Department of Transportation 1983; Jones 1989.

Chapter 9

1. Brodsly 1981.
2. Pivetti 1992.
3. Baldwin 1963; DiMento and Ellis 2013; Jacobs 1961; Kay 1998; Rose and Mohl 2012; Swift 2011.
4. Baumbach and Borah 1981, ; Biles 2014; Buel 1972; Bullard, Johnson, and Torres 2004; Connerly 2002; Dewey 2020; Dimento and Ellis 2013; Hodge 1986; Karas 2015; Leavitt 1970; Lieb 2011; McCormick 2020; McNichol 2006; Mohl 2004, 2008, 2012a, 2012b, 2014; Rose and Mohl 2012; Swift 2011; Wells 2011.
5. Rose and Mohl 2012, 108–109.
6. Brinkman and Lin 2019.
7. Brinkman and Lin 2019.

8. Brinkman and Lin 2019.
9. Pivetti 1992.
10. Mohl 2004.
11. Baum-Snow 2007, 2008.
12. Cox, Gordon, and Redfearn 2008.
13. Brinkman and Lin 2019.
14. Blumenberg et al. 2019.
15. Jones 2008.
16. Avila 2014; Manville and Goldman 2017; Mohl 2012b; Sherman 2014.
17. Zettel and Shuldiner 1959.
18. Mohl 2004.
19. DiMento and Ellis 2013.
20. Avila 2014.
21. Karas 2015.
22. Biles, Mohl, and Rose 2014, 154.
23. Baumbach and Borah 1981.
24. Mohl 2014.
25. Mohl 2014, 880.
26. Karas 2015.
27. Mohl 2014.
28. Mohl 2004.
29. California Division of Highways 1958; California Department of Transportation 1991.
30. White and Erickson 2011.
31. Zettel 1958.
32. California Division of Highways 1970.
33. USDOT, FHWA n.d.a. *Highway Statistics* 1991, Table PT-5.
34. Jones and Taylor 1987.
35. USDOT, FHWA 1977.
36. California Division of Highways 1970.
37. Schaeffer 1992.
38. National Academies of Sciences, Engineering, and Medicine 2019.
39. Schaeffer 1992.
40. See, for example, Olmsted, Bartholomew, and Cheney 1924; McClintock 1937.
41. McClintock 1932.
42. TEB 1939; National Interregional Highway Committee 1944.
43. California Division of Highways 1970.
44. California Division of Highways 1975.
45. California Division of Highways 1970.
46. USDOT, FHWA 1977.
47. DiMento and Ellis 2013; Zamora 1989.
48. Heppenheimer 1991.
49. DiMento, Van Hegel, and Ryan 1996; Garrett 2006.
50. Los Angeles Metropolitan Transit Authority n.d.
51. Zamora 1989.
52. Pivetti 1992.
53. Brooks and Liscow 2020.
54. Brooks and Liscow 2020.

55. USDOC, BPR 1962–1966, *Highway Statistics 1960–64*, Tables F-2, SMB-2; USDOT, FHWA, BPR 1967-n.d.a. *Highway Statistics 1965–68*, Tables F-2, HF-2, SMB-2; USDOT, FHWA n.d.a. *Highway Statistics 1969*, Tables HF-2, SMB-2.
56. USDOT, FHWA n.d.a. *Highway Statistics 1970–77*, Tables HF-2, SMB-2.
57. Pivetti 1992.
58. USDOT, FHWA n.d.a. *Highway Statistics 1983*, Table FE-101.
59. USDOT n.d.a. *Highway Statistics 2000*, Table FE-221.
60. USDOT, FHWA n.d.a *Highway Statistics 1991*, Table FE-221.
61. USDOC, BPR 1953, 1963.
62. The Pew Environment Group 2011.

Chapter 10

1. Calculated from the National Transit Database 2019 and the American Community Survey 2019.
2. Morrow, Jr. 2019.
3. Morrow, Jr. 2019.
4. Taylor and Morris 2015.
5. APTA 2019
6. USDOT 2018.
7. Weiner 2013, 14.
8. Sciara and Handy 2017, 142.
9. Burrows 2009.
10. EPA n.d.
11. USDOT, FHWA 1977.
12. USDOT 2020a.
13. Holtz-Eakin and Wachs 2011.
14. Taylor and Schweitzer 2005.
15. USDOT 2007.
16. Duncan 2021a.
17. Sciara 2012a, 2012b, 2012c.
18. Duncan 2021a.
19. ASCE 2021.
20. Knopman et al. 2017.
21. Schaper, 2017.
22. NTSB 2008.
23. Rogers 2019.
24. National Academies of Sciences, Engineering, and Medicine, 2019.
25. National Academies of Sciences, Engineering, and Medicine, 2019, 207.
26. Davis 2018; Murse 2018.
27. USDOT, FHWA 1977.
28. USDOT 2013.
29. USDOT 2017.
30. McMahon 2019.
31. Vlasic 2012.
32. Davenport 2018; Roberts 2018.

33. Lewis and Westervelt 2020.
34. Schultz and Atkinson 2009; National Surface Transportation Policy and Revenue Study Commission 2008; National Transportation Policy Project 2011.
35. Hubler et al. 2021.
36. Stein 2021.
37. Lewis and Westervelt 2020.
38. USDOT, FHWA n.d.a. *Highway Statistics 2019*, Table FE-221.
39. Office of Policy and Governmental Affairs 2017, Table 8.
40. USDOT, FHWA n.d.a. *Highway Statistics 2019*, Table FE-221.
41. Nixon and Agrawal 2018.
42. USDOT, FHWA n.d.a. *Highway Statistics Summary to 1985*, Table MF-205, n.5.
43. Bowman and Mikesell 1985.
44. Ang-Olson, Wachs, and Taylor 2000.
45. USDOT, FHWA n.d.a. *Highway Statistics Summary to 1985*, Table MF-205, n.5.
46. Rall et al. 2011; Workman and Rall 2012.
47. Rall et al. 2011; Workman and Rall 2012.
48. USDOT, FHWA n.d.a. *Highway Statistics 2019*, Table MF-205.
49. USDOT, FHWA n.d.a. *Highway Statistics 2000, 2010*, Tables LGB-2, SB-2.
50. Wall Street Journal 2021.
51. Laska and Puentes 2019.
52. Lederman et al. 2018b.
53. Crabbe et al. 2005.
54. Hannay and Wachs 2007.
55. Lederman et al. 2018a, 2018b.
56. Jones and Bock 2017.
57. Wachs 2018.
58. USDOT 2019.
59. Small, Winston, and Evans 1991.
60. Manville and Goldman 2017.
61. Schweitzer and Taylor 2008.
62. Poole 2018.
63. Mastako, Laurence, and Sullivan 1998; Sullivan and Harake 1998; Sullivan and Burris 2006.
64. USDOT 2021.
65. Poole 2012.
66. Mastako, Laurence, and Sullivan 1998; USDOT 2020b.
67. Manville 2019.
68. Schweitzer and Taylor 2008.
69. Manville 2021.
70. Taylor and Kalauskas 2010.

Chapter 11

1. Mohl 2012b.
2. Rose and Mohl 2012.
3. CNU 2021a.
4. Popovich, Williams, and Lu 2021.

5. Mohl 2012b.
6. CNU 2021b.
7. Dewey 2020; Duncan 2021b.
8. Biden 2021, n.p.
9. Popovich, Williams, and Lu 2021.
10. USDOT n.d.a. *Highway Statistics 1992, 2019*, Table HM-72.
11. National Academies of Sciences, Engineering, and Medicine, 2019.
12. Friedlaender 1965; Keeler and Ying 1988; Boarnet 1997; Fernald 1999; Gramlich 2001; Shatz et al. 2011.
13. Shatz, et al. 2011, 20.
14. Shatz, et al. 2011.
15. Keeler and Ying 1988.
16. Nadiri and Mamuneas 1994.
17. Duranton and Turner 2012.
18. Cox and Love 1996.
19. Allen and Arkolakis 2014.
20. USDOT n.d.a., *Highways Statistics 2019*, Tables FI-220, VM-202.
21. Cox and Love 1996.
22. Kopecky and Suen 2010.
23. Aschauer 1989.
24. Boarnet 1997; Duranton et al. 2014; Fernald 1999; Harmatuck 1996; Leff Yaffe 2019; Mamuneas and Nadiri 2006; Nadiri and Mamuneas 1994.
25. Duranton and Turner 2012.
26. Brugge et al. 2007; Hu et al. 2009; Karner et al. 2010; Rioux et al. 2010.
27. Anderson 2020.
28. Hoek et al. 2002.
29. Gauderman et al. 2007.
30. Rosenbloom et al. 2012.
31. Brugge et al. 2007.
32. Singh et al. 2018.
33. Nelson 2008.
34. Bateman et al. 2001.
35. Kim et al. 2007.
36. Andersson et al. 2010.
37. Brinkman and Lin 2019.
38. Bateman et al 2001.
39. Houston et al. 2004.
40. Manville and Goldman 2017.
41. Manville and Goldman 2017, 335.
42. See, for example, Bateman et al. 2001.
43. Seo 2019.
44. Bowes and Ihlanfeldt 2001.
45. Ryan 2005.
46. Kim et al. 2007.
47. Andersson et al. 2010.
48. Li and Saphores 2012.
49. Brinkman and Lin 2019.

50. Walsh 2019.
51. Bernhard 2020.
52. Blumenberg et al. 2019.
53. Circella and Mokhtarian 2017.
54. getAbstract 2020; Watkins 2021.
55. Florida and Ozimek 2021.
56. Eno Center for Transportation 2021b.
57. Millard-Ball, 2019.

References

Adler, Sy. 1987. "Why BART but No LART? The Political Economy of Rail Rapid Transit Planning in the Los Angeles and San Francisco Metropolitan Areas, 1945–1957." *Planning Perspectives* 2 (2): 149–174.

Agg, Thomas R., and John E. Brindley. 1927. *Highway Administration and Finance*. New York, NY: McGraw-Hill.

Alchon, Guy. 1985. *The Invisible Hand of Planning: Capitalism, Social Science, and the State in the 1920s*. Princeton, NJ: Princeton University Press.

Allen, Treb, and Costas Arkolakis. 2014. "Trade and the Topography of the Spatial Economy." *The Quarterly Journal of Economics* 129 (3): 1085–1140.

Altshuler, Alan A. 1965a. *Locating the Intercity Freeway*. Indianapolis, IN: Bobbs-Merrill.

Altshuler, Alan A. 1965b. *The City Planning Process: A Political Analysis*. Ithaca, NY: Cornell University Press.

American Association of State Highway Officials (AASHO). 1945. *A Policy on Design Standards: Interstate System, Primary System, Secondary and Feeder Roads*. Washington, DC: American Association of State Highway Officials.

American Community Survey. 2019. *2019: American Community Survey 5-year Estimate*. Washington, DC: US Census Bureau.

American Petroleum Industries Committee (APIC). 1933. *First Annual Report of the American Petroleum Industries Committee*. New York, NY: American Petroleum Industries Committee.

American Public Transportation Association (APTA). 2019. *2019 Public Transportation Fact Book Appendix A: Historical Tables*. Washington, DC: American Public Transit Association.

American Society of Civil Engineers (ASCE). 2021. "2021 Report Cards for America's Infrastructure." *Infrastructurereportcard*. https://infrastructurereportcard.org/. Accessed March 10, 2021.

Ammann and Whitney Consulting Engineers, and Nathan Cherniack. 1952. *Preliminary Plan for a Comprehensive Expressway System for the City of Milwaukee*. Milwaukee, WI: Commissioner of Public Works and the Director of Expressways.

Anderson, Michael L. 2020. "As the Wind Blows: The Effects of Long-Term Exposure to Air Pollution on Mortality." *Journal of the European Economic Association* 18 (4): 1886–1927.

Andersson, Henrik, Lina Jonsson, and Mikael Ögren. 2010. "Property Prices and Exposure to Multiple Noise Sources: Hedonic Regression with Road and Railway Noise." *Environmental and Resource Economics* 45 (1): 73–89.

Andrews, W. Earle. 1945. *Detroit Expressway and Transit System*. New York, NY: Detroit Transportation Board.

Ang-Olson, Jeffrey, Martin Wachs, and Brian D. Taylor. 2000. "Variable-Rate State Gasoline Taxes." *Transportation Quarterly* 54 (1): 55–68.

Aschauer, David Alan. 1989. "Is Public Expenditure Productive." *Journal of Monetary Economics* 23: 177–200.

Automobile Club of Southern California (ACSC). 1937. *Traffic Survey of Los Angeles Metropolitan Area*. Los Angeles: Automobile Club of Southern California.

Avila, Eric. 2014. *The Folklore of the Freeway: Race and Revolt in the Modernist City*. Minneapolis: University of Minnesota Press.

Baldwin, James. 1963. "Urban Renewal . . . Means Negro Removal. ~ James Baldwin (1963)." *Vince Graham Channel—YouTube.* https://www.youtube.com/watch?v=T8Abhj17kYU. Accessed March 2, 2021.

Bartholomew, Harland. 1917. *A Major Street Plan for St. Louis.* St. Louis, MO: St. Louis City Plan Commission.

Bartholomew, Harland. 1921. *A Major Street Plan for Pittsburgh.* Pittsburgh, PA: Citizens Committee on City Plan of Pittsburgh.

Bartholomew, Harland. 1924. "Alleviation and Remedy of Street Congestion." *Engineering News-Record* 92 (18): 766–767.

Bassett, Edward. 1930. "The Freeway—A New Kind of Thoroughfare." *The American City,* February 1930: 95.

Bateman, Ian, Brett Day, Iain Lake, and Andrew Lovett. 2001. *The Effect of Road Traffic on Residential Property Values: A Literature Review and Hedonic Pricing Study.* Edinburgh, Scotland: The Scottish Executive and The Stationary Office.

Baumbach, Richard O., and William E. Borah. 1981. *The Second Battle of New Orleans: A History of the Vieux Carré Riverfront-Expressway.* Tuscaloosa: University of Alabama Press.

Baum-Snow, Nathaniel. 2007. "Did Highways Cause Suburbanization?" *The Quarterly Journal of Economics* 122 (2): 775–805.

Baum-Snow, Nathaniel. 2008. "Reply to Cox, Gordon and Redfearn's Comment on 'Did Highways Cause Suburbanization.'" *Econ Journal Watch* 5: 46–50.

Bayor, Ronald. 1996. *Race and the Shaping of Twentieth-Century Atlanta.* Chapel Hill: University of North Carolina Press.

Bernhard, Adrienne. 2020. "Flying Cars May Seem Futuristic—But from Commercial Jetpacks to Personal Air Taxis, They Are Already Here. Here's How They Could Transform the Way We Commute, Work and Live." *Future Inc.*https://www.bbc.com/future/article/20201111-the-flying-car-is-here-vtols-jetpacks-and-air-taxis. Accessed March 5, 2021.

Biden, Joseph R. 2021. "Memorandum on Redressing Our Nation's and the Federal Government's History of Discriminatory Housing Practices and Policies." *The White House.* https://www.whitehouse.gov/briefing-room/presidential-actions/2021/01/26/memoran dum-on-redressing-our-nations-and-the-federal-governments-history-of-discriminatory-housing-practices-and-policies/. Accessed May 23, 2021.

Biles, R. 2014. "Expressways before the Interstates: The Case of Detroit, 1945–1956." *Journal of Urban History* 40 (5): 843–854.

Biles, R., Raymond A. Mohl, and Mark H. Rose. 2014. "Revisiting the Urban Interstates: Politics, Policy, and Culture since World War II." *Journal of Urban History* 40 (5): 827–830.

Blanchard, Arthur. 1919. *American Highway Engineers Handbook.* New York, NY: John Wiley and Sons.

Blumenberg, Evelyn, Anne Brown, Kelcie Ralph, Brian D. Taylor, and Carole Voulgaris. 2019. "A Resurgence in Urban Living? Trends in Residential Location Patterns of Young and Older Adults since 2000." *Urban Geography* 40 (9): 1375–1397.

Boarnet, Marlon G. 1997. "Highways and Economic Productivity: Interpreting Recent Evidence." *Journal of Planning Literature* 11 (4): 476–486.

Bottles, Scott. 1987. *Los Angeles and the Automobile: The Making of the Modern City.* Los Angeles and Berkeley: University of California Press.

Bowes, David R., and Keith R. Ihlanfeldt. 2001. "Identifying the Impacts of Rail Transit Stations on Residential Property Values." *Journal of Urban Economics* 50 (1): 1–25.

Bowman, John, and John Mikesell. 1985. "Recent Changes in State Gasoline Taxation: An Analysis of Structure and Rates." *National Tax Journal* 36 (2): 163–182.

Bramlett, N. Kent. 1982. *The Evolution of Highway-User Charge Principals.* Washington, DC: Federal Highway Administration.

Brinkman, Jeffrey, and Jeffrey Lin. 2019. "Freeway Revolts." Working paper WP 19-29. Philadelphia: Federal Reserve Bank of Philadelphia.

Brodsly, David. 1981. *L.A. Freeway, An Appreciative Essay*. Berkeley: University of California Press.

Brooks, Leah, and Zachary D. Liscow. 2020. *Infrastructure Costs*. Rochester, NY: SSRN.

Brown, Jeffrey R. 1998. *Trapped in the Past: The Gas Tax and Highway Finance*. Master's thesis, University of California, Los Angeles.

Brown, Jeffrey R. 2003. *The Numbers Game: The Politics of Surface Transportation Finance*. PhD dissertation, University of California, Los Angeles.

Brown, Jeffrey R. 2005. "A Tale of Two Visions: Harland Bartholomew, Robert Moses, and the Development of the American Freeway." *Journal of Planning History* 4 (1): 3–32.

Brown, Jeffrey R. 2006. "From Traffic Regulation to Limited Ways: The Effort to Build a Science of Transportation Planning." *Journal of Planning History* 5 (1): 3–34.

Brown, Jeffrey R., Michele DiFrancia, Mary C. Hill, Phillip Law, Jeffrey Olson, Brian D. Taylor, Martin Wachs, and Asha Weinstein. 1999. *The Future of California Highway Finance*. Berkeley: California Policy Research Center, University of California.

Brown, Jeffrey R., Eric A. Morris, and Brian D. Taylor. 2009. "Planning for Cars in Cities: Planners, Engineers and Freeways in the 20th Century." *Journal of the American Planning Association* 75 (2): 161–77.

Bruegmann, Robert. 2006. *Sprawl: A Compact History*. Chicago, IL: University of Chicago Press.

Brugge, D., J. L. Durant, and C. Rioux. 2007. "Near-Highway Pollutants in Motor Vehicle Exhaust: A Review of Epidemiologic Evidence of Cardiac and Pulmonary Health Risks." *Environmental Health* 6 (1): 1–12.

Buel, Robert A. *1972. Dead End: The Automobile in Mass Transportation*. Baltimore, MD: Penguin Books.

Bullard, Robert, Glenn Johnson, and Angel Torres. 2004. *Highway Robbery: Transportation Racism and New Routes to Equity*. Boston, MA: South End Press.

Burby, John. 1971. *The Great American Motion Sickness; or, Why You Can't Get There from Here*. Boston, MA: Little, Brown.

Burch, Philip H. 1962. *Highway Revenue and Expenditure Policy in the United States*. New Brunswick, NJ: Rutgers University Press.

Bureau of Public Roads (BPR). 1939. *Toll Roads and Free Roads*. H. Doc. 272. Washington, DC: 76th Congress, 1st session.

Bureau of Public Roads (BPR). 1955. *General Location of National System of Interstate Highways*. Washington, DC: U.S. Department of Commerce.

Burnham, Daniel, and Edward H. Bennett. 1909. *Plan of Chicago*. Chicago, IL: The Commercial Club of Chicago.

Burnham, John C. 1961. "The Gasoline Tax and the Automobile Revolution." *Mississippi Valley Historical Review* 48 (3): 435–459.

Burrows, Matthew. 2009. "The Clean Air Act: Citizen Suits, Attorneys' Fees, and the Separate Public Interest Requirement." *Boston College Environmental Affairs Law Review* 36 (1): 103–134.

California Department of Public Works, and Business and Transportation Agency. 1973. *Statistical Reports of the Department of Public Works Pertaining to the Division of Highways, 1963–1973*. Sacramento: California Department of Public Works.

California Department of Transportation. 1983. *State Highway Program: Financial Statements and Statistical Reports*. Sacramento: California Department of Transportation.

California Department of Transportation. 1991. *Annual Financial Statements of Miscellaneous Statistical Reports*. Sacramento: California Department of Transportation.

California Division of Highways. 1958. *The California Freeway System: A Report to the Joint Interim Committee on Highway Problems of the California Legislature in Conformity with*

Senate Concurrent Resolution No. 26 1957 Legislature. Sacramento: California Division of Highways.

California Division of Highways. 1970. *Spiraling Costs: A Report of the Causes and Effects of Increasing Highway Project Costs and on Recommended Courses of Action*. Sacramento: California Division of Highways.

California Division of Highways. 1975. *The Highway Program in Crisis: How Did We Get Where We Are Today?* Sacramento: California Division of Highways.

California Legislature. 1945. *Journal of the Assembly*. Sacramento: State Printing Office.

California Legislature. 1947a. *Journal of the Assembly*. Sacramento: State Printing Office.

California Legislature. 1947b. *Journal of the Senate*. Sacramento: State Printing Office.

California State Division of Highways. 1943. *First Critical Deficiency Report*. Sacramento: California State Division of Highways.

Caro, Robert. 1974. *The Power Broker: Robert Moses and the Fall of New York*. New York, NY: Vintage.

Chandra, Amitabh, and Eric Thompson. 2000. "Does Public Infrastructure Affect Economic Activity? Evidence from the Rural Interstate Highway System." *Regional Science and Urban Economics* 30 (4): 457–490.

Cheney, Charles. 1921. *Major Street Plan, Boulevard and Park System for Portland, Oregon*. Portland, OR: City Planning Commission.

Cheney, Charles. 1928. *Major Traffic Street Plan and Report: Riverside, California*. Riverside, CA: Riverside City Planning Commission.

Chicago Plan Commission. 1925. *Through Traffic Streets*. Chicago, IL: Chicago Plan Commission.

Chicago Plan Commission. 1943. *Proposed Expressway Development Program (Initial Stage) for the City of Chicago*. Chicago, IL: Chicago Plan Commission.

Chudacoff, Howard P., and Judith E. Smith. 2005. *The Evolution of American Urban Society* (6th edition). Upper Saddle River, NJ: Pearson Prentice Hall.

Circella, Giovanni, and Patricia L. Mokhtarian. 2017. "Impacts of Information and Communications Technology," in *The Geography of Urban Transportation* (4th edition), Genevieve Giuliano and Susan Hanson (eds.). New York, NY: Guilford Press, 86–109.

City of Philadelphia Traffic and Transportation Board. 1955. *Plan and Program*. Philadelphia, PA: City of Philadelphia Traffic and Transportation Board.

City Plan Commission (Kansas City, MO). 1951. *Expressways of Greater Kansas City: An Engineering Report for the Missouri State Highway Department and the Bureau of Public Roads, Department of Commerce*. Kansas City, MO: City Plan Commission.

City Plan Commission of St. Louis. 1912. *Central Traffic Parkway*. St. Louis, MO: St. Louis City Plan Commission.

City Planning Commission (Cincinnati, OH). 1951. *The Expressway System for Metropolitan Cincinnati*. Cincinnati, OH: City Planning Commission.

Collier, Randolph. 1949. *The Legislature Takes a Look at California Highway Needs and Other Addresses*. Sacramento: Senate of the State of California.

Committee on Roads. 1937. *Report to the House of Representatives*. Washington, DC: United States House of Representatives.

Commonwealth Club of California. 1946. *Metropolitan Freeways and Mass Transportation*. Transactions of the Commonwealth Club of California. San Francisco.

Congress for New Urbanism (CNU). 2021a. "Completed Highways to Boulevards Projects." *Congress for New Urbanism*. https://www.cnu.org/our-projects/highways-boulevards/completed-h2b-projects. Accessed February 21, 2021.

Congress for New Urbanism (CNU). 2021b. "Oakland | Mandela Parkway." *Congress for New Urbanism*. https://www.cnu.org/oakland-mandela-parkway. Accessed February 21, 2021.

Congressional Budget Office (CBO). 1978. *Highway Assistance Programs: A Historical Perspective*. Washington, DC: Congressional Budget Office.

Connerly, Charles E. 2002. "From Racial Zoning to Community Empowerment: The Interstate Highway System and the African American Community in Birmingham, Alabama." *Journal of Planning Education and Research* 22: 99–114.

Cook, Joan. 1989. "Harland Bartholomew, 100, Dean of City Planners." *New York Times*, sec. Obituaries, December 7, 1989: 22.

Cox, Wendell, P. Gordon, and C. L. Redfearn. 2008. "Highway Penetration of Central Cities: Not a Major Cause of Suburbanization." *Econ Journal Watch* 5: 32–45.

Cox, Wendell, and Jean Love. 1996. *The Best Investment a Nation Ever Made: A Tribute to the Dwight D. Eisenhower System of Interstate and Defense Highways*. Washington, DC: American Highway Users Alliance.

CQ Press, ed. 1965. "Congress and the Nation 1945–1964: A Review of Government and Politics in the Postwar Years." In *Vol. 1: Congress and the Nation*. Washington, DC: Congressional Quarterly Service, 530.

Crabbe, Amber, Rachel Hiatt, Susan D. Poliwka, and Martin Wachs. 2005. "Local Transportation Sales Taxes: California's Experiment in Transportation Finance." *Public Budgeting & Finance* 25 (3): 91–121.

Crawford, Finla G. 1932. *The Administration of the Gasoline Tax in the United States*. New York, NY: Municipal Administration Service.

Crawford, Finla G. 1939. *Motor Fuel Taxation in the United States*. Baltimore, MD: Lord Baltimore Press.

Creese, Walter. 1994. *The Legacy of Raymond Unwin: A Human Pattern for Planning*. Cambridge, MA: MIT Press.

Davenport, Coral. 2018. "Trump Administration Unveils Its Plan to Relax Car Pollution Rules." *New York Times*, sec. Climate and Environment, August 2, 2018. https://www.nytimes.com/2018/08/02/climate/trump-auto-emissions-california.html. Accessed March 2, 2021.

Davies, Pete. 2002. *American Road: The Story of an Epic Transcontinental Journey at the Dawn of the Motor Age*. New York, NY: Henry Holt.

Davis, Carl. 2018. "An Unhappy Anniversary: Federal Gas Tax Reaches 25 Years of Stagnation." *Just Taxes* (blog). Institute on Taxation and Economic Policy. September 25, 2018. https://itep.org/an-unhappy-anniversary-federal-gas-tax-reaches-25-years-of-stagnation/. Accessed March 2, 2021.

De Leuw Cather and Company, and Ladislas Segoe and Associates. 1948. *A Report to the City Planning Commission on a Transportation Plan for San Francisco*. San Francisco, CA: De Leuw, Cather and Co.

De Leuw, Charles E. 1939. *A Comprehensive Superhighway Plan for the City of Chicago*. Chicago, IL: Department of Superhighways.

Department of City Planning, City and County of San Francisco. 1951. *Trafficways Plan*. San Francisco, CA: City and County of San Francisco.

Dewey, Caitlin. 2020. "Advocates Rally to Tear Down Highways That Bulldozed Black Neighborhoods Stateline, an Initiative of The Pew Charitable Trusts." July 28, 2020. https://www.pewtrusts.org/en/research-and-analysis/blogs/stateline/2020/07/28/advocates-rally-to-tear-down-highways-that-bulldozed-black-neighborhoods. Accessed July 17, 2021.

DiMento, Joseph, and Cliff Ellis. 2013. *Changing Lanes: Visions and Histories of Urban Freeways*. Cambridge, MA: MIT Press.

DiMento, Joseph, Drucilla Van Hegel, and Sherry Ryan. 1996. "The Century Freeway: Design by Court Decree." *Access* 9 (Fall 1996): 7–12.

Duany, Andres, Elizabeth Plater-Zyberk, and Jeff Speck. 2010. *Suburban Nation: The Rise and Decline of the American Dream*. New York, NY: North Point Press.

Duffy, John. 1968. *A History of Public Health in New York City 1625–1866*. New York, NY: Russell Sage Foundation.

Duffy, John. 1974. *A History of Public Health in New York City 1866–1966*. New York, NY: Russell Sage Foundation.

Duffy, John. 1990. *The Sanitarians: A History of American Public Health*. Chicago, IL: University of Illinois Press.

Duranton, Gilles, and Matthew A. Turner. 2012. "Urban Growth and Transportation." *The Review of Economic Studies* 79 (4): 1407–1440.

Duranton, Gilles, Peter M. Morrow, and Matthew A. Turner. 2014. "Roads and Trade: Evidence from the US." *The Review of Economic Studies* 81 (2): 681–724.

Duncan, Ian. 2021a. "As Democrats Bring Back Earmarks For Transportation Projects, Billions of Dollars from Years Ago Sits Unused." *Washington Post*, sec. Transportation. March 3, 2021.https://www.washingtonpost.com/local/trafficandcommuting/earmarks-transportation/2021/03/03/68ae6f06-7b8d-11eb-85cd-9b7fa90c8873_story.html. Accessed March 8, 2021.

Duncan, Ian. 2021b. "A Woman Called for a Highway's Removal in a Black Neighborhood: The White House Singled It Out in Its Infrastructure Plan." *Washington Post*, sec. Transportation. April 1, 2021. https://www.washingtonpost.com/local/trafficandcommuting/highway-removal-infrastructure/2021/03/31/effd6a26-9234-11eb-a74e-1f4cf89fd948_story.html. Accessed July 10, 2021.

Dunn, James A. 1998. *Driving Forces: The Automobile, Its Enemies, and the Politics of Mobility*. Washington, DC: Brookings Institution Press.

East-West Gateway Council of Governments (EWGCOG). 2017. "Bartholomew's Best-Laid Plans for St. Louis Go Awry." *East-West Gateway Council of Governments*. July 27, 2017. https://www.ewgateway.org/bartholomews-best-laid-plans/. Accessed October 31, 2021.

Ellis, Clifford. 1990. *Visions of Urban Freeways*. Doctoral dissertation, University of California, Berkeley.

Engineering News Record. 1960. "Construction Cost Index." *Engineering News Record* 164 (12): 76.

Eno Center for Transportation. 2014. *How We Pay for Transportation: The Life and Death of the Highway Trust Fund*. Washington, DC: Eno Center for Transportation.

Eno Center for Transportation. 2021a. "About Eno/Our History." *Eno Center for Transportation*. https://www.enotrans.org/about-eno/mission-history/. Accessed March 2, 2021.

Eno Center for Transportation. 2021b. *Saving Time and Making Cents: A Blueprint for Building Transit Better*. https://projectdelivery.enotrans.org/wp-content/uploads/2021/07/Saving-Time-and-Making-Cents-A-Blueprint-for-Building-Transit-Better.pdf. Accessed November 9, 2021.

Fairbank, J. 1937. "Objects and Methods of the State-Wide Highway Planning Surveys." *American Highways* XVI (1) 1937: 22–26.

Federal Works Agency (FWA), Public Roads Administration (PRA). 1947a. *Highway Statistics Summary to 1945*. Washington, DC: United States Government Printing Office.

Federal Works Agency (FWA), Public Roads Administration (PRA). 1947b. *Highway Statistics 1946*. Washington, DC: United States Government Printing Office.

Federal Works Agency (FWA), Public Roads Administration (PRA). 1948. *Highway Statistics 1947*. Washington, DC: United States Government Printing Office.

Federal Works Agency (FWA), Public Roads Administration (PRA). 1949. *Highway Practice in the United States of America*. Washington, DC: United States Government Printing Office.

Fein, Michael R. 2008. *Paving the Way: New York Road Building and the American State, 1880–1956*. Lawrence: University Press of Kansas.

Fernald, John G. 1999. "Roads to Prosperity? Assessing the Link between Public Capital and Productivity." *The American Economic Review* 89 (3): 619–638.

Florida, Richard, and Adam Ozimek. 2021. "How Remote Work Is Reshaping America's Urban Geography." *Wall Street Journal*, March 5. https://www.wsj.com/articles/how-remote-work-is-reshaping-americas-urban-geography-11614960100

Forkenbrock, David J., and Norman S. J. Foster. 1990. "Economic Benefits of a Corridor Highway Investment." *Transportation Research Part A* 24 (4): 303–312.

Foster, Mark. 1981. *From Streetcar to Superhighway: American City Planners and Urban Transportation, 1900–1940*. Philadelphia, PA: Temple University Press.

Friedlaender, Ann Fetter. 1965. *The Interstate Highway System: A Study in Public Investment*. Amsterdam: North-Holland.

Garrett, Mark Evan. 2006. *The Struggle for Transit Justice: Race, Space, and Social Equity in Los Angeles*. PhD dissertation, University of California, Los Angeles.

Gauderman, W. James, Hita Vora, Rob McConnell, Kiros Berhane, Frank Gilliland, Duncan Thomas, Fred Lurmann, et al. 2007. "Effect of Exposure to Traffic on Lung Development from 10 to 18 Years of Age: A Cohort Study." *The Lancet* 369 (9561): 571–577.

getAbstract. 2020. "A Majority of US Employees Want Remote Work Arrangement to Stay." https://journal.getabstract.com/wp-content/uploads/2020/04/ga_remote_survey_2020_compressed.pdf. Accessed July 16, 2021.

Gifford, Jonathan L. 1983. *An Analysis of the Federal Role in the Planning, Design and Deployment of Rural Roads, Toll Roads and Urban Freeways*. Berkeley: University of California.

Gifford, Jonathan L. 1984. "The Innovation of the Interstate Highway System." *Transportation Research A* 18 (4): 319–332.

Gifford, Jonathan L. 1991. "Historical Antecedents and Development Impacts of Highways of National Significance: The Conflict between Technical and Political Criteria." Presented at the *Transportation Research Board Annual Meeting*. Washington, DC.

Glaeser, Edward L., and Janet E. Kohlhase. 2004. "Cities, Regions and the Decline of Transport Costs." *Papers in Regional Science* 83 (1): 197–228.

Gladwell, Malcom. 2019. *Talking to Strangers: What We Should Know about the People We Don't Know*. New York, NY: Little, Brown.

Gordon, Robert J. 2016. *The Rise and Fall of American Growth: The U.S. Standard of Living since the Civil War*. Princeton, NJ, and Oxford: Princeton University Press.

Gramlich, Edward. 2001. "Infrastructure and Economic Development, Remarks by Governor Edward M. Gramlich." Presented at the *Texas Trade Corridors New Economy Conference*, San Antonio, TX, August 3.

Gutfreund, Owen D. 2004. *Twentieth-Century Sprawl: Highways and the Reshaping of the American Landscape*. New York, NY: Oxford University Press.

Hannay, Robert, and Martin Wachs. 2007. "Factors Influencing Support for Local Transportation Sales Tax Measures." *Transportation* 34: 17–35.

Harland Bartholomew and Associates. 1927. *A Proposed Plan for a System of Major Traffic Highways: Oakland, California*. Oakland: Major Highway and Traffic Committee of One Hundred.

Harland Bartholomew and Associates. 1928a. *A Plan for the City of Vancouver, British Columbia*. Vancouver: City of Vancouver.

Harland Bartholomew and Associates. 1928b. *Major Street Report for Sacramento, California*. Sacramento: City Planning Commission.

Harland Bartholomew and Associates. 1930. *A System of Major Highways for Saint Louis County, Missouri*. St. Louis: Harland Bartholomew and Associates.

Harland Bartholomew and Associates. 1942. *Report on the Comprehensive System of Highways, St Louis County, Missouri*. St. Louis: Harland Bartholomew and Associates.

Harland Bartholomew and Associates. 1947. *A Report on Freeways and Major Streets in Eden Township Alameda County*. Prepared for the Board of Supervisors County of Alameda California. St. Louis, MO: Harland Bartholomew and Associates.

Harland Bartholomew and Associates. 1954. *City of Atlanta and Fulton County Georgia Major Thoroughfare Plan*. Municipal Board, City of Atlanta: Georgia State Department of Highways.

Harmatuck, Donald J. 1996. "The Influence of Transportation Infrastructure on Economic Development." *Logistics and Transportation Review* 32 (1): 63–76.

Harvey, Greig W. 1994. "Transportation Pricing and Travel Behavior." In *Curbing Gridlock*, Committee for Study on Urban Transportation Congestion Pricing. Washington, DC: National Academy Press, Vol. 1, 89–114.

Heathcott, Joseph. 2005. "'The Whole City Is Our Laboratory': Harland Bartholomew and the Production of Urban Knowledge." *Journal of Planning History* 4 (4): 322–355.

Heathcott, Joseph, and Marie Agnes Murphy. 2005. "Corridors of Flight, Zones of Renewal: Industry, Planning, and Policy in the Making of Metropolitan St. Louis, 1940–1980." *Journal of Urban History* 31 (2): 151–189.

Hebert, Richard. 1972. *Highways to Nowhere: The Politics of City Transportation*. Indianapolis, IN: Bobbs-Merrill.

Heppenheimer, Thomas A. 1991. "The Rise of the Interstates: How America Built the Largest Network of Engineered Structures on Earth." *American Heritage of Invention and Technology* 7 (2): 8–18.

Higgens-Evanston, R. Rudy. 2002. "Financing a Second Era of Internal Improvements." *Social Science History* 26 (4): 623–651.

Highway Research Board. 1925. *Report of Committee on Highway Finance*. Washington, DC: Highway Research Board Proceedings.

Highway Education Board. 1929. *Highways Handbook*. Washington, DC: Highways Education Board.

Hill, Curtis. 1917. "Traffic Ways." *National Conference on City Planning Proceedings 1917*, 60–63. New York.

Hilles, William. 1958. *The Good Roads Movement in the United States*. Master's thesis, Duke University.

Hines, Thomas. 1979. *Burnham of Chicago: Architect and Planner*. Chicago, IL: University of Chicago Press.

Hodge, David. 1986. "Social Impacts of Urban Transportation Decisions: Equity Issues," in *The Geography of Urban Transportation*, Susan Hanson (ed.). New York, NY: Guilford Press, 303–327.

Hoek, Gerard, Bert Brunekreef, Sandra Goldbohm, Paul Fischer, and Piet A. van den Brandt. 2002. "Association between Mortality and Indicators of Traffic-Related Air Pollution in the Netherlands: A Cohort Study." *The Lancet* 360 (9341): 1203–1209.

Holt, W. Stull. 1923. *The Bureau of Public Roads: Its History, Activities and Organization*. Baltimore, MD: Johns Hopkins Press.

Holtz-Eakin, Douglas, and Martin Wachs. 2011. *Strengthening Connections between Transportation Investments and Economic Growth*. Washington, DC: Bipartisan Policy Center.

Houston, Douglas, Jun Hu, Paul Ong, and Arthur Winer. 2004. "Structural Disparities of Urban Traffic in Southern California." *Journal of Urban Affairs* 26 (5): 565–592.

Hu, S., S. Fruin, K. Kozawa, S. Mara, S. E. Paulson, and A. M. Winer. 2009. "A Wide Area of Air Pollutant Impact Downwind of a Freeway during Pre-sunrise Hours." *Atmospheric Environment* 43 (16): 2541–2549.

Hubler, Shawn, Emily Cochrane, and Zach Montague. 2021. "This Is Where the States Want Billions of Dollars in Infrastructure Funding Spent." *New York Times*, November 6, 2021. https://www.nytimes.com/2021/11/06/us/states-infrastructure-bill-funding.html. Accessed November 8, 2021.

H. W. Lochner and Company, and De Leuw, Cather & Company. 1946. *Highway and Transportation Plan for Atlanta, Georgia*. Chicago, IL: State Highway Department of Georgia and the Public Roads Administration, Federal Works Agency.

Ingram, Tammy. 2014. *Dixie Highway: Road Building and the Making of the Modern South, 1900–1930*. Chapel Hill: University of North Carolina Press.

Jackson, Kenneth T. 1987. *Crabgrass Frontier: The Suburbanization of the United States*. Oxford: Oxford University Press.

Jackson, Nathan. 2021. "Harland Bartholomew: Destroyer of the Urban Fabric of St. Louis." *NextSTL*. April 10, 2021. https://nextstl.com/2021/04/harland-bartholomew-destroyer-of-the-urban-fabric-of-st-louis/. Accessed October 31, 2021.

Jacobs, Allan B. 1993. *Great Streets*. Cambridge, MA: MIT Press.

Jacobs, Allan B., Elizabeth Macdonald, and Yodan Rofe. 2002. *The Boulevard Book: History, Evolution, Design of Multiway Boulevards*. Cambridge, MA: MIT Press.

Jacobs, Jane. 1961. *The Death and Life of Great American Cities*. New York, NY: Random House.

Johnson, David. 1995. *Planning the Great Metropolis: The 1929 Regional Plan of New York and Its Environs*. London: Routledge.

Joint Board for the Metropolitan Master Highway Plan. 1948. *The Master Highway Plan for the Boston Metropolitan Area*. Boston, MA: Joint Board.

Jones, David. 1985. *Urban Transit Policy: An Economic and Political History*. Englewood Cliffs, NJ: Prentice-Hall.

Jones, David. 1989. *California's Freeway Era in Historical Perspective*. Sacramento: California Department of Transportation.

Jones, David, and Brian D. Taylor. 1987. *Mission and Mix: A Study of the Changing Tasks and Staffing Requirements of the California Department of Transportation*. Berkeley: University of California Institute of Transportation Studies.

Jones, David W. 2008. *Mass Motorization and Mass Transit: An American History and Policy Analysis*. Bloomington: Indiana University Press.

Jones, Kathryn and Maureen Bock. 2017. *Oregon's Road Usage Charge*. Salem: Oregon Department of Transportation.

Karàs, David. 2015. "Highway to Inequity: The Disparate Impact of the Interstate Highway System on Poor and Minority Communities in American Cities." *New Visions for Public Affairs* 7 (April 2015): 9–21.

Karner, A. A., D. S. Eisinger, and D. Niemeir. 2010. "Near-Roadway Air Quality: Synthesizing the Findings from Real-World Data." *Environmental Science and Technology* 44 (14): 5334–5344.

Karnes, Thomas L. 2009. *Asphalt and Politics: A History of the American Highway System*. Jefferson, NC: McFarland.

Kay, Jane Holtz. 1998. *Asphalt Nation: How the Auto Took over America and How We Can Take It Back*. Berkeley: University of California Press.

Keeler, Theodore E., and John S. Ying. 1988. "Measuring the Benefits of a Large Public Investment." *Journal of Public Economics* 36: 69–85.

Kelley, Ben. 1971. *The Pavers and the Paved: The Real Cost of America's Highway Program*. New York, NY: Donald W. Brown.

Kennedy, Donald. 1946. *Engineering Facts and a Future Program*. Sacramento: California Legislature.

Kim, Kwang Sik, Sung Joong Park, and Young-Jun Kweon. 2007. "Highway Traffic Noise Effects on Land Price in an Urban Area." *Transportation Research Part D: Transport and Environment* 12 (4): 275–280.

Klein, Daniel. 1990. "The Voluntary Provision of Public Goods? The Turnpike Companies of Early America." *Economic Inquiry* 28 (October), 788–812.

Knopman, Debra, Martin Wachs, Benjamin M. Miller, Scott G. Davis, and Katherine Pfrommer. 2017. *Not Everything Is Broken: The Future of U.S. Transportation and Water Infrastructure Funding and Finance.* Santa Monica, CA: RAND.

Knowles, Morris. 1925. *City Planning as a Permanent Solution of the Traffic Problem.* Baltimore, MD: Norman, Remington.

Kopecky, Karen A., and Richard M. H. Suen. 2010. "A Quantitative Analysis of Suburbanization and the Diffusion of the Automobile." *International Economic Review* 51 (4): 1003–1037.

Laska, A., and R. Puentes. 2019. *Eno Brief: Transportation at the Ballot Box.* Washington, DC: Eno Center for Transportation.

Leavitt, Helen. 1970. *Superhighway-Superhoax.* Garden City, NY: Doubleday.

Lederman, Jaimee, Anne Brown, Brian D. Taylor, and Martin Wachs. 2018a. "Arguing over Transportation Sales Taxes: An Analysis of Equity Debates in Transportation Ballot Measures." *Urban Affairs Review* 56 (2): 640–670.

Lederman, Jaimee, Anne Brown, Brian D. Taylor, and Martin Wachs. 2018b. "Lessons Learned from 40 Years of Local Option Transportation Sales Taxes in California." *Transportation Research Record: Journal of the Transportation Research Board* 2672 (4): 13–22.

Leff Yaffe, Daniel. 2019. "The Interstate Multiplier." NBER Working Paper, February 22. http://conference.nber.org/conf_papers/f117288.pdf. Accessed September 15, 2021.

Levin, Melvin R., and Norman A. Abend. 1971. *Bureaucrats in Collision: Case Studies in Area Transportation Planning.* Cambridge, MA: MIT Press.

Lewis, David. 1997. *Divided Highways: Building the Interstate Highways, Transforming American Life.* New York, NY: Viking.

Lewis, Paul, and Marla Westervelt. 2020. "Embracing the General Fund Future: Turning Revenue Constraints into Opportunities." *TR News* 329 (September–October): 36–39.

Li, Wei, and Jean-Daniel Saphores. 2012. "Assessing Impacts of Freeway Truck Traffic on Residential Property Values: Southern California Case Study." *Transportation Research Record* 2288 (1): 48–56.

Lieb, E. 2011. 'White Man's Lane': Hollowing Out the Highway Ghetto in Baltimore," in *Baltimore '68: Riots and Rebirth in an American City*, J. Elfenbein, E. Nix, and T. Hollowak (eds.). Philadelphia, PA: Temple University Press, 51–69.

Lindbloom, Charles. 1959. *The Science of Muddling Through Public Administration Review* 19 (2) (Spring): 79–88.

Lindman, Bertram. 1946. *A Proposed System of Highway Financing for the State of California.* Sacramento: California Legislature.

Longstreth, Richard W. 1997. *City Center to Regional Mall: Architecture, the Automobile, and Retailing in Los Angeles, 1920–1950.* Cambridge, MA: MIT Press.

Longstreth, Richard W. 1999. *The Drive-in, the Supermarket, and the Transformation of Commercial Space in Los Angeles, 1914–1941.* Cambridge, MA: MIT Press.

Los Angeles County Regional Planning Commission. 1943. *Freeways for the Region.* Los Angeles, CA: Los Angeles County Regional Planning Commission.

Los Angeles Department of City Planning. 1941. *Master Plan of Parkways.* Los Angeles, CA: Los Angeles City Planning Department.

Los Angeles Metropolitan Transit Authority. N.d. "Interactive Estimated Ridership Stats." N.d. http://isotp.metro.net/MetroRidership/IndexRail.aspx. Accessed March 2, 2021.

Los Angeles Traffic Commission (LATC). 1922. *A Selected Traffic Program.* Los Angeles, CA: Los Angeles Traffic Commission.

Lovelace, Eldridge. 1993. *Harland Bartholomew: His Contributions to American Urban Planning.* Urbana, IL: Department of Urban and Regional Planning.

Lupo, Alan, Frank Colcord, and Edmund P. Fowler. 1971. *Rites of Way: The Politics of Transportation in Boston and the U.S. City.* Boston, MA: Little, Brown.

MacDonald, Thomas H. 1936. "Roads We Should Have." Presented at the *Annual Meeting of the Councilors of the American Automobile Association*, Washington, DC.

MacDonald, Thomas H. 1941. "Flatten Out Those Traffic Peaks: Highways of Tomorrow Will Avoid Big City Congestion and Provide Safe Speed in the Country." *Motor*, 76 (4) 1941: 102.

MacDonald, Thomas H. 1954. "The Engineer's Relation to Highway Transportation." Presented at the *Sixth Salzberg Memorial Lecture*, Texas A&M University, College Station, TX.

Maguire, Charles, and Associates. 1947. *Expressway System for Metropolitan Providence.* Providence, RI: State Department of Public Works and the Public Roads Administration.

Mamuneas, Theofanis P., and M. Ishaq Nadiri. 2006. *Production, Consumption and the Rates of Return to Highway Infrastructure Capital.* University of Cyprus, New York University, and National Bureau of Economic Research.

Manville, Michael. 2019. "Longer View: The Fairness of Congestion Pricing." *Transfers Magazine* 3 (Spring 2019). https://transfersmagazine.org/magazine-article/issue-3/longer-view-the-fairness-of-congestion-pricing/ Accessed May 8, 2021.

Manville, Michael. 2021. *How and Why Would Congestion Pricing Work?* Los Angeles: University of California, Los Angeles, Institute of Transportation Studies.

Manville, Michael, and Emily Goldman. 2017. "Would Congestion Pricing Harm the Poor? Do Free Roads Help the Poor?" *Journal of Planning Education and Research* 38 (3): 329–344.

Marshall, Stephen. 2005. *Streets and Patterns.* New York, NY: Spon Press.

Mastako, Kimberley Allyn, R. Rillet Laurence, and Edward C. Sullivan. 1998. "Commuter Behavior on California State Route 91 after Introducing Variable-Toll Express Lanes." *Transportation Research Record: Journal of the Transportation Research Board* 1649 (1): 47–54.

McClintock, Miller. 1925. *Street Traffic Control.* New York, NY: McGraw-Hill.

McClintock, Miller. 1926. "Conducting a Traffic Survey." *The American City* 35 (6): 772–776.

McClintock, Miller. 1927. "The Traffic Survey," in *Planning For City Traffic*, Austin F. Macdonald (ed.). Vol. 133. Philadelphia, PA: Annals of the American Academy of Political and Social Science, 8–18.

McClintock, Miller. 1931. *A Traffic Plan for the Embarcadero.* San Francisco, CA: San Francisco Traffic Survey Committee.

McClintock, Miller. 1932. "Limited Ways: A Plan for the Greater Chicago Traffic Area." Chicago, IL: Committee on Traffic and Public Safety.

McClintock, Miller. 1937. "Report on the San Francisco Citywide Traffic Survey." WPA Project 6108-5863. San Francisco, CA: Department of Public Works, City and County of San Francisco.

McCormick, Kathleen. 2020. "Deconstruction Ahead: How Urban Highway Removal Is Changing Our Cities." *Land Lines.* Lincoln Institute, April 2020. https://www.lincolni nst.edu/sites/default/files/pubfiles/deconstruction-ahead-lla200406.pdf. Accessed July 17, 2021.

McCullough, David. 1992. *Truman.* New York, NY: Simon & Schuster.

McMahon, Tim. 2019. "Average Annual Inflation Rates by Decade." *InflationData.Com.* https:// inflationdata.com/Inflation/Inflation/DecadeInflation.asp. Accessed March 2, 2021.

McNichol, Dan. 2006. *The Roads That Built America.* New York: Sterling.

McShane, Clay. 1975. *American Cities and the Coming of the Automobile.* Doctoral dissertation, University of Wisconsin, Madison.

McShane, Clay. 1994. *Down the Asphalt Path: The Automobile and the American City.* New York, NY: Columbia University Press.

McShane, Clay. 1999. "The Origins and Globalization of Traffic Control Signals." *Journal of Urban History* 25 (2): 379–404.

McShane, Clay, and Joel A. Tarr. 1997. "The Centrality of the Horse in the 19th Century American City," in *The Making of Urban America* (2nd edition), Raymond A. Mohl (ed.). Oxford: SR Books, 105–130.

Melluso, Angelo. 2020. "A Man Drove Solo across America in 25 Hours 55 Minutes in a Rental Mustang." *Road & Track*, June 19, 2020. https://www.roadandtrack.com/car-culture/a32917 037/a-man-drove-solo-across-america-in-25-hours-55-minutes-in-a-rental-mustang/. Accessed October 31, 2021.

Metropolitan Transportation Engineering Board. 1958. *Proposed Freeway and Expressway System for Los Angeles, Orange and Ventura Counties.* Los Angeles: California Department of Public Works.

Michaels, Guy. 2008. "The Effect of Trade on the Demand for Skill: Evidence from the Interstate Highway System." *The Review of Economics and Statistics* 90 (4): 683–701.

Millard-Ball, Adam. 2019. "The Autonomous Vehicle Parking Problem." *Transport Policy* 75: 99–108.

Milowski, Daniel. 2018. "Could New Legislation Lead to a Route 66 Revival?" *The Conversation*, June 29. https://theconversation.com/could-new-legislation-lead-to-a-route-66-economic-revival-98601. Accessed October 5, 2020.

Mitchell, Daniel J. B. 2006. "Earl Warren's Fight for California's Freeways: Setting a Path for the Nation." *Southern California Quarterly* 88 (2): 205–238.

Mohl, Raymond A. 2004. "Stop the Road: Freeway Revolts in American Cities." *Journal of Urban History* 30 (5): 674–706.

Mohl, Raymond A. 2008. "The Interstates and the Cities: The U.S. Department of Transportation and the Freeway Revolt, 1966–1973." *Journal of Policy History* 20 (2): 193–236 [reprinted in Rose and Mohl, 2012].

Mohl, Raymond A. 2012a. "Planned Destruction: The Interstates and Central City Housing," in *The Making of Urban America*, Raymond A. Mohl and Roger Biles (eds.). New York: Roman & Littlefield, 226–245.

Mohl, Raymond A. 2012b. "The Expressway Teardown Movement in American Cities: Rethinking Postwar Highway Policy in the Post-Interstate Era." *Journal of Planning History* 11 (1): 89–103.

Mohl, Raymond A. 2014. "Citizen Activism and Freeway Revolts in Memphis And Nashville: The Road to Litigation." *Journal of Urban History* 40 (5): 870–893.

Morris, Eric A. 2006. *From Horse Power to Horsepower.* Master's thesis, University of California, Los Angeles.

Morris, Eric A. 2007. "From Horse to Horsepower." *Access* 30: 2–9.

Morris, Eric A., Jeffrey R. Brown, and Brian D. Taylor. 2016. "Negotiating a Financial Package for Freeways: How California's Collier–Burns Highway Act Helped Pave the Way for the Era of the American Interstate Highway." *Transportation Research Record* 2552 (1): 16–22.

Morrow, William S., Jr. 2019. "Urban Mass Transportation Acts: Major Acts of Congress." *Encyclopedia.com.* https://www.encyclopedia.com/history/encyclopedias-almanacs-tran scripts-and-maps/urban-mass-transportation-acts. Accessed March 2, 2021.

Moses, Robert (Director). 1938. *Construction Program: Arterial Parkways in the Metropolitan Area.* New York, NY: Department of Parks, City of New York.

Moses, Robert (Director). 1939. *Arterial Plan for Pittsburgh.* Pittsburgh, PA.

Moses, Robert (Director). 1941. *Gowanus Improvement.* New York: Triborough Bridge and Tunnel Authority.

Moses, Robert (Director). 1943. *Portland Improvement.* Portland, OR.

Moses, Robert (Director). 1944. *Baltimore Freeway and Expressway Plan.* Baltimore, MD.

Moses, Robert (Director). 1946. *Arterial Plan for New Orleans.* Prepared for the Department of Highways of the State of Louisiana. New Orleans.

Moses, Robert (Director). 1951. *New York City Traffic Relief.* New York, NY: Triborough Bridge and Tunnel Authority.

Moses, Robert (Director). 1953. *Recent Projects.* New York, NY: Triborough Bridge and Tunnel Authority.

Moses, Robert (Director). 1970. *Public Works: A Dangerous Trade.* New York, NY: McGraw-Hill.

Moses, Robert, and Andrews & Clark Consulting Engineers. 1949. *Arterial Plan for Hartford.* New York, NY.

Mowbray, A. Q. 1969. *The Road to Ruin.* Philadelphia, PA: Lippincott.

Murse, Tom. 2018. "US Federal Government Gasoline Tax since 1933: How Much Has the Tax Increased over the Years?" *ThoughtCo*, October 3. https://www.thoughtco.com/history-of-the-us-federal-gas-tax-3321598. Accessed March 2, 2021.

Nadiri, M. Ishaq, and Theofanis P. Mamuneas. 1994. "The Effects of Public Infrastructure and R&D Capital on the Cost Structure and Performance of U.S. Manufacturing Industries." *The Review of Economics and Statistics* 76 (1): 22–37.

National Academies of Sciences, Engineering, and Medicine. 2019. *Renewing the National Commitment to the Interstate Highway System: A Foundation for the Future.* Washington, DC: The National Academies Press. https://doi.org/10.17226/25334. Accessed July 17, 2021.

National Interregional Highway Committee. 1944. "Interregional Highways: Report and Recommendations of the National Interregional Highway Committee." House Document No. 379. Washington, DC: United States Government Printing Office.

National Surface Transportation Policy and Revenue Study Commission. 2008. "Transportation for Tomorrow." Washington, DC: National Surface Transportation Policy and Revenue Study Commission.

National Transit Database. 2019. *2019 Database Files.* Washington, DC: Federal Transit Administration.

National Transportation Policy Project. 2011. "Performance Driven: Achieving Wiser Investment in Transportation." *Bipartisan Policy Center.* https://bipartisanpolicy.org/wp-content/uploads/2019/03/BPC_Transportation_0.pdf. Accessed March 2, 2021.

National Transportation Safety Board (NTSB). 2008. *Collapse of I-35W Highway Bridge, Minneapolis, Minnesota, August 1, 2007. Highway Accident Report NTSB/HAR-08/03.* Washington, DC: National Transportation Safety Board.

Nelson, Jon P. 2008. "Hedonic Property Value Studies of Transportation Noise: Aircraft and Road Traffic." In *Hedonic Methods in Housing Markets,* Andrea Baranzini, José Ramirez, Caroline Schaerer, and Philippe Thalmann (eds.). New York, NY: Springer, 57–82.

Nixon, Hillary, and Asha Weinstein Agrawal. 2018. "Would Americans Pay More in Taxes for Better Transportation? Answers from Seven Years of National Survey Data." *Transportation* 46: 819–840.

Nolen, John. 1926. *A Comprehensive City Plan for San Diego, California.* San Diego: City Planning Commission.

Nolen, John. 1930. *A Report on a Major Street Plan for the City of San Diego, CA.* San Diego: City Planning Commission.

Norton, Peter D. 2008. *Fighting Traffic: The Dawn of the Motor Age in the American City.* Cambridge, MA: MIT Press.

Office of Policy and Governmental Affairs. 2017. "Funding Federal-Aid Highways." Publication No. FHWA-PL-17-011. U.S. Department of Transportation, Federal Highway Administration. https://www.fhwa.dot.gov/policy/olsp/fundingfederalaid/07.cfm. Accessed July 17, 2021.

Olmsted, Frederick Law. 1911. *Pittsburgh Main Thoroughfares and the DownTown District: Improvements Necessary to Meet the City's Present and Future Needs.* Pittsburgh, PA: Pittsburgh Civic Commission.

Olmsted, Frederick Law, Harland Bartholomew, and Charles Cheney. 1924. *A Major Street Plan for Los Angeles*. Los Angeles, CA: Committee on Los Angeles Plan of Major Highways of the Traffic Commission of the City and County of Los Angeles.

Oregon State Highway Department. 1955. "Freeway and Expressway System Portland Metropolitan Area 1955." Technical Report No. 55-5. Traffic Engineering Division and Planning Survey Section, Oregon State Highway Department, in cooperation with the Bureau of Public Roads. Salem, Oregon.

Orlin, Glenn S. 1992. *Evolution of the American Urban Parkway*. Washington, DC: George Washington University.

Oum, Tae Hoon, William G. Waters, and Jong-Say Yong. 1992. "Concepts of Price Elasticities of Transport Demand and Recent Empirical Estimates: An Interpretative Survey." *Journal of Transport Economics and Policy* 26 (2): 139–154.

Pant, Mohan, and Shjui Fumo. 2005. "The Grid and Modular Measures in the Town Planning of Mohenjodaro and Kathmandu Valley: A Study on Modular Measures in Block and Plot Divisions in the Planning of Mohenjodaro and Sirkap (Pakistan), and Thimi (Kathmandu Valley)." *Journal of Asian Architecture and Building Engineering* 4 (1): 51–59.

Paxson, Frederic. 1946. "The Highway Movement, 1916–1935." *The American Historical Review* 51 (2): 236–253.

PB Consult, Inc. 2007. *Future Options for the National System of Interstate Defense Highways, Task 10 Final Report*. Washington, DC: National Cooperative Highway Research Program, Transportation Research Board of The National Academies.

Pennsylvania Turnpike Commission. 2021. "Turnpike History." https://www.paturnpike.com/yourTurnpike/ptc_history.aspx. Accessed November 7, 2021.

Peterson, Jon A. 2003. *The Birth of City Planning in the United States, 1840–1917*. Baltimore, MD: Johns Hopkins University Press.

Petroski, Henry. 2016. *The Road Taken: The History and Future of America's Infrastructure*. New York, NY: Bloomsbury.

Pivetti, Charles. 1992. Highway System Engineer, California Department of Transportation. Personal communication.

Poole, Robert. 2012. "VMT Charges and the Future of Toll Roads." *Tollways*, 2012: 7–15.

Poole, Robert W. 2018. *Rethinking America's Highways: A 21st Century Vision for Better Infrastructure*. Chicago, IL: University of Chicago Press.

Popovich, Nadja, Josh Williams, and Denise Lu. 2021. "Can Removing Highways Fix America's Cities?" *New York Times*, May 21, 2021. https://www.nytimes.com/interactive/2021/05/27/climate/us-cities-highway-removal.html. Accessed July 10, 2021.

President's Advisory Committee on a National Highway Program. 1955. *A 10 Year National Highway Program: A Report to the President*. Washington, DC: U.S. Government Printing Office.

Price, Nelson. 1949. *Digest of Testimony and Reports Considered in Enacting the Collier-Burns Highway Act of 1947*. Sacramento: California Legislature.

Purcell, Charles H. 1939. "Annual Convention Address by the President of the Association." *American Highways* 18 (1) 1939: 1–5.

Purcell, Charles H. 1940. "California Highway Program Requires More Federal Aid for Projects within Cities—Part I." *California Highways and Public Works* 18 (May) (5): 26.

Rall, Jaime, Alice Wheet, Nicholas J. Farber, and James B. Reed. 2011. *Transportation Governance and Finance: A 50-State Review of State Legislatures and Departments of Transportation*. Washington, DC: National Conference of State Legislatures and The AASHTO Center For Excellence in Project Finance. http://www.ncsl.org/documents/transportation/FULL-REPORT.pdf. Accessed July 17, 2021.

Rapid Transit Commission. 1924. *Proposed Super-Highway Plan for Greater Detroit*. Detroit, MI: Rapid Transit Commission.

Rapid Transit Commission. 1949. *Rapid Transit Plan for Metropolitan Detroit*. Detroit, MI: Rapid Transit Commission.

Regional Plan Association. 1929. *Regional Plan of New York and Its Environs*. New York, NY: Regional Plan Association.

Richmond, Jonathan. 2005. *Transport of Delight: The Mythical Conception of Rail Transit in Los Angeles*. Akron, OH: University of Akron Press.

Rioux, Christine, David Gute, Doug Brugge, Scott Peterson, and Barbara Parmenter. 2010. "Characterizing Urban Traffic Exposure Using Transportation Planning Tools." *Journal of Urban Health* 87 (2): 167–188.

Roberts, David. 2018. "Trump Is Freezing Obama's Fuel Economy Standards. Here's What That Could Do. Quantifying the Damage to Our Air and Pockets." *Vox*, August 2, 2018. https://www.vox.com/energy-and-environment/2018/5/3/17314000/trump-epa-cars-trucks-fuel-economy-cafe-standards. Accessed July 17, 2021.

Roberts, Gerrylynn K., and Phillip Steadman. 2000. *American Cities and Technology: Wilderness to Wired City*. New York, NY: Routledge Press.

Robinson, Charles Mulford. 1916. *City Planning: With Special Reference to the Planning of Streets and Lots*. New York, NY: G. P. Putnam's Sons.

Rodrigue, Jean-Paul, and Theo Notteboom. 2013. "Transport Supply and Demand," in *Geography of Transport Systems* (3rd edition), Jean-Paul Rodrigue (ed.). New York, NY: Routledge, 243–254.

Rogers, Katie. 2019. "How 'Infrastructure Week' Became a Long-Running Joke" *New York Times*, sec. White House Memo, May 22, 2019. https://www.nytimes.com/2019/05/22/us/politics/trump-infrastructure-week.html. Accessed March 10, 2021.

Rose, Mark. 1979. *Interstate: Express Highway Politics, 1941–1956*. Lawrence: Regent Press of Kansas.

Rose, Mark. 1990. *Interstate: Express Highway Politics 1939–1989*. Knoxville: University of Tennessee Press.

Rose, Mark, and Raymond A. Mohl. 2012. *Interstate: Highway Politics and Policy since 1939*. Knoxville: University of Tennessee Press.

Rose, Mark, and Bruce Seely. 1990. "Getting the Interstate System Built: Road Engineers and the Implementation of Public Policy." *Journal of Policy History* 2 (1): 23–55.

Rosenbloom, Joshua I., Elissa H. Wilker, Kenneth J. Mukamal, Joel Schwartz, and Murray A. Mittleman. 2012. "Residential Proximity to Major Roadway and 10-Year All-Cause Mortality after Myocardial Infarction." *Circulation* 125 (18): 2197–2203.

Ryan, Sherry. 2005. "The Value of Access to Highways and Light Rail Transit: Evidence for Industrial and Office Firms." *Urban Studies* 42 (4): 751–764.

Schaeffer, William. 1992. Retired Deputy Director, California Department of Transportation. Personal communication.

Schaper, David. 2017. "10 Years after Bridge Collapse, America Is Still Crumbling" *npr*, sec. National. August 1, 2017. https://www.npr.org/2017/08/01/540669701/10-years-after-bridge-collapse-america-is-still-crumbling. Accessed March 10, 2021.

Schultz, Martin, and Robert D. Atkinson. 2009. *Paying Our Way: A New Framework for Transportation Finance*. Washington, DC: National Surface Transportation Infrastructure Financing Commission.

Schultz, Stanley. 1989. *Constructing Urban Culture: American Cities and City Planning, 1800–1920*. Philadelphia, PA: Temple University Press.

Schwartz, Gary T. 1976. "Urban Freeways and the Interstate System." *Southern California Law Review* 49 (3): 406–513.

Schweitzer, Lisa, and Brian D. Taylor. 2008. "Just Pricing: The Distributional Effects of Congestion Pricing and Sales Taxes." *Transportation* 35(6): 797–812.

Sciara, Gian-Claudia. 2012a. "Financing Congressional Earmarks: Implications for Transport Policy and Planning." *Transportation Research Part A: Policy and Practice* 46 (8): 1328–1342.

Sciara, Gian-Claudia. 2012b. "Peering Inside the Pork Barrel: A Study of Congressional Earmarking in Transportation." *Public Works Management and Policy* 17 (3): 217–237.

Sciara, Gian-Claudia. 2012c. "Planning for Unplanned Pork: The Consequences of Congressional Earmarking for Regional Transportation Planning." *Journal of the American Planning Association* 78 (3): 239–255.

Sciara, Gian-Claudia, and Susan Handy. 2017. "Regional Transportation Planning," in *Geography of Urban Transportation* (4th edition), Genevieve Giuliano and Susan Hanson (eds.). New York, NY: Guilford Press, 139–163.

Scott, Mel. 1995. *American City Planning since 1890*. Chicago, IL: American Planning Association.

Seely, Bruce E. 1987. *Building the American Highway System: Engineers as Policy Makers*. Philadelphia, PA: Temple University Press.

Seo, Sarah A. 2019. *Policing the Open Road: How Cars Transformed American Freedom*. Cambridge, MA: Harvard University Press.

Shatz, Howard J., Karin E. Kitchens, Sandra Rosenbloom, and Martin Wachs. 2011. *Highway Infrastructure and the Economy: Implications for Federal Policy*. Santa Monica, CA: RAND.

Sheridan, Lawrence. 1927. "Planning and Re-Planning the Street System," in *Planning for City Traffic*, Austin F. Macdonald (ed.). Vol. 133. Annals of the American Academy of Political and Social Science. Philadelphia, PA: The American Academy of Political and Social Science, 28–33.

Sherman, Bradford P. 2014. "Racial Bias and Interstate Highway Planning: A Mixed Methods Approach." *CUREJ (College Undergraduate Research Electronic Journal), University of Pennsylvania* 176 (January): 28–33.

Silver, Christopher. 1984. *Twentieth-Century Richmond: Planning, Politics, and Race*. Knoxville: University of Tennessee Press.

Singh, Devi, Neeraj Kumari, and Pooja Sharma. 2018. "A Review of Adverse Effects of Road Traffic Noise on Human Health." *Fluctuation and Noise Letters* 17 (1): 1830001–1332.

Small, Kenneth, and Clifford Winston. 1999. "The Demand for Transportation: Models and Applications," in *Essays in Transportation Economics and Policy: A Handbook in Honor of John R. Meyer*, Jose A. Gómez-Ibáñez, William B. Tye, and Clifford Winston (eds.). Washington DC: Brookings Institute, 11–55.

Small, Kenneth, Clifford Winston, and Carol A. Evans. 1989. *Road Work: A New Highway Pricing and Investment Policy*. Washington, DC: The Brookings Institution Press.

Snell, Ronald. 2009. *State Finance in the Great Depression*. Washington, DC: National Conference of State Legislatures.

Sorin, Gretchen. 2020. *Driving While Black: African American Travel and the Road to Civil Rights*. New York, NY: Liveright.

Southworth, Michael, and Eran Ben-Joseph. 2003. *Streets and the Shaping of Towns and Cities*. Washington, DC: Island Press.

St. Clair, David J. 1986. *The Motorization of American Cities*. New York, NY: Praeger.

State Road Department of Florida. 1947. "A Traffic Survey Report and Limited Access Highway Plan for the Tampa Metropolitan Area." Division of Research and Records of the State Road Department of Florida in Cooperation with the Public Roads Administration, Federal Works Agency.

Stein, Jeff. 2021. "Patience and Persistence Pay Off as Biden Gets Infrastructure Deal across Finish Line." *Washington Post*, November 6, 2021. https://www.washingtonpost.com/us-pol icy/2021/11/06/biden-infrastructure-deal/. Accessed November 8, 2021.

Sullivan, Edward C., and Mark W. Burris. 2006. "Benefit-Cost Analysis of Variable Pricing Projects: SR-91 Express Lanes." *Journal of Transportation Engineering* 132 (3): 191–198.

Sullivan, Edward C., and Joe El Harake. 1998. "California Route 91 Toll Lanes Impacts and Other Observations." *Transportation Research Record: Journal of the Transportation Research Board* 1649 (1): 55–62.

Swan, Herbert S. 1931. "The Parkway as Traffic Artery, Part 1." *The American City* 45 (4) 1931: 84–86.

Swift, Earl. 2011. *The Big Roads: The Untold Story of the Engineers, Visionaries, and Trailblazers Who Created the American Superhighways*. Boston and New York: Houghton Mifflin Harcourt.

Tarr, Joel A. 1996. "The Horse: Polluter of the City," in *The Search for the Ultimate Sink: Urban Pollution in Historical Perspective*, Joel A. Tarr (ed.). Akron, OH: Akron University Press, 323–334.

Taylor, Brian D. 1992. *When Finance Leads Planning*. PhD dissertation, University of California, Los Angeles.

Taylor, Brian D. 1995. "Public Perceptions, Fiscal Realities, and Freeway Planning: The California Case." *Journal of the American Planning Association* 61 (1): 43–56.

Taylor, Brian D. 2000. "When Finance Leads Planning: Urban Planning, Highway Planning, and Metropolitan Freeways." *Journal of Planning Education and Research* 20 (2): 196–214.

Taylor, Brian D., and Eric Morris. 2015. "Public Transportation Objectives and Rider Demographics: Are Transit's Priorities Poor Public Policy?" *Transportation* 42 (2): 347–367.

Taylor, Brian D., and Lisa Schweitzer. 2005. "Assessing the Experience of Mandated Collaborative Inter-Jurisdictional Planning in the United States." *Transport Policy* 12 (6): 500–511.

Taylor, Brian D., and Rebecca Kalauskas. 2010. "Addressing Equity in Political Debates over Road Pricing: Lessons from Recent Projects." *Journal of the Transportation Research Board* 2187 (1): 44–52.

Technical Committee of the Council. 1947. *Traffic, Transit and Thoroughfare Improvements for San Francisco*. San Francisco, CA: Mayor's Administrative Transportation Planning Council, City and County of San Francisco.

The American City. 1924. "Los Angeles Making Scientific Study to Relieve Congestion." *The American City* 31 (3) 1924: 196.

The American City. 1933. "Extraordinary Development of Express Highways in the New York Region." *The American City* 48 (7) 1933: 40.

The Pew Environment Group. 2011. *History of Fuel Economy, One Decade of Innovation, Two Decades of Inaction*. Philadelphia, PA: The Pew Environment Group.

Transportation Engineering Board (TEB). 1939. *A Transit Program for the Los Angeles Metropolitan Area*. Los Angeles, CA: City of Los Angeles.

Turner, Daniel. 1925. "The Detroit Superhighway Project: A Unique Departure in Transportation Planning." *American City* 32 (4): 373–376.

Unwin, Raymond. 1994. *Town Planning in Practice: An Introduction to the Art of Designing Cities and Suburbs*. New York, NY: Princeton Architectural Press.

USA Facts. 2022. *How has the population changed in California?*, updated July 2022. https://usafacts.org/data/topics/people-society/population-and-demographics/our-changing-population/state/california?endDate=1981-01-01&startDate=1980-01-01. Accessed 25 September 2022.

U.S. Bureau of Labor Statistics, 2021. "Consumer Price Index." https://www.bls.gov/cpi/. Accessed July 17, 2021.

U.S. Census Bureau. 2019a. "Gazetteer Files: 2019." https://www.census.gov/geographies/reference-files/time-series/geo/gazetteer-files.2019.html. Accessed February 21, 2021.

U.S. Census Bureau. 2019b. "Quick Facts: New York City, New York." https://www.census.gov/quickfacts/fact/table/newyorkcitynewyork/PST045219. Accessed February 21, 2021.

U.S. Census Bureau. 2021. "National Intercensal Tables, Historical National Population Estimates: July 1, 1900 to July 1, 1999." https://www.census.gov/data/tables/time-series/demo/popest/pre-1980-national.html. Accessed July 17, 2021.

U.S. Congress. 1932. *Congressional Record*. Washington, DC: Government Printing Office.

U.S. Congress. 1937. *Congressional Record*. Washington, DC: Government Printing Office.

U.S. Congress. 1944. *Congressional Record*. Washington, DC: Government Printing Office.

U.S. Congress. 1948. *Congressional Record*. Washington, DC: Government Printing Office.

U.S. Congress. 1949. *Congressional Record*. Washington, DC: Government Printing Office.

U.S. Congress. 1951. *Congressional Record*. Washington, DC: Government Printing Office.

U.S. Congress. 1955. *Congressional Record*. Washington, DC: Government Printing Office.

U.S. Congress. 1956. *Congressional Record*. Washington, DC: Government Printing Office.

U.S. Congress. 1960. *Congressional Record*. Washington, DC: Government Printing Office.

U.S. Department of Commerce (USDOC), Bureau of Public Roads (BPR). 1950–1966. *Highway Statistics 1948–1964 [series]*. Washington, DC: United States Government Printing Office. https://www.fhwa.dot.gov/policyinformation/statistics.cfm. Accessed September 21, 2021.

U.S. Department of Commerce (USDOC), Bureau of Public Roads (BPR).1967. *Highway Statistics Summary to 1965*. Washington, DC: United States Government Printing Office. https://www.fhwa.dot.gov/policyinformation/statistics.cfm.

U.S. Department of Transportation (USDOT). 2007. *Review of Congressional Earmarks within Department of Transportation Programs*. AV-2007–066. Washington, DC: U.S. Department of Transportation.

U.S. Department of Transportation (USDOT), Federal Highway Administration (FHWA), Bureau of Public Roads (BPR). 1967a–n.d. *Highway Statistics 1965–1968 [series]*, Washington, DC: United States Government Printing Office. https://www.fhwa.dot.gov/policyinformation/hsspubsarc.cfm. Accessed September 12, 2021.

U.S. Department of Transportation (USDOT), Federal Highway Administration (FHWA), Bureau of Public Roads (BPR). 1967b. *Highway Statistics Summary to 1965*. Washington, DC: United States Government Printing Office. https://www.fhwa.dot.gov/policyinformation/hsspubsarc.cfm. Accessed September 12, 2021.

U.S. Department of Transportation (USDOT), Federal Highway Administration (FHWA). n.d.a. *Highway Statistics 1969–2019 [series]*. Washington, DC: United States Government Printing Office. https://www.fhwa.dot.gov/policyinformation/statistics.cfm. Accessed September 12, 2021.

U.S. Department of Transportation (USDOT), Federal Highway Administration (FHWA). n.d.a. *Highway Statistics Summary to 1975*. Washington, DC: United States Government Printing Office. https://www.fhwa.dot.gov/policyinformation/hsspubsarc.cfm. Accessed September 12, 2021.

U.S. Department of Transportation (USDOT), Federal Highway Administration (FHWA). n.d.a. *Highway Statistics Summary to 1985*. Washington, DC: United States Government Printing Office. https://www.fhwa.dot.gov/policyinformation/hsspubsarc.cfm. Accessed September 12, 2021.

U.S. Department of Transportation (USDOT), Federal Highway Administration (FHWA). 1977. *America's Highways 1776–1976: A History of the Federal-Aid Program*. Washington DC: United States Government Printing Office.

U.S. Department of Transportation (USDOT), Federal Highway Administration (FHWA). 1984. *America on the Move: The Story of the Federal-Aid Highway Program*. Washington, DC: Department of Transportation, Office of Public Affairs.

U.S. Department of Transportation (USDOT), Federal Highway Administration (FHWA). 1997. *Highway Statistics Summary to 1995*. Washington, DC: United States Government Printing Office. https://www.fhwa.dot.gov/policyinformation/statistics.cfm. Accessed September 12, 2021.

U.S. Department of Transportation (USDOT), Federal Highway Administration (FHWA). 2013. "MAP-21—Moving Ahead for Progress in the 21st Century: Highway Trust Fund and Taxes." Washington, DC: U.S. Department of Transportation. https://www.fhwa.dot.gov/map21/factsheets/htf.cfm. Accessed March 2, 2021.

U.S. Department of Transportation (USDOT), Federal Highway Administration (FHWA). 2017. "Fixing America's Surface Transportation Act or 'FAST Act:' Highway Trust Fund and Taxes." Washington, DC: U.S. Department of Transportation. https://www.fhwa.dot.gov/fast act/factsheets/htffs.cfm. Accessed March 2, 2021.

U.S. Department of Transportation (USDOT), Federal Highway Administration (FHWA). 2018. "Summary of Travel Trends: 2017 National Household Travel Survey." Washington, DC: U.S. Department of Transportation. http://nhts.ornl.gov. Accessed July 17, 2021.

U.S. Department of Transportation (USDOT), Federal Highway Administration (FHWA). 2019. "FAST Act Section 6020: Surface Transportation System Funding Alternatives (STSFA) Biennial Report." Washington, DC: U.S. Department of Transportation. https://ops.fhwa.dot.gov/fastact/stsfa/reports/stsfarpt19/index.htm. Accessed September 21, 2021.

U.S. Department of Transportation (USDOT), Federal Highway Administration (FHWA). 2020a. "Legislation, Regulations, and Guidance: Intermodal Surface Transportation Efficiency Act of 1991 Information." Washington, DC: U.S. Department of Transportation. https://www.fhwa.dot.gov/planning/public_involvement/archive/legislation/istea.cfm. Accessed March 2, 2021.

U.S. Department of Transportation (USDOT), Federal Highway Administration (FHWA). 2020b. "Report on the Value Pricing Pilot Program Through April 2018." Washington, DC: U.S. Department of Transportation. https://https://ops.fhwa.dot.gov/congestionpricing/value_pricing/pubs_reports/rpttocongress/vppp18rpt/ch2.htm. Accessed September 12, 2021.

U.S. Department of Transportation (USDOT), Federal Highway Administration (FHWA). 2021. "Value Pricing Pilot Program." FHWA-PL-99-014 HPTS/3-99(5M)E. Washington, DC: U.S. Department of Transportation. https://ops.fhwa.dot.gov/congestionpricing/value_pricing/. Accessed September 12, 2021.

U.S. Environmental Protection Agency (EPA). n.d. "What Is the National Environmental Policy Act?" Washington DC. U.S. Environmental Protection Agency. https://www.epa.gov/nepa/what-national-environmental-policy-act. Accessed September 2021.

U.S. House of Representatives, Committee on Ways and Means. 1956. *Hearings on HR 9075, Highway Revenue Act of 1956.* Washington, DC: United States House of Representatives, Congress of the United States.

U.S. House of Representatives, Public Works Committee. 1955. *Hearings on 4260.* Washington, DC: Committee on Public Works, United States House of Representatives, Congress of the United States.

U.S. Senate Finance Committee. 1956. *Hearings on HR 10660, Highway Revenue Act of 1956.* Washington, DC: United States Senate, Congress of the United States.

U.S. Senate Public Works Committee. 1955. *Hearings on HR 4260.* Washington, DC: United States Senate, Congress of the United States.

Vail, Wesley. 1955. *The Legislative History of the Collier-Burns Highway Act of 1947.* Master's thesis, Stanford University.

Vance, J. C. 1988. "Rights of Abutting Property Owner Upon Conversion of Uncontrolled-Access Road into Limited Access Highway," in *Selected Studies in Highway Law.* Vol. 2, Robert W. Cunliffe, John C. Vance, Larry W. Thomas (eds.). Washington, DC: Transportation Research Board.

Vance, James E., Jr. 1990. *Capturing the Horizon: The Historical Geography of Transportation since the Sixteenth Century.* Baltimore, MD, and London: Johns Hopkins University Press.

Vlasic, Bill. 2012. "U.S. Sets Higher Fuel Efficiency Standards." *New York Times*, sec. Business, August 28, 2012. https://www.nytimes.com/2012/08/29/business/energy-environment/obama-unveils-tighter-fuel-efficiency-standards.html?module=inline. Accessed July 17, 2021.

Wachs, Martin. 1984. "Autos, Transit, and the Sprawl of Los Angeles: The 1920s." *Journal of the American Planning Association* 50 (3): 297–310.

Wachs, Martin. 2018. "Raising Revenue for California Transportation: Are Direct User Fees in Our Future?" in *California Policy Options: 2018*, D. Mitchell (ed.). Los Angeles: UCLA Lewis Center for Regional Policy Studies, 26–49.

Wall Street Journal. 2021. "Prime Rate History." *fedprimerate*. http://www.fedprimerate.com/wall_street_journal_prime_rate_history.htm. Accessed March 10, 2021.

Walsh, Kelley. 2019. "12 Cool Technologies That 'The Jetsons" Predicted for 2062 That We Have Right Now." *EmergingEdTech*. https://www.emergingedtech.com/2019/11/10-cool-technologies-the-jetsons-predicted-for-2062-that-we-have-right-now/. Accessed March 5, 2021.

Watkins, Hannah. 2021. "The Problem Isn't the Office—It's the Commute." *Hubble*. https://hubblehq.com/blog/impact-of-commute-time-on-work-preferences. Accessed June 30, 2021.

Wells, C. W. 2011. "From Freeway to Parkway: Federal Law, Grassroots Environmental Protest, and the Evolving Design of Interstate-35E In Saint Paul, Minnesota." *Journal of Planning History* 11 (1): 8–26.

Weiner, Edward. 2013. *Urban Transportation Planning in the United States: History, Policy, and Practice* (4th edition). New York, NY: Springer.

Weingroff, Richard F. 1996. "Federal-Aid Highway Act of 1956: Creating the Interstate System." *Public Roads* 60 (1): 10–17.

Weingroff, Richard F. 2000. "The Genie in the Bottle: The Interstate System and Urban Problems, 1939–1957." *Public Roads* 64 (2) (October): 2–15.

Weingroff, Richard F. 2017a. "'Clearly Vicious as a Matter of Policy': The Fight against Federal-Aid." U.S. Department of Transportation, Federal Highway Administration. https://www.fhwa.dot.gov/infrastructure/hwyhist01.cfm. Accessed September 12, 2021

Weingroff, Richard F. 2017b. "Designating the Urban Interstates." United States Federal Highway Administration. https://www.fhwa.dot.gov/infrastructure/fairbank.cfm Accessed July 17, 2021.

Weingroff, Richard F. 2017c. "Good Roads Everywhere: Charles Henry Davis and the National Highways Association." *Highway History*. https://www.fhwa.dot.gov/infrastructure/davis.cfm. Accessed July 17, 2021.

Weingroff, Richard F. 2017d. "Moving the Goods: As the Interstate Era Begins." U.S. Department of Transportation, Federal Highway Administration. https://www.fhwa.dot.gov/interstate/freight.cfm. Accessed March 2, 2021.

White, Karen, and Ralph Erickson. 2011. "New Cost Estimating Tool." *Public Roads* 75 (1). https://highways.dot.gov/public-roads/julyaugust-2011/new-cost-estimating-tool

Whitten, Robert. 1930. *Report on a Thoroughfare Plan for Boston*. Boston, MA: Boston City Planning Board.

Whitten, Robert. 1932. "The Expressway in the Region." *City Planning* 8 (1): 23–27.

Wikipedia. 2021. "Cannonball Run Challenge." *Wikipedia*. https://en.wikipedia.org/wiki/Cannonball_Run_challenge. Accessed October 31, 2021.

Workman, Simon, and Jaime Rall. 2012. "Motor Fuel Sales Taxes and Other Taxes on Fuel Distributors or Suppliers." National Conference of State Legislatures. June 2012. http://www.ncsl.org/research/transportation/fuel-sales-taxes-and-other-related-taxes.aspx. Accessed July 17, 2021.

Young, Hugh. 1928. "Ten-Mile $60,000,000 Motor Express Highway Proposed for Chicago." *The American City* 38 (3) 1928: 91–92.

Zamora, Anthony N. R. 1989. "The Century Freeway Consent Decree." *Southern California Law Review* 62: 1805–1844.

Zettel, Richard. 1946. *An Analysis of Taxation for Highway Purposes in California, 1895–1946.* Sacramento, CA: State Printing Office.

Zettel, Richard. 1958. *Appendix B: The California Freeway Program: An Economic and Fiscal Analysis.* Sacramento: Joint Interim Committee on Highway Problems, California Legislature.

Zettel, Richard, and Joint Interim Committee on Highway Problems. 1959. *The California Freeway Program: An Economic and Fiscal Analysis.* Sacramento: California Legislature.

Zettel, Richard, and Senate Transportation Committee. 1980. *Highway Cost Allocation and Tax Recovery in California.* Sacramento: California Legislature.

Zettel, Richard, and Paul Shuldiner. 1959. *Freeway Location Conflicts in California.* Berkeley: University of California Institute of Transportation and Traffic Engineering.

Index

For the benefit of digital users, indexed terms that span two pages (e.g., 52–53) may, on occasion, appear on only one of those pages.

Tables and figures are indicated by *t* and *f* following the page number

costs imposed principle and (*see* costs imposed principle)

donor/donee states and (*see* Federal transportation spending: donor/donee states)

drivers' license fees (*see* drivers' license fees)

enduring legacy, 293

federal motor fuel taxes and (*see* federal motor fuel taxes)

federal/state matching ratio, 69, 77

Clay Committee and (*see* Clay Committee: federal/state matching ratio)

federal transportation spending and (*see* federal transportation spending)

freeways, financing of (*see* freeways)

gas taxes (*see* motor fuel taxes)

general fund financing of urban streets (*see* general funds to fund highways)

graduated weight-based vehicle fees (*see* graduated weight-based vehicle fees)

Great Depression and (*see* Great Depression)

Interstate Highways System and (*see* Interstate Highway System)

limited spending on rural roads, 26–27, 59–60, 76

local option taxes (*see* local option taxes [LOTs])

Los Angeles plan and, 50

marginal social cost pricing and (*see* marginal social cost pricing)

mass transportation and (*see* mass transportation)

mileage-based user fees (*see* mileage-based user fees)

motor fuel taxes (*see* motor fuel taxes)

poll tax finance of rural roads, 59–60, 80

post-WWII spending on highways, 174–77, 178–80, 180*f*

property tax financing of rural roads (*see* property tax: financing of rural roads and)

property tax financing of urban streets (*see* property tax: financing of urban streets and)

recommended changes post-WWII, 175, 176

selling public lands for intercity roads, 23–24, 25

special assessments for urban streets (*see* special assessments)

Toll Roads and Free Roads report and, 147–48

tolls and (*see* tolls)

trust funds and (*see* trust funds)

urban motorists cross-subsidizing rural motorists, 119

user fees, 83, 85, 157, 164, 176, 206, 256, 292

vehicle registration fees (*see* motor vehicle excise taxes)

transportation planning profession

3C planning process and (*see* 3C planning process)

accommodating land use and (*see* urban planning)

City Beautiful movement and (*see* City Beautiful movement)

City Practical movement and (*see* City Practical movement)

data collection and (*see* traffic modeling)

fight against congestion and, 291–93

Interregional Highways report and (*see* *Interregional Highways* report)

local authorities and (*see* local authorities and transportation planning)

plans for cities, 46–53, 91, 97–119, 270

rise of traffic consulting field, 31, 37–40, 269

technocratic outlook of, 38–39

traffic modeling and (*see* traffic modeling)

Transportation Research Board (TRB)

poor state of infrastructure and, 251–52

trucking

benefits of freeways to, 279–80

California legislation and (*see* California: truck weight fees and, *and* Collier-Burns Committee *and* Collier-Burns Highway Act)

diesel fuel taxes and, 168, 171, 172, 173, 187–88, 253

goods movement funding, 285

incentives to overload trucks, 71

lobbying for better roads by (*see* Highway Lobby)

rise of trucking industry, 91

road damage and, 71, 74–75, 178, 187–88, 253, 265

weight-based fees and, 82–84, 120, 168, 170, 171, 172, 173, 178, 188, 191–92

Printed in the USA/Agawam, MA
January 25, 2023

804923.019